CURSED VICTORY

CURSED VICTORY

ISRAEL AND THE OCCUPIED TERRITORIES:

A HISTORY

AHRON BREGMAN

PEGASUS BOOKS
NEW YORK LONDON

CURSED VICTORY

Pegasus Books LLC
80 Broad Street, 5th Floor
New York, NY 10004

First Pegasus Books hardcover edition May 2015

ISBN: 978-1-60598-780-4

10 9 8 7 6 5 4 3 2 1

Printed in the United States of America
Distributed by W. W. Norton & Company, Inc.

For
Miriam Eshkol

Contents

PART ONE
The First Decade, 1967–1977

PART TWO
The Second Decade, 1977–1987

Preface to the American Edition

Shortly after the release of *Cursed Victory* in the UK, in the summer of 2014, an all-out war broke out between Israel and the Palestinians in the Gaza Strip. The roots of this fierce clash, which came to be known in Israel and elsewhere as Operation *Protective Edge,* were to be found in Israel's continuing occupation and the brutal pressure its army put especially on the Gaza Strip, where nearly two million Palestinians live in appalling conditions.

Israel, as we have seen, officially evacuated the Gaza Strip in 2005 under Prime Minister Sharon, declaring that it was no longer an occupied land and that Israel had no obligations under international human rights law towards Gaza's population. However the majority of the international community, including the UN, did not accept that this was a legitimate evacuation, since Israel, even after the departure of its troops and settlements, effectively continued to control the Gaza Strip from the outside through various methods. It did so from the sky by using electronic devices such as surveillance balloons, floating as high as 300 metres above the Gaza Strip, to collect data about every corner of the Strip and its people. This intelligence was then used by pilots to assassinate Palestinian activists Israel deemed "terrorists" by firing missiles at them from helicopters and dropping bombs on them from aeroplanes.

Gazans, over the years, became accustomed to the constant overhead buzzing of helicopters, planes, and particularly the notorious drones—unpiloted air vehicles, used by the Israelis for surveillance and attacks. A Gazan named Yamin explains in an interview that: "when we hear an Apache [helicopter] or an Israeli F16 [jet] we know that it will only be there for a while and we can go into our houses for safety. Drones, however, are in the air 24 hours a day so the people don't hide from them. We can't hide 24 hours a day."[1]

Israel also continued to maintain control of the Strip from the sea where its navy, which constantly patrolled the Mediterranean water along Gaza's coast, effectively sealed off the Strip, preventing anyone from approaching the area by sea. When on one occasion a Turkish flotilla attempted to pass through the Israeli navy to bring food and supplies to aid the Gazans, the Israelis attacked them, killing several people on board and seizing their ship. Above all, Israeli control of the Gazans manifested itself in the monitoring of the entries into and the exits from the Gaza Strip, through which Palestinians could – depending on changing Israeli moods – travel to the West Bank. Often, Gazans asking for exit permits to visit family and friends on the West Bank or to go there on business trips had to "pay back" by providing Israeli officials with intelligence on life in the Gaza Strip and on specific people there, thus effectively becoming collaborators with Israel's remote-control occupation.

IMPOSING A BLOCKADE

The rise to power of Hamas, the Palestinian Islamic movement, in 2007, turned out to be a turning point for Gaza, leading to even harsher Israeli treatment of its people. Regarding Hamas as a sworn enemy, successive Israeli governments attempted to topple its leadership by turning to a tactic which had proved effective in Lebanon in 1982.

At that time, long before the birth of Hamas, Israel's leading Palestinian enemy was Yasser Arafat, who would dispatch his guerrillas to strike at Israel from his then headquarters in Beirut. Keen to disrupt Arafat's activities, Israel invaded Lebanon and, in the summer of 1982, it imposed a blockade on its capital; as an artillery officer I was part of the IDF machine which operated this blockade.

Surrounding Beirut from all sides and controlling it from the air and sea too, the Israeli military cut off electricity and water supplies, and restricted the amount and types of foods, particularly flour, entering the city; at the same time, artillery, aeroplanes, and warships kept bombing large sections of Beirut. The Israelis hoped that the pressure on the capital – the fire, restrictions on food, water, and electricity – would break the morale of the Beirutis and they would then turn their backs on Arafat. It worked well: in August 1982, the Lebanese government – exhausted by the continuing Israeli tactics and the destruction of their capital – demanded that Arafat and his guerrilla leave Beirut, at which point the Palestinian leader relocated to Tunisia.

Since Hamas has come to power in Gaza, the military has implemented the same tactics it did in Lebanon. Taking advantage of its air, sea, and land control of the Strip, Israel has imposed a strict blockade on the Gazans in order to make their lives hell and break their spirit in the hope that they turn their backs on Hamas.

The most visible aspect of the Israeli blockade on Gaza was the restrictions it imposed on the imports of foods; the aim was to allow the Gazans just enough food and no more. The Israelis developed mathematical formulas to measure the number of days it would take the Gazans to run out of each particular product, what the Israelis called "the length of breath." Lower and upper lines were set up to give the army "advance warnings" of "shortages" and "surpluses." If, and when, the "upper line" for a given food item was reached, its import was blocked, only to be topped up when an advance warning was issued, based on the mathematical formula, that the "lower line" was reached. For the Gazans, this heartless system produced food insecurity and total dependence on the good will of the Israelis. At the same time, food items regarded by the Israelis as "luxuries" such as fruit tins disappeared altogether from shop shelves.

Building materials were also restricted under the Israeli blockade: cement, gravel, and steel bars were all banned which, in turn, triggered a severe housing shortage as only a fraction of the 40,000 housing units needed to meet natural population growth and the loss of homes destroyed during previous Israeli attacks could be built. The housing crisis, which was directly caused by the Israeli blockade, had devastating humanitarian consequences, as many Gazans had to live in increasingly cramped living quarters. Gazan Mihdad Abu Ghneimeh, who lived in a house in eastern Gaza City that was partially destroyed in an Israeli attack with 26 extended family members and his wife and seven children all in the same 30 square-metre bedroom, described the dire conditions:

> I am tired of this situation. None of us has any privacy. My wife is obliged to cover her head all day since my extended family also lives with us. All children study in the same room where we all sleep; it has no windows and its door cannot be locked. As my children range from a few months to 14 years old, and they are boys and girls, it is not appropriate for them to live side-by-side. This often results also in fights and tension.[2]

Gaza's farmers were also targeted by the Israeli blockade, as they were totally or partially prevented from accessing land located up to 1,000-1,500 metres from the perimeter fence surrounding Gaza and separating it from Israel; altogether the army restricted farmers' access to 17 percent of the total land mass of the Gaza Strip which is 35 percent of its agricultural land. To stop Palestinian farmers from getting into the banned areas, the Israeli Air Force dropped warning leaflets and bull-dozers would cross the perimeter fence into Gaza to raze to the ground greenhouses and uproot fruit trees; troops would often open fire against farmers trying to access their own lands, thus turning the forbidden areas into killing fields.[3] Farmers lucky enough to be able to access their fields would see much of the fruits and vegetables rot on trees as restrictions on the export of goods out of the Strip were also imposed without any advance warning.

At sea, as of 2007, restrictions on fishing became harsher as the Navy banned fishermen from accessing fishing areas beyond three nautical miles from the shore, which meant that they were banned from fishing in what was 85 percent of the maritime areas they were entitled to according to the Oslo Agreements they signed with Israel back in the early 1990s. While the Israeli blockade failed to convince the Gazans to turn their backs on Hamas, it did cause profound misery and widespread unemployment as many – at certain times up to 40 percent – were out of work.

As long as the regime in Egypt was friendly to Hamas, particularly under Mohamed Morsi, who ruled Egypt from 30 June 2012 to July

2013, food and other supplies still trickled into the Gaza Strip through a system of underground-dug tunnels connecting the Sinai desert and the Gaza Strip. But in June 2014, Abdel Fattah Saeed Hussein Khalil el-Sisi took power in Egypt and, regarding Hamas as too close an ally of the Muslim Brotherhood movement, the opposition in Egypt, quickly distanced himself from Hamas and ordered the military to shut down the tunnels between the Sinai and the Gaza Strip. Thus, Israel's strict blockade and the closing down of the Sinai-Gaza tunnels combined to turn the Gaza Strip into a powder keg waiting to blow. What eventually ignited it were events that took place on the occupied West Bank.

THE POWER KEG EXPLODES

There, in June 2014, three young Israeli settlers were abducted by Palestinian activists associated with Hamas, but not on the instructions of the organization. This event was regarded by the Israeli government of Benjamin Netanyahu as a serious attack on Israel, but also as an opportunity to weaken Hamas on the West Bank, where it was particularly strong in the southern town of Hebron. Subsequently, the government dispatched hundreds of troops into the occupied West Bank to search for the abducted settlers – who were eventually found dead – and also to take advantage of the crisis to strike Hamas.

The measures the army unleashed against Hamas on the West Bank were particularly harsh and indeed humiliating: hundreds of activists, many of whom had nothing to do with the abduction of the three settlers, were arrested and thrown into jails without even standing trial; Hamas centres and institutions were closed down and their computers seized for intelligence purposes. Humiliated and upset by the Israeli clampdown in the West Bank, Hamas in Gaza and other militants, such as Islamic Jihad, started firing rockets against Israeli villages from inside the Strip, also in an attempt to break – once and for all – the eight-year blockade which had become especially unbearable since the closure of the tunnels connecting to the Sinai.

For 45 days, Israel and Hamas traded blows. Hamas used rockets and missiles which reached as far as Tel Aviv; at one point a missile landing close to Israel's international airport led to the suspension of international flights to and from Israel. At the same time, Hamas's infantry fighters tried to penetrate Israeli settlements by using a web of underground tunnels which they had dug under the Israeli nose during the years preceding the war.

The damage Hamas inflicted on Israel was minimal as Israel's effective anti-missile system, the Iron Dome, managed to intercept most of the incoming missiles and the ground and underground attacks Hamas initiated were easily repelled by the better trained and equipped Israeli army which had the technologies to spot the Hamas fighters the moment they emerged out of the tunnels on the Israeli side. The Israelis, on the other hand, inflicted an enormous amount of damage on the Gaza Strip: jets and artillery were used indiscriminately to raze to the ground whole Palestinian neighbourhoods, leaving behind scenes of utter devastation. At the end of the war, some neighbourhoods of the Gaza Strip resembled Dresden during the Second World War, with many of the 2,200 killed Palestinians – mostly innocent civilians – still under the rubble.

AS FOR THE FUTURE

Along with its Gaza blockade, which at the time of writing is still under way, the Israeli government is taking advantage of the wave of revolutions in the Arab world and the fact that world attention is focused particularly on Syria and Iraq to consolidate its hold on the occupied West Bank by building more settlements there. If Israel is not stopped from taking over Palestinian lands and building more settlements, then the prospect of a viable Palestinian state on the West Bank linked to the Gaza Strip would diminish, as the physical separation between Israel and the future Palestine which is necessary in order to create two states will be just too difficult to implement. So what *could* persuade the Israelis to end their remote-control occupation of Gaza and particularly their direct occupation and attempts to swallow up the West Bank?

As I put it in the last chapter of this book, the most viable option to end the occupation is through direct negotiations between Israel and the Palestinians, whereby the parties agree to establish a Palestinian state to live side by side in peace with Israel. But, by now, it is exceedingly clear that the Israelis – the stronger party which is also holding almost all of the assets – will not move unless it is compelled to do so. It is only pressure that would persuade the Israelis to end the occupation; indeed, the lesson of history is that Israel only relinquishes occupied lands and compromises with its enemies when under pressure. The latter should come from two sources: from the Palestinians themselves who, given the Israeli reluctance to compromise, are left with no other option but to embark on a non-violent Gandhi-style third intifada against the occupation; at the time of writing I can clearly detect growing Palestinian resistance to the occupation. The other source of pressure on the Israelis must come from the international community; this must also include boycotts on products and services emanating from Jewish settlements on the occupied territories. Boycotts were effective in ending South Africa's apartheid regime, and there is no reason why they should not have an impact on Israel too.

It is reasonable to believe that, like other occupations before it, the Israeli occupation will, at some point in the future, collapse, and a Palestinian state will emerge on the West Bank and the Gaza Strip. But states are not given to people on silver platters, and the Palestinians will have to keep fighting for one; more importantly, they must be helped in their struggle by the international community which must not stand idly by as the Israeli occupation – one of the cruellest and brutal in modern history – continues.

(Endnotes)

1. In Tom Anderson and Therezia Cooper, "Gaza: Life beneath the drones", in *Gaza Reports*, 25 January 2014.

2. UN office for the Coordination of Humanitarian Affairs Occupied Palestinian Territory, *Easing the Blockade: Assessing the Human impact on the population of the Gaza Strip*, March 2000.

3. OCHA-WFP, *Between the Fence and a Hard Place – The humanitarian Impact of Israeli-imposed restrictions on access to land and sea in the Gaza Strip*, August 2010.

Illustrations

Photographic acknowledgements are given in parentheses.

1. (a) Three Israeli paratroopers look up at the Wailing Wall (David Rubinger/epa/Corbis); (b) Moshe Dayan meets Palestinians near Jerusalem after the Six Day War (Micha Bar Am/Magnum Photos).

2. (a) Syrian refugees flee the mountains with their possessions (Micha Bar Am/Magnum Photos); (b) The Golan Druze community allowed to remain on the Golan use megaphones to call to those on the Syrian side (Micha Bar Am/Magnum Photos).

3. (a) The Israeli army erects checkpoints across the West Bank and the Gaza Strip (AFP/Getty Images); (b) Collaborators help the army by fingering suspects (Micha Bar Am/Magnum Photos).

4. (a) Tensions grow between the settlers and local Palestinians (AFP/Getty Images); (b) The Israeli army erects a barrier across the West Bank (Larry Towel/Magnum Photos).

5. (a) Israeli Prime Minister Menachem Begin and Egyptian President Anwar Sadat (Popperfoto/Getty Images); (b) Israeli troops remove Jewish settlers in the Sinai (Peter Marlow/Magnum Photos).

6. (a) A Palestinian boy throws stones at an Israeli tank (Reuters/Corbis); (b) Palestinian suicide bombers (Abed Omar Qusini/X01203/Reuters/Corbis).

7. (a) Israeli Prime Minister Yitzhak Rabin and Palestinian leader Yasser Arafat sign the Oslo Accords (Gary Hershorn/Reuters/Corbis); (b) The bullet that killed Rabin (AFP/Getty Images; (c) The Song of Peace text which Rabin carried in his coat (Time & Life Pictures/Getty Images).

8. (a) Israeli Prime Minister Ariel Sharon (Getty Images); (b) Arafat is evacuated by helicopter from the West Bank (Ammar Abdullah/Reuters/Corbis).

Maps

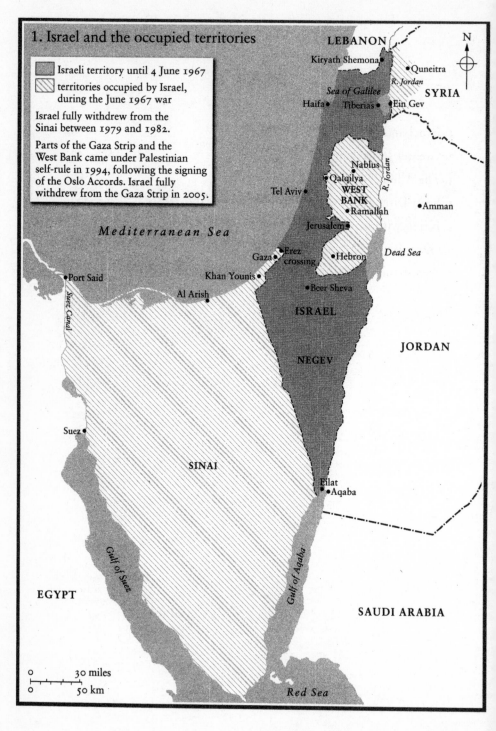

1. Israel and the occupied territories

■ Israeli territory until 4 June 1967
▨ territories occupied by Israel, during the June 1967 war

Israel fully withdrew from the Sinai between 1979 and 1982.

Parts of the Gaza Strip and the West Bank came under Palestinian self-rule in 1994, following the signing of the Oslo Accords. Israel fully withdrew from the Gaza Strip in 2005.

N

LEBANON

Kiryath Shemona
•Quneitra
R. Jordan
SYRIA
Sea of Galilee
Haifa• Tiberias• •Ein Gev

Nablus
•Qalqilya
WEST
BANK
•Ramallah
•Amman

Tel Aviv•

Jerusalem

R. Jordan

Mediterranean Sea

Gaza• •Erez
crossing •Hebron
Dead Sea

•Port Said
Khan Younis•
Al Arish•
•Beer Sheva

Suez Canal

ISRAEL

JORDAN

NEGEV

Suez•

SINAI

Eilat
•Aqaba

Gulf of Suez

Gulf of Aqaba

EGYPT

SAUDI ARABIA

0   30 miles
0   50 km

Red Sea

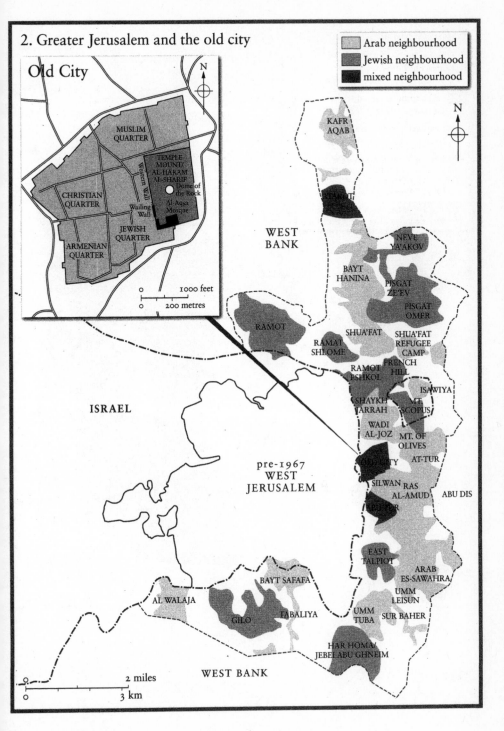

2. Greater Jerusalem and the old city

Old City

Arab neighbourhood
Jewish neighbourhood
mixed neighbourhood

N

MUSLIM
QUARTER

TEMPLE
MOUNT/
AL-HARAM
AL-SHARIF
Dome of
the Rock
Al-Aqsa
Mosque

CHRISTIAN
QUARTER

Western Wall

Wailing
Wall

JEWISH
QUARTER

ARMENIAN
QUARTER

1000 feet

200 metres

N

KAFR
AQAB

WEST
BANK

RAMOT

NEVE
YA'AKOV

BAYT
HANINA

PISGAT
ZE'EV

PISGAT
OMER

RAMAT
SHLOME

SHUA'FAT

SHUA'FAT
REFUGEE
CAMP

ISRAEL

RAMOT
ESHKOL

FRENCH
HILL

SHAYKH
JARRAH

MT.
SCOPUS

ISAWIYA

WADI
AL-JOZ

MT. OF
OLIVES

pre-1967
WEST
JERUSALEM

OLD CITY

AT-TUR

SILWAN

RAS
AL-AMUD

ABU DIS

ABU TUR

EAST
TALPIOT

ARAB
ES-SAWAHRA

BAYT SAFAFA

UMM
LEISUN

AL WALAJA

GILO

TABALIYA

UMM
TUBA

SUR BAHER

HAR HOMA/
JEBEL ABU GHNEIM

2 miles

3 km

WEST BANK

xxi

3. The Allon Plan

- areas to be returned to Jordan under the Allon Plan
- areas to be annexed to Israel under the Allon Plan
- ○ principal Arab towns to return to Jordanian rule
- ▬ link road with free access
- ● Jewish settlements in 1970, to be annexed to Israel
- ■ Jewish settlements built in the two decades after the Allon Plan

20 miles
30 km

N

Mediterranean Sea

ISRAEL

R. Jordan

Jenin

Tulkarm

Qalqilya   Nablus

Ramallah

Jericho

Jerusalem

Bethlehem   Maale

Gush Etzion

Dead Sea

Gaza

Hebron   Kiryath Araba

JORDAN

EGYPT

4. Sinai Disengagement Agreements, 1974 and 1975

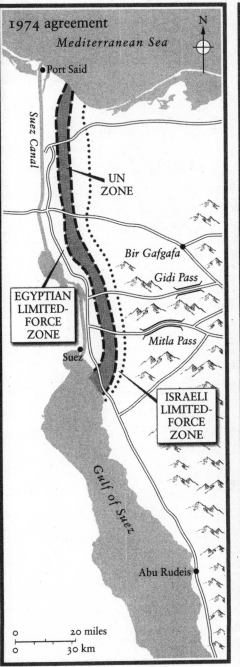

1974 agreement

Mediterranean Sea

N

Port Said

Suez Canal

UN ZONE

Bir Gafgafa

Gidi Pass

EGYPTIAN LIMITED-FORCE ZONE

Mitla Pass

Suez

ISRAELI LIMITED-FORCE ZONE

Gulf of Suez

Abu Rudeis

0   20 miles
0   30 km

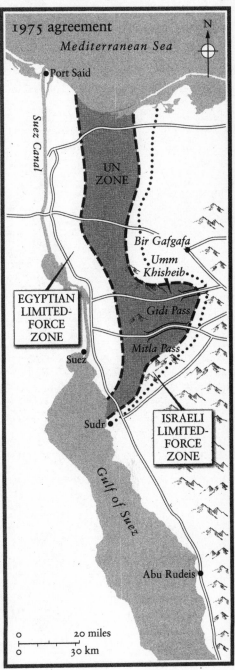

1975 agreement

Mediterranean Sea

N

Port Said

Suez Canal

UN ZONE

Bir Gafgafa

Umm Khisheib

EGYPTIAN LIMITED-FORCE ZONE

Gidi Pass

Mitla Pass

Suez

Sudr

ISRAELI LIMITED-FORCE ZONE

Gulf of Suez

Abu Rudeis

0   20 miles
0   30 km

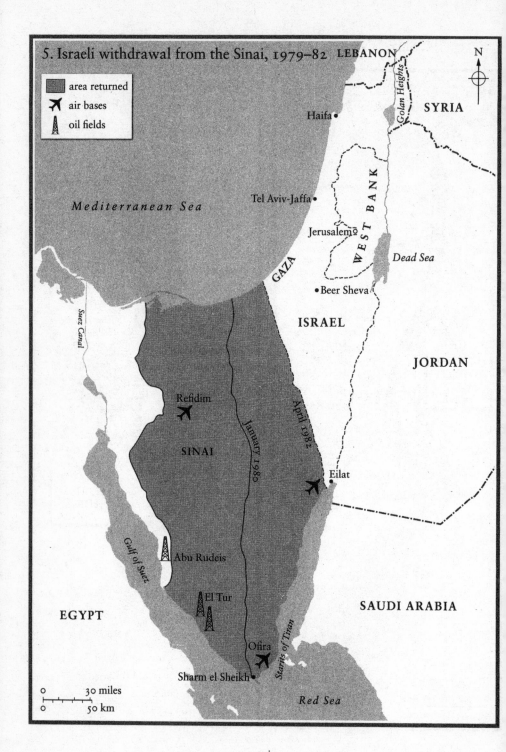

5. Israeli withdrawal from the Sinai, 1979–82

Legend:
- area returned
- ✈ air bases
- oil fields

LEBANON

N

SYRIA

Golan Heights

Mediterranean Sea

Haifa •

WEST BANK

Tel Aviv-Jaffa •

GAZA

Jerusalem •

Dead Sea

• Beer Sheva

ISRAEL

JORDAN

Swez Canal

Refidim ✈

January 1980

April 1982

SINAI

Eilat ✈

Gulf of Suez

Abu Rudeis

El Tur

SAUDI ARABIA

Ofira ✈

Straits of Tiran

EGYPT

Sharm el Sheikh •

Red Sea

0   30 miles
0   50 km

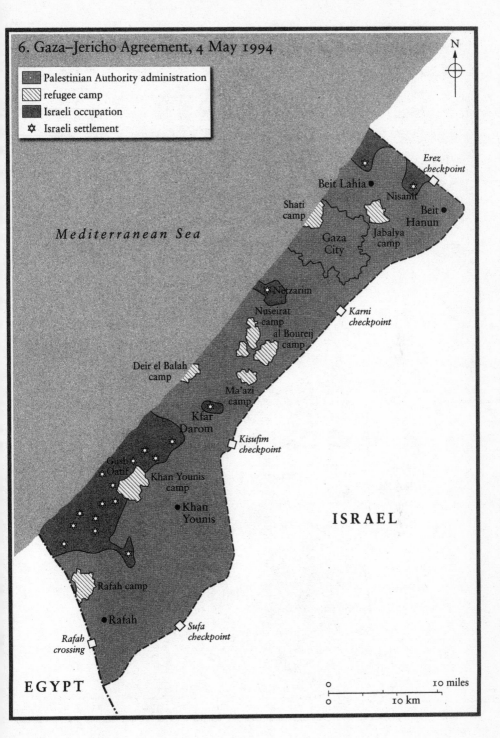

6. Gaza–Jericho Agreement, 4 May 1994

Palestinian Authority administration
refugee camp
Israeli occupation
✿ Israeli settlement

N

Mediterranean Sea

Beit Lahia ●

Nisanit

Erez checkpoint

Shati camp

Gaza City

Jabalya camp

Beit Hanun ●

✿ Netzarim

Nuseirat camp

al Boureij camp

Deir el Balah camp

Ma'azi camp

Kfar Darom

Karni checkpoint

Kisufim checkpoint

Gush Qatif

Khan Younis camp

● Khan Younis

ISRAEL

Rafah camp

● Rafah

Sufa checkpoint

Rafah crossing

EGYPT

0 ——— 10 miles
0 ——— 10 km

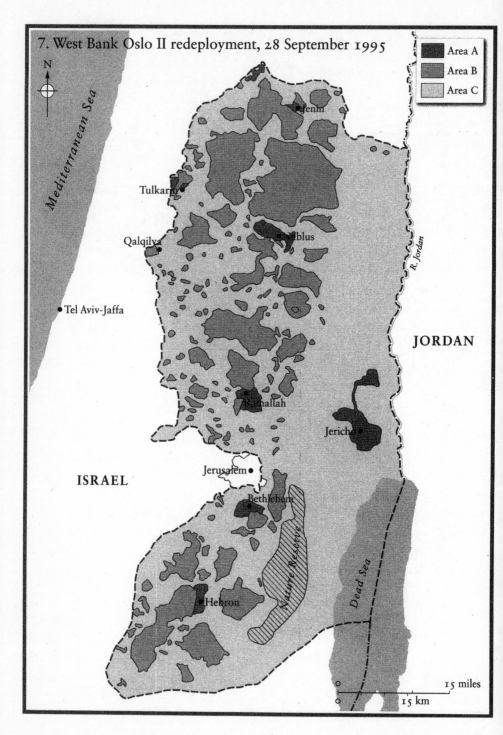

7. West Bank Oslo II redeployment, 28 September 1995

	Area A
	Area B
	Area C

N

Mediterranean Sea

Jenin

Tulkarm

Qalqilya

Nablus

Tel Aviv-Jaffa

R. Jordan

JORDAN

Ramallah

Jericho

Jerusalem

ISRAEL

Bethlehem

Nature Reserve

Dead Sea

Hebron

15 miles

15 km

A Note on Sources

Some of the material I have used in this book, particularly in chapters 9–14, includes 'Top Secret' memos, letters and reports which have never been seen before and are unlikely to be made public in the foreseeable future. Chapter 10, in particular, includes direct quotes from transcripts of telephone conversations between Syrian officials, negotiating in the US, and their masters back home, as well as quotations from telephone conversations between the President of the United States and world leaders, all secretly recorded by Israeli agents, using various electronic devices. However, in order to protect my sources, I often avoid specific references to them. Likewise, the identities of several people have been disguised in order to protect them.

Throughout the book, I have drawn on scores of personal interviews conducted over the last two decades, particularly during the course of my work as an associate producer and academic consultant on two major BBC/PBS television series: the six-part *The Fifty Years War: Israel and the Arabs* and its three-part sequel, *Israel and the Arabs: Elusive Peace*. Full transcripts of these interviews are now available to the public at the Liddell Hart archives, King's College London.

A Personal Note

I was nine years old when Israel occupied the Gaza Strip, Sinai, the Golan Heights, the West Bank and Arab East Jerusalem in those astonishing six days in June 1967, and I can still remember clearly our first family trip to the newly occupied East Jerusalem: by train to Jewish West Jerusalem from our family home near Tel Aviv, then a short taxi drive to the Jaffa Gate, and from there, after changing some Israeli liras to Jordanian dinars, by foot into the Old City.

Colours! That's what I recall of this first trip to Jerusalem. It was all *so* colourful: the bazaars with the Arab vendors and hawkers wearing their chequered *kefiya*s (it was the first time I had seen 'real' Arabs); the sweet shops with their heavily laden silver trays of *kunafa*, a sweet pastry of fine noodles, stuffed with white cheese and soaking in syrup; the wooden handcarts overflowing with fresh fruits and vegetables; the *cakh* – a sesame-seeded, doughnut-shaped roll sold with *za'atar*, a spice blend, wrapped up in a piece of paper ripped from an Arabic newspaper; the magnificent Dome of the Rock, its gold-plated dome twinkling over Temple Mount. Taking off our shoes we walked into the shrine – I still remember the cool and quiet, the heavy carpets underfoot, the Koranic verses inscribed in Arabic on the walls, and here and there the faithful at prayer – kneeling, bending, rising. Then down to the *Kotel*, that part of the Western Wall where generations of Jews have prayed and where I placed a secret wish written on a tiny piece of paper into a crack in the stones. Up at the top of the Wall, out of reach, weeds were sprouting among the ancient stones and pigeons made their nests. I held my dad's hand as we wandered through the narrow, cobbled alleys and covered lanes of the Old City, looking around with wide eyes, climbing on walls and peeping into hidden places. Domes, stone cupolas, red-tiled roofs, steeples, turrets, min-arets, church spires, jasmine, marigolds, geraniums in old tin cans, church bells. As evening came we watched from a high flat roof as Jerusalem turned golden. Although the walls bore the scars of bullets, it did not feel at all like occupation. It was like being abroad, like visiting a foreign land, living in a dream.

It was a decade or so later that I came face to face with the reality of the occupation when, as a young officer in the Israeli army, I was sent to patrol the streets of Gaza. The open sewage, the unpaved dusty streets, the rot and stench, the tetchy dogs barking in dark alleys, the rats (so big) scuttling in the rubbish, and, most of all, the sheer hostil-ity of the local population shocked me to the core. It was then that it dawned on me for the first time that, in fact, *I* was an occupier, *they* the occupied, and the land I was treading on in my army boots was, like it or not, an occupied territory.

Some ten years later again, and by then a civilian and an officer in the reserve, I was in Kathmandu in Nepal while on a long honey-moon, when I found out that war was raging in the occupied territories; it would soon acquire its, by now, well-known name, the *intifada*. And when, in a small corner shop in that most remote and romantic of cities, I spotted in one of the papers a picture of an Israeli soldier beating a Palestinian demonstrator with the butt of his rifle, my hair stood on end. There was something very poignant about this picture: the Palestinian looking up at the Israeli and the soldier look-ing down while raising his rifle. From Kathmandu I sent a letter to the editor of the Israeli newspaper *Haaretz* criticizing the Israelis – my people, my friends – and accusing them of committing the same brutal crimes against the Palestinians that so many other peoples of the world had once wreaked upon Jews. My father-in-law, a professor at Tel Aviv University who was unaware I had sent the letter, spotted it and, at once, phoned the editor to protest. He said that it just did not make any sense that his new son-in-law, a veteran of the 1982 Leba-non war, would say such things, and demanded an apology. The editor replied: 'Professor, the letter is here just in front of me and I can tell you that I have printed it without changing so much as a comma.'

I wrote in my letter that I would not return home before the killing was over. But in the end I had nowhere else to go. In Jerusalem, when

I bumped into a journalist friend of mine at the Hebrew University book shop, he raised an eyebrow and asked: 'Well, what are *you* doing here?' I had no answer. But I did say that should I be called up by the army for a tour of duty in the occupied territories, I would flatly refuse. He printed the exchange a week or so later in the *Haaretz* weekend supplement under the headline 'Ronnie Bregman refuses for the first time'.[1] I felt, at the time, like Joseph, Linda Grant's hero in *Still Here*, did about Vietnam – that the war was wrong, immoral and a disgrace.[2] I could not be a part of it, and as a result, like Joseph, I felt I had to find another country to live in until the insanity came to an end. In my case emigrating would also save me from the unpleasant prospect of being sent to prison for refusing to serve, an unusual act of defiance quite unheard of in those early days of the *intifada*. So it was that not much later I found myself in England, where I still live.

No author, no matter how strict a historian, can detach his work from his own experiences, interests and tastes, and I am sure this book bears the mark of having been written by an insider-outsider who lived through the events covered either at first hand in Israel or at a distance in England. As the reader will see, my attitude towards the occupation is apparent and my criticism pronounced, which, I suppose, will be regarded as unpatriotic by some of my fellow Israelis. Writing this book has made me look again at the period through which I have lived and question things which I have often taken for granted. And like any other writer I have had to make decisions about what to put in and what to leave out: in doing so, I have tried despite my personal feelings to be objective and to focus on what I regard as key turning points and episodes, those which I believe history will come to deem significant.

Many people have helped me along the way. Thanks are due to Daniel Bregman and Tom Raw, who cast their eagle eyes over the text, Dr Nir Resisi for information on the Sinai, Aharon Nathan for his fascinating insights on the Israeli administration of Gaza in the post-1956 war, Rabbis Sylvia Rothschild and Sybil Sheridan for going through my Bible quotations, and Professor Iain Scobbie for his useful comments on the legality of the Israeli occupation. My dear friend Norma Percy suggested that the imaginative Brian Lapping should help a little; as it turned out, he helped quite a lot by suggesting 'Cursed

Victory' as the title for this book. I was lucky to have a dedicated researcher in Daniela Richetova, who provided invaluable help in collecting personal testimonies, thus putting a human face to some of the events described. I should also like to thank my King's College students for taking my MA Occupation class at the War Studies department; I have learnt as much from you as I hope you have from me. At Penguin UK, I would like to thank Stuart Proffitt for accepting my idea to write a book on the Israeli occupation and for showing the patience of a saint in waiting for the final manuscript; my principal editor there, Laura Stickney, for her incisive comments and perceptive insights into earlier drafts of this work and her suggestions for their improvements, which resulted in the current much improved text; Mark Handsley, who was my copy-editor; the managing editor, Richard Duguid, who also produced my previous book for Penguin. I dedicate this book to Miriam Eshkol, wife of the former Israeli prime minister, Levi Eshkol, and my close friend for many years.

A line normally follows here: 'any errors of fact or interpretation are mine alone'; in a book whose subject matter is as fraught as this one I make it with unusual emphasis.

Ahron (Ronnie) Bregman,
London, 2014

Introduction

This is the story of Israel's occupation of the West Bank, Jerusalem, the Golan Heights, the Gaza Strip and the Sinai Peninsula since its sweeping victory over the combined forces of its Jordanian, Syrian and Egyptian neighbours in the Six Day War of 1967. The Sinai was gradually returned to Egypt from 1979 to 1982, following a successful peace deal, and Israel also withdrew its troops and settlements from the Gaza Strip in August 2005; partial withdrawal from the West Bank has occurred at various points since 1993, as a result of the tortuous Oslo peace process with the Palestinians. Yet, at the time of writing, much of the West Bank, Arab East Jerusalem and the Golan Heights remain under tight Israeli control.

The lands Israel seized in 1967 go by many different names, depending largely on one's political colour: 'Palestine' (pro-Palestinian); 'the occupied territories' (broadly left-wing); 'the Liberated Territories' or 'Judea and Samaria' (both right-wing Jewish); 'the Administrative Territories', 'the Territories beyond the Green Line', or, for those truly on the fence and often for brevity's sake, just 'the Territories'. Israel's military capture of these lands in 1967 has been covered extensively elsewhere, and I will not go over that ground again here.[1] However, if we wish to put a finger on the turning point when, in popular Western perception, the Israelis turned from the beleaguered victims of Arab aggression to occupiers, it is the six days from 5 to 11 June 1967. It was during these dramatic days, with Israel showing herself to be more of a Goliath than little David, that world sympathy started shifting from the Israelis to the new underdogs – namely to the people who came under Israel's occupation. From this point of view, and with the benefit of hindsight, it is safe to say that the great 1967 military triumph, which at first seemed such a blessed moment in Israeli – indeed Jewish – history, turned out to be, as the title of this book puts it, a cursed victory.

After seizing these lands Israel placed most of them under a military government, whereby army officers were in direct charge of daily life there, emphasizing that these captured territories would be a 'deposit', lands kept as a bargaining chip until the Arabs recognized Israel's right to exist peacefully in the Middle East, and publicly put an end to their dreams of destroying their neighbour by force.[2] In the meantime, the Israelis assured the world that, with their unique and appalling experience of what it is to be persecuted, the Jewish state would establish a truly 'enlightened occupation' ('Kibush Naor' in Hebrew).

But, as historians of empires everywhere are increasingly aware, an enlightened occupation is a contradiction in terms, 'like a quadrilateral triangle's;[3] and with the passage of time Israel's 'enlightened occupation' turned sour. Like many others before and since, the Israelis had failed to grasp the simple fact that, by definition, no occupation can be enlightened. The relationship between occupier and occupied is always based on fear and violence, humiliation and pain, suffering and oppression – a system of masters and slaves, it can be nothing *but* a negative experience for the occupied, and sometimes also for the individual occupier who is obliged to execute policies he might not necessarily agree with. That Israel – a vibrant and intellectual nation overwhelmingly aware of the pain of history – went down the path of military occupation is in itself quite astonishing. By the late 1960s, the world's former colonial empires were marching away from occupation and colonialism, whereas here, it seemed, the Israelis were attempting to march in the opposite direction.

When, twenty years after the 1967 war, the Palestinians launched an uprising – an *intifada* – in the Gaza Strip and West Bank, Israel claimed it came as a surprise. But a close look at the history of Israel's presence in those lands shows that this rebellion was hardly unexpected. Rather, it was the culmination of continuous resistance to occupation which had started soon after the Israeli army arrived: from the beginning the Israelis faced not only the wrath of militants who physically attacked them, but also that of ordinary men and women – students, teachers, lawyers, engineers, shopkeepers, housewives – in fact, all sections of Palestinian society, who welcomed the

Israelis with naked hostility from the outset. Edward Hodgkin, a former foreign editor of the British *Times* newspaper, visited the West Bank just two years after it was captured and wrote of 'the intensity with which the Israelis are hated everywhere by all sections of the population'.[4] Between 1968 and 1975, 350 incidents of violent resistance a year were recorded in the Palestinian occupied territories; from 1976 to 1982, the number doubled, and from 1982 to 1986 it went up to 3,000. During the first six months of the *intifada*, the number of violent incidents in the Palestinian occupied territories reached a staggering 42,355.[5] These daily acts of resistance led the Israelis to rely increasingly upon coercion and force to sustain the occupation, which in turn resulted in a mounting number of casualties, particularly on the Palestinian side. The annual average of Palestinians killed resisting the occupation from June 1967 to December 1987 was 32; from December 1987 to September 2000, it went up to 106; and from September 2000 to December 2006, it reached 674. The total number of Palestinians killed from 1967 to 2006 was 6,187; compared with 2,178 Israelis killed in the occupied territories and in Israel proper by Palestinian attacks.[6]

As for the non-Palestinian-populated territories seized by Israel in 1967: the vast expanse of the Sinai Peninsula, largely desert, was sparsely populated and remained fairly calm throughout the Israeli occupation; while in the Golan Heights, seized from Syria during the last thirty hours of the 1967 war, the Israelis were able to impose their will with relative ease. This was largely because the population of the Golan was much smaller and less dense than in the West Bank or Gaza, thanks to the mountainous terrain, and the fact that the advancing Israeli army destroyed most of the villages there, forcing the inhabitants to flee further into Syria. As for the Golanis whom the Israelis did allow to remain on the Heights, they were mainly Druze, an offshoot from Muslim tradition and relatively docile, at least at the beginning of the occupation.

The story that follows is about the politics and practice of the Israeli occupation – a narrative history in which I often stop to expand, explain and observe. It fills a surprising gap in the existing literature, which often adopts a thematic rather than a chronological approach.

I strongly believe in narrative history; the eminent historian James Joll once observed that 'It is important to remind the reader of the sequence of events . . . to provide him, so to speak, with a chart with which he can begin to navigate in these stormy seas'.[7]

As we will see, there are three main pillars supporting the Israeli occupation. The first is the use of military force to subjugate the occupied, including the use of military orders, arbitrary arrests, expulsions, torture and prolonged imprisonment. The second consists of laws and bureaucratic regulations, which maintain Israeli control over appointments to official positions, access to employment, restrictions on travel, the issuing of all sorts of licences and permits, including those needed for development and zoning. The third pillar is the establishment of physical facts on the ground; this includes land expropriation, the destruction of Arab villages and the construction of Jewish settlements and military bases, as well as the setting up of security zones, and control over water and other natural resources.[8]

Occupation, as the reader will see, is a much more complex and multi-dimensional phenomenon than it may at first seem. It can perhaps be better understood if seen as made of two circles: an inner circle, namely those areas where occupied and occupier rub shoulders on a daily basis; and an outer circle, where the occupation is argued over at some distance from the scene on the ground – this is where the politicians, diplomats, envoys and their ilk operate. The 'inner' and 'outer' circles are not disconnected; rather they touch and feed each other: the actions of soldiers, militants and civilians on the ground in the occupied territories (the 'inner circle'), of course, impact on the goings-on in the UN conference rooms, expensive hotels and TV studios that are the domain of the outer circle, and vice versa. How many times were delicate political negotiations set back months by a careless bullet from an Israeli rifle, or a maliciously timed Palestinian suicide bomb? And, as we will see, there is no better example of how the outer circle impacts on the inner circle than the Israeli–Palestinian peace summit at Camp David in 2000, whose collapse upset the Palestinians so much that all that was needed was a spark – a trigger (which turned out to be a provocative visit by the then leader of the opposition, Ariel Sharon, to Jerusalem) to push the Palestinians to embark on a massive uprising against the occupation (the second *inti-*

fada), resorting to the use of lethal weapons and suicide bombings. While I deal with *both* the occupied and the occupiers, my focus is necessarily on the latter, as it is in the very nature of its role that the occupier is more often the one driving events. History here as elsewhere is dictated by the victor. All the same, I try to let the reader also hear the voices and understand the experiences – and indeed the pain – of those living under occupation, thus putting a human face to the story.

As I go along, I follow the zigzagging of Israeli policy in the occupied territories, which has swayed between two opposing impulses for more than four decades and has determined the fortunes of millions of ordinary people living under occupation. At one end of the scale, Israeli policy has imposed a de facto annexation of occupied lands (though not of the *people* living there) by constructing large Jewish settlement blocs and installing military hardware. At the other end has been the occasional bout of political will – often as a result either of growing international pressure or of attacks by the occupied – to disengage from the territories, or at least from a good portion of them. There is a persistent tension within Israeli politics and society between these two opposing forces, which has, at times, even led Israeli governments to pursue *both* policies at the same time: offering peace and disengagement, while simultaneously continuing to build settlements. As clearly emerges in the story that follows, Israel's indecision between these two courses has led to much confusion about the fate of the occupied lands.

Another thread running through this narrative is what one might accurately describe as the true tragedy of the Arab–Israeli conflict, and that is one of lost opportunities. Throughout the first four decades of Israel's occupation, there have been many small, tactical errors made by all sides, which could have been corrected, forgotten, or simply brushed past by the unstoppable march of events. But there have also been larger, strategic mistakes, which took the conflict into undesired, unforeseen territory, prolonging the occupation and resulting in unnecessary death and suffering on both sides. Perhaps the biggest of these mistakes was made by Israeli Labor governments during the first decade of the occupation, when they had a unique opportunity to resolve, perhaps once and for all, their long-running conflict with the

Palestinians. This opportunity emerged as a result of the 1967 victory, which, indeed for the first time, brought almost the entire Palestinian nation under Israeli control and was an exceptional moment to tackle the roots of the conflict head on and perhaps offer the Palestinians some concessions which could have provided them with a more digni- fied life and some hope for a better future. This opportunity is not only clear with hindsight; some observers said at the time: 'Now is the shortest possible hour of decision', and 'it will be lost if we fail to exploit it'.[9] Yet in those critical early years of occupation, little pro- gress was made: Levi Eshkol, the Israeli prime minister in power for a couple of years after 1967, formed committee after committee to advise him on the best course, but when it came to acting on that advice – one way or the other – he demurred. One can only speculate why – perhaps it was his lack of self-confidence and his instinct to cling to the lands rather than give them back; or perhaps because, like many others in Israel's government at the time, he was simply at a loss with what to do with this prize that had fallen into Israel's lap. After the 1967 war, Eshkol adopted the habit of making a Churchillian V sign at public occasions; asked by his wife, Miriam, 'Eshkol, what are you doing? Have you gone mad?' the prime minister replied: 'No, this is not a V sign in English. It is a V sign in Yiddish! *Vi Krishen aroys?*' meaning: 'How do we get out of this?'"[10]

Successive governments similarly allowed themselves to drift along, carried by events instead of setting their own course towards a solu- tion to the conflict and the end of occupation. Policy making was largely an ad hoc business, consisting of knee-jerk reactions to par- ticular events or specific pressures with no orderly decision-making process. Public opinion played a major role here: in the wake of the great 1967 military victory over the Arabs the Israeli public felt invin- cible and saw no reason to put pressure on its governments to return lands which, many believed, could benefit Israel economically and otherwise. There was also a strong objection among Israelis – reli- gious and secular alike – to returning such places as Jerusalem and Hebron, the cradle of Jewish history.[11] We should also recall that the prime minister invited (in fact, for the first time in Israel's history) right-wing political parties into the 1967 war cabinet and they remained part of his coalition after the war as well, and strongly objected to the return of any occupied land, defined by their ultimate leader, Menachem Begin, as 'liberated' territories, to the Arabs.

Lack of decisive American pressure on Israel to withdraw from lands occupied in 1967 played its role too, as influential American senators such as Robert F. Kennedy, Jacob K. Javitz and others called on the US administration not to pressurize Israel to withdraw before Arab governments agreed to sign a peace treaty.[12] Richard M. Nixon, a contender for the 1968 US presidency, who visited the occupied lands soon after the war, publicly supported a continuous Israeli presence there, arguing that it would make Arab regimes more compliant in the matter of agreeing to peace talks 'within six months'.[13]

Similarly, in the late 1990s, when an opportunity emerged to end the occupation of the Golan Heights and strike a peace deal between Israel and Syria, Israel's leaders fell short of taking that decisive step. In chapter 10, I use unpublished documents to show that, while Syria was indeed willing to make the necessary concessions to get its occupied lands back and sign a peace treaty, Israel, at that time, chose to cling to the occupied land, preferring land to peace. And, as we will see, there have been many more such missed opportunities. Indeed, what the legendary Israeli diplomat Abba Eban once said of the Arabs, namely that they have never missed an opportunity to miss an opportunity, could well apply to Israeli governments too.

I have divided the book into three parts. The first covers the decade of the occupation from 1967 to 1977, and is further subdivided into the four separate geographical areas concerned: the West Bank including Jerusalem; the Gaza Strip; the Sinai; and the Golan Heights. In many ways, I would have preferred to deal with the four areas together – after all, in real life events took place simultaneously across all four regions, frequently impacting on each other – but the volume of events during this first decade, particularly on the occupied West Bank, is so vast that such a comprehensive approach runs the risk of drowning the reader in a confusing mass of facts and details. The second part of the book covers the second decade of the occupation, 1977–1987, ending with the opening salvos of the Palestinian *intifada*, their uprising against the occupation in the Gaza Strip and West Bank. The third part covers the remaining two decades from 1987 to 2007, a most dramatic era where the 'inner' and 'outer' circles of occupation intertwined, with the first and second *intifada*s raging alongside various faltering negotiations towards a settlement, culminating in Israel's unilateral disengagement from some Palestinian territories.

I regard *Cursed Victory* as a 'work in progress', and hope to add to it as the story of Israel's occupation continues to unfold and, I trust, comes to an end in the not-too-distant future. For now, I end the main narrative in 2007, with the last major event being the Israeli withdrawal from the Gaza Strip and four West Bank settlements and the subsequent events in the Gaza Strip, thus providing the reader with four decades of Israeli occupation. I conclude with some reflections on the years since 2007 and thoughts about how things might develop in the future.

The historian W. L. Langer once observed that the utmost mistake a historian can make is to construct a neat, logical pattern when, in actual fact, everything was confusion and contradiction. I hope that my attempt to bring some sense and clarity to the history of the Israeli occupation does not distort the confusion, contradictions and arbitrariness that have been such prominent features of it.

A Note on Occupation

Should the lands Israel seized in 1967 be regarded as 'occupied'? Is Israel an 'occupier'? Finding definitive answers to such questions is harder than one might suppose, but they are important because if Israel is indeed an occupier then, according to international law, it comes under certain obligations towards the land and people it occupies.

The briefer and more general 1907 Hague Convention and the longer, more detailed, 1949 Fourth Geneva Convention to which Israel is a party both require the occupier to abide by numerous rules in the lands it occupies.[1] For instance, the imposition of demographic changes within occupied territory is prohibited: article 49 of the Fourth Geneva Convention states that an occupying force 'shall not deport or transfer parts of its own civilian population into the territory it occupies', and 'individual or mass forcible transfers, as well as deportations . . . from occupied territories . . . are prohibited, regardless of their motive'. These rules are aimed at preventing colonization of conquered territory by citizens of the conquering state by, for instance, erecting settlements there and exploiting the land's resources, such as water. Additionally, an occupier must protect the people it occupies and their property: article 53 of the Fourth Geneva Convention states that 'any destruction by the Occupying Power of real or personal property . . . is prohibited'; the 1907 Hague Convention says, in article 46, that 'Private property cannot be confiscated' by the occupier; for example, private land belonging to the occupied or their houses. It is also – again in article 53 of the Fourth Geneva Convention – the 'duty' of the Occupying Power to ensure 'the food and medical supplies of the population'. Article 56 of the Fourth Geneva

Convention makes clear that 'the occupying force has the duty of ensuring and maintaining . . . the medical and hospital establishments and services, public health and hygiene'. In fact, Section III (Occupied Territories) of the 1949 Fourth Geneva Convention contains more than thirty articles on the duties and obligations of the occupying force.

The concept of occupation, however, does not go undisputed: in the post-1967 victory period, governments of Israel have consistently challenged the status of the Palestinian territory it seized from Jordan as 'occupied'. Instead, as a former legal adviser to the Israeli Foreign Ministry once put it, 'since Israel seized the West Bank . . . this territory has essentially been *disputed* land with the claimants being Israel, Jordan, and the Palestinians . . .'² Accordingly, argue the Israelis, the 1949 Fourth Geneva Convention – all the obligations and duties it requires of occupiers – is not applicable to the West Bank, nor, also, to the Gaza Strip. This view is based on the way the Israelis interpret article 1 of the Geneva Convention, where it is stated that '*The High Contracting Parties* undertake to respect and to ensure respect for the present Convention in all circumstances', and in article 2 of the same Convention where it says, among other things, that 'the present Convention shall apply to all cases of declared war or of any other armed conflict which may arise between two or more of the *High Contracting Parties* . . .' (my emphasis).

Israel interprets the term 'High Contracting Parties', as meaning sovereign rulers of distinct states. They argue that in the *absence* of such a High Contracting Party on the opposing side in a conflict, the rest of the 'contract', namely the entire Geneva Convention, does not apply. This, to be sure, is more than a political statement, but it is also supported by leading legal experts. For instance, a former Chief Justice of the Israeli Supreme Court, Meir Shamgar, argues that, in formal terms, the 1949 Geneva Convention cannot be applicable to the West Bank and Gaza Strip because the Convention is based, as Shamgar explains, on the assumption that there had been a sovereign who was ousted and that he had been a legitimate sovereign. The Israelis insist that neither the Kingdom of Jordan, which held the West Bank prior to 1967, nor Egypt, which ruled the Gaza Strip, could be regarded as the sovereign rulers in those territories and, thus, cannot be regarded as 'High Contracting Parties'. Both Jordan and Egypt, the Israelis maintain, illegally invaded Palestine in 1948; Egypt never formally annexed the Gaza Strip after it seized it, and Jordan's annexation of the West Bank in 1950 (see chapter 1) was never recognized by the international community, except Great Britain and Pakistan. This 'missing reversioner' argument, as it is better known, which maintains that neither Jordan nor Egypt possessed sovereignty over the West Bank and Gaza Strip, and that Israel, therefore, does not have the status of occupant, is used by Israel to dismiss the applicability of the Fourth Geneva Convention to these lands.

Furthermore, the Israelis claim that the demarcation lines drawn up between Israel and her neighbours at the end of the first Arab–Israeli war of 1948, the so-called 'Green Line', should not be regarded as proper 'borders', rather as armistice lines. This, they go on to argue, means that Israel's troops crossed no internationally recognized borders during the 1967 war. Additionally, they claim, Israel went to war in 1967 in self-defence; writing in 1970, the former US State Department Legal Advisor, Stephen Schwebel, who went on to head the International Court of Justice in The Hague, observed that, where the prior holder of territory had seized that territory unlawfully (as according to the Israelis did Egypt and Jordan), the state which, subsequently, takes that territory in the lawful exercise of self-defence (as the Israelis claim they did in 1967) has, against that prior holder, 'better title'. This suggests that Israel's claim to Gaza and the West Bank is stronger than that of Jordan or Egypt. Finally, from a historical perspective, the Israelis argue that, at least on the West Bank, Jews have a stronger claim than do Palestinians, as the Land of Israel has played a far more important role in Jewish history than in Palestinian or Arab history, and there has been a continuous Jewish presence there for at least three millennia; this, to be sure, is strongly disputed by Arabs, not least since they have formed the vast majority of the population on the land for many generations.

It is important to note that although the Israelis insist that the 1949 Fourth Geneva and, the 1907 Conventions do not apply to the West Bank and Gaza Strip, they have nonetheless pledged to observe the

Conventions' *humanitarian* provisions in these 'disputed' lands. Even this has been problematic, however, as the vagueness and strictly voluntary nature of this commitment can, in effect, allow Israel to pick and choose which provisions it applies at any given time.[3]

The vast majority of legal experts reject the main tenet of the Israeli argument, namely that the Fourth Geneva Convention and the Hague Convention are not applicable just because the previous status of the territories may have been slightly different from what those who negotiated the Conventions had in mind. In truth, behind closed doors, Israeli leaders do recognize that their view that Palestinian areas under their control since 1967 are not occupied lands is not convincing, and can hardly be sustained. In a 1967 'Top Secret' letter to the prime minister's office and a 'Most Urgent' memorandum, a Foreign Ministry legal adviser, Theodor Meron, noted that the international community rejects Israel's argument that 'the [West] Bank is not "normal" occupied territory', and goes on to say that 'certain actions taken by Israel are even inconsistent with [its own] claim that the [West] Bank is not occupied territory'.[4]

It is quite safe to say that the Israeli government and its defenders stand relatively alone in their denial of the nature of the occupation and, indeed, where Israel has sought to obfuscate or redefine what that occupation means, others see no room for interpretation. The UN General Assembly, for instance, has resolved that the situation in the lands seized by Israel in 1967 is one of occupation, and has urged it to respect the principles contained in the Fourth Geneva and other Conventions.[5] And the UN's International Court of Justice, for the most part a sober, mainstream, conservative legal organ, is unequivocally clear, both its individual judges and as a whole, that 'Few propositions can be said to command an almost universal acceptance . . . as the proposition that Israel's presence in the Palestinian territory of the West Bank including East Jerusalem and Gaza is one of military occupation governed by the applicable international regime of military occupation'.[6]

The view I adopt here, in common with the UN and most international observers, is that, notwithstanding the Israeli legal argument, the West Bank and the Gaza Strip are occupied lands and, hence, the 1949 Geneva and other Conventions should be applied there. The same is true also in relation to the Golan Heights and the Sinai Peninsula, which are unequivocally occupied, as these regions were until the 1967 war under the sovereignty of Syria and Egypt, which are, legally, the High Contracting Parties there.

PART ONE

The First Decade, 1967–1977

I

West Bank and Jerusalem

The kidney-shaped 'West Bank', roughly 110 kilometres long and fifty kilometres wide, is quite literally the land abutting the western bank of the River Jordan, and it was the heartland of old Palestine, which stretched to the north, west and south of the West Bank.

Geographically, the West Bank is not homogeneous: its southern part (the biblical Judea) is harsh and arid, whereas its northern section (Samaria) is gentler and more fertile. Demographically and culturally, the West Bank is composed of three distinctive sectors. Life in the south revolves around the conservative town of Hebron (Al Khalil in Arabic), which is home to an intensely traditional Muslim community. The second sector, in the centre, focuses on Jerusalem (Al Quds in Arabic) and is relatively cosmopolitan thanks to that city's unique status, worldwide fame and constant stream of tourists. In the north is an area dominated by Nablus, the largest West Bank town after Jerusalem, where people are more politically conscious and nationalistic and there exist a sophisticated intelligentsia and thriving merchant and landowning classes.

For four centuries, from 1517 to 1917, the area was part of the Ottoman Empire, but during the First World War it was occupied, along with the rest of Palestine, by the British. Thirty years on, the British withdrew from Palestine, and the Jewish community there, which was less than half of the non-Jewish population of Palestine, defeated the latter in a short civil war and then proceeded to declare independence, on 14 May 1948. A war immediately broke out between the newly established Israel and its Arab neighbours, who objected to Israel's existence and wished to restore the defeated Arab populations of Palestine; in the course of this war King Abdullah's

Trans-Jordanian forces crossed the River Jordan and seized the West Bank along with the Arab sector of Jerusalem, including some of Islam's most important shrines. Subsequently, in April 1950, King Abdullah's parliament passed an Act of Unification, which incorporated the occupied West Bank of the River Jordan and Jerusalem into the four-year-old Hashemite Kingdom of Jordan.

There was wide disapproval of this unilateral annexation among the international community, including the Arab League, the forum representing Arab nations, as this annexed part of Palestine had been allotted by the UN in November 1947 to the Arabs of Palestine to form part of a proposed Arab state to live side by side with a Jewish state;[1] only Great Britain and Pakistan would recognize the annexation. In the face of such criticism, King Abdullah made it plain that the West Bank annexation was neither immutable nor irrevocable, and that he would hold the area as a pledge until 'the liberation of Palestine' from the Israelis.[2]

The West Bankers themselves, on the whole, were ambivalent towards their new overlord, although they regarded the Hashemite regime as the lesser of two evils compared to potential rule by Israel. They suspected the king had a hidden agenda to weaken Palestinian identity; and, in addition, they had long regarded themselves as more advanced, sophisticated and better educated than their new masters, whom they often dubbed 'backward Bedouins of the desert'. Nonetheless, there was – and this did not escape the West Bankers – much sense in joining together the East and West Banks of the River Jordan. For West Bankers had, up till now, often looked westwards for their trade and contacts with the world – towards the Mediterranean coast. But the establishment of the State of Israel created a barrier, effectively cutting the West Bank off from its traditional trade routes and thus forcing its people to look to the east for new trade and contacts – to Jordan and beyond. From this point of view, annexation with the East Bank and incorporation of the remaining part of old Palestine into Jordan proper made sense, though it is safe to say that few West Bankers regarded themselves as primarily Jordanian.

Gradually, many West Bankers became reconciled to the Hashe-mite government, particularly during the 1960s when Jordan enjoyed an annual growth rate of as much as 23 per cent, some of which prosperity inevitably spilled over to the West Bank. That King Abdullah's grandson, Hussein bin Talal, who succeeded to the throne in 1952 (Abdullah was assassinated in Jerusalem on 20 July 1951) was attentive to the needs of the West Bank helped enormously in integrating the region into his kingdom. This relative harmony, how-ever, came to an abrupt end when, in 1967, some seventeen years after annexation, the advancing Israeli army occupied Arab East Jerusalem and the West Bank, and blew up the bridges over the River Jordan, thus symbolically, and indeed physically, re-separating the two banks.

When the Israelis marched into the West Bank the area had a popula-tion of 670,000 Palestinians, including 35,000 in East Jerusalem.[3] The pace of life in this traditional land, where the extended family and community played a central role, was slow and, in 1967, it was not uncommon to see women drawing water from a well, or farmers ploughing fields with a wooden plough pulled by a pair of oxen. But with the war this land and its people endured swift, indeed, dramatic changes, with the Israelis demolishing entire villages, as was the case for example in the Latrun area.

In the 1948 war, the salient of Latrun, halfway between Tel Aviv and Jerusalem, witnessed ferocious fighting as the Israelis threw in wave after wave of troops in repeated attempts to capture this stra-tegic point from the Jordanian Legion – but to no avail. Now, in 1967, the Israelis were finally successful: they dislodged the Jor-danians and took control of Latrun along with the area around it, including the nearby Palestinian villages of Imwas, Beit Nuba and Yalu.

Until 1967 life in these villages was simple and mundane, as the eighty-year-old Aishe, from the village of Yalu, recalls:

The people got along well together. They used to sit together ... There was a central square where people coming home from work would go. They would take coffee and sugar, and have fun in the square together.

5

When a visitor would come to the square he would be invited to lunch and dinner. The lunch host would slaughter a sheep and feed everyone in the square.[4]

What happened in and around these villages in 1967 we know from Amos Kenan, an Israeli soldier and in later years a leading writer, who recalls how 'The commander of my platoon said that it had been decided to blow up these villages ... [in order] ... to punish these murderers' dens and ... to deprive infiltrators of a base in future.'[5] He and his colleagues were instructed to search the villages, take any armed men prisoner, and 'any unarmed persons should be given time to pack their belongings and then ... to get moving'. Heavy machinery was then brought in, turning the villages into heaps of rubble; in Imwas 375 houses were demolished, in Yalu 535 and in Beit Nuba 550; 10,000 Palestinians became refugees and were never allowed back to their land, some of which was later distributed among Israelis and on the rest of which a national park was built.[6] The events in Latrun were not, however, exceptional; the wholesale demolition of West Bank Palestinian villages was widespread during and in the aftermath of the 1967 war in breach of the international laws of war. Yet the most dramatic and significant changes would take place in Jerusalem.

CHANGING JERUSALEM

For Palestinians, East Jerusalem was not only a holy place, but also an important commercial, administrative and cultural centre and the natural connection for transport between the northern and southern halves of the West Bank. As in the Latrun area and elsewhere, in Jerusalem local military commanders took matters into their own hands and sought to make changes to the facts on the ground without troubling the consciences of their commanders in the military or in government. Thus, Chaim Herzog, Jerusalem's first military governor after the war, and a future president of Israel, upon his first visit to the holy Wailing Wall ordered the removal of a urinal which was placed right up against the Wall. A trivial and benign act, this nonetheless paved the way to other more significant changes. 'We concluded',

Herzog recalls, 'that we should take advantage of the opportunity to clear the entire area in front of the [Wailing] Wall. It was a historic opportunity . . .'[7] Immediately in front of the Wall there were 200-odd houses of the ancient Magharbeh Quarter (the Harat al-Magharibah, or the Moroccan Quarter), its Muslim inhabitants the beneficiaries of an ancient Islamic foundation, originally established in 1193. However, located as it was so close to the Wall, the Magharbeh Quarter left little room for the Jews who gathered there to pray; pre-1967 postcards show how tight the area just in front of the Wall had been.

On 10 June, on his second visit to the area, General Herzog, working with General Uzi Narkiss, ordered his troops to demolish the entire Magharbeh Quarter with a view to creating a plaza in front of the Wall that would be able to accommodate many hundreds at once. Herzog would later admit that he had not been authorized by anyone and neither did he seek authorization for the demolition, justifying his decision by his concerns about losing the opportunity if he waited too long for approval from the government. Narkiss, in a similar vein, wrote: 'In certain situations, you don't need to involve the upper ranks.'[8] Concerned about the legality of the demolition, the mayor of Jewish West Jerusalem, Teddy Kollek, who accompanied the generals on their visits to Jerusalem, consulted the minister of justice, who told him: 'I don't know what the legal status is. Do it quickly and may the God of Israel be with you.'[9]

Subsequently, officers passed from door to door giving residents of the Magharbeh Quarter notice to empty their homes within two hours; 135 Arab families (around 650 people) were forced to evacuate before bulldozers moved in to knock down the houses. Some refused to leave and were buried alive in the wreckage: in a 1999 interview, Major Eitan Ben-Moshe, the Israeli officer in charge of the demolition, described how 'After we finished demolishing the neighbourhood we found some bodies of the residents who refused to leave their homes . . .'[10] Those who did get out had little time to carry much with them; Mahmoud Masloukhi, who grew up in the Quarter and was thirty-four and recently married in 1967, gathered his family and they fled with 'just the clothes on our backs', carrying with them black-and-white photographs.[11] Another resident, Muhammad Abdel-Haq, describes how in the days after the demolition his wife and child would return to the site of their home, where the clear-up operation continued for a few more days, and wait for the Israeli bulldozer to clear the rubble somewhere 'so that we might retrieve clothes and other belongings which we did not have time to take with us'; they repeated this ritual every day for a week.[12] As roughly half of the neighbourhood's residents traced a lineage back to Morocco, many returned there with the assistance of Morocco's King Hassan II; others found places in the Shufat refugee camp in northern Jerusalem.

The largest potential flashpoint in recently occupied East Jerusalem was clearly the Temple Mount/Haram al-Sharif compound. This was originally the site of the Jewish temple built by King Solomon in the tenth century BC, then rebuilt 400 years later before finally being destroyed by the Romans in AD 70. Some seven centuries later Muslims constructed on the same spot the al-Aqsa mosque and the Dome of the Rock, which was built on a raised rocky surface from where, according to Islamic tradition, the prophet Mohammed ascended to heaven; it is considered the third-holiest shrine in Islam. Now, however, with the Temple Mount/Haram al-Sharif compound in Israeli hands following the defeat there of Jordanian forces, there was a growing concern that religious fanatics, of either faith, would claim the site as their own and provoke bloodshed. Aware of this danger, the defence minister, Moshe Dayan, intervened.

At fifty-two, Dayan was one of Israel's greatest war heroes. He proved himself in Israel's 1948 war of independence as a daring field commander and eight years later, aged only forty-one and by then the highest-ranking officer in the Israeli army – its Chief of Staff – he led his troops from the front in a successful attack on Egypt, coordinated with France and Britain. With his trademark black eye-patch (he had lost an eye in battle) Dayan looked like a modern pirate and he was one of Israel's most colourful and controversial characters: a brave, charismatic individual, egocentric, ambitious, cynical, arrogant and hedonistic. Dayan's nomination to the post of defence minister came on the eve of the 1967 war, and it was under his direction that Israel's armed forces achieved their great victory over the Arabs.

A few days after the end of the war, Dayan went to East Jerusalem to speak to the Muslim Council, the body in charge of the holy Muslim properties on the Mount. He made it clear that he expected all religious peoples to have free access to the Temple Mount/Haram al-Sharif and that, while overall security would be Israel's responsibility, the country would not interfere in any other way; Muslims could continue to run their shrines as they had done before the war. Acknowledging that allowing Jews to pray in the compound might be seen as a provocation, Dayan assured the Muslim leaders that Jews would be banned from praying on the Mount itself; they would only be allowed access to the Wailing Wall at the foot of the Haram. In his memoirs Dayan notes that while the Muslim leaders 'were not overjoyed' with their new rules, they had little choice but to accept.[13] On 23 June, 5,000 Muslims, including 1,000 from Israel proper (until this time Arabs living in Israel had not been allowed access to the holy site), took part in Friday prayers on the Haram.

Israel's interests in Jerusalem, as it soon became apparent, were very ambitious. What Israel sought above all was a complete geographical and demographic transformation: to enlarge the city's municipal borders, bring together the Arab East and Jewish West sectors, and turn a hitherto divided Jerusalem into one united city ruled by Israel.

Back in 1947, the international community had proposed that Jerusalem be given special status as a *corpus separatum* and be kept united. But as a result of the 1948 war it was partitioned between Israel and Jordan: West Jerusalem, an area of thirty-eight square kilometres, came under Israeli control, while East Jerusalem, an area of six square kilometres, was ruled by Jordan. Later, the parties erected a fence, separating the two city's sections, with belts of mines laid along each side; there were only two entry points in this formidable barrier, under UN supervision, one at the Mandelbaum Gate, the other on Mount Zion, through which only diplomats were allowed to pass and, on holy days, pilgrims too.

Now, however, the government set up a special ministerial committee to look into ways of creating an Israeli-controlled unified Jerusalem. Some proposals discussed by the committee went so far as to suggest that as much as two thirds of the wider West Bank around Jerusalem be incorporated into an enlarged city.[14] In these discussions, Dayan turned out to be a moderating voice. 'What is this?' he commented on one proposal. 'A plan for a city or for a state?'[15] On another occasion he remarked: 'I know the Jews' big appetite ... [but] I'm not in favour of [annexing] ... villages with 20,000 [Arab] inhabitants [to Jerusalem].'[16]

On 26 June 1967, the committee brought its final proposal before the government for approval. This plan would lead to a de facto annexation of East Jerusalem as Israel's laws would be imposed there, and the raising of the city's combined territory from forty-four square kilometres before 1967 to a staggering 108.8 square kilometres.[17] The ministers approved the plan and they then turned to debating how best to announce the annexation to the world. Unlike in later years, in the 1960s the Israelis were still quite tuned to international mood and opinion, and understood that their expanding the boundaries of Jerusalem would violate international law and upset much of the international community. Ministers therefore sought to downplay the event by reporting it to the Israeli press as merely a series of small administrative matters, so that the bigger picture 'won't get too much publicity and commentary'.[18] The head of the committee, the justice minister, Ya'acov Shimshon Shapira, reported to the committee that after discussing the matter with a number of journalists he felt that 'All the journalists [are] sympathetic [and would play the matter down], apart from one editor who thinks that it's more important that his readers know what's happening than it is to keep this secret.' To ensure that the story was also downplayed in the foreign press the minister suggested that 'the censor should not allow anything about the unification of Jerusalem to be published or telegraphed abroad ...' In the meantime, the Foreign Ministry instructed its representatives abroad to avoid using the word 'annexation' and, instead, to describe the action taken by the government as an 'administrative step', aimed at facilitating the running of electricity and water supplies, public transportation, and education and health services; that the steps were 'municipal integration' rather than 'annexation'.

Many dubbed the new boundaries of Jerusalem 'the Arak and cigarette border', as it was fixed in such a way as to leave the Palestinian factories producing alcohol and cigarettes – products considered undesirable for the then puritan Israel – outside the municipal boundaries; these new boundaries were also drawn in a way that would ensure that the annexed land contained as few Palestinians as possible in an attempt to keep Jerusalem as Jewish as possible.

With the new maps drawn, on 29 June 1967 the Israelis issued an order for the dissolution of the eight-member elected council of Arab East Jerusalem, adding that all Arab municipal personnel in all departments of the city administration were henceforth 'temporary employees of the [Israeli] Municipality of Jerusalem until such time as it is decided to appoint them through the Municipality of Jerusalem on the basis of job applications'. The order concluded by 'thank[ing] Mr. Ruhi al-Khatib [the mayor of Arab Jerusalem since 1957] and the members of the Municipal Council for their services during the period of transition from the entry of the IDF [Israel Defence Force, into Arab East Jerusalem] to this day'.[19] With that the enlarged city came under the baton of Teddy Kollek, the first Jewish mayor of a united Jerusalem.

In the annexed area Palestinians were granted permanent residency status, allowing them to live there and work in Israel, vote in municipal elections, be eligible for the welfare benefits provided by Israel, and travel freely throughout Israel and the occupied territories; those wishing to receive full Israeli citizenship could do so if they agreed to swear allegiance to Israel, give up any other citizenship – they often had Jordanian citizenship – and demonstrate some command of Hebrew.

Dayan, in an especially daring move, simultaneously ordered the removal of all the concrete barriers, barbed wire and minefields that had divided Arab East and Jewish West Jerusalem since the 1950s, and to allow Arabs and Israelis access to each other. The defence minister's decision initially aroused opposition from the police and Mayor Kollek, all of whom feared bloodshed, but he persisted, and all barriers separating the two sectors of Jerusalem were torn down, leading to an immediate cross-migration of peoples. That night Mayor Kollek wired Dayan: 'You were right,' he said. 'The city is one huge carnival – all Arabs are in the Zion Square [in Jewish West Jerusalem] and all Jews are in the [Arab East Jerusalem's] bazaars'.[20] There was no bloodshed.

In spite of the government's efforts to obscure their intentions, the changes in Jerusalem could not be concealed from the eyes of the wider world: on 4 July 1967, the UN General Assembly adopted resolution 2253 (ES-V), calling upon Israel 'to rescind all measures already taken [and] to desist forthwith from taking any action which would alter the status of Jerusalem'. The Israelis dismissed these claims. Abba Eban, Israel's foreign minister, dispatched a letter to the UN Secretary General, U Thant, repeating the Israeli mantra that 'the term "annexation" is out of place', and proceeded to present the Israeli view that the measures adopted related to the integration of Jerusalem 'in the administrative and municipal spheres'.[21]

The Palestinians living in the now occupied West Bank and Jerusalem were at first simply stunned – indeed, June–July 1967 came to be known as the 'months of shock' – but once recovered they went on to raise the banner of protest against the Israeli annexation, with demonstrations taking place in Jerusalem and elsewhere. On 26 August, eight Arab notables, led by the dismissed mayor of East Jerusalem, Ruhi al-Khatib, issued a memorandum which they distributed among fellow Palestinians and also sent to the UN, protesting against the measures taken by the army against Jerusalem. The memo delineates some of the means by which the Israelis sought to turn their annexation into a new reality on the ground:

> The Israeli occupation authorities . . . have proceeded with and given effect to annexation measures without heeding world public opinion and against the wishes of the Arab inhabitants, thus violating fundamental and elementary international law relating to occupied countries . . . They have . . . permitted access to [churches and mosques] during hours of prayer. We must also protest the complete lack of decorum in dress and behaviour shown by both men and women [which] offended the religious sensibilities of the faithful . . . The Jewish Municipality demolished many Arab buildings . . . and it is continually taking similar measures in order to erase the last trace of the demarcation lines between the two sectors [of Jerusalem] . . . All the Jordanian laws in force in the Arab sector of the city have been repealed and replaced by Israeli measures and laws, in violation of international law, which stipulates that the laws in force in the occupied territories must be respected . . . The failure of the occupation authorities to prevent desecration of the holy places has led to the burglary of one of the largest and holiest

churches in the world. The priceless, diamond-studded crown of the Statue of the Virgin, Our Lady of Sorrows, on Calvary itself was stolen ... The occupying forces destroyed a large plastics factory inside the [city] walls, where 200 manual and clerical workers were employed ... the buildings were demolished and the machinery was pillaged.

They ended their letter by proclaiming that:

The inhabitants of the Arab sector of Jerusalem and those of the West Bank resolutely proclaim their opposition to all the measures which the Israeli occupation authorities have taken ... this annexation, even camouflaged under the cloak of 'administrative measures', was carried out against their will and against their wishes. In no event shall we submit to it or accept it.[22]

In the face of growing protest, Dayan advised the army to deploy 'at least four to six tanks' in sensitive flashpoints like Jerusalem, Nablus, Hebron and other locations to deter potential rioters. 'We must be in a position to immediately put them down,' he said.[23] Such advice from Dayan was unexpected because, as we shall now see, it ran against the grain of his philosophy about how the Israeli occupation should be handled.

DAYAN'S INVISIBLE OCCUPATION

Moshe Dayan was not only 'the Sultan of the Territories', as he was often dubbed – perhaps the single most influential figure in the fate of the lands Israel seized in 1967 – but also the only minister in government with previous experience in dealing with Arab populations under occupation. After the 1956 war, as the army's Chief of Staff he was in charge of the occupied Gaza Strip, which Israel had just seized from Egypt and would keep for a year. Perhaps the most important feature of Dayan's tenure there was his reluctance to intervene in the daily life of the Gazans. On one occasion, when the local population embarked on a general strike to protest against the occupation – shutting down schools and shops – Dayan summoned Gaza City's mayor and told him: 'If you close the shops, only your people will suffer. If the schools are shut, it's to your children's disadvantage. We will not interfere ...'[24]

Dayan learnt further lessons a decade later, in 1966, when he followed the American army in Vietnam as a reporter, recording his experiences in a largely overlooked book titled *Vietnam Diary*. In it, he is highly critical of the Americans' conduct and their attempt, as Dayan saw it, to impose American culture, values and ways of life on the Vietnamese; he could not comprehend, he wrote, why it was important to the Americans that Vietnamese children play baseball. Rather than meddling in Vietnamese life, he observed, American forces would have enjoyed much greater success if they had simply left the locals to their own devices.

This background sheds light on Dayan's instructions to Jerusalem's military governor, Chaim Herzog, immediately after the occupation of the city, when he urged him to refrain from intervening in Palestinian daily life. 'Don't try to rule the Arabs,' he warned the general, 'Let them rule themselves . . . I want a policy whereby an Arab can be born, live, and die without ever seeing an Israeli official.'[25] In the same spirit, when he met military commanders five days after the end of the war, Dayan urged them:

> Don't boss [the Arabs]. Leave them alone. Don't [try to] educate them and don't [try to] teach them. With regard to security . . . Go ahead – a strong arm. [But then] leave them alone. Let them move around freely, on foot and by car. Let them go to their fields, to their businesses . . . And besides, why are there so many soldiers in the town [of Nablus]? Get out of town. Deploy out of town. You don't have to be seen. The city must appear as if it hasn't been occupied . . . Give them the feeling that the war is over and that nothing has changed.[26]

Dayan also instructed that Israeli flags be removed from headquarters and military bases in the West Bank, since it was, as he told them, 'a loathed symbol to the Arab side, and we do not want to make matters worse with an unnecessary provocation'.[27]

Dayan, as he himself often explained, cherished Arab culture; before the war, he would often meet heads of Arab villages in Israel for talks, and visit the Bedouin tribes who roam the Negev desert in southern Israel with their flocks, go into their tents, sit on the ground and eat and drink with them. For this reason, many have claimed that his policies during the early days of the occupation were borne of magnanimity. It is my view, however, that his policy was not magnanimous, but Machiavellian: he thought that an 'invisible occupation', where his troops were not seen and there were no overt symbols of occupation such as Israeli flags, would foster apathy among the Palestinians, diminishing their appetite for change, and thus let Israel hold on to the occupied lands permanently. Although secular, Dayan nevertheless regarded the West Bank – Judea and Samaria – as the cradle of Jewish history and wanted Israel to keep it for good, but he also knew that a more visible form of occupation would only foment resistance. And in case resistance to the occupation did occur, what Dayan wished was that Palestinian parents should deal with this resistance, rather than his troops. On one occasion, when young people on the West Bank, particularly young girls, embarked on demonstrations against the occupation, Dayan summoned local Palestinian leaders and told them:

> We are not going to clash with these girls. These girls . . . they have a home and parents . . . There are many differences between us, but one thing we have in common – you have daughters and I have a daughter. It never occurred to me . . . that we would not be able to control our daughters or that they would not do as we wished.[28]

Dayan's invisible occupation had another dimension in that he turned a blind eye to a measured Jordanian meddling in West Bank affairs by allowing the Jordanian dinar to continue as one of the legal tenders there. Israel was reluctant to invest in the occupied lands and, as far as Dayan was concerned, if Jordanian funds could help support the West Bank, so much the better. Indeed, King Hussein continued paying salaries to civil servants – to teachers, health professionals, judges and bureaucrats, hoping that by funnelling funds to the occupied West Bank he could continue to exert influence in lands which he still hoped would be returned to him one day; also, ensuring the occupied West Bankers were comfortable financially would be an incentive for them to stay put rather than emigrate across the River Jordan into Jordan proper, already over-populated with Palestinian refugees.[29]

ONE-WAY BRIDGES

It had been Dayan's decision to blow up the bridges over the River Jordan during the 1967 war, but once the West Bank was securely in Israeli hands, he decided to allow again the free movement of goods and people across the river as before the war.

What came to be known as Dayan's 'Open Bridges' policy is often hailed as 'liberal', but in fact it is – again – another aspect of his 'invisible occupation' working at its best. He thought, and for good reason, that allowing Palestinians to cross freely to Jordan and return to their homes in the occupied territories could help ensure that they did not feel the occupation impinging on their daily lives; that the situation, as far as they were concerned, was much the same as it had been before the war and there was, therefore, no need to resist it. And furthermore, if Palestinians did feel the pressure of occupation, then crossing the river could provide a 'safety valve', giving them somewhere to go to let off steam and relax. Perhaps Dayan also calculated that by allowing free movement across the river he might be able to thin out the occupied territories' Arab population – after all, the Israelis preferred the land without its native people – as those who left, such as students travelling abroad to study, might choose not to return home, where jobs were scarce, salaries low and career opportunities limited. Free movement across the river could also provide a stick as well as a carrot – if Palestinians caused trouble, the privilege of crossing the River Jordan could be withdrawn at any moment, giving them, as Dayan often put it, 'something to lose'.

Like many of Israel's 'policies' in the occupied territories, however, Open Bridges was neither planned nor discussed in government, nor in any other forum. In Israel, the government is formally in charge of the military, but with no effective advisory body on security matters (like, for example, an American-style National Security Council) it is very much dependent on the military, and here again the Open Bridges policy developed from bottom to top – from the military to the government.

This policy originated in the ingenuity of a certain Lieutenant Colonel Yisrael Eytan, the newly appointed military governor of Samaria in the north of the West Bank who, in the immediate aftermath of the war, had to grapple with an unexpected and intractable problem: what to do with a surplus of fruit and vegetables – some 80,000 tons of watermelons, melons, grapes, tomatoes, olives and cucumbers – cut off from their traditional market in Jordan, and rotting on trees and in boxes on the West Bank. While some of the produce was sold to Israeli and European markets, and the Israeli military increased its own daily ration of fruit and vegetables – Israel even managed to offload some to the US army – there was still a large surplus.

It was at this juncture that a certain Palestinian by the name of Abu Hashem, a wealthy farmer from Nablus, and the landlord of 500 hectares of crops in the Jordan Valley, approached the Lieutenant Colonel, pointing out that, although the bridges over the River Jordan still lay in ruins, during the summer months the river could easily be forded by motor vehicle at several points; should the army allow the produce to be exported to Jordan, the problem of the surplus would soon be solved. And with government policy on the matter yet to be formed – as on many other issues – Lt Col. Eytan spread the news among local West Bank farmers that the army would turn a blind eye to the 'exporting' of crops to the East Bank. Subsequently, in the last week of June 1967, as the Israeli army watched from a distance, two trucks from Jenin, in the northern West Bank, loaded with produce, made their way through the river at a shallow point near Tel Abu Zuz to meet a small convoy on the opposite shore, where, within minutes, all the produce was unloaded and loaded again onto the awaiting Jordanian trucks.

From this humble beginning, trade soon flourished and by the first week of July ten trucks had crossed the river, with ten more in the second week. Soon, the army began organizing the crossing, taking registration numbers and noting when the vehicles returned; on the Sabbath, when Jews are not permitted to carry out any work, pre-prepared slips were handed over to drivers, which were given back on their return and recorded, on the following day, in the 'Book of Crossings'. Before long, hundreds of trucks were crossing the river to Jordan, carrying vegetables, fruit, olive oil, plastic containers made in Bethlehem, building stone from quarries in Ramallah, furniture and household goods.

Dayan came to Tel Abu Zuz, which had become known as 'the vegetable market', on 2 August, and gives a vivid account of the scene in his memoirs: 'An extraordinary sight, a Hollywood Wild West scene except that instead of cowboys, cattle, and horse-drawn wagons converging on a river ford, there was a huge assembly of heavily laden trucks, vans, and carts being towed across by tractor'.[30]

What was initially an ad hoc solution to a surplus of crops gradually developed, now under Dayan's personal supervision, into the Open Bridges policy under which not only goods but also *people* were allowed to cross the River Jordan in both directions. And as the encroaching winter would see water levels in the river rise and make it impassable, Dayan dispatched an emissary, Hamdi Canaan, the mayor of Nablus, who knew Jordan's King Hussein well, to see if Hussein would agree to erect permanent bridges over the river. The emissary later reported back that the king would cooperate on the matter and, subsequently, the Jordanian Legion threw two Bailey bridges across the Jordan: one just east of Jericho to serve the inhabitants of Jerusalem, Bethlehem and Hebron; the other near the old Damiya Bridge to serve Nablus, Jenin and the other towns and villages in the northern West Bank.

For a while, these measures helped to create an atmosphere of normality, thus allowing the army to stay out of sight, in line with Dayan's philosophy of invisible occupation; but other developments on the occupied West Bank would soon prove far less encouraging.

OPERATION REFUGEE

The war on the West Bank was brief, but the army was quite successful in encouraging Palestinian populations to emigrate from there to Jordan; here, as elsewhere, Israel wished to have the land without its people. The vast majority of those who emigrated were refugees of the first Arab–Israeli war, namely Palestinians who in 1948 fled from Palestine; now, in 1967, they became refugees a second time. Hajji Fatima Da'en had an experience typical of second-time Palestinian refugees; she recalls how, upon arriving on the West Bank in 1948, 'We built new homes and we planted grapes and figs and apples and plums and everything.' But in 1967 'the Jews came and kicked us out. They took what we had planted and threw us out . . .'[31] Other West Bankers followed suit, many of them apprehensive that if they stayed put, they would be cut off from their relatives or from jobs on the East Bank. Indeed, as a result of the war, many Palestinian families were forcibly divided, with part of the family on the East Bank and the other on the West. The Palestinian Ra'ida Shehadeh from the West Bank Kalandia refugee camp recalls: 'We were two sisters and a boy . . . my parents separated by the [1967] war . . . My mother went to Jordan and my father stayed living here . . .'[32]

In Jerusalem, which was an integral part of the West Bank, the army was particularly proactive, providing, from just after the war, daily buses from the Old City's Damascus Gate to Jordan. The Israeli army's General Narkiss testified how he placed several buses in Jerusalem, writing on them 'To Amman – Free of Charge'. This transfer, organized entirely by military commanders on the ground and flying in the face of international law, was not challenged by the government. Once at the bridges over the River Jordan, the Palestinians would sign a departure statement declaring that they had left willingly. This was rarely the case, however, as one former Israeli soldier whose job it was to collect signatures at the bridges recounts:

> We forced them to sign . . . a bus would get [to the bridge] with only men . . . aged 20 to 70, accompanied by soldiers. We were told that these were saboteurs and it would be better if they were out of the country . . . [The Palestinian men] did not want to leave, and were dragged from the buses while being kicked and hit with rifle butts. By the time they reached my [signing] stall, they were usually already completely blurred and they would not care any longer about the signing . . . frightened, they would cross to the other side running . . . When someone would refuse to give me his hand [the soldiers] would beat him up badly. Then I would forcibly take his thumb, immerse it in ink and fingerprint him . . .[33]

Israel's foreign minister, Abba Eban, privately urged the government to ease off any transfer of Palestinians that might be seen as forcible, and even to allow some of those who had already left to return to the West Bank ahead of a September UN General Assembly that was to deliberate the Middle East crisis. Concerned that international focus on a refugee crisis might distract from a debate about responsibility for the outbreak of the 1967 war, which Eban not unreasonably wished to place squarely on the Arabs, he felt it would be wise to modify the policy of transfer.

In response, on 2 July, the government publicly launched 'Operation Refugee', aimed at allowing some Palestinians who had recently departed to return to their homes within a month. But it turned out to be a lengthy process, as the deportees had first to fill in an application form (while still in Jordan), which would then be considered by the Israelis. To make matters worse, on the ground, the whole process was hampered by bureaucracy and squabbling between Israeli and Jordanian officials over technicalities. While Amman, for instance, wished the refugees to use Red Cross application forms – the actual physical process and organization of the return had been delegated to the International Committee of the Red Cross – Israel insisted on forms bearing the insignia of the Israeli state. The truth is that, while the Israelis realized that they should not upset world opinion too much at this point in time, they still wished to see the refugees stay in Jordan and even encourage more to leave. 'We want emigration [out of the West Bank] . . . we want to create a new map,' Dayan is recorded as saying, and 'our intention [is] to encourage emigration . . . Anyone who has got practical ideas or proposals how to encourage emigration let him speak up. No idea or proposal is to be dismissed out of hand.'[34] Military governors, in the meantime, encouraged their subordinates 'not to meet every request [the West Bankers] send our way', as they did not want to make life too comfortable for the Palestinians. Instead, they sought ways to 'to increase Arab emigration . . .'[35]

Thus, with every Israeli effort directed towards encouraging emigration, and the process for refugees to return to the West Bank slow and difficult, it is no surprise that while it is estimated that somewhere between 175,000 and 250,000 Palestinians left during and immediately after the war, only a fraction, perhaps 14,000 in all, were allowed to return.

THE BATTLE OF THE BOOKS

Whereas at a strategic level the Israeli government was slow to decide what exactly to do with the occupied territories, at a tactical level –

on the ground – it was incredibly active. Israeli bureaucracy, for example, quickly penetrated all avenues of Palestinian life and closely monitored them, counting refrigerators, livestock, tractors, shops, cars and other goods, registering letters sent to and from various regions of the West Bank and abroad, even scrutinizing the eating habits of Palestinians and the nutritional value of their food basket, before producing detailed lists and statistics. One area, however, where they sought not only to monitor and record but also to actively *remould* was the Palestinian education system.

Soon after the war, a special cabinet committee set up a new education curriculum for schools in the occupied territories, particularly in Arab East Jerusalem, which Israel, as shown, effectively annexed and wanted to mesh into its own education system. It also approved scrutiny and, where necessary, censorship of textbooks which contained animosity to Israel and to Jews, or material that engendered a Palestinian national identity. This decision went hand in hand with Military Order No. 101, which specified that the military censor must approve all reading materials – books and periodicals – on the West Bank.

The task of scrutinizing the Palestinian schools' textbooks fell on the Israeli Ministry of Education, which, after going through the material, judged sixty out of 120 Palestinian textbooks to contain some degree of anti-Israeli or anti-Jewish vitriol, of which forty-nine were serious enough to be banned from all schools. On other occasions, the officials also rephrased passages they deemed inappropriate; for instance, the line in a grammar book which read: 'Our unity will frighten the enemy' was replaced with 'Our success will please our parents', and a poem called 'Beautiful Jaffa' was removed simply because it contained a reference to a visit of the prophet Mohammed to Jerusalem.

Angered over the meddling in their education system, 200 teachers in the northern West Bank town of Jenin signed a petition of protest, criticizing the Israelis for changing textbooks that had been used for the past twenty years under the Jordanians. This set off a wave of further petitions, protests and proclamations throughout the West Bank. A leaflet distributed in Jerusalem, on 17 August, claimed that the books of the Arab minority schools in Israel, which were to be introduced in East Jerusalem, 'offend the Arabs', a reference to the fact that the books used in Israel adopt a Zionist narrative, particularly with regard to the 1948 war, which the Arabs call the *Nakba*: the catastrophe. Three days later, a trade strike was staged in East Jerusalem, and in Tulkarm, Qalqilya and Nablus leaflets were distributed calling on pupils to strike and absent themselves from schools on 1 September, the first day of the new academic year. Rashid Maree, the education department supervisor in the Nablus area, in the north West Bank, reported to the military that schools would not open because too many books had been banned and teachers preferred the Jordanian school programme; the military promptly arrested Maree and held him for three months without trial.

Throughout these disturbances Moshe Dayan had tried to keep his cool, telling military commanders: 'Let them strike if they want.' Still, he was aware that such demonstrations were devastating to Israel's public image abroad, sending a message that not all was well in the occupied territories. Veering between the instinct just to 'shrug our shoulders' and the opposite approach of heavy-handed confrontation, Dayan eventually opted for the latter. 'Our overt position vis-à-vis the Arabs is that the reopening of the schools and resumption of studies is *their* business. We will not force them to study,' he told the military. 'All the same, we must make it clear to them that we view the strike itself as an act of disobedience . . . it is of the utmost importance to break the school strike. This, without doubt, would count as an achievement and victory for us.'[36]

By mid-September the school strike was still in full swing; however, while across most of the West Bank the protests gradually died out, in Nablus it held, and was well observed, turning the town into the standard bearer of defiance against the occupation for the entire West Bank.

Nablus, or Shechem as it was known in biblical times, has always been a special place for both Jews and Arabs. According to the Bible it was there that Abraham came in about 1850 BC and learned in a revelation that the land he had entered and chosen as his new home was the very land which had been predetermined in the counsels of God to be given to him and his descendants (Genesis 12:6–7); Jacob purchased a field there (Genesis 33:18–19); Joshua gathered his people there to renew their covenant (Joshua 8:30–35, 24:1–29); and it is where Joseph was buried (Joshua 24:32). Joseph's Tomb is one of the three most important Jewish holy sites in the Land of Israel, along with Temple Mount in Jerusalem and the Tomb of the Patriarchs in Hebron. However, when in 1967 Nablus was seized from Jordan, it was an Arab town – a centre of commerce and industry with various factories, most notably the Al Bader (Full Moon) soap factory, which has been operating there for over 250 years.

Under Jordanian rule, Nablus, and the district around it, was favoured with a large proportion of what little investment was granted to the West Bank, in the hope that it could be set against East Jerusalem, making it difficult for the latter to become too dominant, lest it challenge Amman's authority. Yet, for foreign occupiers, Nablus has always been a headache; a stronghold of Arab nationalism, it was more hostile to outsiders and rebellious to their rule than any other West Bank town, as the Israelis now discovered. And with Nablus leading the opposition against Israeli interference in the Palestinian education system, the military went on to use punitive measures to make an example of it, so that other towns and cities could see the fate of those resisting the occupation. Forced now to all but abandon his 'invisible' occupation, Dayan, on 21 September, gave the army the green light to sort out Nablus.

The next day, the district commander, Colonel Zvi Ofer, summoned Mayor Canaan to notify him of any sanctions and punitive measures the army would impose on Nablus. But the mayor declined the invitation and failed to show up; he later explained that at his previous meeting with the Colonel the officer had snubbed him by refusing to shake his hand. A few hours later, army jeeps rolled into town, announcing through loudspeakers a curfew from five in the afternoon to seven in the morning 'until further notice'; loudspeakers in the mosque minarets usually used to summon Muslims to prayer now repeated the curfew hours. Engineers then shut down Nablus's telephone system, so that each family would be isolated within its own home, and when night fell, troops carried out searches in private houses and institutions. The troops – novice occupiers – were given precise instructions on how to conduct searches:

> During the search one must constantly observe the people's responses; these will often serve as a reliable guide for those searching . . . walls and floors are often hiding places. Therefore, searchers must knock on every wall and floor and listen to the sound. A dull echo indicates the possibility of a hiding place . . .[37]

In the meantime, public transportation was shut down and the military chose twenty shops – among them Mayor Canaan's own – that had taken part in strikes, and sealed them off 'until further notice'; the business licences of some wholesalers were also revoked. Israeli accountants were brought in to go over municipal financial records, looking for irregularities and evidence of corruption.

With the military operation in full swing, Nablus's economic status as the centre of commercial activity in the northern West Bank was sidelined. The army also shut the Damiya Bridge, the main route to Jordan, thus forcing Nablus residents and merchants to take a much longer and more circuitous route.

Mayor Canaan, on the first evening of the military operation, convened Nablus's municipal council to demand that the army cancel all sanctions. However, when he phoned for an urgent audience with the military governor to deliver the council's request, he could not get through; the governor, he was told, was 'busy'. On 23 September, Canaan explained to the Israeli-based *Maariv* newspaper why Nablus, of all towns, staged strikes against the Israelis. 'Nablus,' he explained, 'is more turbulent. The people enjoy a higher standard of education and are thus more alive to political problems.'

That day, during the first hours of curfew, a military vehicle came under fire near Nablus. It returned fire and summoned two tanks, which shelled the house from where the shots came, before troops burst inside, killing a Palestinian and arresting another. A helicopter pursued some other Palestinians fleeing the scene who led them to a cave where thirteen saboteurs and a large quantity of arms and explosives were discovered. This incident played straight into the hands of the military: now the defence minister could justify the heavy-handed treatment of Nablus on security grounds. With that, the army further tightened its squeeze: it laid a siege, allowing no one to enter or leave town, and it increased the number of searches and arrests.

Gradually, the army's draconian actions began to take their toll on Nablus: food prices spiralled, and the usually lively market was all but abandoned. Council officials watched with growing concern as neighbouring Jenin prospered at their expense, its wholesalers taking over the suspended wholesale trade of Nablus and providing the northern West Bank with agricultural produce. Pressure on him mounting, Mayor Canaan asked for a special audience with Dayan, which took place on 11 October 1967 in Jerusalem. It was a difficult encounter. The mayor said to the defence minister: 'It's been a long time since Nablus has known such heavy and drastic measures as those recently imposed. The iron fist removes all good will the people might have felt towards the occupying forces.'[38] Dayan replied that he did not expect the residents of Nablus to 'love' the Israelis, but they must maintain the normal routine of life. He added: 'The choice you have is either orderly life or rebellion. But you should know that if you choose rebellion, we'll have no other option but to break you.'[39] Canaan capitulated. He suggested the Palestinian grievances over Israeli interference in the education system could be dealt with by setting up a meeting with representatives of the Israeli Ministry of Education to discuss the principles upon which school books were censored, and, crucially, he undertook to ensure the opening of schools no later than 5 November 1967.

Dayan and the army had won: they broke the strike, bringing Nablus to its knees, and asserting their authority over its people. That same evening the curfew and other sanctions were lifted and, after twenty-five harsh days, life started to return to normality in Nablus. As for the controversial books: in the end, fifty-nine out of seventy-eight banned textbooks were reprinted with some modifications and stamped with 'This book is authorized as a textbook by the Military Commander'; and with the release of teachers and students who had been arrested, all schools then reopened. But the episode served as a reminder of resentments simmering beneath the surface of everyday life, and how easily they could boil over into open resistance. It also set the scene for growing Israeli censorship, which, in coming years, would become a major feature of the occupation. As the Palestinian poet and critic Muhammed Albatrawi attested:

> Every word of mine goes through the censorship office. In my poems, I am forbidden to write Yafa, the Arabic name for the city Jaffa, and must use the Hebrew for Yafo. I can't write Askalan and must write Ashkelon. Sometimes I write a simple love song and the great Israeli censor decides it is a nationalist Palestinian poem. For this reason I try to write with great clarity, so that they won't mistakenly ascribe to me other intentions and red-pencil whole lines and verses. I have to guess and take into account what the Israeli censor will think, and refrain from getting him angry at me . . . I never know in advance how the censor will react: sometimes I write something risky and he approves it without a comment, and sometimes I write something totally innocent and it is banned completely. It can drive you crazy, because there is no logic in it.[40]

Ali Alkhalili, a Palestinian intellectual, recalls a similar experience:

> If you don't want all the copies of your book to be confiscated immediately upon publication, you must send the manuscript to the censor . . . What happens to me now . . . is that I find myself, to my horror, developing a little Israeli censor inside me, who keeps an eye on me. It has suddenly become clear to me that in a way I am no longer a free man . . . when he [the censor] has any doubts, he prefers to delete. Sometimes I can feel how angry he is at me by how deep his pen has gouged the manuscript . . . he is like an executioner. Words, after all, are things full of life, of humanity, and his job is to cut their heads off.[41]

THE ORGANIZATION OF THE OCCUPATION

On 13 October 1967, just a couple of days after Dayan lifted his siege on Nablus following the capitulation of Mayor Canaan, the cabinet approved 'Operational Principles for the Administered Territories'.[42] Written in terse military style these new guidelines incorporated lessons learnt from the Nablus strike, and provide a fascinating insight into the philosophy of the occupation, particularly on the West Bank.

The purpose of the new guidelines, as stated in Article 1, was to ensure 'efficient military and administrative control of the Administered Territories'. Encouraging Palestinians to emigrate from the occupied territories is a thread that runs throughout the document, as in Article 2, for instance, where the military is called upon to conduct 'a policy of free travel' for Palestinians by positively responding to their 'requests to leave for study and/or employment abroad . . .' At the same time, 'no permits should be granted to Arabs from the outside for the purpose of settling in the Administered Territories'.

As taxation in Israel was high, it was regarded as an effective tool that should play 'a significant role' in encouraging Palestinian departures across the borders. The guidelines also called on the military to foster a belief among Palestinians that Israel was intending to administer the territories 'for a long time'; presumably because those who wrote the document thought that rebellion arises from uncertainty, and if West Bankers believed that Israel was there to stay then they would either depart or behave. Interestingly, around this time, Israeli hotel owners were sent to the West Bank to discuss travel packages with hotel owners in Jericho and elsewhere, most likely as a way of convincing the West Bankers that Israel was indeed intending to stay on for good.

The document also instructed the army to strengthen and deepen an awareness of the 'great military defeat' of the Arabs in the Six Day War, presumably in order to deter the Palestinians from challenging it; and show 'indifference' towards manifestations of civil disobedience. But at the same time – and typical of the contradictions often found in Israeli policies in the occupied territories – the guidelines also emphasized that military intelligence should use all efforts to identify those who incite rebellion and punish them, preferably by physically removing them from the West Bank and deporting them across the River Jordan into Jordan.

Any Palestinian collaboration with the military, such as those informants who furnish the Israelis with intelligence, the document says, should be 'rewarded', and the military should adopt a policy of 'recompense and protection' for locals willing to help the occupation. On the other hand, any support ordinary Palestinians give to resistance against the occupation should be suppressed, and any town or village that fosters resistance or serves as a base for terrorism should not be eligible for grants, loans or other benefits.

Physical attacks on the army, the guidelines stated, should not be tolerated, and if violence does occur then: '(a) A swift and harsh response is highly important. (b) Suspects should be arrested . . . (c) Houses serving terrorists should be demolished. And (d) publication of every violent incident should be permitted for the sake of internal Israeli morale.'

The new guidelines also stressed that the West Bank economy should weigh as little as possible on the Israeli budget and, while 'avoiding conditions of poverty and famine that would encourage subversion and invite international political pressure on Israel', no investment in the occupied territories should be encouraged. Finally, say the new guidelines, 'Our administration . . . should always have a military façade', and any contacts, particularly with women, 'must be avoided'. The latter prohibition, as it is put in another military handbook published around this time, is due to the danger of sexually transmitted diseases, 'which are extremely common in the enemy countries'.[43]

Alongside these general principles, a complex regime of permits gradually became a prominent and much resented feature of the occupation. Palestinians were required to obtain permits and licences for virtually everything: for engaging in financial activities, building homes, travelling abroad, studying, living outside a village or city where one is registered, grazing livestock in certain areas – even growing certain kinds of fruits and vegetables. As Nadia Abu-Zahra and Adah Kay put it in *Unfree in Palestine*, 'A Palestinian cannot plant a tomato . . . [nor] plant an eggplant without such a permit. You cannot whitewash your house. You can't fix a pane of glass. You can't sink a well. You can't wear a shirt that has the colours of the Palestinian flag. You can't have a cassette in your house which has Palestinian national songs.'[44] Obtaining a permit often entailed a long process that included filling in forms, paying fees (which became an important source of income funding the occupation) and, frequently, having to pass a lengthy interview.

The permit regime and other activities conducted by the occupation had a legal façade, whereby the Supreme Court of Israel became the ultimate arbitrator between the occupied peoples and the occupying authorities. This institution, perhaps the most respectable in Israel, not only reviewed policies in the occupied territories, but also heard scores of cases brought by Palestinians; these varied from challenging house demolitions by the army, which were often used as a collective punishment against the Palestinians, extended curfews, deportations from the occupied territories to Jordan and elsewhere, to accusations of torture. The sociologist Baruch Kimmerling observes that, by hearing these cases, the court not only bestowed on the occupation an enlightened face but it also committed a 'judicial annexation' of the territories, producing an image of 'legality'.[45] And David Kretzmer, in *The Occupation of Justice*, points out that in almost all of its judgements relating to the occupied territories, the Supreme Court had decided in favour of the authorities, often on the basis of 'dubious legal arguments'.[46] And thus, what the court actually did was to provide a veneer of justice for the Palestinians, but ultimately it just reinforced the unequal terms of occupier and occupied.

The military government which administered the occupied Palestinian population was manned by Israeli military personnel. Responsibility was divided between a Security and a Civil Branch, with officers in both branches reporting to a regional military governor. The Security Branch was responsible for maintaining law and order and for guaranteeing the safety of Jewish settlers, whose numbers would in subsequent years grow quite dramatically. It established military bases, deployed troops and often imposed collective punishments on Palestinians. The Civil Branch of the military government oversaw industry, commerce, agriculture, labour and financial activities, education, welfare, health and postal matters. Here the military was aided by thousands of Palestinians – school heads, teachers, social workers, doctors, policemen, postal clerks and other bureaucrats – who effectively ran the daily operations of the different civilian institutions. Thus, any ordinary Palestinian coming into contact with the occupying authority – by applying for some permit or other – was likely to encounter another Palestinian rather than an Israeli, which, in turn, helped meet Moshe Dayan's wish that the occupation be as invisible as possible.

CRUSHING THE GUERRILLAS

For the army, grappling with strikes and protests such as those in Nablus was in essence a policing mission, but on the West Bank it also faced insurgents armed with guns. One of the leading Palestinian figures in this war, but by no means the only one, was a certain Yasser Arafat.

His full name was Muhammad Abdul Raouf Arafat al-Qudwa al-Husseini and he was born on 24 August 1929, probably in Cairo, Egypt, the sixth of seven children of a Palestinian merchant. When he was four, his mother died and the family moved to Jerusalem and settled with an uncle in a house near the Wailing Wall and al-Aqsa mosque, where young Arafat witnessed the growing tensions between Jews and Arabs in British Mandatory Palestine.

In 1937, his father married for the second time and the family returned to Cairo, where Arafat grew up. As a child Arafat showed a strong aptitude for leadership: he would gather the children in his neighbourhood and try to force them to march, beating those who did not obey his orders with a stick. During the first Arab–Israeli war, in 1948, Arafat joined a unit of irregular soldiers which fought alongside regular Egyptian forces against Israel in southern Gaza and excelled himself, quickly earning a reputation as a fearless fighter.

Later, as an engineering student in Cairo, he became active in the militant Egyptian Students' Union, as well as in the Palestinian Students' Union, of which, in 1952, he was elected president. In this role he demonstrated the characteristics which would later become so familiar: a tireless, wily, domineering nature and a love of showmanship and the theatrical gesture. It was at this time that Arafat also started wrapping his head in a *kefiya*, a piece of cloth draped over the head, which, as well as hiding his thinning hair, also became his emblem.

In 1958, armed with a Cairo University engineering degree, Arafat travelled to Kuwait, where he got a job as a public works department junior site engineer before setting up his own company, subsequently claiming that he had been well on the way to becoming a millionaire.

In Kuwait, in 1959, with his close friend Abu Jihad, Arafat began publishing a magazine called *Our Palestine* in which he criticized Arab regimes for not doing enough for the Palestinians, and he also called for a 'popular liberation war' to free Palestine. Together they formed the Palestinian National Liberation Movement, Fatah, which as early as January 1965 carried out its first military operation against Israel; it was a rather amateurish affair and failed.

After the Arab defeat in 1967 Arafat, who during the war stayed in Damascus, travelled with a group of colleagues to Jordan and from there approached the River Jordan to cross into the occupied West Bank. He was the first to cross, and as he was only 5 feet 4 inches tall, the water came up to his shoulders, and he had to hold his clothes and rifle above his head. Reaching the other side, he fell to his knees, kissed the ground and waited for the rest of the group, twenty-eight in all, to join him. He then led them through mountains until they reached the northern West Bank, where Arafat established a base.[47] In the coming weeks, he would criss-cross the area in an old Volkswagen car, preaching the Palestinian cause and recruiting young Palestinians to form secret cells to fight the occupation and ignite a war of national liberation; he believed that the Israeli occupation, like the French regimes in Vietnam and Algeria, would ultimately prove vulnerable to insurgency. Attacks carried out by Arafat's recruits included lobbing hand grenades at military patrols, ambushes, hit-and-run attacks, and planting bombs in factories and on railway lines.

Lacking good intelligence, the army at first struggled to conduct an effective counter-insurgency campaign against Arafat and his people, but before long the Shabak (the Hebrew acronym for Israel's General Security Service, equivalent to the FBI in America or MI5 in the UK) deployed in the occupied territories and started gathering intelligence. It recruited a network of collaborators – young and old, poor and rich – insinuating itself into all areas of Palestinian life, penetrating towns and villages, exploiting religious rivalries, and also making extensive use of underworld figures. One way to recruit collaborators from among the Palestinians was through the aforementioned permit regime, since the interviews provided an opportunity for the Shabak to spot likely candidates to enlist. Often, a positive response to a permit request was conditional upon the applicant's willingness to collaborate; the Israelis would also frequently withdraw charges, lighten sentences, or improve imprisonment conditions for Palestinian criminals in return for collaboration. And, of course, given the grinding poverty that prevailed, especially among the West Bank refugees who had lived there since the 1948 war, money was always an important tool for the Shabak in its recruitment efforts. The Palestinian collaborator A.T. explains:

> Since 1967, there is no one in the territories who has requested a service or permit of some kind from the Military Government who did not receive an offer from the Shabak to act as a collaborator in return for his request being fulfilled. That is the nature of the occupation. Whoever wants to get ahead a little in life, whoever has ambitions, encounters the dilemma at a certain stage.[48]

The Shabak also recruited Palestinian women as collaborators by blackmailing them, taking advantage of their vulnerabilities as members of a traditional Palestinian society. The Palestinian activist Hussein 'Awwad explains their methods:

> The authorities recruit women through photographing them naked or engaged in some immoral activity. They threaten that if they do not collaborate, they will show the pictures to their family and publish them in the newspapers. Women who have already been recruited as collaborators tempt other women to have sex with men [and this is secretly filmed by the Israelis], and so it continues.[49]

*

Now, to break up Palestinian resistance, the army – working closely with Shabak and Palestinian collaborators – attempted to hunt down the Palestinian leadership and Yasser Arafat quickly became top of its list of priorities. The Shabak circulated a 'wanted' leaflet among Israeli troops, with a picture of Arafat wearing his *kefiya*. It described him as follows, using his nom de guerre, Abu Amar.

Abu Amar: One of the founders of Fatah, a commander and organizer. Present in the West Bank. A very important figure in the organization.

Description: About 45. Short: 155–160 centimetres. Skin Colour: Brownish. Build: Chubby, bald in the middle of head. Colour of hair at the temples – grey. His moustache is shaved. His bottom lip sticks out. Speech: an Egyptian accent. His movements: nervous. His eyes: constantly moving.

Dress: Traditional Arab – usually wears European clothes. Glasses – it might be that he's wearing glasses now.

Names and nicknames:
Abu Amar.
Yasser Arafat.
Dr Mohamed Rauf.
Dr Yusuf Amar.
Faiz Machmud Arafat.
Well-known in his nickname: 'The Doctor'.

Relatives: In Gaza – Sami Arafat – a cousin and owner of a photo shop.

His origins: From Nablus or Gaza.

Comment: Upon his arrest let the Service know at once.[50]

While Arafat remained elusive, his men – still largely inexperienced and amateurish – played into Israeli hands. They operated in groups that were way too large, knew too much about each other, and blindly trusted the Palestinian population, many of whom had now been bribed or blackmailed into collaborating with the occupation.

The army was also proactive, always seeking to keep the initiative. On 30 October 1967, for instance, it surrounded three refugee camps in Nablus, among them the large Balata camp, and used 'monkeys' for identification of suspects. 'Monkeys' was the Israeli name for Palestinians rounded up in previous raids on the northern West Bank who had been convinced, one way or another, to help the army; their heads covered with a sack with two peepholes for their eyes, so that they could not be identified by fellow Palestinians, they would finger suspects.

To deter locals from supporting the guerrillas, the army also employed collective punishment, acting against whole villages where Fatah members had been found. In the last fortnight of November 1967, for instance, the army blew up scores of houses in the village of Jiftlig, after finding out that villagers had been sheltering the guerrillas.

Gradually, the army managed to push most of the insurgents across the River Jordan to the East Bank and to starve the remaining cells of arms by stepping up surveillance and searches of vehicles crossing from Jordan to the West Bank. While Dayan's Open Bridge policy continued as before, the army would only allow a restricted list of known vehicles to pass and return, and required that these vehicles be stripped bare of all removable panels, including upholstery, to make it easier for the guards at the bridges to search for guns. Some types of goods, previously imported, were now banned altogether, such as the olive-wood logs used by the carving industry in the Bethlehem area that could easily conceal weapons, and for the same reason the empty wooden crates that had carried citrus fruit from the West Bank to Jordan could no longer be brought back. Cosmetics, various tubes, sprays and canisters, and even cigarette packages were banned and anything brought in over the bridges was fully and carefully examined – body searches also being carried out – including all the personal effects of thousands of returning residents and visitors.

Dayan's Open Bridges policy had once been seen as a 'safety valve', giving West Bankers somewhere to go to let off steam away from their occupiers; but queuing for long hours in the heat of the Jordan Valley, particularly in the summer months, to be subjected to the most rigorous body examination before re-entering the West Bank, only increased Palestinian resentment towards the occupation. The Palestinian author Raja Shehade recalls his cousin's complaints after coming for a simple visit:

> He cursed me for two days after his arrival, and accused me of being responsible for everything that happened to him at the Allenby Bridge when he came from Jordan. The cries of the children when he was stripped for a body search; the sight of a corpse, in transfer for burial in the West Bank, taken out of its coffin for a security search; the stink of the feet of travellers after hours of waiting for their shoes, which had

been sent for X-ray examination; the heartrending wails of a mother whose fourteen-year-old son had been taken for interrogation and had not yet been returned. All this, and the long hours that each person waits for his name to be called . . .[51]

SETTLEMENTS

During the Ottoman era (1517–1917) and the British rule in Palestine (1917–1948) Jews hardly settled in the area we now call the West Bank. Instead, religious Jews, emigrating to the Land of Israel, settled mainly in the four holy cities – Jerusalem, Tiberias, Tzefat or Hebron – while secular Zionist pioneers established themselves mainly along the Mediterranean coastal plain and the Jezreel Valley, which received more rainfall and where it was simpler to purchase land and generally less inhabited. Land in eastern Palestine – which was less fertile and whose ownership was more evenly distributed among individual Palestinian farmers, clans and villages, all generally reluctant to sell to outsiders – was less attractive for settlement.

However, after the 1967 victory, the land seized west of the River Jordan became an irresistible destination for Israeli settlers: first, because some felt strong religious connections to the area, regarding it as the ancestral Land of Israel, promised to the Jewish people by God; and second, whereas in Israel proper there remained little land available for settlement and what *was* available was in undesired areas such as in the Negev desert, on the occupied West Bank there seemed to be large empty tracts awaiting development.

In government, the driving force for settling the occupied lands was the deputy prime minister, Yigal Allon, who put his ideas into the Allon Plan of 13 July 1967.

THE ALLON PLAN *VS* THE DAYAN PLAN

Allon, a former military general who distinguished himself in the 1948 war, was chiefly concerned with national security, which he believed Jewish settlements on the West Bank could protect. He proposed that Israel annex a strip of land, between ten and fifteen kilometres wide, along the entire western bank of the River Jordan, and establish a dense belt of settlements there. These villages, combined with the physical barrier of the river, would constitute a buffer between Israel, Jordan and the wider threat of invasion by Arab armies, such as those of Iraq or Syria, from the east.[52] Allon's plan also called for the construction of Jewish urban neighbourhoods in Arab East Jerusalem, and he had some ideas regarding the Gaza Strip too (see chapter 2).

Allon sought to redraw Israel's borders by annexing land, but, at the same time, avoiding any increase in the number of Palestinians themselves; Israel, as he saw it, could not afford to absorb the large, fast-growing Palestinian population of the occupied territories without threatening its Jewish character. Hence, while Israel would annex the strip of land along the River Jordan, it would not annex the rest of the West Bank, instead letting its populated areas rule themselves as an autonomous region – they would be self-governing when it came to running Palestinian daily life.[53] After all, for 400 years of Middle Eastern rule the Ottomans had provided the region's minority groups – Jews, Christians and others – substantial political, judicial and economic autonomy, and it worked quite well.

Soon after, however, Allon amended his plan by replacing his idea to offer the lands to the Palestinians in favour of giving it to King Hussein of Jordan. Under this new version, Israel would annex the strip of lands needed for its security, mainly along the river, and offer Jordan's King Hussein the Palestinian-populated lands to be linked to his kingdom by a corridor around Jericho (see map 3). We can offer a range of explanations why Allon decided to replace a Palestinian option with a Jordanian one, though the main reason was probably American pressure, which at that time insisted that any arrangement Israel wished to offer regarding the West Bank must be concluded with Washington's own ally King Hussein, by whom it was occupied during the war. In one of many governmental debates about whether to adopt a Palestinian or a Jordanian option the prime minister was quite clear in stating that he would rather have a deal with the king because 'this is what the Americans prefer'.[54]

Allon's offer came, however, with some strings. First, the king would have to agree that the West Bank portion given to him would remain permanently demilitarized; he would not deploy military forces there which could threaten Israel's security. Second, the king would have to grant Israel permission to enter these areas in pursuit of Palestinian terrorists should they use them as a jumping-off pad from which to attack Israel. Third, the king would have to acknowledge Israel's sovereignty in Arab East Jerusalem and the areas it would annex along the River Jordan. Finally, as Israel also wished to annex some of the Gaza Strip's land, the king would have to agree to absorb those Palestinians who would be transferred from there to his lands.[55] To lure King Hussein to accept this plan, Allon proposed allowing him a land route between the rump of the West Bank and the northern Gaza Strip, thus providing Jordan access to the Mediterranean – a crucial benefit it had lost after the creation of Israel in 1948.

Dayan strongly opposed Allon's plan, not least simply because the two were arch-rivals; they had both contended for the post of defence minister in the run-up to the 1967 war and that Dayan eventually won had only increased tensions between them.

Dayan's objection to Allon's plan was, however, more than a personal whim; he felt that squeezing the Palestinians in the West Bank between a line of settlements and Israel proper could not work. 'They are not fools,' Dayan insisted, 'If we are to sandwich the Arabs of Palestine . . . it [will] mean the detachment of the West Bank from Jordan . . .'[56] Instead, Dayan proposed his own plan, which, in many ways, was a mirror image of Allon's.

Dayan thought that the mountain ridge that runs along the centre of the West Bank, *not* the lowlands along the River Jordan, was the strategic land Israel needed for its security. He therefore proposed building 'fists' of settlements further to the west, punching out from Israel proper deep into the mountain ranges of the West Bank. He envisaged five large blocs, stretching from Jenin in the north, through Nablus, Ramallah and to Mount Hebron in the south, each 'fist' – a block of settlements – to be accompanied by military bases and all linked to Israel by a system of roads, along with connections for electricity, water and communications. With Jewish settlements cheek by jowl with Palestinian population centres, Israel would continue to maintain control of the entire West Bank land – but the Palestinians living on it, according to Dayan's plan, would continue to be subjects of the Hashemite Kingdom of Jordan, as they had been since the annexation of this area by King Abdullah in 1950. And unlike in the Allon plan, the Palestinians would not feel 'sandwiched' between Jewish settlements along the river and Israel proper, and therefore might find the disruptions of war and occupation to be less marked, as they could still move freely in line with Dayan's Open Bridges policy to Jordan and back.

Allon's and Dayan's plans represented two very different philosophies of occupation which would continue to compete in the coming years: Allon sought to annex the bare minimum of occupied land to ensure Israel's security needs, and a complete divorce from Palestinian Arabs and the lands they were living on. Dayan, on the other hand, wished to keep the entire occupied West Bank because, as he often put it, 'this is Judea and Samaria . . . our homeland' and, unlike Allon, he did not feel that Israel should divorce from the Palestinians. He thought that Jews and Palestinians (the latter as Jordanian subjects) could live side by side, integrated. By integration, he meant that Palestinians would become, over time, *dependent* on Israel for their livelihoods, and, he believed, as they meshed into the Israeli economy, they would become less nationalistic and resistant to the Israeli presence. Dayan did not disguise his views; as he told the Palestinian poet Fadwa Tuqan: 'It is analogous to the relationship between a man and the woman he's abducted, who doesn't love him and doesn't want to marry him. Once their children are born, they view the man as their father and the woman as their mother. The abduction no longer has any significance for them. You too as a people do not want us today, but we are imposing ourselves upon you.'[57] In filmed interviews, Dayan would often hold up his fingers crossed together and say he would like to generate a situation in the occupied territories whereby it would be as hard to separate the territories from Israel 'as it is to separate my crossed fingers'.

The government, however, rejected Dayan's programme, hesitant about his 'integration' ideas. One of Dayan's colleagues and a close ally, Shimon Peres, later observed: 'Moshe [Dayan]'s view, that if we learn "to live with the Arabs and not above them" we could in fact control the territories, or in other words: if we change our attitude to the Arabs we will not have to change the map – all of these were optical and historic mistakes.'[58] Perhaps another reason for governmental opposition to Dayan's plan was that it proposed that Israel should sit *away* from the River Jordan, namely on the mountains to the west of it, and therefore went against the grain of the Israeli strategic thinking that the frontier is where Jews *actually* sit and not where a line is drawn on a map.

As for Allon's plan, the government neither formally adopted nor rejected it, perhaps because it simply could not make up its mind, or because remaining vague on its territorial aspirations could have enabled it to rebuff criticism that its policies ran against the international law of occupation, which would not permit substantial changes on the ground to occupied lands. After all, even the US, Israel's closest ally, made it clear that it could not support the implementation of the Allon Plan, as Washington would only approve 'really minor changes on security grounds', and here the Allon Plan seemed to suggest Israel's security needs were being linked with 'substantial territorial acquisitions'.[59] Nonetheless, the Allon Plan became the unofficial blueprint for settlement building under successive Labor governments.

LEGALIZING THE LAND GRAB

Since new settlements required land free of existing inhabitants or owners, the Israeli government proceeded to compose a legal–bureaucratic structure of laws in order to allow the 'legal' acquisition of Palestinian land. The idea was to set up a system whereby land could be converted from *private* into *state* property and then settlements and bypass roads could be built on it, thus creating facts on the ground.

The main foundation for this legal system became the (British) Emergency Law (1945) and the Law of Closed Areas (1949), which allowed the army to close off any area of land for military manoeuvres for undefined periods of time. Similarly, the Law of Taking Action (1953) permitted the state to confiscate any land not being cultivated by its Palestinian owners to be used by the military for defence purposes. After taking over the land, the military would then hand it to settlers to build settlements.

There were other methods of seizing land for settlement building, such as declaring it 'absentee property'; Military Order No. 58 defines absentee property as 'property whose legal owner, or whoever is granted the power to control it by law, left the area prior to [its occupation by the army on] 7 June 1967 or subsequently'; during the first few years of the occupation, the Israelis registered about 7.5 per cent of the West Bank as absentee property, as much of it belonged to West Bankers who either became refugees as a result of the war and crossed, mainly, into Jordan, or perhaps were out of the country during the war and thereafter were not allowed to return. Another method the military would use to take over Palestinian land was to declare it the property of a hostile state; Military Order No. 59, issued on 31 July 1967, declares that any land or property belonging to a hostile state should become Israeli state property. In fact, all lands were considered property of the state unless the Palestinian claimants could prove ownership; this, however, was frequently difficult, as many West Bank transactions were never recorded, with ownership often based on informal agreements or inheritances stretching back generations.

And what about settlers to take over the confiscated Palestinian land? As shown earlier, the 1949 Fourth Geneva Convention prohibits transfer of the occupier's civilian population into territories under its occupation, but does allow military personnel into these areas. To circumvent the Convention, the government used the Nahal Brigade – a military unit combining active military service with civilian service. Wearing uniforms they were given the task of erecting ghost 'military camps' on Palestinian land that had been confiscated for 'military purposes', and when these camps were established facts on the ground, they were transferred into civilian hands – turning into proper settlements.

Despite the range of laws ostensibly enabling Palestinian land to be confiscated for settlement building, Israel's policy during the first decade of the occupation was, by and large and compared to what would come later, restricted. The rule of thumb was that settlements should be erected away from Palestinian population centres and the main consideration in approving a scheme was national security; namely, how a village in this or that location could contribute to Israel's overall protection from a potential Arab invasion from across the River Jordan. But there were some 'special cases'; one of those, which took place in Hebron, was, perhaps, the most notorious.

STAND-OFF IN HEBRON

Situated some thirty-two kilometres south of Jerusalem and built across several hills and wadis, Hebron has always held significance for both Muslims and Jews. For the latter it is the second-holiest place after Jerusalem; 'Hebron' derives from the Hebrew word 'haver' ('friend'), a description of the Patriarch Abraham, who was considered to be a friend of God. The Arabic word for Hebron, 'Al Khalil', literally means 'the friend' and also refers to Abraham, whom Muslims, similarly, describe as a friend of God. According to the Bible it was at Hebron that God made a covenant with Abraham that he would greatly 'increase your numbers' (Genesis 17), and it was there that for 400 silver shekels Abraham purchased from Ephron the Hittite a cave and the adjoining field as a family tomb (Genesis 23). According to the Bible, the Cave of Machpelah is where Abraham himself is buried along with Isaac, Jacob, Sarah, Rebecca and Leah.[60] Abraham, of course, was the father of the Muslims' forebear, Ishmael, which makes the Cave of the Patriarchs important for Muslims also, hence the construction of the Ibrahimi mosque which now stands over the cave.

Throughout the centuries a small Jewish community had lived among the Arabs of Hebron; their number increased towards the end of the nineteenth century with the arrival of Eastern European Jews. But the Jews of Hebron have always been hated by their neighbours, who regarded them as arrogant colonialists; in the wave of ethnic violence that swept Palestine in August 1929, sixty-seven Jews were killed by Arabs in Hebron, and their community and its synagogues destroyed. The survivors fled to Jerusalem; there they stayed until, in 1931, thirty-one Jewish families returned to Hebron to re-establish their community. This effort, however, was short-lived as, on 26 April

1936, fearing repeated bloodshed, the Mandatory British authorities evacuated the Jewish families. In the 1948 war, the Jordanian Arab Legion captured Hebron, and in 1950, along with the entire West Bank, incorporated it into the Hashemite Kingdom of Jordan.

Seventeen years later, on the fourth day of the 1967 war, Hebron was captured by Israeli forces; and with Jews wishing to return to re-establish their community in what by now was all but an Arab – traditional and conservative – town, a conflict over Hebron seemed unavoidable.

Troubles indeed emerged on 12 April 1968, when 40–45 religious Jews arrived at Hebron to celebrate the Jewish festival of Passover. They were brought together by an unassuming advertisement in the papers a few days before which called on families or singles wishing to resettle ancient Hebron to contact Moshe Levinger; a 35-year-old rabbi, Levinger was an extremist, possessed of a messianic zeal to reclaim Hebron for the Jewish people. The military commander in charge of this area, General Narkiss, allowed them to enter Hebron on condition that they leave town promptly the following day. Given that the group set off to Hebron with plenty of luggage, including fridges, washing machines and other appliances, the General must have known their true intentions. With permission granted, Levinger led his people into the small El-Haled Hotel, which was run by the Palestinian Qawasmi family.

The visitors were excited and, as Rabbi Levinger's wife, Miriam, recalls, 'Everyone was deliriously happy, as if the Messiah was just around the corner . . . as if they were personally touched by God.'[61] They cleaned and koshered the kitchen allotted to them and celebrated the Passover Seder, but, on the next day, instead of leaving Hebron as promised they hoisted an Israeli flag over the hotel and announced they would settle in town for good. When they set up a makeshift seminary on the second floor, Fahed Qawasmi, the hotel owner, demanded that they leave, but they refused. On 21 April, Hebron's mayor, Muhammad Ali al-Ja'abri, wrote to the prime minister, Levi Eshkol, and the defence minister to complain about the group's intrusion, expressing his hope, though with a touch of sarcasm, that the day would come when the Jews of Hebron could return to live in their old homes, and the Arab refugees could return to their former homes in Palestine which they had left in 1948.

The person best equipped to deal with the problem, Dayan, was temporarily out of action, lying in hospital, recovering from a serious accident. In his absence, the matter was left in the hands of the prime minister, who was greatly influenced by Dayan's rival Allon, who persuaded his colleagues to let the settlers stay on in Hebron, much to Dayan's dismay.[62] In an interview years later, Dayan observed that 'Allon did not care about [the Hebron settlers], but about Moshe Dayan, and that I was against this wild settlement was sufficient for him to do everything he could so that these people would stay there'.[63]

By the time Dayan was discharged from hospital the Hebron affair was a *fait accompli* and Dayan felt he had no other option but to come to a compromise with the settlers, who agreed to move to a military compound at the edge of town. Dayan perhaps hoped that uncomfortable conditions in a military base would deter the settlers, but in the end he seriously underestimated their determination; they sweated out the tough conditions in camp, playing a waiting game with Dayan and the army. Finally, in 1970, under mounting pressure in government by ministers sympathetic to the settlers, Dayan agreed to let them establish a settlement just east of Hebron's centre. Subsequently, Kiriath Arba – an alternative biblical name for Hebron ('Now the name of Hebron formerly was Kiriath-Arba . . .' Joshua 14:15) – was set up on twenty-five hectares of private land expropriated from its Palestinian owner on the orders of the military governor for 'security reasons'. To begin with a 'military base' was set up there, and in 1971, after 250 units had been built, the first settlers started moving into the settlement.

When Dayan, in a conversation with the settlers, urged them not to raise their children to hate the Arabs, the settlers replied: 'The Arabs must know that there is a master here – the Jewish people. It rules over *Eretz Israel* . . . The Arabs are temporary dwellers who happened to live in this country . . .'[64] Dayan knew full well that it had been a grave error to compromise with the settlers, one which he regretted for the rest of his life. 'I did not fulfill my duty as defence minister,' he would later observe, 'in that I did not prevent this pirate settlement in

Hebron. I understood its significance, that it was a catastrophe and that I should have threatened resignation . . . but I did not do so, and for this I am really sorry.'[65]

The settler movement had scored a highly visible victory which, in Dayan's own words, had 'dangerous implications for the future',[66] as it demonstrated that a small but committed group of people could impose its will on the government. Indeed, the settlers learnt that sheer obstinacy could win out, and the Hebron affair set a precedent for future wildcat occupations by settler groups elsewhere on the West Bank.

PERSUADING A KING

In the meantime, away from the occupied territories, in the weeks and months following the 1967 war and well into 1968 Israeli officials held a series of meetings in London and Paris with King Hussein of Jordan. One such meeting took place on 3 May 1968 and involved Israel's foreign minister, Abba Eban, the king and just two aides. Eban attempted to present Israel's thoughts about a possible peace deal with Jordan, along the lines of the Allon Plan, whereby responsibility for the occupied West Bank could be divided between Israel and Jordan; Eban now sought some clarifications: could the king sign a separate peace treaty with Israel, even if other countries like Egypt and Syria refused to do so themselves? Could he ensure an end to terrorist activities against Israel?[67] The king, after listening to Eban's presentation, promised to get back with his thoughts about a dividing plan and Eban clearly interpreted the king's polished manners and politeness as a sign that the meeting went well; indeed, even before getting Hussein's formal reply, Eban advised the cabinet that the next meeting should be between Hussein and the prime minister.[68] But Eshkol was in no particular hurry and refused Eban's suggestion that he meet the king in person, lest this give too much momentum to the talks and, perhaps, force Israel to compromise on the land.

Instead, on 27 September 1968, the ministers Eban and Allon met the king, so that Allon could present his Plan as a 'personal' and unofficial one, rather than a governmental proposal to the king.[69] Allon was bold: 'The king is responsible for the [1967] war . . .' he said to King Hussein, 'you lost the war and you should bear the consequences.'[70] They had a thorough discussion of Allon's ideas and, as was his custom, the king promised that he would consider the matter thoroughly before getting back to the Israelis. His response came a while later in the shape of a six-point document which described the Allon Plan as 'wholly unacceptable'. The king's emissaries explained that any future peace programme had to be one that the king 'could explain to the Arab world . . . and . . . one that the Arab world could accept . . .'[71] More meetings involving the king, Eban and Allon and a few aides to discuss the Israeli offers, notably on 19 November 1968, aboard an Israeli ship, failed to reach a deal.

Perhaps it was the euphoria of victory that made the Israelis think, wrongly as it turned out, that a defeated King Hussein would accept any offer they put his way, or that over time, faced with a choice between losing the entire West Bank or accepting the little Israel was ready to offer him, the king would soften his position and accept the Allon Plan. It is more likely, however, that the Israelis offered very little, both in their negotiations with local Palestinians and later with the king, safe in the knowledge that their offers would be rejected and they could then cling to the lands. For the king, a bare minimum was to recover the West Bank with only minor territorial changes on a reciprocal basis, and clearly he could not possibly give up on his responsibility for the Muslim and Christian parts of Jerusalem, which the Israelis were determined to keep under their control, along with much of West Bank land. But Hussein probably concluded that it would be wise to keep the Israelis engaged, lest they strike a deal with the local Palestinian leadership behind his back, or, even worse, offer them some form of sovereignty on lands he was still hoping to reclaim.

COLONIALIZATION

On the West Bank, in the meantime, the occupation radically transformed the local economy: the tourist trade, previously a major sector and an important earner of foreign currency, was particularly badly hit. Before the war the West Bank attracted tourists from across the world who would flock to see the holy sites, particularly in Jerusalem. Anwar al-Khatib al-Tamimi, governor of the Jerusalem District until 1967, remembers how:

> Up until the Israeli attack [in 1967] Jerusalem had been thriving . . . The city's hotels were full, the markets crowded, the souvenir shops overflowing with visitors, the tourist buses clogging the streets of Jerusalem and the West Bank. We would see dozens of hitchhikers with their backpacks on the roads between towns, thumbing down rides to their next destination . . .[72]

Also, Arab tourists, in particular, would regularly visit the winter resort of Jericho and the summer resort of Ramallah, dubbed the 'Switzerland of Jordan', which was popular with wealthy Jordanians escaping the heat of Amman. But, in the aftermath of the war, tourism stopped nearly altogether, as the bridges over the river were in ruins, Israeli rules regarding tourist permission were not yet clear, and there was a general reluctance, particularly on the part of Arab tourists, to holiday in what was now an Israeli-occupied area. While Israeli tourists did help fill the gap – after the war scores of them flocked into Jerusalem and the West Bank – the typical Israeli visitor would only stay for the day, which did little to revive the West Bank hotel industry and services linked to it.

The occupation also transformed the West Bank's agriculture, which, before the war, was a mainstay of the economy and an important export earner. It was a sector based on numerous smallholdings, selling both to a local market and to Jordan across the river. Traditional and old-fashioned, it suffered from not exploiting the advances made elsewhere: 20 per cent of the available land remained uncultivated because no use was made of fertilizers, modern farm equipment or suitable irrigation, and no effort had been made to adapt crops to the season. For a short time after the war the Israelis were quite helpful, making experts and advisers available to guide Palestinian farmers in new farming techniques, such as using plastic covering to protect crops and employing sprinklers and drippers to replace primitive irrigation methods. Under Israeli guidance, new mechanical equipment was also introduced; while before the war there were fewer than 300 tractors on the West Bank, in 1968 their number grew to 460 and ten years later it rose to 1,673. The Israelis also helped with the vaccination of animals. A 1969 military report details how:

> In the course of a veterinary action all cattle herds, about 30,000 heads, were marked, and immunisation shots against foot and mouth disease administered. The cattle are examined for tuberculosis, and sick cows are purchased by the Military Government for slaughtering without loss to the farmer. The entire poultry stock – about half a million heads – received shots against the Newcastle disease ... There has been a radical decline in the mortality of poultry as a result of these injections to a very small number this year in comparison with a 60% loss in the past. Thousands of dogs were destroyed.[73]

These were not necessarily magnanimous measures, as the Israelis had a vested interest in ensuring the health of Palestinian livestock, as viruses and diseases do not take account of borders; also, it was thought, Palestinian dependency on Israeli assistance and a relative prosperity would repress nationalism. Gradually, however, under mounting pressure from Israeli farmers who saw a potential threat to their profits from a modernized West Bank system of agriculture, the government dropped its assistance for Palestinian farmers. Furthermore, it took measures to protect Israel's agriculture sector by blocking crop imports from the West Bank into Israel; instead they were directed to the East Bank – to Jordan and beyond – at a time when Israeli farmers were allowed unlimited access to markets on the West Bank. And the government also took measures to ensure that the Palestinian agricultural sector supplemented rather than competed with Israel's own, by encouraging West Bank farmers to produce low-profit crops, which were neglected in Israel.

What hit West Bank agriculture more than anything else, however, was the Israeli decision, in August 1967, to transfer control of water supplies to the military authorities (as it would do on the Golan in March 1968 and in the Gaza Strip in December 1974). This, in turn, led to severe restrictions on drilling new wells; again, the permit system was employed and a lengthy and complicated bureaucratic process was put in place, in which the vast majority of applications submitted by Palestinians desperate for more water were denied and the few granted were only for domestic use. In 1975, Israel tightened the screw even further by setting quotas for extracting water from existing wells and installed meters to enforce the new rules, all of which resulted in too small an amount of water to maintain a vigorous Palestinian agriculture.

Similarly, in industry, the Israelis encouraged the West Bankers to focus on industries that served, and indeed complemented, the Israeli economy. For instance, in the clothing industry, Israeli manufacturers would provide the material – the cloth and designs – while scores of low-paid Palestinians, often women and children, would labour over the sewing machines. Here, as in other fields, the permit system was used to restructure West Bank industry in line with Israel's needs and avoiding competition.

The occupation also transformed – quite dramatically – the West Bank employment market. When the war ended, unemployment on the West Bank was rife; out of a total Palestinian workforce of 85,700, the numbers of unemployed reached between 30,000 and 50,000. Acknowledging that unemployment might increase resentment against the occupation, Israel attempted to create more jobs, primarily through the Public Works Department; it was arranged that jobs be distributed in such a way as to provide between two and three days of employment a week for as many West Bankers as possible. This, in turn, had some effect and by September 1967 the number of West Bankers unemployed had dropped to 25,000 (30 per cent unemployment), and a year later it went down to 11,500 (14 per cent unemployment).

Although over the following years the Gaza Strip would become the main source of cheap labour for Israel, the first Palestinians to be employed in Israel after the war came from the West Bank. Between 1968 and 1972, twenty-three employment agencies were set up on the West Bank to regulate the job market, apparently in the interests of the workers, but in reality to satisfy the needs of Israeli business and industry, and also to screen workers from the point of view of security: these agencies also often acted on behalf of the Shabak, Israel's internal security agency, by recruiting collaborators to help the occupation, providing it with intelligence.

Gradually, Palestinian labour in Israel concentrated in the construction industry, which became almost wholly dependent on the Palestinian workforce; ironically, the new Jewish settlements established on the West Bank were largely built by Palestinian labourers. Even the *kibbutzim* that had traditionally been based on Jewish work started hiring Palestinian labourers both in agriculture and in industrial plants. At the same time, Israeli workers abandoned unskilled and semi-skilled occupations in construction, services, agriculture and low-tech industries and moved to highly skilled, high-tech, managerial and bureaucratic occupations. Palestinians under the age of seventeen, who could not be legally employed in Israel, turned to the black market, as did those who preferred not to be registered, so as to avoid paying up to 30 per cent of their salaries in taxes, as Israelis do and which is much more than Palestinians would pay on the West Bank. The Palestinian workers found themselves trapped between the official prohibition on them to stay overnight in Israel and their Israeli employers' preference to have them spend the week in Israel and be available for longer hours each day. This, then, led to Palestinian workers being illegally housed in disgraceful conditions, crammed into farm outbuildings, sheds, warehouses and the like. Meanwhile, with so many employed in Israel, West Bank agricultural lands were left untilled, and this, in turn, made it even easier for the army to confiscate the untilled lands for Jewish settlement building.

But then, as typically Palestinians would earn anywhere from 10 to 100 per cent more in Israel than if they worked in the West Bank, the new jobs offered by the Israelis led to rapid economic growth. And with more money in people's pockets, private consumption grew dramatically; West Bankers now bought more gas cookers, refrigerators, television sets and other appliances. On the other hand, this new labour market had a very negative impact on the social fabric of the West Bank, since educated and skilled Palestinians began leaving to seek employment abroad. Thus, teachers, doctors, engineers and other professionals – in fact, the elite of West Bank society – emigrated to Saudi Arabia, Kuwait, Jordan and elsewhere, leaving behind the uneducated proletariat to work in Israel, or do what little they could on the West Bank.

THE PLO: DOWN BUT NOT OUT

As we have seen, in the aftermath of the 1967 war Palestinian insurgents, led by figures such as Arafat, attempted to establish themselves on the West Bank to fight the occupation. But, bit by bit, the army managed to push them out of this area and across the river into Jordan. These guerrillas belonged to different Palestinian factions, with different ideological underpinnings, from Palestinian nationalism (Fatah) to Maoism (PFLP) to a more unalloyed Marxism (PDFLP); but they all came after the 1967 war under the umbrella of the mother grouping, the Palestine Liberation Organization (the PLO), which was a political and paramilitary set-up which since 1969 had been led by Arafat.

From Jordan, after being pushed out of the West Bank by the army, the PLO continued to try and mobilize the West Bankers against the occupation by sending them instructions, money and weapons. At the same time, in Jordan proper, they turned on King Hussein and tried to topple him, hoping that, with the king out of the way, they could turn the Kingdom of Jordan into a hinterland from which to mount guerrilla operations against Israel and, ultimately, liberate Palestine. Jordan, after all, was an ideal location, given its long frontier with Israel and its large and sympathetic Palestinian population. This, however, was a fateful mistake, as the PLO underestimated King Hussein's determination: in September 1970, sick and tired of the Palestinian guerrillas' troublemaking in his kingdom – parts of which they all but ruled – the king turned on them and, in what came to be known as 'Black September', drove the insurgents out of the kingdom and into Lebanon.

The PLO's defeat in Jordan had quite a dramatic impact on the occupied West Bank since the PLO lost much of its influence over policies there. Against this background, the Israeli cabinet, in October 1971, concluded that the time was ripe to hold municipal elections on the West Bank – the first since 1963 – as with the PLO defeat in Jordan, the ministers reasoned, ordinary West Bankers were far less likely to vote for pro-PLO candidates and this, in turn, would leave in power candidates who were relatively moderate and less nationalistic. Under the British Mandate, and also during the Jordanian era from 1948 to

1967, West Bank municipalities were responsible for important functions such as urban planning, granting building permits, water and electricity usage, and more. But under Israeli occupation most of these functions were taken away from them and transferred to the military government. That said, West Bank municipalities did play one crucial role, as the link between the West Bankers and the military government – passing on, for instance, applications for permits and, in so doing, turning themselves into a tool through which the military managed the occupation. This is why it was so critical for the Israelis to have municipal councillors who were not in favour of the PLO, and why they felt it was a good idea to have the elections now that the PLO was relatively weak; also, holding an election would give a liberal veneer to the occupation.

On 19 December 1971, the army issued an order fixing the date of the first round of local elections in all the municipalities in Samaria and Jericho for 28 March 1972; further elections would be held later, once the Israelis had been able to gauge the situation and make plans for how to proceed.

The PLO, however, smelling a rat, was quick to respond by urging West Bankers not to cooperate with the occupation and refrain from voting in the upcoming municipal elections; this was quite effective, particularly in persuading residents of the notoriously nationalist Nablus, on the northern West Bank. Apprehensive, however, that other cities might follow in Nablus's steps, the army summoned the senior members of Nablus's Al Masri and Tuqan clans, bringing them to the Judea and Samaria Area command headquarters in Bet El by helicopter, where they had an audience with Israel's defence minister. Dayan threatened that should they fail to present candidates in the upcoming elections, the military would take control of their private factories and forbid them from shipping their products to Jordan via the bridges; faced with ruin the Nablusis complied.

Queues on election day were long: 84 per cent of eligible voters cast their votes, compared with 76 per cent in the previous, 1963, elections; and as the Israelis had rightly predicted, the PLO candidates fared badly and the moderate candidates managed to retain the majority of seats in most municipalities. Pleased with these election results, the Israelis went ahead, five weeks later, with elections in the rest of the

West Bank, where again PLO candidates fared badly and moderate Palestinians continued to dominate West Bank municipalities.

Israel kept up its pressure on the PLO and in April 1973 assassinated three of its leaders in Beirut. But the government underestimated the dormant support that the Palestinian guerrillas still enjoyed in the occupied territories; the assassinations unleashed a storm of protest, leading to vast demonstrations on the West Bank, during which the PLO flag was displayed in place of the Jordanian banner that had previously been used as a rallying point. At the same time, internationally, the organization was gaining a more powerful profile; on 14 October, the UN General Assembly, where there were many representatives of Muslim countries sympathetic to the Palestinian plight, invited the PLO to attend assembly meetings on the question of Israel–Palestine, granting it Observer Status at the UN. Two weeks later, an Arab summit meeting in Rabat, Morocco, declared the PLO – rather than Jordan – 'the sole legitimate representative of the Palestinian people'.[74] Finally, Arafat was invited to speak to the UN General Assembly in New York in what became known as his 'gun and olive branch' speech. 'I have come bearing an olive branch and a freedom fighter's gun,' he told the assembly. 'Do not let the olive branch fall from my hand.' The speech was met with jubilation in the occupied Palestinian lands, where thousands poured into the streets to express their support for the PLO and to denounce the Israeli occupation.[75] The Israeli army reacted harshly by imposing long curfews, making more than 200 arrests, and sentencing 132 Palestinians for up to six months in jail with fines.[76]

Thus, despite its setbacks in Jordan in September 1970 and in the municipal elections in 1972, the PLO was clearly holding its ground on the occupied West Bank, and even managed to rekindle a spirit of resistance, at a time when the Jordanian king's influence seemed to be on the wane. And then came the climax of the PLO success, when in 1976 the Israeli military government called again for municipal elections on the West Bank.

Whereas in 1972, as shown, the PLO had boycotted the ballot and been defeated by moderate candidates, many of whom, generally speaking, tended to cooperate with the occupation, now the PLO had learnt from its past mistake and rigorously promoted its own candidates, organizing them into the 'National Bloc'. The army, in turn, attempted to stop this bloc from promoting its agenda, short of banning it outright, by interfering directly in the election campaign – prohibiting posters bearing the Palestinian flag and breaking up demonstrations in support of known PLO candidates.

In Hebron, concern had mounted within the military government that the PLO candidate might defeat the moderate, anti-nationalist incumbent, Muhammad Ali al-Ja'abri, a close ally of Israel and instrumental in allowing the smooth functioning of the occupation. [77] In the 1972 election, Ja'abri had been the only candidate and, as no list of candidates was offered to challenge him, he was automatically elected; but now he faced a challenge from Dr Ahmad Hamzi Natshe, a pro-PLO candidate. Shimon Peres, by now defence minister, allowed the military to make what he called 'a limited intervention' in Hebron, to help Muhammad Ali al-Ja'abri, and subsequently, on 27 March 1976, the army deported Dr Natshe, removing him physically from Hebron, having charged him with inciting and organizing strikes.[78] This blatant intervention in the Palestinian election campaign turned out to be counterproductive, leading, as it did, to growing resentment among Hebronites, so much so that al-Ja'abri withdrew from the campaign altogether.

On election day, 12 April, 63,000 men and women voted, representing 72.3 per cent of the potential voters. The PLO did spectacularly well throughout the West Bank, whereas the moderate Israeli allies, leftovers from the former Jordanian regime, were defeated and swept out of power. Out of 191 contested seats, the PLO's National Bloc captured a staggering 148, with the only major success for the anti-nationalists being in Christian Bethlehem, where Elias Freij was elected mayor.[79]

In the wake of these elections, a new brand of leaders emerged on the West Bank: generally young, militant, more radical, sporting a new political style and forthright in their support for the PLO. Of the newly appointed mayors, eight were known for their nationalist positions, compared to just three in the 1972 elections; eighteen of the new councillors had been involved in what the army called 'terrorist activities' against the occupation; of them nine had spent time in Israeli jails, and one was in prison at the time of his election. The most radical changes took place in the nationalist Nablus and Hebron; in the former, the pro-PLO candidates won all the seats in the council except for one, and the newly appointed mayor, Bassam Shaka, was open in his hostility to Israel. In Hebron, the era of the moderate al-Ja'abri ended, as he was succeeded by the pro-PLO Fahed Kawasmeh.

The elections demonstrated that most of the West Bank's population had developed strong nationalist feelings under the occupation; that they supported the PLO as their voice, and rejected Jordan's policies regarding the West Bank; Jordanian influence was now in free fall. The newly elected pro-PLO leaders, unlike their predecessors, who often resented each other, worked closely together, coordinating their moves against the occupation and staging, within weeks of their election, a series of protests and demonstrations against land expropriation and Jewish settlement building.

The PLO victory so stunned the Israelis that, for the next decade, they would refrain from holding any further municipal elections on the West Bank lest they reaffirm the widespread support for the Palestinian nationalist forces.

THE FACE OF OCCUPATION

As the occupation's first decade drew to a close, it was clear that it was anything but as enlightened as the Israelis had declared it would be. While Israel did allow local municipal elections, the army nonetheless curtailed political freedom, muzzled the press, used censorship and, at the same time, facilitated the building of settlements on occupied land – all in defiance of international law. Although successive Labor governments had attempted to channel the building of settlements to the Jordan valley, away from Palestinian-populated areas, mounting pressure by religious groups, one called Gush Emunim, had forced its hand and resulted in settlements right next to Palestinian-populated areas; by May 1977 there were twenty-four settlements on the West Bank with 3,200 settlers (not including Jerusalem).

The first decade of occupation saw relative prosperity for the West

Bank, but, in many ways, it was an artificial economy – the result of funds sent home by Palestinian workers with jobs in Israel and monies channelled in by King Hussein, keen to hold on to his gradually declining influence in the area. It was during this first decade of occupation that the West Bank economy was converted into a colonial-style economy, providing cheap labour for Israel, forced to buy Israeli manufactured goods, and not able to compete with subsidized Israeli farming, while at the same time Israeli control of water dramatically handicapped Palestinian agriculture.

Politically, although hesitant attempts were made to settle the Israeli–Palestinian conflict by implementing ideas such as the aforementioned Allon Plan, the Dayan plan and more, these gradually gave way to a more institutionalized military control of land and people.

2

Gaza Strip

Wedged between modern Israel and the Mediterranean Sea, and with a short border with Egypt at its southern end, the Gaza Strip is relatively small and roughly rectangular: forty kilometres long and between 6.4 and twelve kilometres wide, with a total area of 360 square kilometres. Historically, politically and religiously it is far less important than the West Bank, which explains why the Strip is often referred to as 'the stepchild of the West Bank'.

The area was not distinct from the rest of Palestine either during the Ottoman period (1517–1917), when it formed part of the independent Sanjak of Jerusalem, or during the British period of rule (1917–1948), when it formed the southern district of Mandatory Palestine. When, in November 1947, the UN proposed to partition Palestine between Arabs and Jews, it allotted an L-shaped area around Gaza to the Arabs. However, heavy fighting between Israelis and Egyptians during the 1948 war reduced this area, resulting in two thirds of it being incorporated into Israel, while the remaining land, consisting mainly of Gaza City and some other small towns and villages, fell into Egyptian hands. Following the signing of the Egyptian–Israeli Armistice Agreement on 24 February 1949, which ended the war, the area captured by Egypt came to be known as the 'Gaza Strip'.

Whereas the Gaza Strip as a political entity is, therefore, a relatively recent innovation, its eponymous unofficial capital, Gaza City, is one of the oldest cities on earth. Lying on the *Via Maris*, the Way of the Sea, an ancient road running from Egypt along the coast of Palestine to Phoenicia, in the north of the ancient kingdom of Canaan, which had its heartland in what is now Lebanon and Syria but extended south to encompass the entire Sinai Peninsula, Gaza was turned by geography into an irresistible target for invaders: from the Israelites through the Egyptians, Assyrians, Scythians, Babylonians, Persians, Romans, Muslims, Crusaders and Mamelukes to the Ottomans and the British. Nowadays Gaza is by far the largest city in the Strip, and an important trade and communications centre for the whole area.

The birth of the Gaza Strip as a distinct political region in 1948 was traumatic for the people who lived there, as the social and economic makeup of the area was irrevocably altered by two critical, indeed disastrous, events. The first was the complete loss of the Strip's productive hinterland – grazing lands and plots used for agriculture – all of which now fell into, and became part of, the newly created State of Israel. The fall of Palestine also meant that traditional trade links between the Gaza area and such important centres as Beer Sheva and Jerusalem were cut off, and employment opportunities, especially in Haifa and Jaffa, disappeared almost overnight, as the labour force could no longer travel to what was now within Israel.

The second event that made the birth of the Gaza Strip so traumatic was the sudden and massive influx of refugees, particularly from Palestine's coastal towns, which radically transformed the composition of the Strip's population. Up until 1948 the dominant people in the Gaza area were the indigenous Gazans, totalling around 80,000 and led by a small but wealthy elite of landowning families, traditionally dependent on export trade for income. But the arrival of 200,000 refugees fleeing the war in Palestine transformed this reality overnight; the newcomers settled into makeshift camps, often in the orchards dotted around Gaza. Whole villages were literally uprooted from Palestine and transplanted into the Gaza Strip, where life often mirrored the society and hierarchy of the old village life in Palestine.

The newcomer refugees were mainly of low social economic class: the poorest, least skilled and least privileged of all the groups that had left Palestine in 1947–8. Their tragedy was that they could not be sustained in the Gaza region, where half the land consisted of unproductive sand dunes, and the tiny size of the area, which lacked natural resources, could not provide them with jobs or land to rebuild their life. Thus thousands of Palestinians suddenly found themselves reliant on the charity of the international community, which was spearheaded by the United Nations Relief and Works Agency (UNRWA), an arm of the United Nations set up in 1950 specifically to help Palestinian refugees.

By 1952, UNRWA had established eight camps in the Strip and assumed total responsibility for the refugees, providing them with food rations, health care and education, and employing many of them in its administration. Although an improvement, the new conditions were far from being idyllic; this indeed was the time – the early 1950s – when the Gaza Strip gradually sank into poverty and destitution. The relationship between the original inhabitants of the Strip, now a minority, and the newly arrived refugees became strained, even hostile, though in the long term the two groups would be united by their growing antagonism towards Israel.

After the 1948 war, Egypt ruled the Strip from Cairo through a special military administration, headed by an Egyptian military governor based in Gaza City. It was not a benevolent rule: Egypt's King Farouk, distrustful of the Palestinians, instructed his administrators to quash any sign of insurgency and keep a tight rein on the refugee population. All public offices, social services, and legal, judicial and commercial activities came under the aegis of the military governor, and Egyptians held all high-level administrative positions and had control over all important appointments in every sphere of Palestinian life. The result was almost total stagnation, both socially and economically, with perhaps the only flourishing industry being the smuggling of products from the Sinai to the Gaza Strip conducted by Bedouins. Then came June 1967: the Strip fell into victorious Israeli hands, and the army proceeded to install a military government in the al-Majlis al-Tashri building in Gaza City, where the Egyptian governor had sat until a few weeks previously.

MILITARY GOVERNMENT AND DEPORTATIONS

This new Israeli administration was tasked by the defence minister, Dayan, with ensuring security and restoring public services. Before the war, all public services had been provided by Palestinian municipal councils in such places as Rafah, Deir el Balah and Khan Younis. These councils drew their authority from the 1934 Municipal Corporation Ordinance enacted under the British Mandate, which had given them authority to oversee services: from urban planning to water usage and allocation, electricity, sewage disposal, public transportation, expenditure of public funds and so on. Now, however, the military government issued Military Orders Nos. 194 and 236, invalidating the earlier status of the councils and transferring authority over local government to the army. This technical change in the law was aimed at weakening local Palestinian leadership, making it dependent on the goodwill of the occupation, which the army, of course, granted only in return for good behaviour.

The military government offered Israeli citizenship to the indigenous residents of the Gaza Strip (most of them rejected it), but not to the Palestinian refugees. The reason for this promise is to be found in the Allon Plan, the scheme that, as discussed earlier, attempted to share responsibility for the West Bank with King Hussein of Jordan, but which also had laid out the future for the Gaza Strip. As the deputy prime minister, the brains behind the scheme, explained: 'The Gaza Strip with its indigenous residents will [eventually] become an integral part of Israel.' This, however, Allon went on, would take place only after the refugees 'were settled out of it'.[1]

The thinking behind Allon's proposal for the Gaza Strip was strategic in nature, namely that Israel would annex the bulk of the land in the southern section of the Strip, with its lush citrus groves and sparse indigenous population in small towns, which could then be easily settled by Jews to form a buffer zone with Egypt and the Sinai desert (it was already assumed that Israel would most probably return the Sinai to Egypt). The northern part of the Strip, including the heavily populated Gaza City, would, according to Allon's strategy, be given to King Hussein along with parts of the West Bank. The Israelis hoped that the king would take the refugees of the Gaza Strip – particularly those in the southern areas Israel sought to annex – and settle them on the East Bank of the River Jordan, or in the West Bank areas given to him. Alternatively, the Israelis thought, the evacuated refugees could be settled in Al Arish, a town in the northern Sinai where there were empty houses left by Egyptians who had lived there and who had run away when Israel occupied the Sinai in 1967.

This wholesale shifting of people for colonial strategic ends was a prominent feature of the era that followed the 1967 war and the Israelis made no secret of their annoyance that their newly captured lands came complete with people already living there. The prime minister, soon after the war, openly said that as a result of the war 'we got a dowry [by which Eshkol meant new lands]. The problem is that with the dowry came a bride [Arab populations], and we don't want to have this bride . . .'² Eshkol often described the Gaza Strip as 'a rose with lots of thorns', because of its large Arab population, and to an audience he said, on 12 November 1967, that 'We should allow the Arabs [of] Gaza to leave.'³ But Eshkol was realistic enough to assume that the Palestinians would not 'leave' without being encouraged to do so and he therefore appointed a certain Ada Sereni to oversee a scheme in which Gazan refugees would be given a few hundred dollars in return for leaving the Strip willingly. He said to Sereni that he was in favour of all of them going, 'even to the moon', and he would often phone her to inquire: 'How many Arabs have you driven out today?'⁴ He instructed her to find 'ways and paths that will help the Arabs [of the Strip] to emigrate', even proposing to channel them to such places as South America and Australia, as 'it's possible to move people to there such that no one could even know about their existence in the world'.⁵ But, as Sereni would later report to him, while Brazil and Australia sought immigrants, 'when they hear they're Arabs, they're not interested . . .'⁶

To lure the Gazans out of the Strip, Israel offered them jobs on the West Bank, in the hope that a prolonged sojourn in the more prosperous region would encourage permanent relocation. Since unemployment in the Strip was rife after the war, many of Gaza's refugees took up the offer and moved to the West Bank, where the Israelis employed them on various projects, including the construction of a twenty-five-kilometre road along the Dead Sea. A special camp was erected for them not far from Jericho, an area, we should recall, that was destined to go to Jordan according to the Allon Plan. However, to the dismay of the Israelis, when construction ended most of the Gazans opted to return to the Strip rather than stay on in the West Bank.

With the refugees seemingly reluctant to leave voluntarily, the army began resorting to forceful deportations. The first to be dealt with were the families of between 25,000 and 50,000 workers who, at the outbreak of the war, happened to be outside the Gaza Strip in work or otherwise. By preventing these Gazans from returning to their homes in the Strip, the army effectively forced their families to leave the Gaza Strip if they ever wanted to be reunited; once out, they would not be allowed to return. A more direct campaign of ethnic cleansing also took place. Abu Hassan, a resident of the Gaza Strip in 1967, recalls his own forced exit:

> A few weeks after the Strip had been occupied, the Israelis embarked on a programme of forced deportation. On one occasion, the Israeli army rounded up all the men from my Quarter and herded us into Jaffa school. The Israelis had two local mukhtars [Palestinian village elders] with them who told the officer in charge each man's profession – 'he's a labourer, that one's a teacher' and so on. The Israelis picked out the ones they wanted, put them on trucks and sent them to Jordan.[7]

Later, in August 1968, the Israeli government appointed a special committee whose task it was to plan the transfer of between 150,000 and 250,000 refugees from the Strip to the West Bank.[8] Statistics show that between June 1967 and December 1968 the Gaza Strip lost a staggering 25 per cent of its pre-war population.

Jordan's King Hussein, in the meantime, begged the UN and Washington to help stop the influx of refugees coming from the occupied territories into his kingdom, as the new arrivals were exacerbating social unease in Jordan, where the vast majority of the population were already Palestinians. But the Israelis would not stem the flow of refugees, and in October 1969 they launched an official policy whereby Gaza Strip refugees would be, as the Israelis put it, 'encouraged to move to refugee camps in the West Bank which were close to available jobs in Israel and the West Bank itself . . .'[9] What the Israelis failed to mention, however, was that these camps were also close to Jordan.

Thus, by various methods the Israelis, after June 1967, had managed to significantly thin the Gaza Strip's population. But in the end their efforts were ineffective; thanks to the Strip's high birth rate, the population had recovered to its pre-war level by December 1976.[10]

CRUSHING THE GAZA INSURGENCY

The Gaza Strip, in the immediate post-war era, was hit by a wave of brutalization as Palestinian activists took the law into their own hands, attacking fellow Palestinians to deter them from cooperating with the occupation or taking up jobs in Israel; buses and taxis ferrying Gazans to Israel were frequently attacked. Militants also struck against those they deemed to be collaborating with the occupation, whom they would torture in gruesome ways and leave to die on the streets.

As long as the militants only attacked fellow Palestinians, Dayan chose to ignore them, but when Israelis too were targeted, this rapidly changed. The straw that broke the camel's back was an assault on a Jewish family visiting Gaza on 2 January 1971 which killed two infants. After this, Ariel Sharon, the military general responsible for the Gaza Strip, approached the defence minister, telling him, 'if we don't respond now, we are going to lose control [in the Gaza Strip]'. Dayan replied, according to Sharon: 'You can start.'[11] This was the green light for Sharon to embark on his brutal campaign against the Gaza militants, still notorious in Palestinian memory.

Ariel Scheinerman (he would later change his name to Sharon) was born in 1928 in a village called Kfar Malal in British Mandated Palestine. His childhood was not happy, mainly because his parents' arrogant behaviour towards their Jewish neighbours led to their being isolated in this tiny settlement. When Sharon was six years old, his father armed his son with a big stick to protect himself and the boy always carried it with him. Sharon's attitude toward the Arabs of Palestine was shaped by the experiences of his parents; a year before he was born, Arab rioters attacked Kfar Malal and caused much damage, and during the Palestine riots from 1936 to 1939 the population of Kfar Malal was on a constant alert.

In Israel's 1948 war of independence Sharon fought and was badly wounded; later, in the early 1950s, he formed a small, highly trained commando outfit called Unit 101, leading it in attacks on Arab villages. On many occasions he would go beyond the scope of what was ordered, planned and accepted by his superiors, but he would always explain these departures as the result of 'unexpected enemy resistance' and the need to save the lives of his soldiers or to avoid leaving behind the wounded and killed. The former prime minister David Ben-Gurion, who liked Sharon very much, considered him a compulsive liar. 'If Sharon would get rid of his faults, such as not telling the truth,' Ben-Gurion noted in his diaries, 'he would be an exemplary military leader.'[12] In the 1967 war Sharon distinguished himself fighting the Egyptians in the Sinai, and by the end of the war his image as Israel's number one warrior was assured.

A day after the attack on the Jewish family in Gaza, Sharon dispatched his men into Palestinian refugee camps, where his troops imposed a total curfew, carried out house-to-house searches and made arrests. It was a vicious operation, with reports of criminal behaviour among the troops, including robbery; two of Sharon's soldiers were dismissed for unjustified use of force during the raid. Palestinian militants hit back by staging a series of spectacular raids, not so much against the military, which was far too strong for them to confront, but against civilian objectives in Gaza City: they blew up the main Post Office, injuring sixty-one local Palestinians.

Sharon sought not only retaliation for the assault on the Jewish family, but also to rid the Gaza Strip of all resistance and guerrilla groups. His plans taking shape, he then brought in first-rate infantry troops and began training them for what he called 'anti-terrorist guerrilla warfare'.

Dividing the Gaza Strip into small, manageable chunks, sometimes 1.5 kilometres square, laid out so that they divided along natural boundaries, Sharon assigned specific squares to individual squads. He would instruct his troops: 'This one single square is your only problem. It is your job to know this square inside and out, and it is your job to find and kill every terrorist in it.'[13]

Sharon had effectively reversed Dayan's original philosophy of keeping troops out of populated Palestinian centres, and had now brought the army straight into the very heart of Palestinian urban centres, particularly into the refugee camps, which provided the insurgents with safe houses, intelligence, logistic support and a source of recruits. And his tactics were brutal; to minimize any risk to his troops, he instructed that before investigating a suspicious hiding place, be it a house, a bunker or a cave in an orange grove, a hand grenade should be thrown in first, and that any suspects failing to respond to an order to stop should be shot at, with intent to kill. He also set up mixed undercover squads, putting together four or five troops made up of Jews and captured Palestinians who had agreed to cooperate for money or something else. They would then move into the centre of their allocated town or city and the Arabic speakers would engage locals in a conversation, probing for information, while the other undercover troops would wait for any action that developed. This tactic often led to the teams, dressed as local Arabs, snatching suspected guerrillas and removing them for questioning, often then recruiting them to join the Israelis.

In his walks among the orchards and groves of Gaza, Sharon realized that, unlike Israeli farmers, Palestinian farmers did less pruning, less thinning – they intervened less in the natural growth of their trees. As a result, as Sharon put it, 'their groves were beautiful but extremely thick and overgrown, very difficult for a squad of soldiers to penetrate, very easy for a squad of terrorists to hide in'.[14] To improve his troops' field of vision and eliminate potential hiding places, Sharon now ordered Palestinian farmers to cut off the lower branches of all trees in the entire Gaza Strip, where there were about 7,000 hectares of orange groves; occasionally he would order an entire orchard to be uprooted or destroy a whole crop to deny insurgents places of concealment.

Extensive demolition of houses and other buildings also took place. In the Gaza Strip in the 1950s, UNRWA would often provide Palestinian refugee families with a small plot, where they could erect single-storey houses of two rooms and a kitchen and surrounded by a wall and a gate, arranged along symmetric lines of roads in a grid pattern. Over the years, however, and with the growing need for more living space, Palestinians extended their houses upwards and outwards and quite often at the expense of the roads, which became the narrow alleys we can see now in the Strip. This, however, meant that military vehicles could not get down many streets, leaving the troops exposed on foot in their pursuit of insurgents. To tackle this problem, Sharon now introduced the policy of 'thinning', involving the demolition of rows of houses to create a grid of patrol roads that dissected the camps.

Sharon's 'thinning' policy had a dramatic effect on whole areas of the Gaza Strip, not least on the Beach refugee camp. Known locally as 'Shati' and situated on the Mediterranean coast in the Gaza City area, the camp was one of the most crowded of Gaza's eight refugee camps, accommodating those who had fled Lydda, Jaffa, Beer Sheva and other areas of Palestine in 1948. Until Sharon's troops arrived at the Beach camp, Wreckage Street was not a street, just narrow, nameless alleys. But, with the destruction which Sharon's troops now inflicted, the street acquired its name. Ibrahim Ghanim, who lived there at the time, recalls how Sharon's troops:

> came at night and began marking the houses they wanted to demolish with red paint. In the morning they came back, and ordered everyone to leave. I remember all the soldiers shouting at people, Yalla, yalla, yalla, yalla [come on, come on, come on]! They threw everyone's belongings into the street. Then Sharon brought in bulldozers and started flattening the street . . .[15]

By the time the work was done, hundreds of homes were in ruins, not only on Wreckage Street but throughout the Beach camp, leaving hundreds of Palestinians homeless, as they were not allowed to rebuild their houses and were forced to take shelter in schools and other public buildings, or with relatives. Izzeldin Abuelaish, fifteen at the time Sharon's troops destroyed his family's house, recalls in *I Shall Not Hate* how on the night their house was demolished and for several nights thereafter:

> We slept in one room at my uncle's house. My parents and siblings slept in a row on the floor, like pickets on a fence. I was stretched out at everyone else's feet. Our few possessions were stacked in a box outside the door as there was no space in the room to keep them with us . . . Sleeping at everyone's feet felt humiliating . . .[16]

Other Palestinians whose houses were demolished, mainly political activists, were loaded into trucks and dumped in the Sinai near the town of Al Arish, which was at the time controlled by Israel. Statistics show that as many as 15,855 Palestinians were displaced as a result of Sharon's thinning policy.[17]

Under Sharon, the entire Strip was sealed off by a ring of fences, eighty-five kilometres in length, electric street lighting was installed to make better supervision possible, caves and bunkers were blocked or filled in altogether to prevent their use as hiding places, and curfews were periodically imposed on individual towns or refugee camps to allow searches.[18]

The fierceness of the Israeli army patrols terrified the Gazans; trapped between Sharon's terror and the insurgents, many Palestinians often opted to cooperate with the military. Bit by bit Sharon closed the net on the insurgents; a quote attributed to him began to make the rounds – 'The only good terrorist is a dead terrorist' – and roaming the Gaza Strip with a list of wanted militants in hand, he would cross off names as they were eliminated. Sharon's Gaza operation was at its height between July 1971 and February 1972, and in spite of growing unease among the rank and file – clearly some of Sharon's tactics fell into the category of war crimes – his policies did succeed in cutting down the number of violent Palestinian incidents: in June 1971, the army recorded thirty-four terrorist incidents in the Gaza Strip; in December only one; and thereafter there were almost none at all.

With calm restored, Gaza's wealthy citrus growers and land-owning elite, who had also historically formed its political leadership, began to rebuild the Strip. One of them, Rashad al-Shawa, a prosperous citrus merchant, became the mayor of Gaza in September 1971, and with the army's permission he formed a municipal council composed of Gaza's upper classes.[19] In 1972, al-Shawa focused his attention on the economic revitalization of Gaza's citrus industry, which had suffered greatly during the fighting, as well as from a variety of measures imposed by the army, including new trade restrictions and taxes. He also promoted the development of cultural organizations in Gaza, including the Red Crescent Society, a community-based health clinic, a lawyers' association and a women's guidance union.

Gradually, however, al-Shawa's activities came under criticism from both pro-PLO nationalists and the army: while the former viewed him as a stooge of the occupation, even a collaborator, the Israelis thought him too independent. In October 1972, the army removed him from office and Gaza, once again, came under the direct rule of a military governor – unlike the West Bank, where the municipalities were run by local Palestinian leaders who, as shown, had been elected by the population.[20] It was, indeed, a consistent feature of the Israeli occupation that the government vacillated between allowing the Palestinians some measure of self-rule and not giving them too much room to manoeuvre.

COLONIALISM IN GAZA

When the Israelis marched into the Gaza Strip in 1967 its economy, although battered, was still functioning. It was dominated by a service sector, which accounted for the largest share of gross domestic product, followed by agriculture, which was heavily dependent on citrus fruit exports to Eastern Europe through Gaza's small port. The construction industry followed and then the light-industrial sector of crafts and food processing, as well as fishing and other marginal industries. The war, inevitably, was a dreadful blow to the Gaza Strip's economy, since it completely severed the economic links between the Strip and Egypt that had evolved over the previous two decades, and led to the loss of administrative jobs and public works programmes created by the Egyptian authorities. The withdrawal of the Egyptian army in the wake of its defeat and the departure of UN forces on the eve of the war meant that a critical source of foreign currency income was also eliminated. This all led, in the immediate post-war period, to rising unemployment, which was higher than during the pre-war period.

Opening up to the Israeli market gradually improved the situation in the Strip, as Israel, emerging from its pre-war recession, and with some sectors experiencing manpower shortages, needed a low-cost workforce and this came from the Palestinians of the West Bank and Gaza Strip. By the end of 1968, and in a situation quite similar to that in the West Bank, five labour exchanges were set up in Gaza to organize the channelling of workers into Israel. Israel also opened six vocational training centres, where courses were offered to the unskilled, and where Palestinians were trained in sewing, shoemaking, bookkeeping, carpentry, building, car mechanics, welding, scaffolding and ironwork.

The opening of Israel's labour market to the Gazans dramatically affected employment patterns in the Strip, with the number of labourers crossing into Israel rising significantly from 800 in 1968 to 5,900 in 1970. Dayan was delighted, as he was in favour of economic integration with the occupied territories, seeing it as an effective tool to keep the Palestinian population content and the occupied lands calm. He wrote:

> In the refugee camps in the Gaza Strip there [is] a veritable economic revolution. Refugees who for years had spent their time sitting outside their huts playing backgammon and talking politics, and seldom shedding their pyjamas, begin going to work . . . thanks to the high wages in Israel they [are] able to improve not only their standard of living but also their way of life. For the first time they [can] acquire new clothes, furniture and kitchen appliances.[21]

The trend towards employment in Israel gained momentum in 1972, when the government lifted all restrictions on freedom of movement between the Gaza Strip and Israel proper. Also, between 1968 and 1973, twelve Israeli and foreign enterprises were established in the Erez industrial zone, an area of some 40.5 hectares located immediately north of the Gaza Strip, in Israeli territory. Initiated by the government, this project opened 6,000 new jobs for Gazans and was intended to encourage local Palestinian entrepreneurs to build a small industry to complement the Israeli markets; loans were offered and Israel would even allow wealthy Palestinian expatriates to return from exile in order to invest.

The Erez concern and jobs in Israel, as well as the emergence of small industries in the Gaza Strip after the war, led to an impressive annual growth rate of almost 30 per cent between 1967 and 1973, which buoyed the Gazan economy. By 1973, employment in the formerly moribund Strip had reached the unprecedented figure of 98 per cent. But this also meant – and here was the downside – that the Strip became almost totally dependent on Israel for jobs.[22]

For the Gaza agriculture sector, however, it took quite a long time to recover. As on the West Bank, the Israelis, at first, helped introduce new techniques such as drip irrigation, as well as new crops and fertilizers, and they also set up two mechanized packing houses for efficient citrus export. Magnanimity, however, was short-lived: as on the West Bank, once the Israelis realized that by assisting the Gazans they were effectively creating competition for their own products, they began putting up obstacles. Thus, while before 1967 Gaza traditionally marketed its produce directly to parts of Eastern and Western Europe and Singapore, between 1967 and 1974 the Israelis would only allow export through Israel's Citrus Marketing Board. This ultimately meant that Gazan products were sold at less than competitive prices, and under increasingly disadvantageous conditions. Later, between 1974 and 1979, when Gaza citrus was at its maximum yield, the Israelis, in order to stop competition with their own products, banned the Gazans from marketing to Europe, forcing them, instead, to seek alternative markets in the Arab world, which Israel could not enter. Forced out of the European markets, the Gazans did manage to develop a market with Iran that proved quite lucrative, but otherwise Gaza's citrus sector became dependent on moody Israelis who, whenever under the illusion that Gaza competed with them, changed the rules of the game.

The Strip became even more dependent on Israel's goodwill when the government linked it to its national electrical grid, starting with Gaza City in December 1969 and then connecting other towns and cities over the following months. While Palestinians protested that this was an effective annexation of Gaza into Israel and requested an immediate disconnection, the defence minister, Moshe Dayan, rejected their requests by insisting that it was necessary for 'security reasons'. There is little doubt that the more efficient Israeli grid allowed more homes in Gaza to be supplied with electricity – 24,000 in Gaza City alone compared with 5,000 before the war.[23] But it also meant that the Israelis assumed control over a resource that could have been an important source of revenue for the Palestinians, and it also proved an important tool to control the Gazans, as it enabled Israel to turn off the lights should Palestinians fail to accept the occupation, as the Israelis would often do in future years.

Similarly, Israel integrated the water supply of the Gaza Strip into its own national water network, in accordance with the Israel Water Law of 1959, which made all water in the Strip a commodity of the Israeli state. This was supplemented by Military Order No. 158, which required – as by now one would have expected – a licence for digging new wells. For Gazans this caused grave problems as, with no rivers, digging wells was standard practice to collect water. Israel's assumption of control over water resources also hit the citrus sector, which accounted for at least 80 per cent of Gaza's total water consumption.

As Israel became a major provider of jobs to Palestinians and assumed control over water, electricity and other resources, it effectively turned itself into an old-fashioned colonialist, in total control of Palestinian lives.

3
Golan Heights

The origin of the word 'Golan', like many other matters, is in dispute between Arabs and Israelis. A Syrian interpretation is that 'Golan' derives from the Arabic 'Jwal', meaning land filled with dust; it is true that the Golan Heights are often racked by dust storms. The Israeli interpretation of 'Golan' goes back to biblical times, when the town of Golan is referred to in the Bible as 'Ir Miklat', a place of refuge to which those who had committed manslaughter could flee; but neither the town nor the region was ever part of the biblical Land of Israel, rather what the Bible refers to as 'Ever Ha'Yarden', meaning 'the other side of the Jordan'.

The Golan is a mountainous plateau in south-west Syria, sixty-five kilometres in length from north to south, and twenty-five kilometres across at its widest point in the south; it consists of two distinct parts – the Upper Golan in the north, which is covered in volcanic hills, the result of ancient lava flows covering the limestone bedrock of the Heights; and the southern Lower Golan, which is flatter. The area as a whole borders Lebanon to the north, Jordan to the south and Israel to the west.

The most important town on the Golan has always been Quneitra, which means, in Arabic, a small arch or bridge, and refers to the bridge of little arches around which the town was constructed. Quneitra began as an inn ('khan') for travellers and ancient maps give its name as 'Khan-Quneitra'. At the middle of the nineteenth century it was still no more than a *khan*; by the end of the century it had about 1,800 inhabitants, mostly Circassians, a Muslim minority people originally from the Caucasus. By the 1940s, Quneitra had about

5,000 inhabitants, still mostly Circassians, and by 1953 its population had risen to 8,100, but by then the town was gradually losing its Circassian character as Arab merchants, trading with Damascus, began to take over.

In the early 1960s, Quneitra was officially proclaimed as the Golan's district capital and commercial centre and it also became the local centre for the Syrian military, with army headquarters and various camps located around the city, including the HQ of 'Israel Front Command'. On the eve of the 1967 war Quneitra's population stood at 17,000; it had become the 'big city' where Golanis frequently went to hunt for jobs, though they would often still keep their lands and apple orchards and homes in the villages.

Otherwise, and until the arrival of the Israelis, the Golan was a mostly agricultural society, where men worked on small plots, wives and children helping in the fields. At the same time, as a relatively isolated corner of Syria, the Golan's dominant agriculture sector had been backward and underdeveloped; hardly any tractors, harvesters or other modern agricultural machinery could be found in the region before 1967. According to Syrian statistics, agricultural production on the Golan between 1960 and 1966 showed yearly averages of 116,000 tons of grain, 13,000 tons of vegetables, 13,400 tons of milk, 67 tons of wool, 16 tons of honey, 2,000 tons of meat, and 18 million eggs.[1]

Isolation also meant self-reliance as the Golanis had to depend mainly on their land to provide for their daily consumption. Muhammad Jum'a Isa, from the Golan village of Butayah, recalls how, before the Israeli invasion, 'We lived a simple life, without difficulties. Everything was widely available, and all necessities were cheap. All a peasant needs are sugar, tea and tobacco ... [it was a] good poor man's country'.[2] And Fatima al-Ali from the village of al-Asbah remembers a peaceful existence and a close-knit community: 'our village was small ... a simple village ... all of the Golan is plentiful ... its waters, its lands, and its bounty. We used to get our running water from the mill ... in the old days, even with the hardships, life was better ... people cared for each other a lot ...'.[3] This sense of close-knit community which existed on the Golan before the war is also apparent in the testimony of Amina al-Khatib, a Druze who remembers how 'We had excellent relations with the neigbouring villages. Christians, Sunnis, and Druze lived together like brothers. It was only that they prayed in different places. When it came to other matters, we even dressed alike. We celebrated Christian feasts too.'[4] And Omar al-Hajj Khalil, who was born in the Golan village of Ayn Aysha, remembers life which was very close to nature: 'We spent it in the vineyards and the wilderness, chasing after animals and shepherding them, working the land and raising crops . . .'[5]

Before 1967 the Golan boasted 142 primary schools and fifteen high schools, but few attended them because, as Fatima al-Ali explains: 'the school was far away and because each household had about twenty head of livestock, there was a lot of work. Girls had to milk the animals and do household chores. A few of the boys went to school, but the rest were illiterate. Everybody worked the land.'[6]

This simple existence, however, was shattered as in the last thirty hours of the 1967 war Israel initiated a battle against Syria in the course of which its forces climbed the Golan Heights and captured it. This, for the Golanis and their land, brought about a swift, dramatic and most traumatic transformation.

ETHNIC CLEANSING AND THE RISE OF THE DRUZE

On the eve of the war, the Golan had a population of 138,000 Syrians who lived in 139 villages, two cities and sixty-one farms, which were large agricultural domains, many established in Ottoman times.[7] However, during and immediately after the war more than 95 per cent of the Golanis departed, leaving the Heights almost entirely devoid of its people. What caused this mass exodus in such a short time? Did they leave of their own volition, or were they pushed out?

In an article in *Life* magazine, soon after the war, Moshe Dayan explains that – shelled, bombed and fearing for their lives – Syrian Golanis had fled eastwards together with the retreating Syrian army. Indeed, this view holds sway in Israel to this day.[8] For instance, in the Israeli-based *Davar* magazine, on the first anniversary of the capture of the Golan, the journalist Ruth Bondy reported that:

The Arab villages along the [Golan] roads are abandoned . . . Everyone fled, to the last man, before the IDF arrived, out of fear of the savage conqueror. The feeling one gets upon seeing the abandoned villages shifts from contempt for the meager huts that the 'advanced' [Syrian] regime managed to provide its farmers, and sorrow at the sight of the relatively nicely tended houses of the Circassian village . . .

She then wonders, 'Fools, why did they have to flee?'[9] The testimonies of Syrian refugees confirm that indeed some of them left willingly, out of personal fear. As the refugee Fatima al-Ali recalls in a later interview:

The village elders said that those who had daughters should take them away, that people should [also] take their wives away. They said: 'leave everything, including your livestock, and make good your escape with your family'. So everyone was trying to save their women and to take them out of the area so they would be safe . . . A few people took their cattle and sheep with them.[10]

There is no evidence of targeted violence towards women on the part of the Israelis, but such a fear seems to be a dominant reason leading to the departures, as emerges from other testimonies too, including that of Izzat al-Ayoub, a Druze from Majdal Shams. 'The people who left did so out of fear,' he confirms. 'They thought the Israelis would assault their women . . .'[11]

A certain number of Golani civilians decided to leave temporarily, as people often do in times of war, hoping to return when the guns fell silent; but many others, as we can learn from various testimonies by Golanis and indeed Israelis, were expelled by military direct action, as the Israeli preference was to have the land without its native people. One of the methods the Israelis would use to encourage their departure was to scare the Golanis into leaving. Fatima al-Ali recalls how 'Israeli aircraft were diving above our heads to terrorize us and make us leave . . . the Israelis . . . fired their weapons at night to wreak havoc. It was then that we ran away . . . The people of our village scattered . . . Each family went off in a different direction, because they were frightened . . .'[12] A UN special representative, Nils Goran Gussing, who visited the Golan immediately after the fighting, observed in a report of 2 October 1967 that 'it seems clear . . . that certain actions authorized . . . by local [Israeli] military commanders were an important cause of the [Syrian] flight'.[13]

Israeli testimonies also offer an indication of direct action aimed at expulsion; the military commander Emanuel Shaked, who fought on the Golan, recounted how:

> We gathered [the Golanis] in a group. We let them take belongings that they could carry in rucksacks, and sometimes we also helped them with trucks. Most went on foot, and some on wagons with horses . . . Some people protested or shouted, but no one resisted or fought us.[14]

Often, the Israelis would evict whole villages, as was the case with Jubata, in the northern Golan, which had 1,500–2,000 people before the war. One resident, Hammoud Maray, recalls how:

> Roughly about half the people from Jubata left their village and moved to Majdal Shams to hide . . . they had left Jubata because they were afraid of the war. [Then] the Israeli military occupied the village of Jubata and began to forcibly transfer the people who remained; the people who had left Jubata [and came to hide in Majdal Shams] and tried to return . . . were also transferred. The Israeli army began shooting in the air and in the direction of the people, all the time, to frighten the people . . . after the transfer, Jubata became a closed military zone; nobody could return . . .'[15]

This is also confirmed by another testimony, according to which the Israeli army gathered the people of Jubata and instructed them to walk in the direction of Lebanon, firing over their heads in order to frighten them.[16] As on the West Bank, the army made the Golanis sign a document attesting that they left willingly; an Israeli soldier who fought on the Golan in 1967 testified how 'We saw a big group of Syrian civilians, a few hundred people, gathered in front of desks with soldiers sitting behind them. We stopped and asked a soldier what they were doing. He answered they were doing pre-expulsion registration [namely having the Syrians sign they left of their own volition].'[17] Some of the evacuees camped out in their fields, rather than leaving altogether, waiting for the right moment to return to their villages. An Israeli soldier on the Golan recalls how 'We saw hundreds of people in the fields and outside the villages. They watched us from a safe distance, waiting to see what the day would bring . . .'[18] And Fatima al-Ali explains that the people of her village wanted to stay close by 'because of the harvest . . . they wanted to go back [to harvest]'.[19]

But the army would not allow the Golanis to return to their villages. Instead, a few days after the end of the war, on 18 June, Colonel Shmuel Admon, the Israeli commander in charge of the region, issued a military order declaring the entire Golan a 'closed military zone', whereby no one who left would be allowed to return to the area; those violating the order were threatened with up to five years' imprisonment. But many Golanis did try to return, mainly in order to collect left belongings. Mamduh al-Hajj Ahmad's family from the village of Ayn Ziwan left in a hurry as 'we could stay no longer, sitting as the Israelis had killed my paternal aunt's husband . . . so we locked our doors and left on foot after ten days under Israeli occupation . . .' Mamduh, however, returned to his house to collect his textbooks and documents. When he arrived, as he later recalled:

> The village was totally empty. The Israelis had been in our house. They had overturned all the beds and ripped open the mattresses. They had shot our dog . . . I spent one night there, and at dawn, before the first light, I took my books and documents and slipped out as I had entered . . .[20]

Israeli military records show that dozens of Golanis who did try to return to their homes were shot at, or arrested. A military report from September 1967 says that 'Our forces opened fire 22 times to chase away shepherds and infiltrators who approached outposts . . .'[21] It also says that 'Relative to the past weeks, the number of infiltrations from Syrian territory has decreased, due to the alertness of our forces who open fire at [those] who approach.' Another military report, of 27 September, describes how an army unit 'spotted 15 people . . . and fired in their direction . . . they [then] fled'. And yet another report, in early October, cites more than twenty incidents of troops opening fire to stave off Syrian infiltrators. On 3 October, for instance, it is reported that troops 'opened fire at an Arab woman and her child, who tried to cross [into the occupied Golan Heights]. After the shooting, the soldiers tried to apprehend them but they disappeared.' At the time, all of the events covered in the reports were banned from publication by the censor, whereas incidents in which the military encountered armed civilians or combatants on the Golan were given extensive media coverage.

Golanis who did, however, manage to sneak through and reach their former homes often found that there was nowhere to return to, as, in their absence, the Israeli army had been busy demolishing entire villages. General Elad Peled, commander of the military's 36th Division during the war, testifies that 'a few days after the end of the fighting ... we started demolishing villages ... With some of the houses no heavy machinery was even needed as it could be done with just a hoe.' Peled estimates that about 20,000 civilians who remained on the Golan in those early days after the war 'were evacuated or left when they saw that the villages were starting to be destroyed ... and they had nowhere to return to'.

As on the West Bank, much of the destruction was initiated by local commanders, acting without explicit governmental authorization; thus, for instance, the army demolished 80 per cent of the houses in the village of Banyas before the government even knew about it; when the cabinet met on 25 June 1967, one minister, Menachem Begin, wondered: '... is something like that for the consideration of a local commander?'[22] Nonetheless, in the absence of definitive instructions from the government to the contrary, the army's demolition of Syrian villages continued well into 1968.

Six villages, clustered in the north-west sector of the Golan Heights, did escape the destruction, and their 6,000 people, mainly of the Druze sect, were allowed to stay.[23] Why were the Druze spared the fate of other Golanis and their villages left intact? Because the Israelis assumed that, like their kinsmen in Galilee in Israel, the Golan Druze community would be loyal to the State of Israel. It is worth mentioning that since the 1948 war a community of Druze had been living peacefully with the Israelis, the majority of them even serving in the military, as, unlike Israeli-Arabs, they were subject to conscription. Now, in 1967, their intervention with the government persuaded ministers to allow the Golan Druze community to stay in their homes. Also, the local Druze leadership on the Golan, particularly the older generation, urged their people not to flee, recalling the lesson learnt from similar events in 1925–7. Then, during the Great Syrian Revolt against the French who at the time controlled the area, the Druze abandoned their villages, only to find their homes in ruins when they returned.

And thus, whereas before the 1967 war the Druze community was a small minority on the Golan, now, with other Golanis either fleeing or expelled, it turned into the majority on the Heights.

And what was the fate of those who left? Many wandered from place to place before settling down. Mamduh al-Hajj Ahmad, a refugee from the Golan, says that 'the older people found it hard to adapt to a new life. Many of them died from sorrow during the first year. It was very hard.'²⁴ Otherwise, over two thirds of the Golan refugees moved to live in camps and residential areas mainly around Syria's capital, Damascus, while others dispersed across Syria; some remained in villages near the Golan such as Sa'sa and Qatana. Expelled, barred from returning and with most of their villages demolished and thus nowhere to return to, the Golanis were cut off from their land; separation and longing gradually became a main feature of the Golanis' life in exile. Decades after being expelled from the Golan, Izzat al-Ayoub, who had lived in Syria since 1967, explains how:

> The [Israeli] occupation cut me off from my hometown, and my region. I'm an old man now, and though I've forgotten many things in my life I have not forgotten those places I have not seen in thirty-three years, where I've worked in the gardens, herded cattle and sheep, and eaten the food of winter – molasses mixed with snow, and boiled corn. If you give me pen and paper I could draw [my] old [town] house by house, street by street, lane by lane. The town lives in my memory as though I were right now in our stone house with its mud roof where we used to shovel and play in the snow in winter.²⁵

And Amina al-Khatib, originally from the village of Ayn Qunyih, but in 1967 staying in Damascus away from her family on the occupied Golan, explains that

> I have been separated from my family ever since. My mother died, four of my uncles died, and my father died and I did not see a single one of them. Those who were children when I left are married now. My

yearning for the Golan, its land, waters, trees and its people is indescribable . . .'[26]

TRANSFORMATION

In the meantime, the Israelis discontinued Syrian law on the Golan and installed a military government, headed by an officer who started ruling the area by issuing military orders. The overall aim was to extinguish the physical remnants of Syrian presence on the Golan, to take over the land and alter the political, economic and social makeup of the remaining population, erase their Syrian Arab identity and remake them into Israeli citizens.

Assuming full control over the local judiciary and administration, the army dismissed the elected mayors of the remaining villages and appointed new mayors to replace them, also creating fresh village councils through which it wished to impose the new rules and turn the military orders into policies on the ground. Under the Syrians until 1967, Golan villages elected 'collective committees' to represent each village before the authorities in Damascus and it had been through this system that farmers' needs were relayed to Damascus, and assistance then channelled to the Golan villagers. Now, however, the army dissolved the committees, appointing instead a handful of individuals whom they placed in positions of power to act as the paws of the occupation by allowing them to issue licences and permits upon which the Golanis were dependent for many activities. They also allowed these representatives to distribute fertilizers and other necessities to farmers, thus making the Golanis dependent on these individuals and indirectly on the occupation.

The Israelis went on to replace Syrian currency with the Israeli lira, issued special car numberplates, and confiscated Syrian identity cards, replacing them with Israeli military IDs. And as on the West Bank and Gaza Strip, here too the Israelis started intervening at all levels of the educational system by appointing a military officer to run the local Golan school system and replacing the Syrian curriculum with one emphasizing a sense of separate Druze identity, distinct from Syrian. This was part of the Israeli strategy of promoting the remaining Druze as a favoured minority, hoping that they would turn their back on the former Syrian regime and embrace the Israelis. As many teachers had fled the Golan during the war, and the army had dismissed qualified teachers who demonstrated loyalty to the previous regime, there was something of a shortage and the military proceeded to appoint secondary-school students as teachers.

The Golanis looked at all these changes and could do little to oppose them as their numbers on the Golan were marginal and in many ways they owed their continued presence there to the Israelis, who had allowed them to stay in the first place. But it upset them a great deal, as Midhat Salih al-Salih, a Druze who was born in Majdal Shams and grew up on the Golan under Israeli occupation, recalls: 'As I grew up, I started to become conscious of what occupation meant and, in contrast, what freedom meant. I opened my eyes as a child only to see Israeli soldiers in the Golan . . . their repression . . .'[27]

What above all concerned the remaining Syrians on the Golan was that the Israelis would confiscate their lands. The traditional land-holding system there had always been based upon about half of the land being individually owned and the rest collectively held by the villagers to be used mainly for grazing. Now, however, apprehensive that the army would seize the lands not individually held, the Golanis, shortly after the war, divided up the collectively owned lands, planting apple orchards on them. This, in turn, led to the area under cultivation growing quite dramatically and, coming on top of the massive destruction of whole villages and the departure of most of their people, resulted in a considerable transformation of the Golan landscape.

The Israelis proceeded anyway, and in order to turn the expropriation of Golan Heights lands into a 'legal' exercise, the military government issued a range of laws. Under these laws, for example, any piece of land conquered by or surrendered to the armed forces, including land that had been deserted by its inhabitants, could be declared abandoned and turned into 'state land'. As they did on the West Bank, the Israelis also employed the Defence (Emergency) Regulations allowing military commanders to declare any area to be closed for the purposes of these regulations. It was the use of these military laws, combined with tactics such as planting landmines in certain areas to keep the Golanis off land Israel wanted to expropriate, that resulted in as much as 94 per cent of the Heights land being seized by the Israelis; and with so much land at their disposal the Israelis proceeded to build new settlements.

On 3 July 1967, the deputy prime minister, Yigal Allon, submitted to the government (ten days earlier than, and quite separate from, his 'Allon Plan' for the West Bank and Gaza), a plan he called 'Labour Camps on the Golan Heights'. The gist of it was to build work camps on the Heights, because, as he explained, cultivation there, which Allon was confident the government would soon approve, would require the setting up of camps to house the labourers, tools, seed and fertilizer. Whether Allon really intended these 'labour camps' to be temporary structures to house people and tools, or to gradually turn into permanent settlements, is not entirely clear, though he probably gathered that, in due course, the Golan Heights would be given back to Syria – unlike the West Bank, for example, which the Israelis insisted had never belonged to Jordan, they did not ever actually dispute the fact that the Golan belonged to Syria. But, as it was not clear *when* the land would be returned to Syrian hands, Allon probably felt that his labour camps could press Damascus to agree to peace on Israel's terms. This view was also expressed by the Israeli ambassador in Washington, Yitzhak Rabin, who, in response to American criticism, soon after the war, that building settlements confirmed Arab suspicions that Israel did not intend to withdraw from the territories it occupied in 1967, observed that 'the Arabs would be more eager to negotiate the more they saw a danger that they would not get their territories back'.[28]

Whatever their reasoning might have been, the ministers approved Allon's plan, and subsequently, on 19 July, workers moved into a wood next to the abandoned Syrian village of Aleika and started tilling the land. On 27 August, the government approved the building of even more settlements on the Heights, while obfuscating this policy publicly by declaring that 'we don't build permanent settlements'.[29] The latter decision led to the establishment of Snier, on 24 September, and, on 12 October 1967, settlers moved into abandoned Syrian houses in

Quneitra to construct kibbutz Golan, later to be called Merom Golan ('Heights of Golan'); it would be moved to its final, permanent, site on 31 March 1972. This bold settlement initiative in the summer and autumn of 1967 was played out against a background of increasingly belligerent Syrian and other Arab governments' statements which, iron-ically, played into Israeli hands in that the government could claim that the Arabs did not want peace and thus Israel's settlement-building policy was justified as a means of self-defence. While allowing the building of Jewish settlements on the Golan, the government, at the same time, put restrictions and obstacles on building in the Arab sector, as we learn from Mufeed al-Wili, a Druze from Buqata who explains that 'Most of the Israeli projects in the Golan are subsidized [by the government] . . . The land is given free [to the settlers] . . . If we [Druze] want more land, we must buy it or rent it from the Israeli authorities . . . [but] we cannot buy or rent land from the Israelis because we don't consider them the owners of the land . . . how can we rent the land or buy it from those who don't own it?'³⁰ And thus, while the Druze neither built nor expanded existing villages, the Israelis had, by the end of March 1969, ten new Jewish settlements on the Golan.

RESISTANCE AND WAR

In the meantime, resistance to the occupation emerged and, in many ways, turned out to be even more violent than in the Palestinian occu-pied territories as it gradually sucked in the Syrian army with its heavy guns. The Syrians rightly identified the static settlements on the Golan as Israel's soft belly and directed their artillery fire towards them, which stunned the Israeli settlers, who were caught unprepared, both mentally and physically, for attacks in such close proximity.

Occasional exchanges of fire gave way to an all-out war when the Syrians, upset by the continuing Israeli occupation of their land, launched a massive invasion in close coordination with Egypt, which simultaneously attacked Israel from the south on 6 October 1973. This came to be known as the October 1973 war – or the Yom Kippur war – and for those, particularly in Israel, who thought that Arabs would become accustomed to the occupation and forgo their lands, was a reminder that this would not happen. Taking the Israeli army almost totally by surprise, Syrian tanks and troops, supported by air power, broke into the Golan, and overran large areas of the Heights with the aim of physically liberating it from the Israeli occupiers. However, initial Syrian success was short-lived, as the Israelis soon pushed the Syrians back, recapturing Quneitra and all the lost ground – in fact, acquiring even more than they had had before the war.

On 31 May 1974, with American help, Israel and Syria signed an Agreement of Disengagement which put a formal end to the 1973 war, and in which the parties took it upon themselves 'scrupulously' to observe the ceasefire on land, sea and air, and refrain from all military actions against each other. While it was agreed that the Israelis would continue to stay on the majority of the Golan area occupied in 1967, Quneitra, as well as the additional salient Israel captured during the war, would be returned to Syria. An expanded UN force – the United Nations Disengagement Observer Force (UNDOF), was also set up and stationed in a buffer zone between Israeli and Syrian troops.

The success in reaching these agreements, however, was clouded by the Quneitra affair. We have already explained that Quneitra has always been the most important town on the Golan, yet during the war it suffered enormously as the advancing Israelis demolished much of it during their counterattack. Now, however, in the short space of time between the signing of the deals that put an end to the war and the date Quneitra was due to be returned to Syria, Israeli Golan settlers took matters into their own hands, brought in heavy machinery, and with the army turning a blind eye to their actions set about destroying as much of the town as they could. *Le Monde*'s Syria correspondent writing for *The Times* gave a detailed eyewitness description of the destruction inflicted by the Israelis:

> Quneitra is unrecognizable. The houses with their roofs lying on the ground look like gravestones. Parts of the rubble are covered with fresh earth furrowed by bulldozer tracks. Everywhere there are fragments of furniture, discarded kitchen utensils, Hebrew newspapers . . . here a ripped-up mattress, there the springs of an old sofa. On the few sections of wall still standing, Hebrew inscriptions proclaim: 'You want Quneitra, you'll have it destroyed'.[31]

Refusing to take responsibility for the damage Israel asserted that much of it had been caused as a result of the exchange of fire between Israel and Syria, but the world would not accept this groundless claim. On 29 November 1974, the UN adopted a resolution (3240/A) deploring Israel's violation of human rights on the Golan and its deliberate destruction of Quneitra.[32]

One of the lessons Israel learnt from the 1973 war was that its sixteen settlements on the Golan, rather than providing any kind of security, in fact proved to be a major liability for the army before and during the war, as it was necessary to evacuate all of their citizens. Nonetheless, and perhaps in an attempt to demonstrate that the war had not weakened Israel's resolve, the government decided to build even more settlements and bring more people to the Golan to beef up the meagre 600 settlers living there; on 16 July 1974, ministers ordered the building of an urban centre on the Golan to be called Katzrin, to house 5,000 families, with a school and other public amenities. They also agreed to extend the construction of settlements to the centre and northern parts of the Golan, overcoming the problem of the infertile land there by developing industry rather than agriculture.

And to tighten its grip on the Golan even further, Israel, in 1975, built a toughened fence, complete with minefields, which completely separated the occupied Golan from the rest of Syria. Thus, while for some time after the start of the occupation Golanis could cross overland into Syria to visit relatives and friends, now they were cut off from each other by the new obstacle; given that 90 per cent of the Golanis had relatives in Syria this was quite a blow. This dramatic change led to families from both sides gathering at the 'Hills of Shouts', a reference to two hills, just outside the Golan village of Majdal Shams, separated by the ceasefire line, and they would communicate with megaphones to convey news of births, deaths and marriages. The frustration of this practice is apparent in the testimony of Amina al-Khatib, originally from the village of Ayn Qunyih on the Golan but living on the Syrian side of the ceasefire line as a result of the 1967 war:

> There [at the Hill of the shouts] I feel very frustrated. My village is right in front of my eyes, yet I cannot reach it. When I go [to the Hill of the Shouts] . . . they inform me through the megaphone that so and so has

died, that so and so is dying, and I feel great anger. I want to rip up those barbed wires and mines, and I don't care what happens . . .[33]

Interestingly, this effort on the part of the Golanis to keep in touch with relatives and friends across the border in Syria was in stark contrast to the cool relations that had developed between the Golan Druze and the Israeli Druze community. While in the period immediately after the 1967 war Israeli Druze from villages in Galilee rushed to the Golan Heights to re-establish contacts with relatives that had been broken off at the creation of Israel in 1948, gradually tensions grew between the two communities, as political differences emerged and Druze Golanis looked with suspicion at the close relationship between their fellow Druze and the Israeli state.

With the first decade of Israeli occupation drawing to a close, there were twenty-four Jewish settlements on the Golan, including the new city of Katzrin, during where settlers started moving in during the summer of 1977. But Jewish settlement on the Golan never reached critical mass and it remains, to date, quite modest. Unlike many West Bank settlers, who would often commute into Israel proper for jobs and services, on the Golan settlers tended to work locally. In the southern Golan, they survived on farming alone, with meat production, both turkey and beef as well as the cultivation of apples, being an important sector of the economy. In the central and northern Golan, some industry was developed: the manufacture of electronics tuff, (a basic material for construction and road building), firefighting equipment, shoes and sandals, and even the production of wine. Other settlements, notably Neve Ativ, provided tourist facilities, of which the main business was skiing on Mount Hermon.

When Israel seized the Golan in 1967, it was an underdeveloped region; there were very few proper roads, and villages were not connected to either electricity or water supplies. From this point of view, the Jewish settlement of the Golan did lead to the development of infrastructure. But the Golanis – although many of them found jobs in Israel and enjoyed the fruits of infrastructure development – continued to demonstrate loyalty to Syria, regarded themselves as Syrians and opposed the Israeli occupation.

4
Sinai

It is often forgotten that the Sinai Peninsula, which Israel seized from Egypt in 1967, was once part of the occupied territories. This is partly because Israel only ruled the Peninsula for a relatively short period of time, from June 1967 to April 1982, and the changes introduced were relatively small. Also, as the vast expanses of desert that comprise the Sinai Peninsula were only sparsely inhabited, there was as a result little friction between occupier and occupied. But the Sinai Peninsula was still occupied land for fifteen years, and it is worth examining the main features of this occupation, as it did share some similarities with other areas under Israeli control and was regarded by the Israelis as an important additional piece of land in that it enhanced Israel's sense of security and provided it with important natural resources such as oil.

Situated between the Mediterranean Sea to the north, the Red Sea to the south and east and the Suez Canal to the west, the Sinai, a desert area of some 60,000 square kilometres, is an inverted triangle-shaped peninsula; its unofficial administrative capital is Al Arish, in northern Sinai. Egypt, including the Sinai, was judicially Ottoman until 1918 and the Sinai was ruled through the Ottoman representative in Cairo, though the area was more or less autonomous, as the Ottomans were mainly effective in exercising control in big cities rather than in such sparsely inhabited desert areas as the Sinai. Gradually, Egypt and the Sinai came under the British sphere of influence until Egypt gained independence in 1922, when the Sinai fell under direct its administration. Sinai has been recognized as Egyptian territory ever since.

While on the eve of the 1967 war the vast majority of the Egyptian population lay to the west of the Suez Canal, the Sinai was by no means empty land. When Israel captured it the Peninsula had a population of roughly 130,000 people, of whom 100,000 lived in the northern Sinai, where most of the region's annual 100–200 millimetres of rain falls. Bedouins numbered between 11,000 and 12,000 and although they were often on the move, looking for grazing lands for their flocks, they had two permanent villages in the north-west corner of the Peninsula, close to the border with the Gaza Strip: Abu Twila and Sheik Zuid. The former was the main market town for all Bedouins of the region and its inhabitants earned their living by trade, commerce and agriculture. Bedouins in Sheik Zuid earned their living from agriculture and, since they were close to the sea, salt extraction; though smuggling goods from Sinai to the Gaza Strip and elsewhere has always been an additional source of income.

SETTLING THE SINAI

Unlike in other areas occupied in 1967, Israel at first refrained from large-scale settlement building in the Sinai. This reluctance to settle the Sinai reflected the fact that Israel recognized that the Peninsula would eventually have to be returned to its legal owner, Egypt; unlike the Gaza Strip, for instance, which never belonged to Egypt, and the West Bank, which, at least according to the Israelis, never belonged to Jordan. Interestingly, however, some in Israel, notably David Horowitz, the governor of the Bank of Israel, suggested, immediately after the war, that Israel should purchase the Peninsula from Egypt and build new settlements there; Horowitz even discussed the matter with American officials, but nothing came of it. Later, however, in 1969, the government authorized a limited settlement project in the Rafiah Plain ('Pitchat Rafiach' in Hebrew) on the Peninsula's Mediterranean coast, adjoining the Gaza Strip. The thinking behind this initiative was that a bloc of settlements in this north-western part of the Peninsula could serve as a buffer zone, a wedge between the Gaza Strip and the Sinai, so that when the latter was returned to Egypt, a bloc of villages could serve as a physical barrier to prevent the smuggling of weapons from Egypt into the Gaza Strip.

As much of the land earmarked for this settlement project, however, was used by the Bedouin tribes, the army, under General Sharon's guidance, embarked in early 1972 on an operation aimed at clearing the area; it expropriated vast tracts of cultivated Bedouin land, fencing them off for 'security reasons'. Next, Sharon dispatched his troops into the fenced area to physically remove the 1,540 Bedouin families that lived there.[1] It was a cruel eviction: houses were razed to the ground, trees uprooted and wells, dug by the Bedouins to water their fields and flocks, blocked. Most of the evacuees settled in tents on the outskirts of the sealed-off area and by crossing the fence they continued, for a time, to till their fields. The evacuees petitioned Israel's Supreme Court, where the military vigorously defended the decision to evacuate them, and the necessity of turning their lands into a buffer zone to separate the Sinai from the Gaza Strip. In May 1973, the judges reached their conclusions – and there were no great surprises: 'We have no reason to doubt that the military justifications for creating a buffer zone in the Rafiah Plain have been argued before us in complete good faith,' the judges ruled, and continued to say that 'on such matters, certainly the opinion of army men is to be preferred to that of the petitioners' counsel . . .'[2] The petition was rejected, and the Bedouin were not allowed to return to their lands, on which new Jewish settlements were then erected.

As the Sinai Peninsula, like the Golan Heights, was not regarded as part of biblical Eretz Yisrael, the influence of religious settlers, so prominent on the West Bank, was marginal, with only one such settlement being built there, called Atzmona, or Bnei Atzmon. Instead, most of the settlers in the northern Sinai – by the mid-1970s there were thirteen villages – were skilled farmers, sons of old and established collective and cooperative settlements in Israel proper, looking for new land to till.

In these new settlements in northern Sinai, the main sector of the economy was intensive, export-oriented agriculture, mainly flowers and vegetables, which were favoured by climatic conditions and the availability of inexpensive Arab labour, brought in to work in the fields from the nearby Gaza Strip. While the government hoped that the Sinai settlements could be turned into the leading farms to export winter crops, in reality they only ever contributed about 15 per cent of the vegetable and flower exports in the months January to March, which in turn only accounted for about 30 per cent of the year's exports.

In 1973, the government approved the construction of an urban centre in the Sinai called Yamit. It was to be built on the Mediterranean coast and become the southernmost of beach cities on that shore – from Haifa in the north, through Tel Aviv and Ashdod in the south. The ministers envisaged that the new city would have a deepwater port and an airfield, and that residents would be employed through tourism and the provision of other services for nearby settlements. The first settlers moved into Yamit's freshly built houses in 1975, and the place soon attracted more settlers from all over Israel, both secular and religious, seeking desert adventure and a challenge. That the government went ahead and invested in building a city despite the fact that this land would eventually have to be returned to Egypt is quite surprising, but perhaps ministers thought that, in due course, they would manage to persuade Egypt to let this city and the settlements around it stay; or perhaps they regarded the project simply as a lever to put pressure on Egypt to make peace on Israel's preferred terms.

In another corner of the Sinai, in what became known as the Shlomo District, the government approved the construction of a series of settlements, between 1969 and 1975, which it thought could somehow guarantee freedom of navigation for Israeli shipping in the Gulf of Aqaba, which Egypt had a history of disrupting. This led to the construction, in 1971, of two settlements: Neviot and Di-Zahav. Neviot was set up just sixty-eight kilometres south of Eilat, with a hotel, restaurant and diving school, along with agriculture; Di-Zahav was constructed a further eighty kilometres south near the Bedouin village of Dahav, and the settlers were mainly engaged in the tourism industry.

A year later, in 1972, the government approved the construction of a town, to be called Ofira, at the southern tip of the Peninsula, close to Sharm el Sheikh. It soon boasted a power station, water desalination plant and two small factories, aimed at providing employment for the settlers, in addition to two hotels. But the area was much too isolated and never really attracted the average Israeli; at its peak Ofira was home to 1,000 residents and, like other settlements in the south-eastern Sinai, was not regarded as a successful venture. This failure to develop the more isolated parts of Sinai was also to do with the fact that, while the settlements in northern Sinai received massive governmental support – financial and otherwise – settlements in the south-east were largely left to their own devices.

Other Israeli projects in the occupied Sinai included developing the area around Saint Catherine's – one of the oldest monasteries in the world and said to have been built on the spot where Moses saw the burning bush – by constructing, in 1976, a modern air terminal, so it could be better linked to the outside world.

And the Israelis were also after the Sinai's natural resources: disregarding the international law of occupation, they went on to search for oil in the Sinai Peninsula, drilling and developing the Alma oil field, which at its peak provided a quarter of Israel's annual oil consumption. Finally, as the vast expanses of the desert were ideal for military training, gigantic military bases mushroomed there and the air force turned the desert into its main training ground.

WAR AND COMPROMISES IN THE SINAI

Wandering through the vast expanses of the Sinai Peninsula in the years after the 1967 war, one could easily get the impression that all was quiet on this front. However, this was far from the truth, as in the Suez Canal zone, on the western edge of the desert, a bloody battle was raging between Israel and Egypt.

Signs of growing tensions could be detected as early as October 1967, when the Egyptians sank the Israeli destroyer *Eilat* with four missiles fired not far from Port Said, at the northern tip of the Suez Canal. Israel retaliated with artillery against Egypt's oil refineries in the city of Suez, at the southern end of the canal, setting them on fire and causing immense damage. This tit-for-tat exchange gradually developed into a full-blown war of attrition along the length of the Suez Canal and, in June 1969, Egypt's President Gamal Abdel Nasser pledged to escalate the battle in order to free the Sinai from its Israeli occupiers. Subsequently, a few months later, the two sides started trading blows, using fighter jets, tanks and heavy artillery – even dispatching troops to operate on each other's side of the Canal. To protect its troops from Egyptian fire, the Israelis transformed the east bank of the Suez Canal by constructing along it a line of fortifications and bunkers, which they called the Bar-Lev line, after their Chief of Staff, Chaim Bar-Lev.

With shells flying over it the Canal remained closed to shipping, as it had been since the start of the 1967 war. While Nasser failed to get the Sinai back by imposing this war of attrition on the Israelis, he did succeed in exhausting them, and this bloody war ended, so to speak, in a no-score draw, with both sides signing a ceasefire agreement which came into effect on 7 August 1970, after three years of conflict in which 367 Israeli soldiers and more than 10,000 Egyptians and civilians had been killed, with no discernible change to the post-1967 status quo; the Sinai remained under Israeli occupation.

Dayan was well aware that the ceasefire with Egypt was just a temporary respite and that, should Israel insist on keeping the occupied Sinai, the fighting was certain to be renewed. So, soon after the ceasefire came into effect, he proposed to the government that they pull back the army from the Suez Canal and deploy in the Gidi and Mitla passes, some thirty-five kilometres east of the Canal. Such a partial end of the Sinai occupation, he argued, would reduce the probability of frontier incidents, as it would be an incentive for Egypt's President Gamal Abdel Nasser to reopen the Suez Canal – an important source of revenue for Egypt – to international shipping. Operating the Canal, Dayan maintained, would make it unprofitable for Egypt to renew hostilities against Israel as this would shut down the Canal again and Egypt would lose important income. But Dayan's political rivals, notably the deputy prime minister, Yigal Allon, objected and the prime minister, Golda Meir, sided with Allon against Dayan, saying she could not understand how Dayan could possibly propose giving up part of the Sinai 'for nothing'; the military also opposed a withdrawal from the desert, and the idea was dropped. But Egypt would not accept Israel's continuing occupation of its land, and President

Nasser's successor, as of September 1970, Anwar al-Sadat, was determined to get it back.

One of thirteen children, Anwar al-Sadat was born in 1918 in the town of Mit Abul Kom some sixty-five kilometres north of Cairo. When he was eighteen, he enrolled at a military school, where he did quite well, but never really excelled himself. Upon graduation he was sent to a distant outpost, where he met Gamal Abdel Nasser, with whom, along with some other officers, he formed the Free Officers group, which in July 1952 overthrew the Egyptian monarchy. Thereafter, Sadat and Nasser, who soon after the Free Officers' coup became president of Egypt, worked quite well together, although it would only be following Nasser's death that Sadat – unknown and untested – really emerged for the first time out of his predecessor's shadow. At first, Sadat was not taken seriously either by his arch-enemy, Israel, or by the superpowers of the time – the Americans and the Russians – or even by his own people. But over time he proved to be bold and decisive.

One of the first things Sadat did was to approach the White House for help in persuading Israel to pull back from the Sinai; at least, from some parts of it initially. The US response, albeit unofficial, came from the Secretary of State, Henry Kissinger, who, according to Egyptian sources, led Sadat to understand that only some sort of a crisis could bring about bold US intervention and with it a diplomatic process which might lead to the end of the Sinai occupation.[3] With Kissinger's advice ringing in his ears, President Sadat assembled an army of 200,000 in the Suez Canal zone and on the afternoon of 6 October 1973, the holiday of Yom Kippur in Israel, he sent 130,000 of them across the Canal to tackle the 450 Israeli troops who were manning the Bar-Lev defensive line; this Yom Kippur war, as shown in the previous chapter, was coordinated with Syria.

While Sadat's forces were successful in crossing the Canal and penetrating ten kilometres into the occupied desert, the Israelis managed to recover quickly: they checked the invaders, launched a counter-attack, and made their own crossing of the Canal, penetrating as deep as twenty kilometres into Egypt proper. Three weeks later, the war was over and Israeli and Egyptian forces were quite tangled up, with

Israeli troops stationed on the west bank of the Suez Canal and Egyptian on its eastern side. With the fighting phase over, it was time for diplomacy.

The beginning of the end of the Sinai occupation

Active American diplomacy, spearheaded by Henry Kissinger, led on 11 November 1973 to the signing of a six-point ceasefire agreement between Israel and Egypt which put a stop to the war and, in hindsight, can be seen as the beginning of the end of Israel's occupation of the Sinai. Point 2 of that agreement called on the parties to embark on discussions to disengage their tangled forces.[4] After weeks of negotiations, the countries' Chiefs of Staff met in the desert on 18 January 1974 and signed a military disengagement agreement that came to be known as the Sinai Separation of Forces Agreement, or Sinai I.[5]

They decided to 'scrupulously observe the ceasefire ... [and] refrain from all military or paramilitary actions against each other ...' Israel agreed to withdraw forces from the western bank of the Suez Canal and redeploy them behind a line in the Sinai some twenty-five kilometres from the water line in positions just west of the Gidi and Mitla passes – the Sinai's most defensible barriers (see map 4). This, interestingly enough, was more or less what Dayan had proposed a couple of years earlier; had his suggested redeployment of troops been accepted by Golda Meir at the time, perhaps the October 1973 Yom Kippur war could have been averted; another missed opportunity that resulted in an unnecessary conflict.

Israel's withdrawal and deployment away from the Suez Canal were an historic event, as it was the first time Israel had pulled out from any territory it had occupied in 1967. Egypt, for its part, agreed to establish new positions in a zone east of the canal, inside the Sinai, along a ten-kilometre-wide strip where arms and personnel would be limited. Israel reciprocated by agreeing to similar limits in the area it still occupied. In the desert between the two armies, a UN Zone was established, occupied by a United Nations Emergency Force (UNEF), whose task was to monitor the restrictions Israel and Egypt had placed upon themselves. The Israelis were keen that Sadat start operating the Suez Canal, believing that with ships sailing up and down it the probability of another confrontation would be significantly reduced; but for now Sadat would not agree to do so.

The Sinai I deal was regarded, especially by Egypt, not just as a ceasefire agreement but as 'a first step towards a final just and durable peace . . .'[6] Egypt, therefore, wished to see more Israeli withdrawals from the occupied Sinai, and to achieve this end President Sadat turned to the US for help.

'Reassessment'

Sadat's minister of foreign affairs, Ismail Fahmy, accompanied by Dr Ashraf Marwan, the former President Nasser's son-in-law and by now Sadat's Secretary for Foreign Contacts, met the US Secretary of State on 13 August 1974, at the State Department in Washington. Their aim was to ensure that Israel proceeded with further withdrawals from the Sinai. In the meeting Kissinger explained the difficulties Washington was facing in trying to press Israel to withdraw from more of the occupied Sinai: for one thing, the US president, Gerald Ford, had only been in office for a week; and the second problem was the perceived weaknesses of the Israeli government.

Kissinger explained that the US could not get into a brawl with Israel, 'as the new President doesn't yet have confidence in the substance . . . There is no sense triggering him into a confrontation [with Israel] before he's confident in the substance . . .'[7] The Israeli government, meanwhile, led by Yitzhak Rabin since 1974, was, in Kissinger's words, 'a very weak government conducted by very immature people. I am disappointed in Rabin . . . Maybe some people have a ceiling above which they can't go . . . he has no charisma . . . Rabin is an intellectual general; that is the worst. It takes him months to learn something . . .'[8] But the Egyptian visitors continued to demand further Israeli withdrawals from the Sinai. 'This will be tough,' Kissinger said. 'The Israelis are not eager to make another move [beyond the withdrawals agreed in Sinai I]'.[9] Kissinger then asked: 'What quid pro quo can you offer [the Israelis, if they withdraw]?' Fahmy replied: 'Peace.' This, clearly, was a strong word. After all, like President Nasser before him, Sadat demanded Israel's withdrawal to the 1967 borders, but had never offered a full bilateral peace deal before Israel also sorted out its conflict with the Palestinians. 'You'll offer peace?' Kissinger pressed the Egyptian diplomat, which caused Fahmy to retreat quickly. Kissinger summarized: 'First we have to let the president [Ford] get himself established. Then we will work out a common strategy ... The President has all the powers now, but he is not really president until he makes something stick.'[10]

President Ford gradually got into his stride, and with his confidence growing began to put pressure on Israel to make further withdrawals in the Sinai. He went as far as threatening a 'reassessment' of US–Israeli relations, a hint that he might withhold part of the enormous US financial and military aid package to Israel. This was a bold policy which made Israel mobilize its friends in America: on 9 December 1974, seventy-one senators sent a letter to the president protesting and warning that 'we wish to reaffirm the commitment to the survival and integrity of the state of Israel that has been the bipartisan basis of American policy over 26 years and under five administrations ... we urge that you reiterate our nation's long-standing commitment to Israel's security by a policy of continued military supplies and diplomatic and economic support . . .'[11] The president retreated; but not for long.

Three months later, in March 1975, he gave his Secretary of State, Henry Kissinger, the green light to make yet another major effort to achieve a second Egyptian–Israeli disengagement agreement, leading on from Sinai I, by pressuring the Israelis to withdraw deeper into the occupied Sinai. But the Israeli government would not move and Kissinger's mission ended in tatters.

President Ford used the opportunity publicly to blame Israel for the stalemate, and then went ahead with his threat to 'reassess' America's relationship with it. Washington delayed consideration of all future economic assistance, froze Israeli requests for F-15 aircraft, delayed delivery of already promised Lance missiles, and would not enter into new arms commitments to Israel while the reassessment was underway. Israel in turn mobilized its supporters in the US and, on 23 May 1975, seventy-five senators sent a joint letter to President Ford demanding continued strong economic, political and military aid to Israel. For the time being, President Ford stood his ground.

Sinai II

In order to support Ford's efforts, on 5 June 1975 Egypt's President Anwar Sadat opened the Suez Canal to international shipping. This unexpected move put enormous pressure on Israel to reciprocate with further troop withdrawals, and, with continued US demands for Israel to compromise, indirect negotiations between Israel and Egypt reached a climax on 4 September 1975, when the parties signed the Sinai Interim Agreement, or Sinai II, as it is better known (see map 4).

Under its terms, Israel agreed to end the occupation of yet another chunk of the occupied Sinai by withdrawing its forces to between thirty and sixty-five kilometres east of the Suez Canal and redeploying them *east* of the Gidi and Mitla passes. Israel also agreed to pull out from the oil fields of Abu Rudeis, which lay on the western edge of the desert, and from which it had been pumping oil since soon after the 1967 war.

Following the model of Sinai I, the two sides agreed upon a demilitarized buffer zone, along with zones of limited armaments between their two armies. Sadat pledged not to use force to settle outstanding differences with Israel, to permit passage of non-military cargo to Israel through the Suez Canal, and to work to relax the boycott of Israeli companies, which had been particularly intense since the 1973 war. For its part, the US pledged to set up and pay for stations manned by 200 Americans to protect both sides from violations and effectively replace UN peacekeeping in the Sinai, which Israel, since the signing of Sinai I, opposed as being prejudiced against itself.

For Israel, however, the most important element of the deal came in the form of secret US aid commitments, described as 'mind boggling' by some American officials. Indeed, while what was offered to the Israelis in return for their Sinai withdrawal was not quite an American blank cheque, though it came close: the United States committed itself to making every effort to be fully responsive 'on an on-going and long-term basis' – by getting an annual Congress approval – to Israel's military equipment and other defence requirements.[12] This meant permanent large-scale military and financial support, a contingency plan for meeting Israel's military needs in any emergency, and a pledge to preserve and consolidate Israel's military superiority by furnishing it with the most advanced and sophisticated weaponry, such as F-15 fighters, that America could offer.[13] In a secret letter Washington also pledged neither to recognize nor to negotiate with the PLO as long as the organization rejected UN Resolutions 242 and 338, which, among other things, recognized Israel's right to exist, and failed to renounce violence against Israel; the latter demand on the Palestinians – to cease their resistance to an illegal occupation as a precondition for being allowed to negotiate an end to this occupation – is quite extraordinary. And as Israel was giving up some of the Sinai oil, Secretary of State Kissinger pledged, on behalf of the US, that America would guarantee for five years that Israel would be able to obtain all its domestic oil needs from the US, and that America would construct in Israel storage facilities capable of storing one year's supply of oil – this despite the fact that Israel's extraction of Egyptian oil from the occupied Sinai had been illegal under international law. At Israel's request, Washington also undertook not to put forward any peace proposals without first making 'every effort to coordinate with Israel its proposal with a view to refraining from putting forth proposals that Israel would consider unsatisfactory'.[14] This, of course, was a significant concession since it gave Israel a direct input into – indeed power of veto over – the formulation of US Middle East policies.

It seems that there is no other example in history of one nation guaranteeing another such enormous amounts of wealth and such an array of commitments as the US did in return for Israel's signature on the Sinai II agreement. Indeed, Israel's defence minister at the time, Shimon Peres, summed up the benefits to Israel by saying that 'We gave up a little to get a lot.'[15]

By 22 February 1976, implementation of Sinai II, which included an Israeli withdrawal in the Sinai and a redeployment of Israeli and Egyptian forces in new locations, was complete. Overall, Sinai II – and indeed Sinai I – was a giant step towards an end to the Sinai occupation. The Israeli government broke one of its own taboos, demonstrating that it was willing to return lands occupied in 1967, though it would be fair to comment here that in comparison to the

West Bank, for example, the Sinai was relatively worthless and thus easy to give up. Sadat, for his part, showed that it was possible to extract concessions from the Israelis, though they came with a heavy price tag and lengthy negotiation. No less important, the series of deals done between Israel and Egypt since the end of the 1973 war also demonstrate Washington's critical role in helping end Israeli occupation and secure peace deals with its neighbours. While, quite clearly, the primary responsibility for that rests with the parties themselves, the US proved in the post-1973 war period that it could have a pivotal role in brokering agreements, using its diplomatic and financial clout to push both parties in the direction of reconciliation.

PART TWO

The Second Decade, 1977–1987

5
Likud Years

Some years are singled out for fame far beyond the common lot. For Israelis and Arabs 1977 was clearly such a year and the two people who turned it into such a special time were President Sadat of Egypt, already in his seventh year in office, and Menachem Begin.

Born in Brest-Litovsk in Russia in 1913, Begin was an ardent Zionist from an early age, and after graduating with a law degree from the University of Warsaw he became a lawyer. His parents and other relatives were murdered by the Nazis in the Holocaust, an experience that would inform Begin's later political life and worldview. In 1942, Begin emigrated to British Mandatory Palestine, where he was incensed by the British policy of restricting Jewish immigration and became a pivotal player in the fight against the British in Palestine, leading an underground terrorist group known as the Irgun and carrying out outrageous acts of violence against both the British and the Arabs. In 1946, Begin's Irgun killed ninety-one British by blowing up a wing of the King David Hotel in Jerusalem, where British headquarters was located; and in the 1948 war his people took an active part in the infamous massacre of Arabs in the village of Deir Yassin near Jerusalem, an incident that accelerated the Arab exodus from Palestine on the eve of the founding of the State of Israel.

Begin spent most of his political career leading the right-wing opposition in the Knesset to Labor rule and now, in the 1977 election, at the head of a right-wing nationalist bloc called the Likud, he brought about a revolution in Israeli politics by becoming the first Israeli prime minister from the right, thus ending almost three decades of Labor hegemony.

Begin was a fanatical believer in the historic right of Jews to biblical

Eretz Yisrael, the heart of which was the West Bank, to which he would only ever refer by its biblical name, 'Judea and Samaria'. This name had been officially adopted back in December 1967, when the military government issued an order stating that 'the Judea and Samaria Region' shall be identical in meaning to the term 'the West Bank Region', a phrase that was seen as linking the area with the 'East Bank' and therefore implying Jordanian sovereignty. Back then this change in terminology was little used, but now, by referring publicly to 'Judea and Samaria', Begin attempted to link past and future, implying that these areas were an indissoluble part of Israel, which had, as expressed in the Likud platform, to be settled by 'both urban and rural settlements'.[1]

First, though, Begin had to set up a coalition government, and two appointments, in particular, would be significant for the fate of the occupied territories. One was Moshe Dayan, once a bastion of the Labor movement and until 1973 the most influential figure in all matters related to the occupied territories, whom Begin now invited to serve as his foreign minister. Dayan, who had been relegated to the political wilderness for having failed to foresee the 1973 Egyptian–Syrian attack, saw an opportunity to repair his tarnished reputation.[2] The other significant recruit to the government was a former army general, Ariel Sharon, whom Begin made minister of agriculture and, most crucially, head of the ministerial committee responsible for settlements in the occupied territories. And with parliamentary approval of Begin's government a new chapter opened in the history of Israel and its relations with the occupied territories.

A CRUCIAL MEETING IN RABAT

Like prime ministers before him, Begin would have preferred a solution to the Israeli–Palestinian dispute to form part of a larger Israeli–Jordanian deal; the idea of having an independent Palestinian state wedged between Israel and Jordan in Judea and Samaria was for Begin, as for many others in the 1970s, unthinkable. To confirm whether a deal could be struck with Jordan, the prime minister dispatched his new foreign minister to meet secretly with Jordan's King

Hussein. They saw each other in London on 22 August 1977, but Dayan found the king adamant that he would only sign a deal with Israel if offered a tangible concession, namely a substantial Israeli withdrawal from the West Bank, including East Jerusalem; for Begin this was a non-starter.[3]

In truth, however, neither Jordan nor the Palestinians were Begin's first priority. Rather, he believed in 'Egypt first': a peace deal with Egypt would effectively put an end to the danger of Israel's destruction, as it would take out of the circle of war the Arab country with the strongest army, and pave the way for others to follow suit. The prime minister turned to King Hassan II of Morocco to see if he could set up a discreet top-level Egyptian–Israeli meeting to discuss their differences. King Hassan was well placed to act as the go-between, as Morocco, home to the largest Jewish community of any country in the Arab world, was closer to Israel than any other Arab country, and Hassan himself was also on good terms with Egypt's President Anwar Sadat. Within days King Hassan had returned with Sadat's response: Sadat would dispatch his deputy prime minister, Muhamed Hassen el-Tohami, to meet the Israeli foreign minister in Morocco.

The two men met on 16 September 1977. An excerpt from an internal Mossad (the Israeli intelligence agency) report sets the scene:

> Foreign Minister [Dayan] arrived in Rabat on a special flight at 19:15 . . . accompanied by his bodyguard . . . On their arrival the visitors were taken to the king's guest house . . . The group was received by the Court Minister whereupon Dayan could remove his disguise [a wig and rimmed glasses]. The guests sat in a half circle where tea tables were scattered . . . The meeting went on for four hours without a break, and it continued even when the king left to see his mother who had come to visit him.[4]

It emerges from this secret report that Dayan and Tohami talked mainly about how Israel and Egypt could strike a deal whereby Egypt would offer full peace and Israel, in return, would end the Sinai occupation. They also discussed the Palestinian issue, since if Egypt failed to act on this, it would be blamed across the Arab world for betraying the Palestinian cause. While they discussed various ideas, on one point they seemed to agree, namely that the PLO and its head, Arafat, were entirely disruptive and posed 'a danger to Israel's future, as well as endangering the king of Jordan'. This is because the PLO claimed not only the West Bank and the Gaza Strip for the Palestinians, but Israel too, and it was aggressive in its approach towards some Arab regimes, notably the monarchy in Jordan, where it had strong support as most Jordanians are Palestinians. To ensure that the PLO did not disturb any peace efforts, nor attempt as it did in the early 1970s to topple King Hussein, Tohami suggested that other Arab countries, namely Saudi Arabia and Egypt, which had a certain influence on Arafat due to their political backing of the PLO, and their financial support to the organization, 'could together control the radicals [i.e. the PLO] and keep the king of Jordan on his throne'.

Dayan flew straight back to Israel from Rabat to report to the prime minister in person, before heading to the US for a prearranged meeting with President Jimmy Carter. Even if Carter knew about Dayan's secret meeting with Tohami in Morocco from his own intelligence services, it appears that he did not register it as a significant event. In his meeting with Dayan, he was blunt, warning his guest that Israel was taking 'a very adamant stand and that the Arab side appears to be more flexible'; he was also furious about Israel's continuing policy of settlement building, which Begin's Likud was determined to accelerate.[5] Dayan was taken aback – Israeli leaders were not accustomed to such an uncompromising stance from the White House. Yet President Carter, a Southerner who moved in a social setting that was relatively free of Jewish influence, was less sensitive than his predecessors to the Jewish lobby in the US, which stood by Israel almost automatically.

The rocky road to ending the Sinai occupation

In Egypt, meanwhile, President Sadat was developing a plan of his own. His emissary Tohami had reported back positively on the secret meeting with the foreign minister in Rabat in September, telling the president about the possible peace deal they had outlined together.

Mohamed Heikal, a leading Egyptian journalist, observed that exactly how Tohami presented his conversation with Dayan is unknown, but 'Sadat *understood* the message to be that Israel was prepared to withdraw from Egyptian territory'.[6] Not long after, on 21 October 1977, and perhaps by pure coincidence, President Carter sent Sadat a handwritten letter, with a 'personal appeal for your support'.[7] In it Carter reminded Sadat of a meeting they had had in the White House where Sadat had promised Carter that 'at a crucial moment . . . when obstacles arose in our common search for peace in the Middle East', the president would be able to count on Sadat. Now, Carter went on to say, 'We have reached such a moment, and I need your help . . . the time has now come to move forward [on the peace process . . .]'

Sadat was inclined toward bold gestures, and the possibilities raised at Tohami's meeting with Dayan had clearly sparked his imagination. Combined with this and the heartfelt letter from President Carter was a crucial third factor: the promise he saw in the newly elected Israeli prime minister, Begin. Sadat viewed him as a strong leader who could be trusted to make hard decisions. He reached this conclusion in part following a meeting with a mutual friend of theirs, the Romanian president Nicolai Ceauşescu. On a visit to Romania in September 1977, Sadat asked the Romanian leader: 'You've already seen Begin . . . tell me: first, in your view, does he want peace? And, secondly, is he strong [enough to deliver]?'[8] Ceauşescu confirmed that Begin was both interested in peace and that he was a strong leader. This was the reassurance Sadat needed, and he now resolved to make a daring move – he would publicly offer direct, open peace talks with Israel.

He did so on 9 November 1977, during a speech to Egypt's National Assembly, when he stunned his audience by announcing that he was prepared to go 'to the ends of the earth if this will prevent one soldier, one officer, among my sons from being wounded – not being killed, just wounded'.[9] He added: 'Israel will be astonished . . . that I am ready to go to their own house, to the Knesset itself, to talk to them'. Sadat's dramatic statement ushered in a new diplomatic phase in which Sadat became the prime mover, forcing Begin to respond to his initiatives, leaving the USA, at least for the time being, as a mere spectator, and keeping the USSR, which Sadat despised, totally out of the picture.

Obliged to react to Sadat's challenge, Begin invited him to come to Jerusalem, though in both Begin's public statements and his formal written invitation, there was none of the boldness shown by Sadat. This, perhaps, is not surprising, as in many ways the two men were poles apart and had little in common in terms of personality and style: Sadat was warm and outgoing, extravagant and impatient with details, while Begin was solemn, formal, pedantic and annoyingly legalistic. But now they were to march together.

An unpleasant surprise in Jerusalem

Anwar Sadat landed in Ben Gurion airport near Tel Aviv on 19 November, where he was met by the prime minister and many of Israel's past and present leaders. From there they travelled to Jerusalem for talks, where things took a turn for the worse, as Sadat began to realize that something was profoundly wrong. He had understood from his emissary, Tohami, that in the September meeting with Dayan, in Rabat, the Israeli foreign minister had promised that Israel would withdraw from the Sinai and abandon its settlements there. Now, at their Jerusalem meeting, Begin told Sadat simply that that was not the case. Dayan – also present – added that in his secret meeting with Tohami he had promised nothing of the kind. Sadat insisted: 'Tohami said you were ready to withdraw', to which Dayan replied: 'Mr President, I did not say that', and a little while later, 'If Tohami said we were prepared to withdraw then he is a liar.'

The transcript of the Rabat meeting supports Dayan's claim; in it he is quoted as saying to Tohami that he considers himself 'no more than Begin's envoy and therefore he would have to bring all the issues to Begin and can't [promise anything] before hearing from Begin . . .'[10] As for Jewish settlements in the Sinai, it seems, according to the transcript, that what Dayan had in mind was for Israel to keep them, particularly the Yamit bloc, which would be the buffer zone between the Sinai and the Gaza Strip, even after Israel's withdrawal from the rest of the desert, and to have Israeli military patrols securing them. Dayan told Tohami, 'What would be the fate of our settlements . . . if we withdrew? Would you let them stay there under your sovereignty?'[11] The transcript, of course, does not convey Dayan's tone – whether he sounded conciliatory, somehow implying to Tohami that if Egypt pressed the matter, Israel would withdraw even from the settlements; or whether he was stern and inflexible. The transcript is written in the third person in Hebrew, and is more of a summary of what the foreign minister said to Tohami; those who knew Dayan would attest that one could never be certain of the true meaning of his words, and his formulations often seemed deliberately obscure, as did his tone. But whatever the explanation for this confusion, the fact is that Sadat – although clearly distressed by this unexpected turn of events – was already in Jerusalem, his peace initiative in full swing.

The climax of Sadat's visit was on the next day at the Knesset, where, in front of a packed house, he unveiled his peace programme. At the heart of the plan was his pledge that 'we really and truly welcome you to live among us in peace and security.'[12] But, in return, Israel would have to play its part in the deal: to withdraw *fully* from the Sinai and other occupied Arab lands, including Arab East Jerusalem, and to tackle head on the Palestinian situation, which was, as Sadat put it, 'the crux of the problem', by allowing, among other things, an independent Palestinian state and return of Palestinian refugees to Israel proper. Sadat refrained, however, from mentioning the PLO, knowing that it would extract a strong response and be counterproductive.

Sadat's demands stunned his Israeli listeners so much that the defence minister, Ezer Weizman, scribbled a note and passed it to Begin to say: 'We have to prepare for war.'[13] In retrospect it is difficult for us to appreciate why Sadat's idea of a full Israeli withdrawal from the occupied territories, particularly from Arab East Jerusalem, and allowing a Palestinian right of return – all issues which, at the time of writing, are discussed in peace negotiations – were perceived by his listeners to be so harsh; but, in 1977, these were all matters that remained strictly taboo.

Forty-three hours after landing in Israel, Sadat returned to Cairo. Looking back, by far the most important achievement of his trip was that in one grand gesture he had managed to breach a psychological barrier of mutual suspicion, distrust, fear, hate and misunderstanding that had for so long existed between Israel and Egypt. Sadat, we now know, strongly objected to having any substantive agenda for his

Israeli trip: the visit in itself, as he made clear to his advisers, *was* the agenda. And now Israelis and Egyptians could, at long last, get to grips with the substance of their dispute, at the heart of which was the issue of Israel's surrender of the occupied lands in return for Arab acceptance of the country's right to exist. But it would not be a straightforward journey.

Convincing the Americans

Begin visited Washington on 17 December, where he laid out to President Carter Israel's official response to Sadat's peace initiative. It was the ever ingenious Dayan who urged the prime minister to present Israel's response to Washington rather than directly to Sadat, so as 'to keep our coordination with the Americans and ensure that they are on our side'.[14] Also, Egypt – and the Arabs in general – as Dayan saw it and with which Begin agreed, could be more flexible in accepting proposals put to them by the US rather than directly by Israel.

In Washington, it was apparent that what the prime minister sought was a separate treaty with Egypt, something which, quite clearly, Sadat did not want to happen, as he needed a solution also to the Palestinian problem, lest he be blamed for abandoning the Palestinian cause. Now, in his meeting with Carter, what Begin proposed on the Sinai were relatively forthcoming if not entirely generous ideas. He said that while Israel would end its occupation there, it would insist on keeping its thirteen Sinai settlements, which at the time were home to 4,000 settlers; it would be, Begin proposed, a special zone administered by the United Nations and patrolled by an Israeli security contingent.[15] Much of the Sinai Peninsula, Begin went on to explain, would be demilitarized – very few, if any, Egyptian forces would be allowed close to the border with Israel – and Israel would insist on early-warning stations in key positions in the Sinai to give it notice of any imminent Egyptian attack. The Straits of Tiran – a source of previous tensions between Israel and Egypt – would be declared international water, never to be blocked to Israeli shipping.

Since he was aware that he would have to offer Sadat something on the Palestinian front too, the prime minister presented to Carter a twenty-two-point Palestinian autonomy programme. At the heart of this was the idea that, while Israel would grant *personal* autonomy to the Palestinian *people* living in the West Bank and Gaza Strip, whereby they could run their own lives without any Israeli intervention, the Palestinians, on the other hand, would have no territorial control, as the land itself would remain in Israel's possession, and there would be no sovereign there other than Israel.[16] Begin's autonomy programme envisaged an administrative council of eleven Palestinians, elected by a general, direct, personal, equal and secret ballot. It would set up departments to deal with various civic spheres of activity, hitherto controlled by the Israeli military, such as education, commerce, tourism, agriculture, health and so on, while security and foreign affairs – the most important attributes of sovereignty – would continue to be performed by Israel. Begin proposed that this Palestinian Council would operate from the sleepy town of Bethlehem – obviously not from Jerusalem, which Israel regarded as its capital – would serve for terms of four years and 'will name one of its members to represent it before the Government of Israel for the purpose of discussion of common issues'.[17]

The fine details of the plan Begin proposed in Washington would be negotiated between Israel, Egypt, Jordan and local Palestinian leaders living in the lands under Israeli control – the PLO would be excluded – and, at the end of a negotiating period, residents of the West Bank and the Gaza Strip would have the free option to receive either Israeli or Jordanian citizenship and, accordingly, would be allowed to vote for state institutions.

While President Carter and his team were not thrilled with Begin's autonomy proposal, which they regarded as an attempt to swallow up for good the Palestinian lands, offering the Palestinians mere autonomy rather than sovereignty, they went on to declare the programme as a 'fair basis' for further negotiations and a 'realistic starting point for negotiations'.[18] However, when reports of the Begin plan reached Egypt's President Sadat he was bitterly disappointed, feeling that the prime minister's approach was unhelpful and that Begin had failed to reciprocate his generous gesture. After all, as Sadat saw it, by making his visit to Jerusalem he had given Israel the legitimacy it was looking for in the Arab world. Sadat had hoped that his move would so impress the Israelis that they would be more forthcoming and provide him with what he really needed to conduct a peace deal – a helping hand to fight off opposition at home and in the Arab world, which at that time was led by the Steadfastness Front of Syria, Iraq, Algeria, Libya and South Yemen. But all Begin offered him was a finger, not a hand, and Sadat's faith in the prime minister was now seriously diminished.

A clash in Ismailiya

The two leaders held a summit meeting on 25 December, in Ismailiya on the western bank of the Suez Canal in Egypt; Sadat would not invite Begin to Cairo, as he was uncertain what reception the people of his capital might give the prime minister. The magic and drama of Sadat's visit to Jerusalem was by now a fading memory; there were no bands, no Israeli flags, no greeting for the Israeli delegation, and the meetings themselves did not go well.

Sadat's insistence on linking the end of the Sinai occupation with Israel's withdrawal from the other lands it acquired in 1967 was steadfastly opposed by Begin, who went on to reject the Egyptian president's request that Israel accept the principle of 'the inadmissibility of the acquisition of territory by war'. Begin – the pedantic lawyer – realized, of course, that were he to acknowledge this principle then it would require him to relinquish all occupied lands; for if it is inadmissible to acquire territory by war, then the Golan Heights, the West Bank, Arab East Jerusalem and the Gaza Strip, which Israel acquired in the 1967 war, would all have to be relinquished in addition to the Sinai. Begin insisted that the principle of 'the inadmissibility of the acquisition of territory by war' should not be applied because in 1967, as he put it, Israel fought a 'defensive war' and international law – as he interpreted it – does recognize the acquisition of territory by the side which came under attack. Otherwise, as Begin argued and would continue to insist in the weeks and months ahead, for potential aggressors it would always be a win–win situation: if their aggression succeeded then they would gain, and if it failed they would get back what they had lost in their failed attempt on the basis of the principle of 'the inadmissibility of the acquisition of territory by war'.

On top of this major disagreement was the prime minister's continuing insistence that Israel should be allowed to retain its Jewish settlements in the Sinai, not so much the isolated Sinai settlements but the Yamit bloc, which strategically could be a wedge between Egypt's Sinai and the Gaza Strip, preventing the potential smuggling, mainly by the Sinai Bedouins, of arms to the Strip. A furious Sadat rejected this request out of hand. 'If I tell my people that Begin wants to leave his settlements in the Sinai,' he told the prime minister, 'they will stone me . . .'[19]

The joint statement of their discussions made at the end of their summit by the host reflected the gulf that remained between the parties on many issues, particularly on the future of the Palestinians. 'The view of Egypt', Sadat read out, 'is that in the West Bank and Gaza there should be established a Palestinian state. The Israeli view is that the Arab Palestinians living in Judea, Samaria and the Gaza Strip should enjoy self-government'.[20] So a stalemate, and a further deterioration of the atmosphere that had seemed so promising only a month before. And things were about to get worse still.

Retrograde steps

Shortly after meeting Sadat at Ismailiya, Begin put up new obstacles when his government, heeding a proposal from the agricultural minister, Ariel Sharon, decided to establish twenty new settlements in the occupied Sinai. It clearly wanted to create more facts on the ground that it could use as bargaining chips in talks with Egypt – offering to give up these new Sinai settlements in return for being allowed to keep the existing ones, particularly in the Yamit bloc. 'We've got to try [this tactic],' said Dayan, who supported Sharon's idea.[21] Subsequently, heavy machinery started work in the Sinai and newspapers ran the headlines, 'Sharon Builds New Settlements in the Sinai'. The timing was disastrous, coinciding, probably on purpose, with a visit by the US president, Jimmy Carter, to Cairo, where both he and Sadat were furious, suspecting that Begin was deliberately fouling the peace process.[22] They saw through Begin's bargaining tactic and, if anything, views in Egypt hardened: in an interview with the Egyptian magazine *October*, Sadat openly pledged that he would not allow a single Israeli settlement to remain on Egyptian soil and if the prime minister wished to plough the villages before Israel left the Sinai, then he was free to do so.

This, however, failed to impress the Israelis, who kept building more settlements in the Sinai, where in 1978 alone between 150 and 200 new families moved into the growing town of Yamit, upsetting not only Sadat, but also Washington. There, on 10 February, the Secretary of State, Cyrus Vance, made a strong statement to the effect that Jewish settlements built on occupied lands were contrary to international law. In response, Begin's government said that Israel's settlement programme was 'in full harmony with international law and that it always has been legal, legitimate and essential'; Israel called on the United States to 'reconsider its position'.[23]

In a series of meetings between President Carter and Begin in Washington, on 21–22 March, the president was outraged and in fighting mood. 'I am discouraged about the prospects for the future,' he told the prime minister. 'I will have to make a report to members of the Congress . . . and I am going to tell them . . . that you are not willing to stop expansion or the creation of new settlements; you are not willing to give up the settlements in the Sinai . . .'[24]

ENDGAME AT CAMP DAVID

It was no big surprise that by the summer of 1978 Sadat's peace initiative, which had started with such great hopes in Jerusalem the previous year, was running out of steam. For President Sadat, still offended by Begin's cold shoulder, the final straw came on 23 July, when the prime minister turned down Sadat's personal request to make some modest goodwill gestures in support of the peace process by symbolically pulling out of some of the Sinai land. 'Not even one grain of desert sand,' Begin retorted. 'Nobody can get anything for nothing.'[25] With that President Carter decided to take one last gamble.

He sent a handwritten and confidential letter to President Sadat on 3 August, in which he expressed his growing frustration with the 'little progress' in the peace process and added that, 'as soon as possible, I would like to meet personally with you and Prime Minister Begin . . . at Camp David [the president's retreat in Maryland, US] . . . My hope is that the three of us, along with our top advisors, can work together in relative seclusion.'[26] He wrote a similar letter to Begin. Carter's was a high-risk strategy as the issues at stake were difficult to resolve: on the one hand, Sadat's insistence on an end to the Israeli occupation of the entire Sinai, a solution to the Palestinian problem which would include dealing with such sensitive issues as the future of Jerusalem, and the Palestinian demand to have a right of return to old Palestine; on the other hand, Begin's attempt at minimizing the price he would have to pay for a peace with Egypt. And the danger was that if such a high-level summit failed then hope for any resolution would all but disappear.

It turned out to be an invitation neither Sadat nor Begin could refuse, so the two men, accompanied by their delegates, arrived in Camp David on 5 September 1978. No substantial talks were held on that day, but even during the brief preliminary encounters with the two leaders, Carter found Sadat to be warm, enthusiastic and open, while, in contrast, the prime minister was as rigid as ever – unimaginative, preoccupied with technicalities, and generally unhelpful.[27]

The next day, President Carter brought Sadat and Begin together for a face-to-face meeting with no aides; it was a tough and unpleasant encounter.[28] As part of a peace deal with Egypt, Sadat read from a pre-prepared speech, Israel would have to withdraw from the Sinai, including from airfields and Jewish settlements it had constructed there since 1967, and from Arab East Jerusalem (the latter, in particular, Sadat must have known was a red rag to a bull, rejected as unacceptable by the vast majority of the Israeli public). Israel, Sadat went on to read, should also allow Palestinian self-determination (another non-starter for most Israelis as this, at the time, was regarded as a direct threat to Israel's security), agree to provide a right of return to Israel for Palestinian refugees (something most Israelis, left or right, would not have agreed to then or now), and pay full compensation for the damage Israel's forces had caused and for exploitation of the natural resources of the occupied territories (extracting oil in the Sinai, for instance). Sadat also insisted that a deal regarding the Palestinians should be signed *before* one was signed between Israel and Egypt on the Sinai so that, insofar as the Palestinians were concerned, 'people will not say that I betrayed them'.[29] Begin would later remark that he needed 'a lot of self restraint in order not to explode', as he was listening to Sadat reading from what he sarcastically referred to as 'the *tzetalé*', a piece of paper, in Yiddish.[30]

In a follow-up meeting, the prime minister responded to Sadat's presentation, going through his document paragraph by paragraph and rejecting it out of hand. He would not accept Sadat's plan regarding the Palestinians as this, the prime minister explained, would lead to a Palestinian state, to which Begin objected. Nor would he evacuate the Jewish settlers in the Sinai as 'There is a national consensus [in Israel] on the settlements ... we will not agree to dismantle settlements.' A furious Sadat interjected: 'I can't understand what your settlements do on my land.'[31] Tempers flared when the prime minister said of Sadat's request that Israel should pay compensation that it 'smacks of a victorious state dictating peace to the defeated'. Mistakenly thinking that the prime minister was referring to Egypt as a defeated nation, Sadat shot back: 'A defeated nation? We were, but after [the] October 1973 [war where Egypt succeeded in crossing the Suez Canal] we are defeated no longer.'[32] He added: 'Premier Begin, Security [to Israel] – yes. Land – no!' President Carter later confided in his diary: 'I thought Sadat would explode.'[33]

The defence minister, Ezer Weizman, at Camp David with his prime minister, later summarized the heart of the problem dividing Begin and Sadat:

> Anyone observing the two men could not have overlooked the profound divergence in their attitudes. Both desired peace. But whereas Sadat wanted to take it by storm, capitalizing on the momentum from his visit to Jerusalem to reach his final objective, Begin preferred to creep forward inch by inch. He took the dream of peace and ground it down into the fine, dry powder of details, legal clauses, and quotes from international law.[34]

Concluding after this meeting that the pair could not interact constructively on a personal level, President Carter, from then on, kept Begin and Sadat apart – the two never met face to face again at the summit and Carter took it upon himself to act as go-between, conveying proposals from one side to the other.

Five days into the summit, with little progress achieved, Carter submitted a seventeen-page American draft where the principles of peace
were presented; he first showed it to the Israelis (as the American
would often do) and he then discussed it with the prime minister, who
spoke in grave and sombre tones about Carter's 'unacceptable' proposal. He particularly resisted the idea, still insisted upon by Sadat
and detected in Carter's document, that the phrase 'inadmissibility of
the acquisition of territory by war' be included in the text. As said, if
accepted by Israel, this would have the potential of bringing more
pressure on it to withdraw from the other occupied territories acquired
by war in 1967. And while Carter in his draft paper also tried to act
on the Palestinian front, so that Sadat would not be blamed across the
Middle East for abandoning them, the prime minister still resisted all
attempts to have anything beyond a very limited form of self-rule for
the Palestinians, similar to the one he had presented in Washington
back in December 1977. When Begin went on to outline all the con-
trols, veto rights and privileges that he would retain for Israel over
Palestinian affairs, a frustrated Carter exploded: 'What you want to
do is to make the West Bank part of Israel!'[35] Likewise, the fate of the
Jewish settlements in the Sinai which Israel wanted to keep also continued to daunt the efforts at Camp David: on Friday, 15 September,
Israel's foreign minister, Moshe Dayan, made it clear to Sadat that
Israel had no intention of evacuating its settlements in the Sinai,
whereupon a frustrated Sadat said: 'Yes, yes, I know that well, Moshe.
You want my land . . . But I can't agree to that . . .'[36]

Ten days into the conference, a dissatisfied Carter confronted the two
leaders. Concluding that Begin was unlikely ever to accept the 'inadmissibility of territory by war' phrase in the agreement, Carter, in a
passionate appeal, asked Sadat to let this phrase go and agree instead
to have one stating that UN Resolution 242 'is accepted by all'; Resolution 242 calls on Israel to withdraw from territories it occupied in
the 1967 war, and does mention the 'inadmissibility of territory by
war', and Israel had formally accepted this resolution in 1970. Sadat
agreed and so did Begin; the prime minister would later explain that
as this critical phrase appears merely in the preamble to 242, it is not
– as Begin interpreted it – an operational part of an agreement.

Similarly, Carter gathered that it was unlikely that Sadat would ever agree to have Jewish settlements remaining on his land, nor any Israeli control of other installations in the Sinai, such as airfields. Thus, in a brutal four-and-a-half-hour conversation with the prime minister, Carter demanded that Israel should give up all its settlements in the Sinai, particularly now that Sadat had agreed to drop his demand to have the 'non-acquisition of territory by war' phrase in the emerging treaty. Carter warned the prime minister that a failure at Camp David might well lead to a break in US–Israeli relations and his pressure finally yielded results; as Carter's National Security Advisor, Zbigniew Brzezinski, recalls, 'After a protracted and heated argument, in which Begin shouted "ultimatum", "excessive demands", and "political suicide", the prime minister finally agreed to leave it to the Israeli parliament – the Knesset – to decide on the fate of Jewish settlements.'[37] Leaving it to the Knesset would free Begin from taking a most unpopular decision on a matter that was close to his heart; the assumption was that, at the Knesset, the opposition Labor Party, which generally objects to the building of settlements, would vote for their removal from the Sinai, and Begin's own party would, for the most part, support their prime minister. Carter demanded this pledge in writing and Begin dispatched him a letter, to say that

after my return home I will submit a motion before Israel's Parliament to decide on the following question: If during the negotiations to conclude a peace treaty between Israel and Egypt all outstanding issues are agreed upon, 'are you in favor of the removal of the Israeli settlers from Sinai . . . or are you in favor of keeping the aforementioned settlers in those areas?' The vote, Mr. President, on this issue will be completely free from the usual Parliamentary Party discipline . . .[38]

Since Carter agreed that the US would finance the building of replacement airfields, Begin also consented to abandon the airfields Israel had built in the Sinai.

There was now just one last major stumbling block at Camp David – one that would recur in future negotiations – the fate of Jerusalem. Sadat still insisted on linking any Egyptian–Israeli peace with a wider deal, while Begin favoured a smaller bilateral treaty between Israel and Egypt directly. Now, this problem came to be focused on a dispute over the future of Jerusalem. While the Israelis wished to keep the entire city – Jewish West and Arab East Jerusalem, which they had illegally annexed back in 1967 – under their sole sovereignty, the Egyptians insisted Arab East Jerusalem should be turned over to Arab hands. However, as they failed to reach a compromise, President Carter looked for a diplomatic form of words that could enable both sides to conclude an agreement at Camp David while glossing over the thorny issue of Jerusalem. In the end, they decided to agree not to agree on the matter: Sadat and Begin would send letters to President Carter stating their position on Jerusalem, which the president would then pocket for any future talks and keep as side-letters to the emerging deal. So letters were dispatched, though neither contained much in the way of compromise: Begin stated that Jerusalem was both 'indivisible' and 'the capital of Israel', whereas Sadat reiterated the view that Arab East Jerusalem was an 'indivisible' part of the West Bank and that it should be returned to 'Arab sovereignty'. It was the flimsiest of fig leaves to cover the failure of the negotiations on this point. But it served its purpose: on Sunday, 17 September, in front of the world's TV cameras, Sadat and Begin signed the Camp David Accords in the White House.

The Camp David Accords were not a settlement as such. Rather, they provided a framework and set of principles to guide further talks which, it was hoped, would lead to a permanent peace treaty between Egypt and Israel within a specified deadline. This future treaty would end the Sinai occupation and later, it was hoped, lead – on the basis of 'additional principles' spelled out in the Accords – to the end of Israel's occupation in other areas and peace treaties between Israel, Syria, Lebanon, Jordan and the entire Arab world.

The Accords also set the principles for negotiation on the future of the West Bank and Gaza Strip during a transitional period not exceeding five years. This transitional period, as the Accords stated, would start with the election by the Palestinians of 'a self-governing authority', at which time the Israeli military government 'will be withdrawn'. Then, 'as soon as possible, but not later than the third year after the beginning of the transitional period', negotiations would begin between Israelis, Egyptians, Jordanians and Palestinians from the occupied territories – though not the PLO – 'to determine the final status of the West Bank and Gaza . . .'

While it is true that these negotiations were aimed, according to the Camp David Accords, towards 'full Palestinian autonomy' rather than to a Palestinian *state*, it is safe to say here that the dynamic of the expected final-status negotiations would probably have led to a full-fledged Palestinian state. Israel's Professor Yair Hirschfeld observed that

> Whoever read carefully the Camp David Accords understood that the logic of what had been agreed there would necessarily lead to a two-state solution. The assumption that a Palestinian self-government authority, duly elected by the Palestinians of the West Bank and Gaza, would negotiate . . . for anything else but a Palestinian state is ludicrous.[39]

It seems that Begin – the brains behind the Palestinian autonomy plan – did recognize the danger that negotiations set out by the Camp David Accords could lead to the establishment of a Palestinian state – to which he vehemently objected – rather than a mere Palestinian autonomy. Indeed, on more than one occasion he admitted that any form of Palestinian self-government or Palestinian autonomy would inevitably lead to statehood as 'this is the ironclad logic of things . . .'[40] His aforementioned consent to negotiations aimed at creating a Palestinian autonomy which he surely knew would probably lead to the establishment of a Palestinian state should, therefore, be regarded as tactical; he knew that President Sadat had to do something about the Palestinian problem or he would otherwise be blamed for abandoning the Palestinians. So while Begin was willing to give Sadat the cover he needed, he almost certainly had no intention of going through with the agreed talks aimed at full Palestinian autonomy. Indeed, as we shall later see, once Begin was confident that Israel's peace with Egypt was secure enough, he went all out to demolish the autonomy idea and kill the negotiations aimed at achieving it.

In the meantime, on the ground in the Palestinian occupied territories, opposition to the Camp David Accords was growing. Pro-PLO activists, particularly the mayors of towns such as Ramallah (Karim Khalaf), Nablus (Bassam Shaka), and Tulkarm (Hilmi Hanoun), who had all been elected to office in the 1976 municipal elections, organized themselves and led rallies and demonstrations against the Accords. They resented the fact that the PLO, whom they considered their legitimate leadership, had been bypassed, and they regarded the proposed autonomy plan as an imposed scheme, a substitute for their dream of an independent Palestinian state. The general sentiment among Palestinians was one of betrayal. Nasser Laham, a Palestinian activist from the Dheishe refugee camp near Bethlehem who took part in West Bank demonstrations against the Camp David Accords, explains that 'Many Palestinians felt deceived and cheated by the peace agreement between Egypt and Israel. They felt abandoned and forgotten . . . We were at a loss . . .'[41] Opposition to the Accords was not confined, however, only to the occupied territories; in New York city, on 23 September, as elsewhere around the world, hundreds of Palestinians and their supporters marched, carrying Palestinian flags and colourful banners, with such statements as 'No to the Camp David Pact, Yes to Palestinian National Rights' and 'Carter, Carter, we're not fools: Sadat and Begin are your tools'.[42]

In the face of such local and international opposition and concerned that the PLO would take advantage of it to sabotage the Camp David deal, the Israelis attempted to weaken the pro-PLO elements; they came up with an ingenious scheme to set up an alternative Palestinian leadership which would support the Accords. At the heart of this new thinking was the idea of exploiting the social tensions that existed between different sections of Palestinian society, mainly by giving a voice to the conservative rural peasantry who constituted some 70 per cent of West Bankers and harboured resentment against the urban population that made up the other 30 per cent and dominated West Bank politics, as well as being more radical and supporters of the PLO.

For this purpose, the military set up the 'Village Leagues', starting in the southern West Bank in the Hebron area, where they appointed a local leader named Mustafa Dudin to head a league of seventy-four villages. Dudin, a native Palestinian from the southern West Bank, spent many years on the East Bank of the River Jordan, where he was close to the Jordanian regime, serving as a minister in Jordanian cabinets. He returned to the West Bank in 1975 and became a strong anti-PLO local leader who preferred to see the Palestinian problems sorted out between Israelis and Jordanians by sidelining the PLO. Now the army attempted to strengthen Dudin's position in the rural areas by turning him into the provider of licences and permits – so critical for Palestinians, who, as mentioned, needed written permission for almost any activity they wished to pursue. The army also authorized Dudin to appoint *mukhtar*s (heads of villages) and civil servants, to reduce prison terms for prisoners, and to sell villagers items such as fertilizers at a discount. For pro-PLO Palestinians Dudin was a quisling – a collaborator with the occupation, but given so much power by the military that ordinary Palestinians were compelled to distance themselves from the PLO and work with him if they wished to be granted the goods that were for him to dispose of and which they badly needed. The Israelis then proceeded to copy the Hebron Village League model in other West Bank localities, such as Bethlehem, where they made Bishara Qumsiya head of the organization, and Ramallah, where Yusuf al-Khatib was installed; he was later assassinated by PLO activists.

SEALING THE CAMP DAVID DEAL AND ITS IMPLEMENTATION

Transforming the framework and principles agreed on at Camp David into a detailed peace treaty, in which exact language was needed to describe the new Israeli–Egyptian relationship and the precise nature of the new arrangements for the West Bank and Gaza Strip, was not an easy matter. But personal intervention by President Carter, which also included him shuttling between Jerusalem and Cairo to seal the deal, was finally successful and in a ceremony at the White House on 26 March 1979, Carter, Sadat and Begin put their signatures to a peace treaty that ended thirty years of war between Israel and Egypt.

The agreement the parties signed stipulated that Israel would end its occupation of the Sinai – remove settlements and installations within three years – allowing Egypt to exercise full sovereignty over the Peninsula up to the recognized international border between Egypt and Israel, and to deploy a limited number of troops in the Sinai, mainly close to the Suez Canal.

On 27 May 1979, the Israeli army withdrew from Al Arish in the Sinai, where, as soon as it pulled out, Egyptians ripped down or painted over all the Hebrew signs that remained. President Sadat arrived there soon after the Israelis departed and when he emerged from a local mosque three trussed buffalos were slaughtered and several young men dipped their hands in the animals' blood and waved them, shouting: 'Sadat, Sadat.'[43] Between July and September 1979 the Sinai oilfields were transferred to Egyptian hands, before the parties proceeded with the rest of the agreed deal.

Indeed, Begin vigorously implemented the Israeli–Egyptian treaty in the Sinai; he was reluctant, however, to go through with the Palestinian part of the deal and therefore adopted a minimalist view of the proposed Palestinian autonomy and almost immediately after signing the treaty with Sadat in Washington began to reinterpret the Palestinian components of the deal in such a narrow way that it lost all meaning. He was able to do this because Sadat, try as he might, had ultimately failed to link the two sides of the deal – Palestinian and Egyptian – tightly enough; peace with Egypt was not strictly conditional on progress on the Palestinian issue in the wording of the agreement. And now, the deal with Egypt signed and sealed, there was little incentive for Begin to stick to his promises as regarded the Palestinians, gambling that this would not wreck the peace between Israel and Egypt. Begin made his new approach evident when he appointed the wily veteran National Religious Party leader, Yosef Burg, the interior minister, as his representative to head the ministerial team in the Palestinian autonomy talks, which were taking place in Cairo. He also set up committee after committee that included hardliners to discuss any ideas raised in Cairo, and this bureaucratic structure hindered all progress in the autonomy talks.

But in the Sinai, at least, Israel continued to dismantle its occupation; this reached its climax on 23 April 1982, when the army, supervised by the defence minister, Ariel Sharon, moved in to remove the settlers in the town of Yamit, who had barricaded themselves in their homes. After Yamit had been completely emptied of people, Sharon then brought in heavy machinery and razed the town's buildings to the ground, along with those of the other Sinai settlements. A proposal by the finance minister to sell the settlements to Egypt for $70m–80m had been rejected by Sharon and the prime minister, as they were reluctant to hand over settlements which were built so close to Israel proper; by contrast, in the southern Sinai, the town of Ofira was transferred to Egypt intact, as were the Sinai airfields. The enclave of Taba, some ten kilometres south of Eilat, was also transferred to Egypt, though only after an international arbitration panel, using old maps, ruled, contrary to the Israeli view, that it belonged to Egypt.

And, with that, the Sinai occupation was over.

THE SPRING UPRISING

Back in the occupied territories, particularly on the West Bank, ordinary Palestinians were growing restless. Many were frustrated by the proposed autonomy plan whereby Palestinians could manage their daily lives by running services such as health and education, but would not be allowed to have their own state, and the feeling that the Camp David Accords were aimed at sidelining the PLO, which had not been involved in the negotiations. Another source of discontent was a new body introduced by Sharon in the autumn of 1981 which was called the 'Civil Administration'.

It was intended to oversee all matters bar those relating strictly to security (to remain in the purview of the military government), including responsibility for health, education and welfare, and to help promote the Israeli version of Palestinian self-rule as envisaged in the Camp David Accords, regardless of the formal talks in Cairo. Israel tried to present the new Civil Administration as the withdrawal of the military government, as if it symbolized the end of occupation and a return to normalcy in the Palestinian occupied territories.

It was not, of course; rather it was intended purely to provide the occupation with a civilian façade, a fact that did not escape the Palestinians. Indeed, a close look at the organization of the new Civil Administration clearly shows that, for all practical matters, the new body was subordinated to the military and, at least at its managerial level, was made up mostly of Israelis. Also deeply involved in the running of the new body was the Shabak, Israel's internal security agency, which, behind the scenes, was making the practical day-to-day decisions regarding Palestinians' lives. Suspicion of the new Civil Administration was so strong among Palestinians that its introduction led to a wave of protests across the occupied territories, which went on during the winter of 1981 and well into 1982. In response, Sharon instructed the military to use an iron fist against the rioters; subsequently, the military shut down West Bank newspapers, closed Bir Zeit University – a hub for Palestinian protest against the Civil Administration – and blew up the homes of relatives of convicted rioters.

On 12 March 1982, the mayor of the West Bank town of el Bireh, Ibrahim Tawil, was dismissed and his council dissolved for refusing to meet the head of the Civil Administration, and an Israeli military officer was appointed to head the municipality. A week later, following widespread protests in other West Bank towns and cities, the mayor of Nablus, Bassam Shaka, was dismissed, arrested and ordered by a military court to be deported. Speaking from his cell, where he embarked on a hunger strike, he said: 'Israel has no legitimate right [to expel me] . . . Nablus is my land. I should stay. The Israeli occupiers are the ones who should go.'[44]

In spite of the Israeli military pressure on them, the Palestinians would not give up: on 1 May, twenty-five West Bank mayors issued a joint statement, threatening that if the Civil Administration was not abolished they would shut down all municipal services, which they proceeded to do eight days later. By mid-1982, most of the major towns in the occupied territories were run by Israeli military officers and the army's grip tightened. Likewise, in the Gaza Strip, the army suppressed the riots, putting their organizers behind bars.

The clashes and the army's heavy-handed response would become known as 'The Spring Uprising'. During this period there were more casualties than there had been in the previous fifteen years of Israeli occupation; in 1982 alone, the army killed thirty-one Palestinians and wounded 365. So brutal was Sharon's conduct that it even led to strong opposition within the army rank and file, where senior reserve officers who had been among those carrying out Sharon's policies spoke out against them and said they were leading to 'brutality . . . and indiscriminate collective punishment'.[45]

TROUBLES ON THE GOLAN

Meanwhile, trouble also emerged in the usually calm occupied Golan Heights. We should recall that after the 1967 war, the army had distributed identity cards to the Syrian population of the Golan, but these did not denote Israeli citizenship. Now, in November 1980, the Knesset amended the Law of Nationality, so that Israeli citizenship could be granted to the Golanis. The rationale behind this initiative was that, while making the Golan population citizens of Israel would not have a significant negative impact on the Jewish demography of Israel as the number of Golanis was so low, it would, on the other hand, make it easier for Israel to annex the Golan on the grounds that the majority of its inhabitants were 'Israelis' and reject the view that the Golan was occupied.

But the Golanis objected to the new Israeli policies as many of them continued to regard themselves as Syrians and accepting Israeli citizenship could also lead to serious repercussions for their Syrian relatives; according to Syrian law, acquiring foreign citizenship leads automatically to the loss of Syrian citizenship, and also to any family possessions held in Syria.

To entice the Golanis to embrace Israeli nationality, the Israelis offered special privileges, such as low taxation, higher water quotas and faster responses on building permits; but the vast majority still refused the offer. In fact, the initiative to turn the Golanis into Israelis actually led to growing Syrian nationalism on the Golan. In early March 1981, the leaders of the Druze community, the vast majority of Golanis, called a general meeting in the *khaluwe*, the Druze house of worship in Majdal Shams, which was attended by 6,000 people – over half the entire population of the Golan at the time. There, they drew up their 'national document', declaring that the occupied Golan was 'an integral part of the Arab Syrian territory', and that 'the Syrian Arab nationality is an inherent inseparable character that will pass on from fathers to children'.[46] The Israeli attempt to 'mingle us into the

Israeli entity' to 'deprive us of our Syrian Arab personality' was rejected. Any Golani who seeks to replace his nationality with the Israeli one, the declaration stated, 'humiliates our dignity, violates our national honour, recants our Religion, breaches our traditions and is considered a traitor to our country'. And there was also a penalty: anyone who embraced the Israeli nationality 'shall be apostate and renegade from our religion and social integrity. All and every kind of trading, sharing his sorrows and joys and inter-marriage with him shall be banned until he acknowledges his sin, repents, asks forgiveness from his society and restores his real nationality so that he is reinstated within us.' The declaration was accompanied by a violent campaign against those very few Golanis who did apply for Israeli citizenship, while the army, in the meantime, extracted revenge by imposing sanctions on the Druze community which included inflated taxes and restrictions on travel and on the marketing of agricultural produce in Israel; activists who led the protest against the Israeli citizenship initiative were placed under house arrest.[47]

Tensions subsided somewhat over the summer of 1981, but shot up again when, on 14 December 1981, the government passed yet another law – the Golan Law, which stated that the law, jurisdiction and administration of the State of Israel shall apply to the Golan Heights. This, effectively, meant an outright annexation of them, and the end of military rule there, since the Golan was now turned into part of Israel proper.

The government took this radical measure, in direct violation of international law, in response to growing concerns among some sectors of the Israeli public that, as it had restored the Sinai to Egypt, the government would soon return the Golan to Syria. What increased public concern and in turn led to growing pressure on the government was, among other things, a statement by Moshe Dayan, while still foreign minister, and just three weeks after signing the peace treaty with Egypt, that the Golan would have to be given back to Syria. 'One should distinguish between the Golan Heights, which has always been Syrian territory and thus will be returned to them in due course,' he said, 'and Judea and Samaria', which Dayan had always wanted to keep in Israeli hands.[48]

The response of the non-Jewish inhabitants of the Golan to the Israeli annexation was defiant: they denounced Israeli expansionist policy, and teachers and their students stopped attending schools; there were even some attacks on military vehicles. At the urging of Syria – understandably horrified by the Israeli decision to annex the Heights – the UN Security Council adopted Resolution 497, on 19 December 1981, which stated that the decision taken by Israel was 'null and void' and of no legal effect at an international level. It called for Israel to 'immediately cancel, without any further delay, its decision'.

On 14 February 1982, when it became clear to the Golanis that Israel would not rescind the annexation, thousands gathered at Majdal Shams and declared an open-ended strike to protest against it. As a Druze resident put it at the time: 'We are Syrians and we want to return to our own country . . . I am a Syrian . . . I am not an Israeli . . .'[49] The Israeli response was harsh: the defence minister, Sharon, dispatched hundreds of troops to impose a full blockade on the Golan: cutting off transportation in and out of the area, preventing food from entering, and disconnecting the supply of both water and electricity. The effect of these measures on the Golan and its non-Jewish population was devastating, as Midhat Salih al-Salih, a Druze from Majdal Shams, recalls: 'Disease spread, the children went hungry, and milk ran out in the homes . . .'

At the same time, the new harsh reality had some positive effects, too, as it gave rise to a new collective spirit of self-reliance in meeting community needs on the Golan. According to Midhat Salih al-Salih, 'those who owned goats and cows began to distribute milk to people with babies . . . people devoted all their time to the struggle. They quit their jobs and their only concern was to express their anger and to resist the Israeli measures.'[50] And Nazi Khattir, a farmer from Majdal Shams, recalls how, with the military measures biting, the Golanis 'began to organize ourselves . . . Everyone was given a task . . . Each village was its own unit, separated but together in spirit.'[51] This spirit of defiance and self-reliance in the face of the Israeli measures is also apparent in the testimony of Jameel Awad, from Majdal Shams, who recalls how:

It was winter time and the lack of a sewage system [due to the stoppage of Israeli services on the Golan] meant the village was very dirty. We

126

established a committee to discuss the issue and we decided to construct a sewage system in the village . . . every house had to pay $200 and contribute four work days to the project . . . Before the end of the strike the project was completed.[52]

The military pressed on with its annexation programme and insisted the Golanis accept Israeli identity cards. In response, many Golanis gathered again in Majdal Shams, where they decided to reject the Israeli ID cards and 'excommunicate' the Golanis who accepted them by cutting off any association with them, even for weddings and funerals – a harsh penalty in the small, tight Druze community. The defence minister was as stubborn as ever, dispatching troops to Majdal Shams to distribute the ID cards to the Golanis. Imposing a curfew, the troops moved from house to house to give out the cards, which was not that easy. The Golani Midhat Salih al-Salih recalls how:

> When the Israelis came to our house to deliver citizenships and to withdraw the old military IDs from my father, my mother, and my brother, my father threw the IDs at them, and they threw them back, and my father threw the cards out of the house and shut the door. They picked them up and laid them on our doorstep . . .[53]

When six days later the troops withdrew, Midhat Salih al-Salih recalls: 'People came out of their homes, collected the ID cards, and then burned some of them. They put the rest in a bag and sent them to the headquarters of the Israeli post and said, "These are your citizenship cards, which we are returning to you."'[54]

While the Israelis would not cancel the annexation itself, they did compromise on the nationality issue, finally agreeing to let Golanis keep their Syrian citizenship. The 'nationality' space on their Israeli identity cards which they had to carry was now left blank; the birthplace was specified as the Golan Heights, rather than either Israel or Syria, and nationality on travel documents was 'undefined'.

The strike, which went on for more than five months, became a major event in the occupied Golan's history as it led to great social changes: Golani women were empowered, as they played an active role at the front line during confrontations with the army and police, leading to a dramatic increase in the number of Golani girls finishing secondary school after 1982; and while only one woman went to university prior to the strike, dozens of women studied in universities in Israel and abroad in subsequent years. Perversely the strike also led to a temporary increase in the status and influence of the traditional, religious leadership, which stood firm behind the protest; but they would later be challenged by a more activist secular leadership.

While it was the stubbornness of the Golanis that forced Israel's hand and led it to back down on the nationality issue, Israel's attention also had to shift – and in quite a dramatic way – to the Lebanese front.

LEBANON AND THE DEATH OF THE VILLAGE LEAGUES

In June 1982, the defence minister dispatched his troops to engage the PLO in battle inside Lebanon. Sharon believed that if Israel could defeat Arafat's guerrilla army in Lebanon, and destroy the PLO infrastructure there, then it could force the Palestinians in the West Bank and Gaza to accept permanent subjugation, and forgo their struggle for independence. Following a short and bloody campaign, Israel's forces prevailed, but stopped short of wiping out the PLO leadership altogether; Arafat and other PLO leaders were exiled to Tunisia and elsewhere.

Sharon, the architect of the war, also hoped that defeating the PLO in Lebanon would boost morale among the Village Leagues; this, we should recall, was a system of local councils managed by Palestinians who were hand-picked by Israel to run local city and village administrations, as a counterbalance – in fact, as an alternative – to pro-PLO leadership in the Palestinian occupied territories. By 1982, the Leagues had been extended to six regional districts with their own budgets, armed militias, uniforms and a bi-weekly newspaper, *al-Mira* (the *Mirror*). Now, with Arafat beaten and licking his wounds in exile in Tunis, Sharon summoned the heads of the Village League and advised them 'to set themselves up as the nascent administration of the self-governing authority', which could work with Israel on implementing the Camp David agreements, leading to Palestinian autonomy.[55] But although the seven federated sections of the Village Leagues did show a degree of unity in their opposition to the PLO, they nevertheless proved incapable of arranging themselves into an effective substitute to the PLO, not least as many in Palestinian society regarded them as traitors. Thus, they ultimately failed to provide Israel with an alternative partner to implement a limited Palestinian autonomy in the occupied lands. With Sharon's resignation as defence minister in 1983 (following an investigation into his culpability in the massacre of innocent Palestinians at the Sabra and Shatilla refugee camps in Beirut), the new defence minister, Moshe Arens, entirely dropped the idea of the Village Leagues as a reliable replacement to the PLO and the core of a future autonomous administration, thus putting an end to Israel's futile attempts to divide and rule the Palestinians in the occupied territories.

In Israel's 1984 general election neither the right-wing Likud Party nor Labor won enough seats to form a government, and neither party managed to cobble together a coalition with a Knesset majority, so instead they formed a National Unity government. The coalition agreement called for a rotation between Labor's Shimon Peres and Likud's Yitzhak Shamir whereby each would serve as prime minister for two years and foreign minister for another two years. Peres would be prime minister first and Labor's Yitzhak Rabin would serve as defence minister for the full four years.

This political arrangement ushered in a period of relative calm in the occupied territories since, particularly during the first two years of the rotation, the army showed a more lenient policy than under Sharon. These years saw a significant development of industrial infrastructures in the Palestinian occupied territories: local banks were opened (having been shut in 1967); new hospitals were built and existing health clinics refurbished and modernized; telephone lines were also installed allowing for direct dialling.

As it turned out, this was just an illusion of calm, as shown by numerous clashes in the occupied territories between the army and protesters. These took place in March 1986, on the tenth anniversary of Land Day, a day when Palestinians commemorate a general strike and severe clashes with Israelis that resulted in the deaths of six Arabs in 1976; then again in September, on the fourth anniversary of the Sabra and Shatilla massacre in Lebanon; and again in early December, on the anniversary of the UN General Assembly's original Partition Plan of 29 November 1947. And yet these clashes were a mere pale foreshadow of what was to come: the following year would turn out to be one of the most pivotal and bleakest phases in the history of the occupation with the eruption of a full-blown Palestinian uprising in the Gaza Strip and on the West Bank.

6

Black December, 1987

On 8 December 1987, a vehicle carrying Palestinian labourers returning from a day's work in Israel collided with an Israeli tank transporter;
four Palestinians were instantly killed and seven others injured. The
casualties came from the Jabalya refugee camp, situated just north of
Gaza City, near a village of the same name. Covering an area of 1.4
square kilometres, the camp was set up after the 1948 war to accommodate 35,000 refugees who had fled their homes in southern
Palestine and settled in the Strip. Thirty-nine years on, Jabalya's population had grown to 60,000, turning it into the largest and poorest of
Gaza's eight refugee camps, a hub of popular discontent and, following this unfortunate car crash, the centre of a full-scale rebellion
against the occupation.

The funeral cortège in Jabalya for the accident victims was huge as
thousands of mourners came to pay their last respects. For them this
was no ordinary funeral: rumours had already spread among the
Gazans that the driver of the Israeli truck had hit the Palestinian vehicle deliberately, as revenge for the killing of a relative of his who had
been stabbed in the marketplace in Gaza two days earlier. Accounts
by survivors of the car crash inflamed these rumours; one of them
described how the Israeli driver 'steered his lorry towards our car and
we could see he meant what he did'.[1] Another survivor, Kamal
Qadoura Hamoudeh, speaking from his hospital bed in Gaza, admitted that he was asleep when the accident occurred, but went on to say
he believed the lorry drove over their car on purpose.

It has never been proven whether this is true, but the rumours led
to an ugly atmosphere in Jabalya, and riots, which were exacerbated
by the sight of Israeli troops nearby and incited by calls from mosque

minarets to the rioters ('O, you young people, go at them, don't back off'), continued throughout the night and included direct clashes with Israeli troops.[2]

Riots and clashes were still going on when Hatem Abu Sisi, seventeen years old, left for school the next morning, and he eagerly joined his friends in hurling stones at the troops. The latter opened fire and Hatem was hit by two bullets in the chest. His friends took him to hospital and his elder brother, Gazi, was called. 'I rushed very quickly to Shifa Hospital,' Gazi recalled, five years after the incident, 'and I saw him lying on the bed. His face was covered, and I knew that he was martyred. He was killed. I looked at his face and I said, "May God bless you."'[3] Hatem Abu Sisi became the first boy to be killed in the fighting and his mother, in a later interview, recalled how shortly before Hatem was born she envisioned that he would grow up to be killed by Israeli soldiers and 'in death help set his people free'.[4] Indeed, Hatem's death marked the beginning of the *shuhada* phenomenon, in which young men killed during the uprising were termed *shahid*s – martyrs.

Those December events in the Gaza Strip, we now know, signalled the beginning of a Palestinian uprising that came to be known as the '*intifada*', or 'shaking off'; it would last six years and claim the lives of hundreds of people, the majority of them Palestinians.

In retrospect, could the Israeli army have put a stop to the uprising early on, before it escalated? It is possible, but only if the troops had quickly resorted to a dramatic show of force against the rioters, inflicting on them a devastating and unforgettable blow from which they could not recover. In the event, the army's initial response was hesitant, as it probably assumed that this was just another of the occasional flare-ups of Palestinian riots in the occupied territories that usually exhausted themselves quickly, rather than the beginning of a large-scale uprising. Indeed, the clashes did not appear to be anything out of the ordinary or a break from the past. As we have seen, the Palestinian population had been restless from the very beginning of the occupation, clashing frequently with the military.

Still, it is clear there was a serious intelligence failure on the part of Israel's security services in that they did not foresee the serious troubles ahead and ignored obvious signs of changes on the ground. This is not only evident with the benefit of hindsight, but was being reported at the time: in mid-1987, for instance, Emile Nakhleh, a former CIA official, wrote that 'Gaza resembles a pressure-cooker ready to explode. The Palestinian population is daily becoming more resentful and rebellious. The military occupation responds by becoming more insecure . . .'[5]

It was not only Israel's security forces that were out of touch with reality, but also its politicians, as reflected in the response to the turmoil of Shamir and Rabin, the prime minister and defence minister, both of whom, immediately after rioting began in the occupied territories, blamed Iran, Syria and the PLO for instigating the unrest. In reality, neither Iran nor Syria was involved, and the PLO's leader, Yasser Arafat, in Tunis since 1982, was as surprised as the Israelis and similarly took the riots to be just another instance of the smouldering discontent that had long characterized life in the occupied territories igniting. Events there in fact took a completely different course from the one he had expected: for over twenty years Arafat had preached that the end of the occupation would come through 'the barrel of the gun', as he often put it, and had called for an 'armed struggle'; an unarmed popular resistance was not part of his strategy.

THE RIOTERS

As it turned out, no particular group or individuals were behind the riots: instead it was simply ordinary Gazans who were at the end of their tether with the occupation. They understood that the occupation, in the words of one Palestinian at the time, 'would always take and take and take'.[6] It is true that by 1987 their living conditions were far better than they had been when Israel seized the Strip twenty years earlier, as jobs in Israel meant that Palestinians had more cash in their pockets to spend. All the same, working in Israel also meant that the Gazans, particularly the younger generation, could see the gap between their living conditions and those of the Israelis. 'You can see with your own eyes why we do this,' explained a young protester shortly after the outbreak of the *intifada*. 'You see our houses, the way we live here. We can't live here like human beings . . . This is our statement.'[7]

The daily trips to hunt for jobs in Israel only increased Palestinian frustration: crossing into Israel was a demeaning experience and a bureaucratic nightmare – as so often under the occupation, special permits were required, and queues at the border crossing lasted for hours and often involved humiliation at the hands of Israeli guards. In his book *I Shall Not Hate*, Izzeldin Abuelaish, a doctor and one of a very few Palestinians allowed to work in an Israeli hospital, describes the experience of crossing from the Gaza Strip into Israel. 'It's hard for a civilized people to believe what happens [at the border crossing],' he writes:

> the humiliation, the fear, the physical difficulty, the oppression of knowing that, for no reason, you can be detained, turned back, that you may miss a crucial meeting, scare your family into thinking that perhaps, like thousands of others, you've been arrested . . . crossing is never routine, often erratic, frightening, and exhausting.[8]

Banned from staying overnight in Israel, Palestinian labourers had to make the journey back to Gaza daily and repeat the process; those defying the law and remaining overnight had to hide from the authorities, often in inhuman conditions. Israeli employers only offered Palestinians the undesirable, poorly paid jobs that Israelis shunned and, generally, failed to provide them with even the most basic elements of social security.

There is no doubt that Israel's economic system and policies in the occupied territories – the exploitation of Palestinian labourers, heavy taxation and other such measures – were the real driving force behind the radicalization of the Palestinian public and a major cause of the *intifada*.[9] Rashad al-Shawa, the former mayor of Gaza, expressed this sentiment well when observing that the people of Gaza 'have a sense of injustice and discrimination . . . they work for [Israel] as garbage collectors and dishwashers, and feel like slaves . . .'[10] Indeed, it should come as no surprise that the workers who made the daily migration between Israel and the occupied Gaza Strip constituted the vast majority of the demonstrators in those early days of the uprising

Students were also substantial participants in the December riots.

In the years after 1967 more universities were established in the occupied territories, but, particularly in the Gaza Strip, there were few opportunities after graduation. Many of the young graduates were often over-qualified for the sorts of job on offer either in the occupied territories or in Israel; seeking jobs outside the territories was often not a viable option, as there was no guarantee that they would be allowed to return home. A twenty-year-old Palestinian by the name of Judat, who studied economics at Irbid University in Jordan, recalls having to take up manual jobs in Israel:

> I worked for a while in a pub in Tel Aviv, and I spoke to Israeli students there. They studied exactly the same material I studied. Afterwards, I worked as a dishwasher in a restaurant until I couldn't stand it anymore – they paid me so little, and treated me like a slave – so I came back to the village. You're surprised? We have an Oxford-educated engineer here who works picking oranges and repairing cars. We have some street cleaners with college educations … a dishwasher who has a master's degree in economics. Can you imagine how someone like that feels? [We] went to college. We had great aspirations, and we forgot where we come from. Our parents spent their life's savings on us, sold their herds in order to pay for our studies, and we come back to the village, no longer really belonging here. But they won't accept us anywhere else. I sit and read newspapers all day, hang out with my friends, and grow older.[11]

Bored, unemployed, frustrated, but educated and politically aware, Judat and others like him rose up against the occupation.

And then there were the Islamists. Islamic groups were stronger in the Gaza Strip than on the West Bank, not least because the Gazans, especially those in the overcrowded refugee camps, came from a more traditional, conservative Islamic background than Palestinians on the West Bank, and they were more receptive to the message of Islamic groups. By the 1980s, there were at least eight Islamist factions in Gaza, all offshoots of the Muslim Brotherhood, the Islamic movement established in Egypt in 1924 which was active in the occupied territories, providing health, education services and other charitable work. The largest of these groups was Hamas, or the Islamic Resistance Movement, which was founded in December 1987 by a group of

Palestinian Islamists with the aim of establishing an Islamic state in the area that is now Israel, the West Bank and the Gaza Strip.

By far the most influential figure in Hamas was the wheelchair-bound Sheikh Ahmed Yassin. He was born in 1936 in a small village in southern Palestine, then under the British Mandate. During the first Arab–Israeli war in 1948, the Yassins fled their home in Palestine and settled in the Gaza Strip, where young Ahmed was educated at the Al Carmel primary school, not far from the Shati refugee camp where his family lived, and at the age of thirteen he started working in a restaurant to help support the poor family. At sixteen, Yassin had a sports accident which left him paraplegic, but he continued to make the three-kilometre round trip to school every day by pushing himself along in a wooden cart with six metal wheels. When Yassin finished high school he became a teacher, and although he was never ordained as a sheikh he was known as 'the sheikh' by those who admired him as a teacher and self-educator. Later, Yassin went to university in Cairo, where he joined the Brotherhood. Taken with their ideals, he began to build cells of young activists which would become the core of the Muslim Brotherhood of Palestine. When the Egyptian authorities found out about Yassin's cells they threw him and some of his colleagues into jail. After his release, and back in the Shati refugee camp, Yassin established an Islamic centre, where he taught until he was arrested in June 1984 by the Israeli army after arms were found in his house. Yassin was sentenced to thirteen years in prison, but was released in May 1985 in an exchange of prisoners with the Israelis.

Hamas joined the uprising from the start, issuing its first communiqué in the Gaza Strip on 11 December, and on the West Bank on the 14th. In it, Hamas declared that 'the *intifada* of our steadfast people in the occupied land constitutes a rejection of the occupation and its oppression', and that 'our people know the right path – the path of sacrifice and martyrdom – and would inform the world that the Jews were committing Nazi-style crimes against our people and would drink from the same cup'.[12] Hamas would issue its official Covenant, which called for the destruction of Israel, among other things, the following year, but already in December 1987 its aims were well known to its audience, namely to resist the occupation and establish an Islamic nation in the whole of Palestine where life would be governed by Islamic Sharia law. Although initially established as a branch of the Muslim Brotherhood, Hamas was ideologically distinct from its parent organization on one fundamental point: the centrality of Palestine.

Surprising and short-sighted as it may now seem, the Israeli army, in the years before the *intifada*, actively contributed to the strength of the Islamist groups, regarding them as a counterweight to the secular, nationalistic PLO, which the Israelis considered a greater threat to Israel – rather like America's support for the Mujahideen against the Soviets in Afghanistan, which was ongoing at the time. Thus the army would often treat Muslim leaders with less severity than agitators affiliated with the PLO, and for a time Islamists moved into positions of power, particularly in the Gaza Strip, but also on the West Bank, with tacit Israeli consent. In this way, Israel, like the US in Afghanistan, unwittingly created a Trojan horse that would come back to haunt it.

No wonder then that interrogations carried out by Shabak, the Israeli General Security Service, during the initial phase of the uprising clearly showed that the Islamists were active in the streets. While there were a few posters of Arafat around, and the odd Palestinian flag flying, the slogans demonstrators shouted often had a distinctly religious ring to them.

What further spurred on those who now joined the riots was the fact that, in the years since 1967, the Israelis had attempted to take over what very little the Palestinians had in terms of land and other resources, notably water. The most obvious manifestation of this was the construction of Jewish settlements mostly on land confiscated, as discussed, for 'military purposes', which spoke to fears among Palestinians that their displacement was the ultimate goal of the occupation. On the eve of the *intifada* there were 125 such settlements on the West Bank, home to 63,000 Jews, and eighteen settlements in the Gaza Strip with 2,500 settlers; the number of settlers moving into the occupied territories each year had increased from an annual average of 770 between 1967 and 1977 to 5,960 between 1978 and 1987.[13]

Another deep frustration for Palestinians was their own leaders and fellow Arabs. In the years after 1967, many Palestinians believed that forces outside the occupied territories, mainly the PLO but also Arab neighbours, would resolve the situation and put an end to the occupation.[14] But in 1982, when Sharon defeated Arafat in Lebanon, evicting him and his close circle of leaders to Tunis, Palestinians in the occupied territories lost hope; indeed, during the decade after the PLO's expulsion from Lebanon there was noticeable lack of progress in achieving Palestinian goals. Rumours of corruption among PLO officials and of the good life they were leading in Tunis, whether true or not, frustrated the ordinary Palestinians living under occupation even further.

As for Arab governments, although they had often spoken at great length about the need to end the Israeli occupation, in the 1980s they made little effort in terms of actual action to ease the plight of those living under it. For instance, the most important item on the agenda of the Arab League meeting in Amman in November 1987 – just before the uprising broke out – was Iran rather than the Palestinians. Palestinians had also taken notice that Egypt, the leading Arab power, had made peace and normalized relations with Israel, without any improvement to their own lives. The former mayor of Gaza, Rashad al-Shawa, observed in December 1987 that the Palestinians 'have lost all hope ... They feel the Arab countries are unable to accomplish anything ... that the PLO, which they regarded as their representative, has failed to accomplish anything.'[15] Thus the situation in December 1987, as one Palestinian leader put it, became one whereby 'the resident Palestinians [of the Occupied Territories] don't expect anything from anyone ... now the main question is how those outside [the occupied territories] can redefine their role. Those outside should become the "echo" of those inside'.[16]

Palestinians in the occupied territories had also been watching events in southern Lebanon, where Israel had taken over a wide strip of land along its northern border. This strip was intended to act as a buffer zone to make it difficult for Israel's enemies to infiltrate northern Israel. However, since the mid-1980s, Hezbollah, a Shiite movement that emerged in Lebanon in the wake of the 1982 invasion, had been challenging the Israeli occupation of southern Lebanon with some degree of success. By 1987, Hezbollah had demonstrated that resistance to the might of the Israeli army was possible without high-tech weaponry or huge firepower, and now offered a model for the Palestinians' own struggle.

Not only in Lebanon, but also in the occupied territories, most notably in the Balata refugee camp, certain events took place confirming that indeed the army had lost much of its deterrent effect.

Like the Jabalya camp in the Gaza Strip, Balata, on the northern West Bank, had always been a hotbed of Palestinian nationalism and resistance, often provoking the military into action. This was the case on 31 May 1987, when troops entered the camp to tackle the Shabibah, a youth movement whose members had been harassing local residents suspected of collaborating with the occupation. The troops made some arbitrary arrests and kept the detainees at a local school, but Palestinian women intervened and started marching towards the school, pelting the troops with stones. This was not unusual, for as Amal, a seasoned Palestinian organizer of demonstrations against the occupation, explains: 'When there is a demonstration, the women raise their voices and confuse the soldiers; they bang on pots and pans, blow whistles. Fear is not in the women's heart anymore . . .'[17] Now, in Balata, taken aback, the army retreated, which Palestinians interpreted as a victory, and this incident later came to be known as the 'mini-*intifada*' – a rehearsal for the events of December. Another incident that seemed to confirm that the army was losing its grip took place on 25 November, when a lone daring Palestinian insurgent flew across the Lebanese border in an ultra-light hang-glider, landed in a field near an Israeli army camp, shot dead six soldiers and wounded thirteen, before being shot and killed.

By December, with these successes against the military and the Hezbollah model to embolden them, Palestinians finally felt able to mount serious resistance to the occupation. From Jabalya, where it all started, riots quickly spread to Gaza's other refugee camps – Khan Younis, Al Bourej, Nuseirat, Ma'azi and Rafah, bordering the Sinai – before engulfing the West Bank.

ISRAEL'S BLACK DECEMBER

When finally the Israeli military started to digest this new reality and conclude that they had to react, they realized that they had neither the gear nor the expertise to confront what they now faced – an all-out but unarmed civilian uprising, in which women and children were leading demonstrations.

While other countries might use the police to deal with popular riots, in the occupied territories (except Jerusalem), it had always been the army's task. But, as the then deputy Chief of Staff, Ehud Barak, frankly admitted to the author: 'We were technically unprepared to deal with a violent popular riot on this scale.'[18] The army was slow to send in reinforcements and too selective in its use of the curfew – a cruel, but standard and often quite effective, technique of restoring order in such situations, as it often provides a cooling-off period for all concerned. This meant that the demonstrations continued without respite, feeding off each other. In fact, for most of December troops were instructed not to engage the demonstrators unless active attempts were made to block main routes or attack the army. The Palestinians, in turn, seeing the Israeli troops hang back, took this to mean that they could barricade themselves inside villages and camps, and they proceeded to turn these into 'liberated zones'.

From the very beginning of the uprising, the Palestinians attempted to neutralize Israel's vast military superiority by resorting to primitive weapons, mainly stones; indeed it was around this time that the image of the Palestinian carrying a gun was supplanted by the image of the kids with stones. For these young Palestinians, as Daoud Kuttab explains, throwing stones was seen as 'to be "one of the guys". To hit an Israeli car was to become a hero; and to be arrested and not confess to having done anything was to be a man.'[19] Palestinian girls joined in too: Reem Zaghout, a schoolgirl at the time, later remembered how 'the boys were throwing stones at the soldiers who were passing by . . . [and girls too would] join the boys in throwing stones, blocking the streets, writing on the wall, joining in . . .'[20] Against this background, what the troops really needed was basic and elementary riot gear – shields, helmets, cudgels and tear gas – but these were all in short supply.

The first few weeks of the *intifada*, from 9 to 31 December 1987, were chaotic and violent: twenty-two Palestinians were killed, among them five aged between thirteen and sixteen, and there were also some 320 injured, of whom two thirds were aged between seventeen and twenty-one. The high toll among Palestinian youth reflected the active part they were taking in the uprising: stone throwing had always been a tradition among schoolchildren even before the outbreak of the uprising, but now these young Palestinians also erected impromptu barricades and fired stones at troops from homemade slingshots. Israeli troops, in these early days of the *intifada*, used live ammunition against the demonstrators and in order to injure rather than to kill them were ordered to aim at their legs; but against children even these injuries often turned out to be fatal. In spite of their casualties the Palestinians were united in a new spirit and as one participant recalls: 'everyone participated . . . Everyone! Men, women, children were all seen on the streets demonstrating. There was a harmonious unification of all . . .'[21]

On 22 December, the UN Security Council strongly condemned Israel's violation of human rights in the occupied territories, deploring the army for the killing and wounding of defenceless Palestinian civilians. The General Assembly also demanded that Israel comply with the Fourth Geneva Convention on the Protection of Civilians in Time of War, and it also deplored the military detention of hundreds of Palestinians. At the UN, and elsewhere, it was often only the US and Israel that voted against these resolutions. But given the scale of violence and the clear imbalance in power between the two sides, even the US could not condone Israel's actions, and Israel found itself alone in its opposition. For Israel this was a Black December.

PART THREE

War and Diplomacy, 1987–2007

7
Intifada

Though it began in December 1987 as a spontaneous, popular uprising, the *intifada* by early January 1988 had developed into a full-fledged, organized and orchestrated rebellion. Those directing it were local leaders who had mainly emerged from within the ranks of the various local committees and organizations that had developed under the occupation and, in many ways, represented a cross-section of Palestinian society; some of them were secular and affiliated with the PLO, whereas others were linked with Islamist groups.[1] It is one of the ironies of the occupation that in the pre-*intifada* days, the military allowed these bodies to flourish because they filled in some of the gaps that existed between the population's needs and the actual services that the army was willing to provide. Now, however, this self-help network played a critical role in sustaining and providing local leadership to the uprising.

UNLU

The various local leaders organized themselves under the umbrella of the Unified National Leadership of the Uprising, or UNLU, and took it upon themselves to direct the rebellion. Their main activity, in the opening stages of the uprising, was to issue communiqués, instructing fellow Palestinians when and where to go and what to do. The first UNLU communiqué, issued on 10 January 1988, called on the Palestinians 'to shake the oppressive regime down to its foundations'.[2] It urged the insurgents to block roads in order to prevent the army from moving freely and went on to instruct that 'Stones must land on the heads of the occupying soldiers' and the activists should 'set the ground burning under the feet of the occupiers'.

One interesting element, and a major feature of the developing uprising, was UNLU's instruction to the insurgents to refrain from using firearms; indeed, a close look at the leaflets distributed in the first eighteen months of the uprising shows that 90 per cent of them call for a non-violent approach, with only 4.9 per cent calling for semi-violent tactics, such as throwing Molotov cocktails at the troops.[3] The thinking behind this strategy was to refrain from providing the army with the excuse to unleash its might; it is estimated that no more than 5 per cent of Palestinian activity during the uprising included the use of firearms or explosives.

We should recall that the Palestinian *intifada* took place in an era before the internet and social media, so the communiqués were copied and distributed manually, often by activists who would put them up around the entrances to mosques or other public places, or would plaster them on telephone poles. Later, with the army edging closer to finding the UNLU leadership, they would start transmitting their instructions by telephone, fax or radio.

In Tunis, however, Yasser Arafat and his associates were becoming quite concerned to see that the uprising was being run by local activists, over whom they had little control, and feared the emergence of a new leadership that would render the traditional Arafat-led PLO irrelevant. At the same time, it was plain that the grass roots rebellion was proving far more effective than armed attacks on Israel; Arafat's huge investment in building a regular force, replete with tanks and artillery, stationed in distant Iraq, Sudan and Yemen, looked downright foolish in the light of the results being achieved by children armed with slings and stones. Now, to guarantee that he and the PLO leadership in exile were not left behind, Arafat forced himself on the local leaders: unlike its predecessors, UNLU communiqué no. 3 of 18 January 1988 and all those that came after it were signed off with the words: 'Palestine Liberation Organization – Unified National Leadership of the Palestinian Uprising in the occupied territories', making it clear that the UNLU leadership was acting on behalf of Arafat's PLO.

*

1. (*left*) Three Israeli paratroopers look up at Judaism's holiest shrine, the Wailing Wall, which was occupied in the Six Day War of June 1967. This photograph came to symbolize a great moment in Jewish-Israeli history, but what at first seemed a blessed triumph soon turned out to be a cursed victory. (*below*) Moshe Dayan, Israel's Defence Minister and the most influential figure in the fate of the occupied territories, meets Palestinians near Jerusalem after the war.

2. (*above*) As Israeli troops push deep into the Golan Heights on the last two days of the 1967 war, thousands of Syrian refugees flee the mountains, taking with them as many possessions as they can carry. (*below*) The small Golan Druze community is allowed to remain on the Golan even after the war, as Israel believes that it will be loyal to the Jewish state. Cut off from friends and families in Syria, the remaining Druze keep in touch by climbing a hill on the occupied Golan and shouting, often using megaphones, to those on the Syrian side.

3. (*top*) Freedom is curtailed as the Israeli army erects hundreds of checkpoints across the West Bank and the Gaza Strip to control Palestinian movement in times of unrest. (*above*) Heads covered with a sack so that they cannot be identified by fellow Palestinians, collaborators – 'monkeys', as the Israelis dub them – help the army by fingering suspects.

4. (*top*) As increasing numbers of Jewish settlers take over Palestinian land, tensions build between the settlers and local Palestinians. (*above*) As frustration with the occupation grows and Palestinians escalate their attacks, the Israeli army erects a barrier across the West Bank to block them from entering Israel.

5. (*top*) In spite of their smiles, Israeli Prime Minister Menachem Begin (*right*) and Egyptian President Anwar Sadat (*left*) were never good friends. But they were pragmatic enough to compromise and sign a peace treaty in 1979 that put an end to the Sinai occupation. (*below*) Just before returning the Sinai to Egypt in April 1982, Israeli troops move into the Yamit bloc of settlements to forcefully remove Jewish settlers who barricade themselves in and refuse to leave.

6. From 1987, opposition to the occupation turns more confrontational as Palestinian frustration reaches its peak. (*above*) West Bankers and Gazans challenge the mighty Israeli army with stones and (*below*) by dispatching suicide bombers into Israeli towns and cities.

7. (*above*) In 1993, Israeli Prime Minister Yitzhak Rabin (*left*) and Palestinian leader Yasser Arafat (*right*) sign the Oslo Accords. But not all in Israel agree: a right-wing fanatic, Yigal Amir, who opposes any handover of occupied land to the Palestinians, assassinates Rabin. The photographs below show the bullet that killed the prime minister and the Song of Peace text which he carried in his coat, stained with his blood.

8. (*left*) In response to a bloody Palestinian insurgency, the Israelis elect a hardline prime minister, Ariel Sharon. Blaming Arafat for the violent insurgency, Sharon fights him tooth and nail (*below*) Sharon's victory over Arafat is symbolically achieved when an ailing Arafat is evacuated by helicopter from the West Bank to a Paris hospital, where he dies of a mysterious illness shortly after. The Palestinians blame Sharon for poisoning him.

The war that UNLU was conducting in the Gaza Strip and on the West Bank was directed not only against the army, but also against some of its own people – those viewed as collaborating with the occupation. As we have seen, collaboration is a main feature of the Israeli – in fact of any – occupation, and in the years before the *intifada* the Israelis had established a network of Palestinian informers to provide them with intelligence. Some Palestinians collaborated for money, or in exchange for a family reunification permit, a driving licence, permission to dig a well or build an extension, while others were forced to collaborate after Israeli intelligence collected sensitive information about them and used it for blackmail. Collaborators have always been feared and hated in Palestinian society. Khalid Amayreh, a Palestinian journalist from Dura, explains that 'Collaborators have been a cancer on the collective conscience of the Palestinian people. They are the worst and most diabolical product of the Israeli occupation, and the collective hatred for collaborators cannot be over-estimated.'⁴ The reason for this is that the presence of collaborators increases suspicion and division in Palestinian society by instilling fear in its members. As one Palestinian explains:

> I was aware of informants from when I was very young. Everyone talked about it, and people were also scared to talk with each other about some things. There was a feeling that there were informants all over the place . . . that if you say something it will get to the Israelis and you will be punished for it – arrested.⁵

Now UNLU decreed that collaborating with the occupation would be regarded as treason against the Palestinian people and those caught severely punished. Figures show that from the beginning of 1988 to mid-1989 more than forty Palestinian collaborators were killed – some by mobs, others by special enforcers. Many were killed by mistake, or for personal rather than political motives. As Hussein 'Awwad, a Palestinian activist from the Khan Younis area in the Gaza Strip explains: 'Not every Palestinian killed by Palestinians since the beginning of the *intifada* was a collaborator. Some were eliminated due to personal motives. In some of the cases, errors were made in the eliminations.'⁶

THE ARMY HITS BACK

After its initial lethargy, the army gradually got a grip on the situation and by January began implementing a variety of measures to put down the uprising. Innovation was paramount, particularly in devising new weapons, as it was apparent that the army could not possibly use its sophisticated arsenal against civilians, of whom women and children were a leading force. So the challenge for the military became to balance the need to downgrade its weapons with still keeping a few steps ahead of the Palestinian insurgents. This would result in the development of such 'weapons' as a stone-hurling machine to counter-attack youthful rock throwers, and vehicles equipped to fire canisters of hard rubber balls and small explosive propellants into crowds.[7] As funerals of Palestinians killed would always turn into the focal point for demonstrations, the army would often keep the body, only releasing it late at night for burial. But, in the cat-and-mouse battle between army and Palestinians, the latter, as a Palestinian leader of the *intifada* explains, 'would snatch the body from the hospital and bury it and turn this into a . . . demonstration'.[8]

As the French had done in Algiers in the 1950s, as captured by Gillo Pontecorvo in his classic 1965 film *The Battle of Algiers*, the Israeli army attempted to undermine the leaders of the insurgency in the occupied territories. They disseminated fake communiqués, mimicking those of UNLU, in order to sow confusion among the public, while hunting down the uprising's leaders. The various popular committees and self-help groups that provided middle- and lower-rank cadres and acted as field commands for organizing demonstrations were now banned outright by the military, and membership was regarded as a criminal offence.

With their methodical approach and superior resources, the army and security services, aided by Palestinian informers, gradually tightened the screw on the UNLU leaders, and most were eventually found and either jailed or physically removed from the occupied territories. This latter method – deporting Palestinian leaders – had, in fact, been used by the army since the early days of the occupation: in the period immediately after 1967, deportations would often be to Israel proper, while later those resisting the occupation would be transferred to Jordan. Now, however, the army took detained leaders of the *intifada* to southern Lebanon, which was still under Israeli occupation, and dumped them there unaccompanied; figures show that in 1988 alone the army deported more than fifty Palestinian activists. On the ground these draconic methods had little effect, as new leaders quickly emerged to replace those deported or jailed.

One of the most effective methods used by the military to put down the uprising was the curfew. Curfews, considered a collective punishment under international law, are forbidden; article 3 of the Fourth Geneva Convention is very clear in stating that 'no protected person may be punished for an offence he or she has not personally committed. Collective penalties and likewise all measures of intimidation . . . are prohibited.' But the army proceeded with this method anyway. Figures show that in 1988 no fewer than 1,600 curfew orders were issued in the occupied territories, 118 of them for five days or more; on several occasions the entire Palestinian population in the West Bank and Gaza Strip was placed under curfew. During curfews, Palestinians would be confined to their homes, even instructed to stay away from windows and balconies; often anyone violating the curfew would be shot at. With Palestinians confined to their homes, the army would move around freely, pick up suspects, often jailing them, and, in general, demonstrate to Palestinians the price they would pay for resisting the occupation. For those Palestinians on the receiving end, particularly families with children, periods of curfew have always been a nightmare. Ghazi Bani Odeh, a Palestinian journalist, explains how during curfews 'our life . . . turns into hell. We have no contact with our neighbours. We don't see, hear or speak with anybody.'⁹ And as another Palestinian refugee from Khan Younis in the Gaza Strip recalls: 'The soldiers would come rumbling in their tanks . . . and the whole house would shake like a leaf. They would announce the curfew in the early hours of the morning, always coupled with the foulest language ever, "You son of a . . ." and "Your mother's . . ."'¹⁰

To make it difficult for Palestinians to organize demonstrations the army would also shut down schools; this, however, led to the emergence of Palestinian 'popular schools', where the community would organize teaching sessions. Recalling her school days in Ramallah during the *intifada*, the Palestinian Diana Wahbe explains:

> We used to go to a neighborhood teacher's home and spend our days studying history, Arabic, geography, mathematics, and literature with students from the area. We were a strange mixture of public and private school kids using old books, reading at different levels, solving problems in different ways, and eagerly enjoying our new teachers and classmates. Sometimes, the teacher was arrested for having such schools so we had to find another teacher or a parent willing to help us with our lessons.[11]

In the meantime, the legal system that had been developed to sustain the occupation was fully exploited to suppress the *intifada*. Under the Defence (Emergency) Regulations, a military court could order the detention of a Palestinian suspect for up to six months without a trial in what was called 'administrative detention' or 'preventative detention' or 'internment'. The procedure had been used sporadically between 1967 and 1980, but gradually diminished. In 1985, however, which was a time of active unrest in the occupied territories, it was resumed and, between 1985 and December 1987, an estimated 316 Palestinians were held in administrative detention; now this method was used extensively. It is estimated that at any given time during 1988 between 3,000 and 4,000 Palestinians were being held under administrative detention; those detained included women along with children as young as fourteen or fifteen.[12]

Detaining so many individuals resulted in existing prison facilities being swamped, and the army had to open new ones. Among the more notorious detention centres were Ansar II in Gaza and Ketsiyot Military Detention Centre (Prison 7), also called Ansar III, in the Negev desert. These jails soon turned into political schools for Palestinians, creating a new generation of leaders with a strong bond between them. One prisoner who spent ten years in Israeli jails described how his Palestinian identity was transformed by the experience: 'Before I went to jail,' he recalls, 'I didn't even know I was a Palestinian. There they taught me who I am. Now I have opinions . . .'[13] Outside the prisons, in the Palestinian occupied territories, the prisoners had strong support and the Palestinian leadership would go out of its way to praise their bravery: 'Glory is yours . . . Glory to the martyrs of the uprising behind bars . . .'[14]

Inside the jails, detainees would be interrogated, and torture would be used routinely as a punishment and to obtain information; torture, of course, is not permitted by international and human rights laws.[15] It is estimated that between 1987 and 1994 the Shabak interrogated more than 23,000 Palestinians, using torture regularly. A study by B'Tselem (Israeli Information Centre for Human Rights in the Occupied Territories) found that Palestinian detainees in Israeli jails suffered 'slapping, punching, kicking, hair pulling, beating with clubs or with iron rods, pushing into walls and onto floors'.[16] The report goes on to describe the methods used in jails against the Palestinian detainees as follows:

> Beating the detainee as he is suspended in a closed sack covering the head and tied around the knees; tying the detainee in a twisted position to an outdoor pipe with hands behind the back for hours and, sometimes, in the rain, at night, and during the hot daytime hours; confining the detainee, sometimes for a few days, in the 'lock-up' – a dark, smelly and suffocating cell one-and-a-half by one-and-a-half metres (five by five feet); placing the detainee, sometimes for many hours, in the 'closet' – a narrow cell the height of a person in which one can stand but not move; and depositing the tied-up detainee for many hours in the 'grave' – a kind of box, closed by a door from the top, with only enough room to crouch and no toilet.

N.S., a nineteen-year-old Palestinian student from Ramallah, charged with membership of Hamas, was arrested by the army and interrogated for thirty days in November and December 1993; the following abuses he describes resemble those recounted by detainees in earlier periods:

> *Shabeh* [enforced sitting or standing while blindfolded and handcuffed] consisted mostly of standing from nine in the morning until eight at night in the courtyard. Some days I stood all the time with no food or no visit to the toilet . . . Sometimes I was put in a leaky damp 'closet' [a closet-sized room] for eight or ten hours. In the 'closet' you sit all the time . . . you can't move . . . often people relieved themselves in the 'closet' because they were not allowed to go to the toilet, and

there was no container in there . . . the closets stank very badly. At night you lied in the cells like animals. The mattresses and blankets are filthy and they stink. There is no sun or air. The cell is full of water, because it leaks . . . The blankets are soaked, the mattresses too . . . In the interrogation room the interrogators slapped me and kicked me between the legs . . .[17]

These experiences in Israeli jails, of course, had a profound long-term effect on the detainees; Aysha Odeh, who spent time in Israeli prisons, explains that after leaving prison 'You discover that you cannot get prison out of you. You carry it inside you. It confronts you with every detail. Your life in prison dictates to you your behaviour to the outside world . . . you didn't leave prison; you actually carry it with you.'[18]

To reduce tensions in a particular hot spot, the army would often declare an entire town or a city a 'closed area', which effectively meant that the place was put under siege, cut off from the outside world. This differed from a curfew in that within the so-called 'closed area' inhabitants were permitted to roam freely, but they would not be allowed to get out of town, prevented from doing so by military checkpoints at all exits and entrances. This method of collective punishment became notorious in 1988, when it was imposed on the West Bank village of Kabatiyeh, near Jenin, in retaliation for the killing by locals of a resident suspected of collaborating with the occupation. From 24 February to 3 April 1988, the army cut Kabatiyeh off, bringing the town to its knees: no food was allowed in, telephone lines were cut off, and Kabatiyehs were forbidden from exporting stone from the town's quarries to Jordan, which put most of the villagers out of work. In all, 400 of the 7,000 villagers were detained, and the army also bulldozed the houses of villagers suspected of being directly involved in lynching the suspected informer.[19] With the siege biting hard, the inhabitants reverted to ancient ways of life, using branches pruned from trees instead of kerosene for cooking fuel, and planting small vegetable patches to supplement meagre food supplies.

Perhaps the most draconian method the army would employ to punish Palestinians considered to be instigators of unrest was to demolish their houses. Bulldozing houses was used by the army even before the outbreak of the *intifada*; however, considered a particularly harsh punishment, it had, until 1987, only been used against those who had committed the most serious of offences. It also required the special approval of the defence minister, and tenants were given the opportunity to petition the High Court of Justice. While the courts often refrained from interfering with military security considerations, they demanded that the principle of proportionality be maintained, which is to say that the punitive act of house demolition be administered in proportion to the severity of the crime.[20] But now, with the uprising in full swing, house demolition became commonplace and no longer required special permission from a minister. It was therefore left to the discretion of area military commanders, and figures show that, compared with 1987, when 103 houses were demolished, in 1988 the number rose to a staggering 423. The following testimony of Jalal Abu Luz gives us a glimpse into the devastating effect of house demolitions on one Palestinian family:

> I was shocked at the destruction and devastation . . . I was hysterical, and began to cry and scream. I ran all around . . . I returned to the ruins of my house and sat on a pile of stones and dirt and started to cry . . . People came to comfort me . . . My wife and children came home and saw that the house had turned into a pile of stones. My wife fainted . . . the children started to cry. My children . . . came to sit . . . on the pile of stones, and we all cried until one o'clock in the afternoon . . . For two days the children did not go to school because all their books and notebooks were buried among the ruins . . . the Red Cross began to distribute tents and blankets . . . We received a tent and ten blankets. We put the tent on the stone pile . . . My children later went to school, but their behaviour changed . . . they wet their beds at the relative's house, and screamed in their sleep because of their nightmares.[21]

And Raja Shehade, a Palestinian lawyer, describes the emotions of seeing a house being demolished by the army:

> I saw how the soldiers measured the thickness of the walls in order to decide where to lay the explosives. They did it with such a matter-of-factness . . . and it was horrible. It was like seeing someone measure a live person for a coffin. I looked at the soldiers. So young! It is a challenge for

me to understand how they can do it . . . They simply don't see the family that lives in that house as their brothers, human beings.[22]

The hatred towards the Israelis caused by their policy of house demolition is apparent in the testimony of Mohammed al-Kal'ilah from the West Bank, whose house was demolished because Mohammed was blamed for hiding his 'wanted' son there. 'I could kill a million times the man who ordered my house destroyed,' admits al-Kal'ilah, 'Did I ever do anything like that? Did I ever think like that before? I only wanted to live. Now they have made me like that, too. They have turned me into a murderer'.[23]

ASSASSINATING ABU JIHAD

The measures the Israelis would use to put down the *intifada* – the curfews, mass arrests, house demolitions and so on – had only been directed against Palestinians within the territories under occupation, but in January 1988 the PLO in Tunis began involving itself in the daily running of the uprising. The person in charge was the organization's Chief of Staff, Khalil al-Wazir, also known as Abu Jihad – 'Father of the Struggle'.

He was born in October 1935 in the town of Ramla, Palestine, then under the British Mandate. At the age of thirteen, when Ramla was captured by Israeli troops during the first Arab–Israeli war, Abu Jihad's family was expelled and settled in the Gaza Strip as refugees. There, young Khalil grew up, attended a secondary school run by UNRWA, and took up various jobs to support his poor family. The Egyptian authorities which controlled the Gaza Strip expelled him in 1957 because he was involved in banned political activities and he settled in Saudi Arabia, where he worked as a schoolteacher. In the early 1960s, together with Arafat and a few other activists, Abu Jihad played an instrumental role in founding the Fatah organization, whose aim was to fight Israel and liberate Palestine; a secular movement, it espoused a Palestinian nationalist ideology, adopting the so-called 'armed struggle' as the way forward to liberate all of Palestine from Israel, particularly after the 1967 war.

In 1969, when Arafat became the head of the PLO, the umbrella organization in which Fatah was the largest faction but that also included other Palestinian groups, Abu Jihad was made his top aide and excelled himself in organizing the armed struggle operations against Israel. Abu Jihad was a quiet but efficient organizer and he continued to play a leading military role in 1970–71, when Palestinian guerrilla fighters in Jordan clashed with King Hussein's forces in what came to be known as 'Black September'. Following the PLO defeat at the hands of King Hussein's forces, Abu Jihad, along with Arafat and other Palestinian leaders and commanders, moved into Lebanon and from there he continued to lead the military armed struggle against Israel and was the mastermind behind numerous attacks. During the 1982 Israeli invasion of Lebanon Abu Jihad organized counterattacks in an effort to slow down the invading Israelis, and later, with Israel prevailing in Lebanon, he was exiled, ending up in Tunis, along with other Palestinian leaders, including Arafat.

Even from there Abu Jihad continued to lead the Palestinian armed struggle against the occupation, notably by setting up youth committees in the Palestinian occupied territories to fight the army. Like many others he was taken by surprise when the *intifada* erupted, but he promptly recovered and imposed his leadership on the locals running the *intifada*, soon having them follow his instructions from Tunis. And now, with Abu Jihad playing such a leading role in conducting the Palestinian uprising, the Israelis decided to eliminate him.

On 15 April 1988, Israeli commando units were ferried to the Tunisian shore, where they broke into Abu Jihad's house, and as a certain Nahum Lev recalls: 'I shot him a long burst.'[24] Abu Jihad's wife, Jihan, hearing the commotion, went out to the staircase to investigate and describes how she saw

> three masked men with machine guns . . . the first of the men opened fire on Abu Jihad. He was wounded in his arm and heart. He turned around and fell to the ground. Then four of them, as they started running down the stairs to leave the house, shot him in rotation. Hearing the screams, Hanan, my daughter, woke up. One of the men pushed her aside and said, 'Go to your mother.' There were about seventy-five bullets in Abu Jihad's body – eight of them in his heart.[25]

In the occupied territories fury at the assassination unleashed a massive wave of protests, particularly in the Gaza Strip, where Abu Jihad had been raised. In the immediate wave of riots the army shot dead fourteen and injured more than seventy. In Jerusalem, Palestinians held three days of mourning and a general strike, during which scores of black flags were flown over Palestinian houses. As Abu Jihad was laid to rest in Damascus, mock funerals were held in towns and cities across the occupied territories, and UNLU issued instructions that the Saturday after Abu Jihad's death should be a 'day of rage' in which protests and demonstrations were to be escalated. The assassination, ultimately, did little to alter the course of the uprising, which continued apace, although it did enable the army to arrest scores of Palestinian activists, as during the Tunis operation the Israelis collected documents with lists of activists in the occupied territories.

The escalation of the riots that followed Abu Jihad's assassination had one important repercussion: it strengthened the determination of Jordan's King Hussein to go ahead with what turned out to be one of the most dramatic and decisive decisions he would ever make – one which had a tremendous impact on the future of the occupied territories.

A POLITICAL DIVORCE

King Hussein had continued to channel funds into the West Bank even after Israel seized it from him in 1967: he paid salaries and pensions to civil servants, administered religious endowments, and financed schools, clinics and other institutions. He was keen to maintain his influence in a land he still hoped he would recover. The Israelis turned a blind eye to his meddling, as they hoped that in due course they could share control of the area with Jordan, rather than see an independent Palestinian state established between Israel and Jordan. Indeed, this 'Jordanian option' was a key element in Israeli – particularly left-wing – governments' thinking, as they feared a hostile Palestinian state on the West Bank would be just too close to Israeli centres and could easily disturb daily life. Hussein continued to support the inhabitants of the Palestinian occupied lands even after his fellow Arab heads of state deprived him of the authority to negotiate on behalf of the Palestinians in favour of the PLO at the Arab League conference in Rabat in October 1974; from 1974 to 1988, the king continually tried to get around the Rabat formula and to persuade the Palestinians, the Arab world and the international community that he was the right person to represent the Palestinians in talks on the future of the Palestinian occupied lands. But the *intifada* shuffled the deck, and although the riots were directed primarily against the Israeli occupation, anti-Jordanian feelings, never far from the surface among Palestinians, rose to new heights as well.

On 11 March 1988, for instance, UNLU, the Palestinian leadership in the occupied territories, issued its tenth communiqué, in which it called on Palestinians, among other things, to intensify the pressure against not only the occupying Israeli army but also 'against person-nel of the Jordanian regime', namely Palestinians who felt closer to the Jordanian regime than to the PLO.[26] It also urged the West Bank representatives who still sat in the Jordanian parliament to resign their seats, 'otherwise, there will be no room for them on our land'. These words hurt the king a great deal as, by now, he could clearly see how most West Bankers were openly aligned with the PLO rather than with Jordan, a process that had gathered pace since the 1976 West Bank municipal elections. There was also – and this did not escape the king – a great security risk here, as, with the vast majority of his subjects in Jordan proper of Palestinian origin, the *intifada* could easily spill over the border into his kingdom, and possibly even endanger his own position. Increasingly tired of the cold shoulder with which the Palestinians had met his advances over the years, and deeply concerned about the future of his kingdom, the king decided to take a bold step – to disengage entirely from the West Bank and trans-fer full responsibility to the PLO.

On 28 July 1988, King Hussein scrapped a $1.3bn development plan for the West Bank that had been intended to pay for housing, health, education, cultural and religious projects, justifying stopping the investment on the grounds that this move was designed to allow the PLO more responsibility for the area. Two days later the king dissolved the lower house of Jordan's parliament, where half of the sixty delegates were Palestinians from the West Bank. The coup de grâce finally came on 31 July when, in a dramatic televised address, he announced he was giving up all claims to the area he lost in 1967, and declared that Jordan would sever all administrative and legal ties with the West Bank. He explained that since there is 'a general conviction' that the struggle to liberate the Palestinian lands from Israeli occupation could be enhanced by dismantling the legal and administrative links between the two banks, then 'we [in Jordan] have to fulfill our duty and do what is required from us'.[27] He proclaimed that a future independent Palestinian state would be established 'on the occupied Palestinian land', and he emphasized that he was taking these steps only in response to the wishes of the Palestine Liberation Organization, 'the sole legitimate representative of the Palestinian people . . .'.[28] The king, though, made it plain that disengagement would not include relinquishing Hashemite trusteeship of the holy sites in Jerusalem, which he viewed as a personal and spiritual obligation, as well as a political necessity, since there was no guarantee that Israel would allow Palestinian sovereignty over these holy sites.

And thus, with 'May God's peace and blessings be upon you', the king cut off Jordan's ties to a land it had first seized in 1948, formally annexed in 1950, lost to Israel in 1967, and up until this moment had still hoped to get back; he also put a formal end to his representation of the Palestinians. This move inflicted a mortal blow to Israel's 'Jordanian Option', leaving them with only the PLO as a potential partner for any negotiations over the Palestinian occupied lands.

Hussein's decision gave momentum to the new reality that was forming on the ground, and set in motion events which would turn his disengagement into an irrevocable act.

INDEPENDENCE

With King Hussein washing his hands of the occupied Palestinian territories and local Palestinian leaders pressing the PLO to help translate the success of their insurrection into a clear programme to guide the struggle to independence, pressure was mounting on Arafat, still based in Tunis, to act. He seized the moment on 15 November 1988, the day the Israeli army slapped a total curfew over the occupied territories and East Jerusalem: at a special meeting in Algiers of the Palestinian National Council (PNC), the legislative body of the Palestine Liberation Organization, he declared 'the establishment of the State of Palestine in our Palestinian nation, with holy Jerusalem as its capital'.[29] He then read the Palestinian Declaration of Independence, which had been written by the Palestinian poet Mahmud Darwish:

> Palestine, the land of the three monotheistic faiths, is where the Palestine Arab people was born, on which it grew, developed and excelled. Thus, the Palestine Arab people ensured for itself an everlasting junction between itself, its land, and its history. Resolute throughout that history, the Palestinian Arab people forged its national identity . . .[30]

The state envisioned by Arafat in his declaration of independence was assumed to include the West Bank and the Gaza Strip, about 22 per cent of historic Palestine, and the Arab sector of Jerusalem, which Israel considered its own, having effectively annexed it in June 1967. As these lands were still under military occupation, Arafat's announcement was merely a political declaration of hope and intent without immediate practical meaning.

The PNC approved Arafat's declaration; it also officially accepted UN Security Council Resolution 242 for the first time. This was significant: while in 1970 Israel, albeit reluctantly, had accepted the resolution, which called on it to withdraw from territories it had occupied in 1967, and Arab states such as Egypt and Jordan had also accepted the resolution and thus also the principle that Israel has the right to live peacefully in the Middle East, up until now the PLO had refused to do so. For them to accept the right of Israel to exist, as implied by Resolution 242, meant that they were giving up 78 per cent of old Palestine. By refusing to embrace 242, the PLO had, for many years, made it easy for Israel to dismiss them as 'terrorists' bent on the destruction of Israel: now, however, Arafat transformed the PLO in one bold move and had laid down a challenge to Israel to open negotiations with him.

Arafat was probably realistic enough to assume that his acceptance of Israel's right to exist would not prompt direct talks with the government, as this would entail discussions of a future Palestinian state, something to which Likud's Shamir and indeed the vast majority of Israelis objected. At the same time, Arafat hoped that the US, Israel's important ally and a superpower, at least, would react positively by lifting the ban on talks with the PLO that had been imposed fourteen years before by the Secretary of State at the time, Henry Kissinger. Kissinger had promised the Israelis that the US would not negotiate with the PLO before it accepted UN Resolution 242, explicitly recognized Israel's right to exist and renounced terrorism, as part of a package of promises to induce Israel to withdraw from the Sinai in 1975. And now, the US Secretary of State, George Shultz, made it plain that before the US could proceed with direct talks with the PLO, Arafat would have to meet *all* the above requirements, particularly by explicitly recognizing Israel and renouncing terrorism. Arafat felt he had to comply and so on 7 December 1988 he sent a message to Secretary Shultz declaring that 'The executive committee of the PLO . . . condemns individual, group and state terrorism in all its forms, and will not resort to it.'[31] Then, on 14 December, Arafat convened a press conference, where he declared that the PLO recognized the right of all parties concerned in the Middle East conflict to exist in peace and security, 'including . . . Israel', and he repeated again 'for the record' that 'the PLO renounces terrorism'.[32]

As far as the Americans were concerned, Arafat had finally complied with US demands, and while the Israelis still rejected any negotiations with the PLO, the US acted swiftly, withdrawing its boycott and preparing for dialogue: the US Ambassador to Tunisia, Robert Pelletreau, made contact with PLO headquarters there and on 16 December talks to establish the future relationship between the PLO and the US government commenced in Tunis. They did not, however, get very far as, in May 1989, a Palestinian splinter faction, headed by a certain Muhammad Abbas of the Palestine Liberation Front (PLF), carried out a seaborne attack on a beach near Tel Aviv; Arafat refused to condemn the attack and, in turn, the US broke off dialogue with the PLO.

Indeed, over the coming years the attempts by Arafat to continue the armed struggle against Israel while at the same time moving towards a negotiated political solution with it would gradually erode his credibility, delaying the prospect of a Palestinian state. For now, yet another historic attempt to sort out the Israeli–Palestinian conflict had failed.

BREAKING BONES AND THE SHAMIR PEACE PLAN

All these diplomatic manoeuvres seemed to have little impact on the situation on the ground, where the army and Palestinian activists continued to trade blows. In 1989, the army introduced rubber bullets to its arsenal with which to fight the uprising; these are bullets wrapped in rubber, which softens their impact and results in fewer fatalities. This 'soft' ammunition still caused fatal injuries and maimed many rioters while failing to stop the rebellion.

By now, however, the IDF was coming under intense international criticism for the sheer brutality with which it was dealing with the rioters, leaving the Israelis with little choice but to downgrade their weapons from guns to sticks and cudgels. The army was acting on direct instructions from the defence minister, Rabin, who, on one occasion, told his troops: 'Gentlemen, start using your hands, or clubs, and simply beat the demonstrators in order to restore order.'[33] This became known as Rabin's 'break their bones' policy and so frustrated were the troops that they took the minister's advice too far: the blows they inflicted on Palestinians left many of them permanently handicapped. Breaking bones could also solve another problem for the army; namely, they could put the demonstrators out of action without having to send them to detention camps; Colonel Yehuda Meir instructed his troops to 'break the arms and legs' of Palestinians, 'because the detention camps are full'.[34]

With the brutal realities in the Palestinian occupied territories shown on TV screens across the globe, international pressure on Israel grew dramatically: the Europeans, the UN, the Soviet Union, even the US government – all became impatient with Israel's forceful measures, calling on it to adopt a political initiative, particularly after Arafat's explicit recognition of Israel and renunciation of terrorism.

Under this mounting international pressure, Shamir, on 14 May 1989, came up with a Four Point Plan.[35] It envisaged a two-stage peace process, involving a transitional period of interim agreement between Israel and the Palestinians which would open with local elections in the Gaza Strip and on the West Bank (aimed at sidelining the PLO), then lead to a permanent solution to be discussed between Israel, Egypt and Jordan (again, aimed at sidelining the PLO leadership). At the heart of this programme was the idea of 'self-rule [for the Palestinians], by means of which they will themselves conduct their affairs of daily life'. Israel, according to the Shamir Plan, would remain in charge of security, foreign affairs, and all matters concerning Israeli settlers on the West Bank and in the Gaza Strip.

The Palestinians recognized the Shamir Plan for what it was: an Israeli tactic to kill the idea of a Palestinian state and sideline the PLO. Indeed, we now know that Shamir's offer was only aimed at easing international pressure on Israel, as he himself would later admit: 'We shall not give the Arabs one inch of our land [a reference to the West Bank], even if we have to negotiate for ten years . . .'[36] Elsewhere, Shamir would say about his plan: 'I would have carried out talks for ten years and meanwhile we would have reached half a million [settlers] in Judea and Samaria.'[37] Clearly what Shamir wanted was to gain time, believing that the longer there was no change in the status quo, the more Israel would be confirmed in the possession of the territories under its control. Shamir's thinking reflected his belief that the collapse of the Soviet Union, the emergence of the US as the sole superpower, and the massive wave of high-quality immigrants from the former Soviet Union who were pouring into Israel around this time all strengthened Israel demographically and economically and these underlying trends would, over time, work in Israel's favour. Supporting Shamir, his defence minister, Rabin, warned the Palestinians that they had better embrace the Shamir Plan as Israel 'would have no qualm about significantly increasing the military pressure if the Palestinians refused even to consider Israel's plan – the only one Israel intends to offer'.[38] But even this warning would not deter the Palestinians, who rejected the Shamir Plan out of hand and continued their uprising.

Though unable to totally suppress the *intifada*, by 1990 the army was clearly gaining the upper hand and the euphoric unity Palestinians had felt when the first rocks started flying was starting to break down. The economy may have been the engine behind the outbreak of the *intifada* in 1987, but by the end of the decade it helped lead to its demise. This was the result of the army's measures, combined with the frequent strikes initiated by UNLU, which had left economic conditions in the occupied territories so dire that all ordinary Palestinians wished for was to be able to return to work in Israel and put some food on the table. Figures show that from the beginning of the insurgency the number of Gazans working in Israel declined sharply from 70,000–80,000 in the pre-*intifada* period to 56,000 in 1989, leading to a 13 per cent drop in per capita income within two years of the start of the uprising. Fatigue was setting in and the uprising had lost much of its vitality; workers were drifting back to their jobs in Israel, defying efforts by activists to continue the rebellion. Sari Nusseibeh, a leader of the *intifada*, wrote about its 'ignominious demise', and how 'the cause died from exhaustion. A "whimper" sums it up better than a "bang".'[39] But the Palestinians' political dreams were not to disappear completely. Salvation, in a form that would build on the uprising to bring dramatic political change to the occupied territories, was soon to come from an unexpected quarter – Iraq.

8

Gulf, Madrid, Oslo, 1991–1995

It is an irony of history that of all people it was Iraq's dictator, Saddam Hussein, who played a pivotal role in kick-starting the Middle Eastern peace process in the early 1990s.

In the late 1980s, with his country bankrupt after eight years of fruitless war with Iran, and with oil prices crashing to an all-time low, seriously damaging Iraq's export earnings, Hussein was looking for funds to rebuild his economy and finance an inflated military. In his desperation, he dispatched his troops to invade and occupy his tiny but oil-rich neighbour Kuwait, on 2 August 1990, calculating that by invading Kuwait and taking over its resources he could inflate oil prices and revive Iraq's economy. However, he underestimated the international mood. On the very day Hussein's troops marched into Kuwait the UN took steps to halt his raid: in Resolution 660 the UN Security Council immediately condemned the invasion and demanded Iraq's unconditional withdrawal; a string of more resolutions then followed which also imposed economic sanctions on Iraq.

Hussein reacted to the mounting pressure with a most original, albeit cynical, idea: he proposed a comprehensive solution to 'all issues of occupation . . . in the entire region', calling for Israel's immediate and unconditional withdrawal from the occupied territories, which would be followed by 'the formulation of provisions relating to the situation in Kuwait . . .'[1] His assumption, of course, was that Israel would refuse to withdraw and the issue would then split Arab opinion, thus reducing pressure on him to get out of Kuwait. Not surprisingly, in the occupied territories, Palestinians cheered the Iraqi leader. As Moghi Assad, a twenty-year-old Palestinian student living with eleven family members in a small house in the Azia refugee camp on the West Bank, explained: 'Saddam Hussein . . . gives us hope. He is a hero . . . Saddam is going to help the Palestinians . . . He has the power to tell Israel to move.'[2]

International opposition to the Iraqi invasion was spearheaded by the US president, George H. W. Bush, who was determined not to let Hussein muddy the waters by introducing a linkage between Iraq's withdrawal from Kuwait and Israel's departure from the occupied territories. But his efforts to persuade Arab nations to join a US-led coalition against Iraq, albeit under a UN umbrella, faced serious difficulties: Syria, for instance, seen by many as the keeper of the flame of Arab nationalism, was reluctant to participate as long as Washington ignored the linkage established by Hussein between the end of his and Israel's occupation. Syria's foreign minister, Farouk al-Shara, later recalled in an interview what Syria's President Assad told the Americans: 'there should be no double standards; if we all support the implementation of UN Security Council resolutions relevant to the Gulf, then the same resolutions should be implemented regarding the Arab–Israeli conflict'.[3]

Desperate to have Syria join his coalition, President Bush was forced to move closer to recognizing, however indirectly, the connection between the Israeli and Iraqi cases; in a speech to the UN General Assembly, on 2 October 1990, he declared that the Iraqi withdrawal from occupied Kuwait would pave the way 'for all the states and peoples of the region to settle the conflict that divided the Arabs from Israel'.[4] Then, in a face-to-face meeting in Geneva with Syria's President Hafez al-Assad, on 23 November 1990, President Bush pledged that 'Once we are done dealing with Saddam, once we are done with liberating Kuwait, the United States will turn to the [Arab–Israeli] peace process.'[5] Bush's pledge persuaded Assad; he and other Arab leaders agreed to join the US-led anti-Hussein coalition and even contributed some troops.

On 16 January 1991, the UN coalition attacked Hussein's forces from the air and, on 24 February, opened up the ground offensive; after a hundred-hour battle, the Iraqi forces were defeated and Hussein had agreed to pull out of Kuwait.

In the Palestinian occupied territories, on the day war started in the Gulf the army took advantage of the fact that many foreign correspondents had left Israel and the occupied territories to report on events in Iraq and clamped down on the Palestinians, imposing a comprehensive curfew. During this time, the army went on to arrest hundreds of Palestinians in an attempt to extract intelligence from them to give a final knock-out to the *intifada*. The Israelis used often brutal methods to extract information from the detainees. As an inside source at the Hebron detention centre revealed:

> Plain horror: they would break their clubs on the prisoners' bodies, hit them in the genitals, tie a prisoner up on the cold floor and play soccer with him – literally kick and roll him around. Then they'd give him electric shocks, using the generator or a field telephone, and then push him out to stand for hours in the cold and rain . . . They would crush the prisoners . . . turning them into lumps of meat.[6]

Curfews the army imposed, which had been going on for seven weeks, had a devastating effect on the economy of the occupied territories. The Gaza Strip, in particular, was hard hit, losing at least $84m; of the 140,000 tons of citrus produced by February 1991 (down from 175,000 tons a year before), only 15,000 tons were exported. And as the army would not allow Palestinian labour to enter Israel to hunt for jobs, thousands of families were pushed to the brink of economic collapse; in late February 1991, the sale of red meat in Gaza had dropped by 80 per cent and vegetables by 70 per cent. The worst was still to come: with Palestinians in the occupied territories openly supporting Hussein, and their leader in Tunis, Arafat – always reluctant to move against the mood of his people – using pro-Saddam rhetoric, Saudi Arabia and Kuwait retaliated against Palestinian workers on their lands. We should remember that with few jobs in the occupied territories, Palestinians, particularly West Bankers, often emigrated to Saudi Arabia and Kuwait in search of work. From there they would then send monies back to their families in the occupied territories and these funds have always been a most important pillar of the occupied territories' income. Now, however, disappointed with Palestinian support for the Iraqi dictator, Saudi Arabia and Kuwait kicked out the Palestinian labourers, the majority of whom had nowhere to go but to return to the occupied territories, where they became unemployed. This development had a devastating impact on the economy of the occupied territories.

THE MADRID PEACE CONFERENCE AND AFTER

Meanwhile, President Bush, having led an international and regional coalition to victory over Iraq, was in a strong position to honour his pledge to tackle the Arab–Israeli conflict. His prestige was at its height and this was a unique opportunity to deal with it. So, soon after the war, he dispatched his Secretary of State, James Baker, to the Middle East, tasking him with arranging an international peace conference, where the direct participants would be Israel, Syria, Lebanon, Jordan and the Palestinians; the latter group was to be represented by Palestinian leaders from the occupied territories, rather than the PLO, with whom Israel refused to negotiate. It took Baker eight exhausting months just to persuade the parties to attend a peace conference in Spain to tackle their differences.

The Madrid peace conference from 30 October to 1 November 1991 was the most significant breakthrough in Arab–Israeli peace efforts since President Anwar Sadat's historic visit to Israel in 1977, which led to the end of the Sinai occupation and to the signing of the first peace treaty between Israel and an Arab nation. Now Israelis and their Arab enemies would sit together around the same table to negotiate; all this to take place under the auspices of the United States and the Soviet Union – the latter more of a decorative ornament, as it was a superpower in decline – with the EU and Egypt as full participants and the UN – so distrusted by Israel – as a mere observer.

In his speech to the conference, Shamir declared that 'We pray that this meeting will mark the beginning of a new chapter in the history of the Middle East', but he then qualified his words:

> We know our partners to the negotiations will make territorial demands on Israel, but, as examination of the conflict's long history makes clear, its nature is not territorial. The conflict raged long before Israel acquired Judea, Samaria, Gaza and the Golan in a defensive war. There was no

hint of recognition of Israel before the 1967 war, when the territories in question were not under Israel's control.[7]

Unlike the Israeli delegation, which was led by the prime minister, who went there to protect the assets rather than compromising them, the Syrian was led by Farouk al-Shara, the foreign minister – as narrow-minded as Shamir – who repeated the basic Syrian demand for a full Israeli withdrawal from the entire Golan Heights, and from all other lands under Israeli occupation.

The Palestinian delegation, which was formally part of the Jordanian delegation, was headed by Haidar abdel-Shafi from the Gaza Strip, who called for an end to the Israeli occupation and then listed the most important matters to the Palestinians, namely, establishment of a Palestinian state with Arab East Jerusalem as its capital, and permission for Palestinian refugees who had fled their homes in what was now Israel to return to Israel proper. Although Arafat was not allowed to participate in the conference he was there in spirit, and he made sure to demonstrate, at least to the Palestinian representatives, that he was still in charge. Ghassan Khatib, of the Palestinian delegation, recalls how from Madrid the Palestinians were taken by car to an unstated destination where, on arrival, they found themselves in front of a plane. 'Only when we were on board the plane,' he recalls, 'were we told that we were going to Tunis . . . and there we found Arafat.'[8] Arafat had made his point – he was the one calling the shots.

Often the two days at Madrid resembled a battlefield more than a peace conference and at one stage when the war of words between the parties nearly led to the disintegration of the entire enterprise, Secretary of State Baker had to beg the participants to act more responsibly. 'If you do not seize this historic opportunity,' he urged them, 'no one else will.'[9]

And yet, in spite of the foul atmosphere, the Madrid conference was far from a failure as it managed to create a two-track mechanism for future negotiations, ensuring that rather than a one-off meeting, the summit would become the first phase in a peace process.

The first track was multilateral, where Israel, regional Arab states and other nations outside the region could join in discussions about five key Middle Eastern matters: water, environment, arms control, refugees and economic development; these multilateral talks would commence in Moscow in January 1992. The second – and by far more important track of negotiations – was to be a bilateral one to be held in Washington, where Israel would negotiate separately with each of its Arab neighbours – Syria, Lebanon, Jordan and the Palestinians, the latter continuing to be strictly non-PLO. The Israelis hoped that the local Palestinian leaders would gradually gain stature, sideline the 'outsiders' – the PLO of Tunis – and conclude a peace deal with Israel.

Washington talks

But as talks started in Washington it became apparent that this was wishful thinking since the Palestinian 'insiders' remained highly dependent on the PLO for guidance and instructions, as they had been from the start of this process in Madrid. Furthermore, if Israel hoped that the 'insiders' would be flexible then this also proved to be a wrong-headed assumption as, at the negotiating sessions, the Palestinian negotiators from the occupied territories insisted on discussing the most sensitive issues, the ones Israel would rather leave out, most notably the future status of Jerusalem.

The Israeli–Syrian negotiating room in Washington was similarly stymied. Shamir's representatives showed little magnanimity and no appetite at all to pull out of the occupied Golan, while the Syrians repeated their traditional demand that first, and as a precondition to any negotiations on any other matter related to future Israeli–Syrian relationships, Israel should agree to fully withdraw from the Golan, extending from what the Syrians call the 4 June 1967 line, namely the lines under their control on the eve of the 1967 war.

The catch-22 in the Washington peace negotiations, however, was that Jordan, which had very few issues to settle with Israel, wished to see progress on the Israeli–Palestinian front before it proceeded to sign with Israel, so as not to be blamed for abandoning the Palestinians. Similarly, Lebanon, which had just a few minor territorial issues to settle with Israel, was effectively controlled by the Syrians and could not proceed before the Syrians did. Thus what was really needed in the Washington talks was a breakthrough on the Syrian and Palestinian fronts; alas – on that count – negotiations were similarly not moving forward.

In June 1992, there was a change of leadership in Israel: Shamir's right-wing Likud party was defeated by Yitzhak Rabin's centre-left Labor. It was Rabin's second tenure as prime minister and by now he was more mature and experienced. He pledged, before the general election, that should he form the next government he would strive to reach an agreement with the Palestinians within six to nine months of taking office. This, no doubt, was an ambitious commitment and, indeed, once installed in office, Rabin realized that this was easier said than done, as peace talks in Washington were still deadlocked and an incident on 13 December halted them altogether. On that day, an Israeli soldier was kidnapped and his mutilated body later found; he had been murdered by Hamas militants. The Israeli response to the brutal killing was harsh and out of proportion: the army rounded up 415 Hamas activists in the Palestinian occupied territories, loaded them on buses and drove them to southern Lebanon, which, at the time, was still under Israeli occupation, and abandoned them there on the barren hills. In Washington, in response, the Palestinian delegation walked out of the peace talks, since pressure was mounting on them from Palestinians in the occupied territories not to negotiate with Israel before the 415 activists were allowed to return.

Washington out – Oslo in

About two weeks before the expulsion incident, two people, a Palestinian and an Israeli, who happened to be in London at the same time, met in what would become a milestone in Israeli–Palestinian relations. The Palestinian, Ahmed Qurei, also known as Abu Ala'a, was a PLO member and a close aide of Arafat based in Tunis. The Israeli, Yair Hirschfeld, was a professor of political science, a peace activist and a friend of Yossi Beilin, deputy to the foreign minister, Peres. They were introduced by Hanan Ashrawi, a member of the now suspended Palestinian Washington team, who knew both of them, realized that they would be in London at the same time and suggested that they meet. Acting on her advice, Hirschfeld and Abu Ala'a met at the Cavendish Hotel, near Piccadilly Circus. Hirschfeld arrived early to meet Terje Rød-Larsen, a Norwegian socialist and sometime diplomat with a passionate interest in Israeli–Palestinian relations who also happened to know Abu Ala'a. Larsen, who had heard from Hirschfeld about his forthcoming meeting with the PLO man, suggested that, after meeting Abu Ala'a, and if the two men still wanted to continue the contact, then Larsen would make the necessary arrangements for secret talks to take place in Norway where he was well connected; he then left.

Hirschfeld and Abu Ala'a soon became engaged in conversation and, having discussed how they could help break the stalemate in Washington, they agreed that it was important to meet away from media attention, somewhere where there was no temptation to play to the gallery; they subsequently decided to take advantage of Larsen's offer to meet in Norway. This initial London encounter kicked off what came to be known as the Israeli–Palestinian 'Oslo Channel'.

Back in Tunis, Abu Ala'a reported on his London meetings to Arafat, who was suspicious, but with the Washington talks deadlocked he gave his blessing to the continuation of informal talks, indeed adding that two more PLO officials should join Abu Ala'a in Norway. In Israel, at about the same time, Professor Hirschfeld was getting ready to head to Oslo along with Ron Pundak, one of his former students. So while in Washington Palestinians walked out of talks because of the Hamas December expulsion, in Tunisia and Israel a group of Palestinians and Israelis were getting ready for a secret meeting in Norway. On 22 January 1993, they met in Oslo, where they decided to focus on Gaza first.[10] The idea of starting with Gaza, ending the occupation there and handing it over to the Palestinians so that they could rule themselves, had been floating around for some time now. Gaza was small and relatively self-contained, and giving it up did not pose major security problems to Israel of the same kind as the West Bank; it would make an ideal experiment for Palestinian self-rule.

The idea had been suggested before but the Palestinians had always been suspicious that the Israelis sought to give them Gaza, which was riddled with problems, as a sop, while holding on to the West Bank for ever. For now the matter was not resolved, but, all in all, this first meeting in Norway went well, demonstrating that secret talks have an advantage over open negotiations (like in the now suspended Washington talks); after two more days, the delegates left Oslo and returned home. In Tunis, Abu Ala'a reported to Arafat that the Israelis were serious, while in Israel Hirschfeld reported to the deputy foreign minister, Beilin, who encouraged him to draft a DOP – a Declaration of Principles. Such a text, listing the principles on which a future deal between Israelis and Palestinians could be based, might concentrate the minds of the negotiators in Oslo.

Meeting again in Oslo, Hirschfeld showed the DOP to the Palestinians. At the heart of this document, which the negotiators now turned into the main working paper in Oslo, was the idea of trying to end the Israeli occupation and strike a peace deal on the basis of interim accords – a gradual process, focusing first on areas where there was already more agreement between the parties (such as the future of the Gaza Strip), and leaving the complicated issues to the end of the process. The strategy here was that a gradual process, whereby Israel relinquished land and the Palestinians maintained law and order in the evacuated areas, could enhance confidence and trust and lead to a situation where, within five years, the parties could address the harder issues of their conflict such as the future of Arab East Jerusalem.

In Israel, shortly after, Beilin finally told his boss, Peres, about the meetings with 'Palestinians from Tunis' (meaning the banned PLO) in Oslo. With the talks in Washington still deadlocked, and Rabin's self-imposed pre-election deadline to reach a deal with the Palestinians within six to nine months fast approaching, Peres went to see the prime minister, telling him: 'The talks in Washington have no chance. They're dead. Washington's become a place for exchanging declarations, not for negotiations.'[11] He then informed the prime minister of the two *meshugoim* ('crackpots') who were meeting PLO representatives in Oslo. Although unimpressed, Rabin would not stop the Oslo talks and allowed them to continue.

The March 1993 closure

Meanwhile, back in the occupied territories, tensions between Palestinians and the army were growing, reaching a climax in March 1993 when Palestinian activists killed fifteen Israelis. The army reacted forcefully by dissecting the Palestinian occupied territories into four areas: the north and south of the West Bank, East Jerusalem and the Gaza Strip. They then sealed off the areas from each other and from Israel, imposing a closure that went on for weeks, inflicting a devastating blow on all aspects of Palestinian life. Medical services, for instance, were hit hard, as was the case in such places as the Al Maqassed Hospital in East Jerusalem.

A general hospital serving the population of the West Bank and Gaza Strip and which offered special services not available in other hospitals in the territories, Al Maqassed lost not only many of its patients, but also staff – doctors, nurses and technicians, who could not travel freely, particularly from the Gaza Strip, from where motor vehicles were not allowed to depart. The closure led to a sharp decline in the number of outpatient visits, hospital admissions and surgical operations performed. During the first three weeks of the closure, only approximately 44 per cent of the usual number of patients used outpatient facilities and the number of persons admitted to the hospital declined by 20 per cent. There was also a 50 per cent decline in the number of women residents of the West Bank who gave birth at Al Maqassed Hospital, many now being forced to give birth at home.[12]

The closure also hit the educational system across the Palestinian occupied territories, where teachers and pupils, unable to travel, found it difficult to get to schools. Aref Abdallah al-Khatib, from the village of Hizmeh (4,000 people), in the central West Bank, describes the difficulties caused by the closure: 'The high school-age girls study in Beit Hanina in East Jerusalem, some 8 kilometres from the village,' he explains.

On 19 April, 1993, the army placed a roadblock at the entrance of the village, preventing the girls from reaching school by foot. In addition, some 30 high school students who live in the village and study in various schools in East Jerusalem and Ramallah are unable to get to school. There are some seventy 3–4 year-old children in the village who attend nursery school in Beit Hanina. Since the erection of the roadblock, these children have been unable to reach school. There are teachers at the boys' school who live in Ramallah. These teachers are held up every morning at the roadblock on the Jerusalem–Ramallah road, and thus school begins late every day.[13]

The closure also had a dramatic impact on the Palestinian economy. In its first two months, the primary source of purchasing power in the Gaza Strip turned out to be the monthly salaries of UNRWA, the UN arm operating in the occupied Palestinian lands and employing Palestinians, and civil administration employees. These salaries amounted to $5m per month, a small sum in comparison to a monthly loss of $19m in wages normally paid to 130,000 Palestinian labourers now barred from getting into Israel to work. What made a bad situation even worse was that Gaza's small subcontractors working for the Israeli textile industry were forced to stop production, as the closure prevented them from purchasing raw materials in Israel. So dire was the situation in the occupied territories as a result of the Israeli measures that overall food purchases, except for essential commodities, declined by a massive 50–70 per cent; purchases of items such as clothing plummeted by almost 90 per cent.

There were other economic calamities too: by the end of May Gaza's citrus sector, which, after wages earned in Israel, was the most important source of income for the Strip economy, was hit due to shipping delays caused by the closure. While the army did issue export permits to Jordan, these were valid for only a week, and as security checks at the Allenby Bridge, the border crossing between the West Bank and Jordan, were particularly long, it exceeded the length of the permits. Trucks carrying Gaza produce were caught on the West Bank, unable to cross into Jordan, their cargo of fruit and vegetables rotting and the vehicles themselves detained by the military; towards the end of May, one hundred trucks, accounting for 25 per cent of the entire Palestinian fleet, were detained, resulting in between 25,000 and 30,000 tons of Valencia oranges remaining unpicked, left to rot on the Gaza trees.

Since they were adamantly opposed to Palestinian workers returning to their jobs in Israel, the Israelis tried to create jobs in the Gaza Strip instead, as they realized that unemployment breeds resentment and this would be directed against the occupation. So the military government started employing Palestinians to clean streets and beaches, paint signs, whitewash and dig ditches; by July 1993, 8,700 workers in Gaza and 7,500 in the West Bank were employed as street cleaners and painters, were paid a daily wage of $9, which was half of what they could earn in Israel, and were usually employed for no more than fifteen days at a time.

In the meantime, taking advantage of the closure, the army increased its efforts to search for wanted persons, in the process inflicting terrible atrocities on the Palestinians. Here is the testimony of Bashir Ibrahim Abdallah Rantisi, a 35-year-old Palestinian whose brother, Nabil, had been wanted by the Security Forces:

> On 6 April, 1993, at 3:30 a.m., soldiers knocked at the gate of the house. I got up and opened the gate. The soldiers came in and asked me about Nabil. I said that he wasn't home. They asked where his room was, and I showed it to them. The door of the room was not locked, but they broke it with their guns ... The soldiers dispersed to all the rooms, and began overturning closets and mixing different kinds of food. My brother 'Abd al-Halim was beaten during the search. The soldiers gave him a soup spoon, and ordered him to dig a trench 1.5 meters into the floor. The soldiers spilled three bags of sugar onto the floor, and one soldier gathered some sugar with his hands and sprinkled it onto the knitting machine. One of the soldiers went up onto the roof of the house, where there is a little chicken coop containing a few chickens. He gathered eggs from the coops, went into Nabil's room, and began throwing the eggs at the walls. The soldier broke one egg into a cup, mixed it with bulgur he had taken from the kitchen, opened the lid of the sewing machine, and poured the mixture into the machine. The soldiers left after approximately 3 hours. The soldiers confiscated two axes we use for chopping meat, and took my brother, 'Abd al-Halim, with them ...[144]

This so called 'March Closure' turned out to be one of the occupation's most traumatic periods for the Palestinians.

BACK TO THE NEGOTIATING TABLE

On 27 April 1993, the ninth round of the Washington talks resumed for the first time after the December 1992 Hamas expulsion crisis, and in Oslo, three days later, Israelis and Palestinians met, but now the PLO Oslo team demanded that the Israelis should upgrade the talks. The reason was that, more than three months since the launch of the Oslo talks, Abu Ala'a and his supervisors in Tunis were still unsure whether Professor Hirschfeld and his colleague, Pundak, were officially representing Israel, or bluffing and simply running their own show.

In Israel, the foreign minister, Peres, discussed the PLO demand with the prime minister and they agreed to send a high-level civil servant – Uri Savir, the director general of the Foreign Ministry, which meant that now the Oslo channel had turned from an academic exercise into an official, albeit secret, engagement between the government of the State of Israel and the PLO (not yet formally recognized by the Israelis as representing the Palestinians). Soon, the prime minister added a lawyer by the name of Yoel Singer to the Israeli Oslo team and he himself became involved in coordinating the talks, holding meetings with the Oslo team every Friday afternoon. Mossad, the Israeli intelligence agency, became involved too, by providing the prime minister with critical information from the heart of the PLO headquarters in Tunis. Using one of its agents, a Palestinian by the name of Adnan Yassin, Mossad managed to move a couch and a desk lamp in which microphones were hidden into the office of Arafat's deputy, Abu Mazen, who, along with Arafat, was supervising the Oslo talks. With this critical information at his fingertips, Rabin was able to direct his Oslo negotiators and let them know what to expect from the Palestinian negotiators in the Oslo talks.[15]

By the beginning of August, a draft agreement was ready and accepted by Rabin in Jerusalem and the PLO's leader, Arafat, in Tunis, but some stumbling blocks remained that needed a resolution by the top decision makers in Israel and Tunis. The next crucial moment came in mid-August.

Clinching the deal

Shimon Peres, who had a pre-scheduled trip to Scandinavia, asked the Oslo team's lawyer, Singer, to join him in Sweden to work on the endgame. From Stockholm, Peres phoned Terje Rød-Larsen, the Norwegian facilitator, asking him to come to Stockholm with the Norwegian foreign minister, Johan Holst, who was also deeply involved in the secret negotiations. As Peres himself did not want to speak to Arafat in order not to commit Israel in case the deal collapsed, he asked Holst to be his mouthpiece. With Arafat and his team on the line in Tunis, and Peres, an aide and Singer in Stockholm, they were ready to start negotiating the last remaining points that had prevented the signing of an Israeli–Palestinian agreement. These concerned sensitive issues such as the fate of Jerusalem, refugees, borders, settlements and more, which the Israelis did not even want to mention in the document, unlike the Palestinians, who insisted on having these issues written down and tackled.

They started negotiating in a phone relay late at night; Holst would convey the Israeli position to Tunis, and in Stockholm they would then wait for the Palestinians to call back after conferring with Arafat and others. This climax of the Oslo secret channel was an exercise in painful compromise. The Israelis eventually agreed to mention the sensitive issues of Jerusalem, refugees and settlements in the text, as long as Arafat agreed that discussion of these issues be deferred for future negotiations in order not to bog down the entire process. The thinking was that, over time, as conditions improved for most Palestinians, relationships could be strengthened and suspicions broken down, thereby making the tougher questions easier to resolve – in hindsight, however, things did not turn out that way. Another stumbling block the negotiators now tackled was the control of the crossing points from Egypt to the Gaza Strip and from Jordan to Jericho; Israel sought full control of these crossings to ensure that no weapons or unwanted people passed into the territories under Palestinian jurisdiction. However, control of borders is a symbol of sovereignty and the Palestinians would not concede on this. Eventually, they agreed on the ambiguous formula that the final agreement would include arrangements for coordination between both parties regarding passages; other remaining unresolved issues were tackled in the same pragmatic way.

But what made Israelis and Palestinians succeed in Oslo where they had failed in Washington? One reason was Arafat's fear that local Palestinian leaders, negotiating in Washington, might succeed in striking a deal with Israel, shunning him as the leading Palestinian leader. Another reason was that the parties negotiated in secret, rather than playing to the gallery; indeed, the French diplomat Jules Cambon was right when he observed that the day secrecy is abolished, negotiation of any kind would become impossible.

All that was needed now was an official mutual recognition between the PLO and the State of Israel; the Israelis still regarded the PLO as a terrorist organization and until that point would not, officially, speak to it. This recognition was finally achieved on 9 September, when Arafat sent a letter to Rabin confirming that the PLO recognized the State of Israel, was committed to the peace process, and renounced the use of terrorism and other acts of violence. Arafat also affirmed that those articles of the Palestinian Covenant which denied Israel's right to exist were no longer valid. In response, the prime minister sent a letter saying: 'Mr Chairman, I write to confirm that, in the light of the PLO commitments outlined in your letter, the Government of Israel has decided to recognize the PLO as the representative of the Palestinian people and will commence negotiations with the PLO within the Middle East peace process.'[16] With that, the Israeli government and the PLO could publicly sign the Oslo agreement. They would do so, however, not in small Norway, but in Washington, thus letting the superpower lend the moment significant clout.

A handshake

On the day of the signing ceremony in Washington, on 13 September, the two parties gathered in the Blue Room of the White House. In an interview with the author, the US Secretary of State, Warren Christopher, recalled the events of the day:

> I watched the parties . . . it seemed that Arafat and Rabin were circling the room to avoid each other, their tension was so high . . . I was afraid that when the ceremony took place there would not be a handshake and the president was concerned about the same thing. Finally I summoned up my courage and went over to Prime Minister Rabin and I said, 'You know, Prime Minister, when we get out on the lawn you'll be expected to meet him and greet him out there.' He said, 'I'll do the right thing when I have to' . . . very gruffly.[17]

On the White House lawn, the audience was waiting in the blazing sun. Behind the scenes, Arafat and Rabin were still standing well apart from each other. But when the time came for the ceremony, they moved closer and, together with President Bill Clinton, they then walked across the lawn for the historic signing. The foreign minister, Peres, and the Palestinian leader, Abu Mazen, signed the agreement and then, with Rabin on President Clinton's right and Arafat on the president's left, Arafat made the first move and stretched out his hand to Rabin. President Clinton, placing his hand on Rabin's back, gently encouraged the prime minister to move closer and shake Arafat's hand. When the author interviewed the foreign minister several years later, he recalled Rabin's emotions on that day:

> Rabin didn't want to shake Arafat's hand. It was terrible. The whole world was watching, and could see from Rabin's body language that he did not want to look at Arafat. Finally, though, Rabin shook his hand and Arafat, who is an expert in these matters, hung on to it. After he had finished shaking Rabin's hand, Arafat turned to me, and Rabin whispered in my ear, 'Now it's your turn.' He had gone through hell; now it was my turn.[18]

*

The importance of the text signed in Washington – the Declaration of Principles – cannot be overestimated, as it introduced a novel approach to the solution of the Israeli–Palestinian conflict: gone was the Jordanian option, whereby it was assumed that Jordan could take responsibility for Palestinians' affairs; gone was the autonomy idea for the Palestinians proposed by the former prime minister Menachem Begin in the negotiations with Egypt in 1977–9, which he himself later abandoned. What was now introduced was something the Palestinians had long sought and which, for so long, had been rejected by the Israelis: a two-state solution. True, in the text which was signed in Washington there is no mention of the words 'Palestinian state', and this, later, led to much suspicion that Israel wished to *reorganize* the occupation rather than to end it; that it sought to throw the Palestinians some crumbs in the shape of a limited autonomy, rather than provide them with full independence. What, indeed, exacerbated these doubts was the fact that in coming negotiations which were aimed at turning the text signed in Washington into an action plan, the Israelis would insist on not allowing any symbols of independence to be introduced by the Palestinians: Arafat would not be called 'President', but 'Rais' (which can be translated into 'head'), the Palestinian executive would be called the 'Palestinian Authority' (PA) rather than the 'National Palestinian Authority', and the lands under Palestinian rule would have no international dialling code of their own. But, as Yoram Meital rightly notes, 'most observers concurred that the parties had in fact endorsed a blueprint for the two-state solution . . . no longer a mere autonomy'.[19] And yet, one cannot ignore the fact that the agreement was between two unequal partners: a hugely powerful Israel – militarily and otherwise – and a relatively weak Palestinian body. This imbalance of power, which put Israel in a stronger bargaining position at Oslo and after, was inscribed into the Declaration of Principles through its unequal *timing* of concessions. For while the Palestinians had to act first in providing Israel with what it needed, their own most cherished needs – independence, removal of the occupation and a just solution to the refugee problems – would only come at a much later stage in the process and require more negotiations.

Perhaps the most noticeable benefit for Israel in the wake of the Washington signing was a halt to the Palestinian *intifada*, as one of the agreement's clauses called on the Palestinians, though indirectly, to end their uprising. For the Palestinians, the *intifada* was a long and bloody affair which lost much of its energy as early as 1991, but continued to bubble under the surface well into 1992 and 1993. Statistics show that in the period from December 1987, when the first stones of the uprising started flying, and the signing in September 1993 which marked the end of it, more than 1,000 Palestinians were killed by the army. Thousands more were injured, and 1,473 Palestinian houses were demolished by the army. The Palestinian uprising had been a hugely effective tool in putting pressure on the Israelis to compromise, but now it had to stop; and with that Palestinians lost an important lever, at a time when Israel kept in its hands all the as-yet-to-be-delivered big promises to the Palestinians.

Oslo II – the action plan

The Washington signing was over, but the efforts that had gone into the agreement had resulted in no more than a framework – a Declaration of Principles. It set out core concepts on which a peace agreement could be built, but was not the peace agreement itself; it was merely a guide to subsequent negotiations: first, Yasser Arafat would take control of the Gaza Strip and Jericho area; next, an interim agreement would have to be concluded to extend his rule to other Palestinian areas; two further agreements would then be needed to govern the Israeli army's further redeployments from Palestinian areas; and, finally, negotiations would be held on a permanent settlement of the conflict that would resolve the final borders, the disposition of settlements, a solution to the refugee problem and the future of holy shrines in Jerusalem.

The first item to be negotiated was the withdrawal of the army from the Gaza Strip and Jericho area, and the transfer of these to Palestinian control. On 4 May 1994, Israel and the PLO signed the Gaza–Jericho Agreement (see map 6), which saw an Israeli withdrawal from large tracts of the Gaza Strip (though not from the settlements and military bases there) and from the town of Jericho on the West Bank, and the opening of the gates of Palestine to Arafat. Dressed in his usual military fatigues and *kefiya* headdress, Arafat returned to Gaza on 1 July, after decades in exile, to take over control of Palestinian affairs and head the Palestinian Authority, a quasi-state body. 'Now I am returning to the first free Palestinians lands,' Arafat declared. 'You have to imagine how it is moving my heart, my feelings.'

· By August, the Palestinian Authority had taken upon itself responsibility for the Palestinian educational system, health institutions and social welfare organizations. It began regulating, licensing, supervising, and developing the tourist industry and started collecting income tax. Salaries for all public servants were now paid by the PA, thus radically scaling down direct contact between the Israelis and the Palestinians.

Despite these achievements, a growing disappointment was felt among many Palestinians that even with the army withdrawal from some areas, the occupation in effect continued. This was not untrue: in education, for instance, Israel continued to have a say about the Palestinian curriculum, and could veto the inclusion of certain topics, particularly in disciplines such as history and geography. As far as the Palestinian legal system was concerned there were also severe limitations, as Arafat's Palestinian Authority could only confirm secondary legislation and the Palestinian judicial position was effectively subordinated to Israel. In the economic sphere, Arafat's Palestinian Authority had even less autonomy: although the Paris Protocol on Economic Relations signed between Israel and the PLO in April 1994 presented the economic relations between Israel and the Palestinian Authority as if these were relations between two equal parties, in practice it reflected more of the unequal relations that had existed during the occupation. So although 1994 is seen as a critical time in Palestinian history when they effectively started ruling themselves, on the ground it was a very limited self-rule, confined to a very little geographical area – some of the Gaza Strip and the Jericho area – and which existed in the shadow of a continuing Israeli occupation.

In early 1995, negotiations began on further Israeli withdrawals from occupied West Bank lands, which were to become known as the Oslo II talks. Here, the task was much more complicated as, unlike the Gaza Strip, where there were only a dozen or so Jewish settlements, on the West Bank there were more than a hundred settlements, which Israel would not abandon at this stage. A further complication was that the West Bank included Hebron, the second most sacred town for Jews and also holy to Muslims, and where 400 Jews – the hard core of Jewish settlers, many of them extremists – lived alongside a huge majority Arab population.

For now, the Israeli and Palestinian negotiators decided to divide the West Bank into three areas (see map 7). The first, which they called 'Area A', comprised about 3 per cent of the West Bank and included all Palestinian cities and their surrounding areas, with no Israeli settlements at all. This area, they decided, would come under full Palestinian Authority control – the PA would be allowed to run all spheres of life there. The second area they called 'Area B'; it comprised about 25 per cent of the West Bank and included many Palestinian towns and villages, but no Israeli settlements; in this area, they decided, Arafat's PA would be responsible for civilian matters: education, health and so on, and there would be joint Israeli–Palestinian security control. Lastly, 72 per cent of the West Bank, to be called 'Area C', where all the settlements were built and there were hardly any Palestinians at all, would continue to be ruled by the Israelis. The idea was that over time more and more 'B' and 'C' areas would be transferred to Palestinian rule to become their Palestinian state.

On 28 September, the 314-page Oslo II Agreement was signed in Washington and during the following months Israeli troops withdrew from six major West Bank cities and hundreds of villages, transferring them to Palestinian control.

When the army left, however, transferring responsibility for Palestinian populations to Arafat's Palestinian Authority, it soon became apparent that Arafat and the ministers who now ran the PA, mainly members of the Fatah movement, the biggest Palestinian political faction within the PLO, were not ready for governance, and they had no solid institutions at their disposal to look after the welfare of the Palestinians, who now came under their responsibility. In his book *The Iron Cage*, the Palestinian scholar Rashid Khalidi observed that 'it is not entirely surprising that this should have been the case: most of the leaders of the PLO, from Arafat on down, had spent their entire careers in the atmosphere of a clandestine, underground liberation movement, and proved to be poorly suited for the task of state building, for transparent governance, or for a stable structure of governance based on law'.[20]

What further distracted Arafat and the Palestinian leadership from the task in hand was their growing suspicion that they had fallen into an Israeli trap, and that Israel had no intention of completely withdrawing from the remaining occupied lands, mainly from areas 'B' and 'C'. They had good reason to be suspicious, as the Israelis, although they did draw their forces back from some areas, went on to construct bypass roads to enable Jewish settlers to travel between settlements without having to pass through the areas now controlled by the Palestinian Authority. This, ironically, increased – and quite dramatically – the number of settlers since, not having to cross through Palestinian-populated areas, they felt safer than before and, as a result, many more joined the settlements, which expanded massively during this period. And as more land was needed to build new settlements for the newcomers, and land was also needed to construct the new network of bypass roads – which was designed exclusively for the use of Jewish settlers and from where Palestinians were barred – it was expropriated from Palestinians. Thus, surrounded by a thick system of new roads and many new settlements and settlers, Palestinians, particularly on the West Bank, felt more and more as though they were living in small cantons isolated from each other, and that the occupation – rather than ending – was hardening.

THE SONG OF PEACE

On 4 November, Rabin attended a rally in support of the peace process in Tel Aviv. Also attending that night was a right-wing Jewish zealot, Yigal Amir, who angrily opposed the concessions made by the prime minister to the Palestinians and Israeli withdrawals. Amir was armed with a gun, which was not uncommon in Israel. The following is the testimony of Peres to the author in an interview for the BBC TV series *The Fifty Years War*, describing what happened on this dramatic evening:

> When we came to the rally Yitzhak [Rabin] could not believe his eyes. It was an immense rally attended by tens of thousands of people. And he was overjoyed. I had never, in my life, seen him so happy. We had known each other for fifty years and he had never, never hugged me. At the rally, for the first time in his life, he hugged me. I had never heard him singing before. But, at the rally, he stood and sang . . . Yitzhak was given a paper with the words of the 'Song of Peace' written on it. After we had sung, he folded it and put it in his jacket pocket . . . When the rally was over . . . we said goodbye to each other. I began to descend the staircase. My car was parked a little way in front of Yitzhak's . . . I got into my car, closed the door, and then suddenly heard three shots. 'Stop,' I said to my driver. I wanted to get out. But my security men said: 'Absolutely not.' And, sounding the sirens, they drove away wildly. We didn't know yet what had happened. We only knew that Yitzhak was being taken to hospital. I demanded to be taken there immediately. The head of the hospital came to me and said that Yitzhak was dead.

Grief-stricken, Peres went to the room, where, as he describes:

> Yitzhak was lying on the bed. His body was covered with a sheet up to his shoulders. On his face was an expression of peace – and an ironical sort of a smile, a special smile. I kissed his forehead and said: 'Goodbye'.[21]

*

The assassination of the prime minister did not kill the Israeli–Palestinian peace process, but it did significantly slow it down, robbing it of much of its vitality and momentum. Rabin, as shown, was not the original brains behind the Oslo process, as those who initially negotiated it did so without his knowledge, let alone his approval. But when Rabin did eventually identify the potential of the Oslo process, compared with the stalled Washington talks, he took over and directed it personally. Above all, he was the leader trusted by the majority of Israelis to combine peace with security; and his death now was certain to create a vacuum which it would be difficult to fill.

9
Missed Opportunities, 1995–1999

Rabin was succeeded for a short time by his Labor colleague Peres, but, keen to get a direct mandate from the people rather than be seen merely as Rabin's successor, Peres called for new elections. It was a high-risk strategy, in particular for Peres, who had a history of losing general elections – in fact, he never won a single national election in his life. Now, again, even with national sympathy at its height in the wake of Rabin's death, Peres lost the election to the right-wing Likud party, led by Benjamin Netanyahu.

At the age of forty-six, Netanyahu, affectionately known as Bibi, was articulate and well-spoken. He was the first Israeli prime minister born in Israel after the founding of the state but spent many years in the United States, where his father, Ben Zion Netanyahu, was a university professor. For many years Netanyahu lived in the shadow of his older brother, Yonatan, who was killed in 1976 while serving as the commander of the elite army unit Sayeret Matkal during a hostage-rescue mission ('Operation Entebbe'), in which his unit rescued more than 100 hostages hijacked by Palestinians to Uganda. Although Benjamin Netanyahu himself was not a war hero, he did, nonetheless, participate in the 1967 and the 1973 wars and as a commando he took part in small operations behind enemy lines. Where he did excel was in diplomacy; he held many diplomatic posts and came to be known as the eloquent Israeli ambassador to the United Nations from 1984 to 1988.

Now, as the new prime minister of Israel, Netanyahu surrounded himself with tough Likud party ministers, such as Ariel Sharon and Benjamin Begin, son of the late prime minister, Menachem Begin. While Netanyahu acknowledged that he would have to proceed with the Oslo peace process and respect agreements signed by his predecessors, he did so only begrudgingly. It was not only that he inherited a peace process which he had aggressively opposed while in opposition, but he also struggled to conceal his extreme disdain for Arafat. And while, after his election victory, Netanyahu rang Egypt's president Hosni Mubarak, Jordan's King Hussein and other world leaders to talk to them, he could not bring himself to phone Arafat.

Terje Rød-Larsen, the UN envoy who had been instrumental in facilitating the Oslo agreements, was now working behind the scenes to bring Netanyahu and Arafat together. He saw the prime minister on 16 August 1996 and informed him that '[Arafat] is keen to meet up with you . . .'[1] And although Netanyahu remained reluctant, he realized he could not avoid it; after all, Israel had officially recognized the PLO as the legitimate representative of the Palestinian people and Arafat was now in charge of the Palestinian Authority in the areas evacuated by Israel.

The two leaders finally met on 4 September 1996, at Erez, on the border between Israel and the Gaza Strip. It was a civilized affair, more of a photo opportunity than any serious discussion of substance, but it passed by seemingly without incident.

THE TUNNEL RIOTS

Soon after, however, all hell broke loose when, on 24 September, Netanyahu approved excavations that would open an ancient Herodian tunnel located at a particularly sensitive place underneath Jerusalem's Old City, running from the Western Wall plaza close to the mosques on Haram al-Sharif. For years Israel had kept the tunnel's northern entrance near the Via Dolorosa closed to avoid provoking Palestinians, who were suspicious of any Israeli attempt to change the status quo in Jerusalem, or even to dig under the Haram al-Sharif lest this was in order to cause its mosques and shrines to collapse. However, its having only one entrance meant that visitors to the tunnel were forced to return the same way they entered, squeezing past people moving in the other direction; opening the northern exit at Via Dolorosa would thus ease congestion and enable visitors to enter the tunnel's southern entrance, walk its length and get out through its far end without having to retrace their steps. But it was no secret that by allowing the Via Dolorosa entrance in the Muslim quarter of the Old City to be opened, the prime minister also wished to make a political statement regarding Israel's claims to Jerusalem, and to express, as he put it, 'our sovereignty over Jerusalem'.[2]

The Palestinians got the message loud and clear. Arafat called for a mass demonstration against the act and a general strike, claiming that opening the entrance was a 'big crime against our religious and holy places'.[3] When the entrance was opened, a battle between Palestinian militants and Israeli police duly ensued in which the number of casualties was staggering: seventy-nine Palestinians and fifteen Israelis were killed, and hundreds more lay injured in hospital; it was the worst fatal incident of its kind in East Jerusalem since its occupation by Israel in 1967. The prime minister, on a visit in Europe at the time, cut short his trip and rushed back home to address the crisis. From the airport, as he told the author in an interview, he phoned Arafat, warning him that should the Palestinian leader fail to quieten the streets and stop Palestinian rioters then Israel would 'bring in tanks' to fight the rioters.[4] What Netanyahu expected Arafat to do was to put down Palestinian riots which the prime minister himself had provoked; no wonder that Arafat was reluctant to cooperate.

In Washington, in the meantime, President Bill Clinton was deeply distressed over the derailment of the peace process. He urged the prime minister to reconsider his decision to meddle with the tunnel, and then summoned him and Arafat to the White House to discuss how they could resolve the crisis. In a pre-meeting with Secretary of State Warren Christopher, Netanyahu insisted that he would not close the tunnel; otherwise, as he put it: 'Arafat will conclude that whenever he is unhappy with Israel's moves it is worthwhile for him to resort to violence . . .'[5] Later, in the White House Map Room, Clinton brought the two leaders together and, after a heated debate, a degree of compromise emerged: while Netanyahu would not reverse the situation in Jerusalem, he would compensate Arafat, indirectly, by pledging to give new momentum to negotiations on the town of Hebron, a left-over obligation from the previous Israeli government.

DIVIDING HEBRON

As we have seen, ancient Hebron, the traditional birthplace of the biblical patriarch Abraham, is a city sacred to Jews and Muslims alike. While between 1929 and 1967 very few Jews lived in Hebron, after its capture from Jordan in 1967 Jewish settlers began gradually to penetrate its centre, and by the 1990s a Jewish community of some 450 lived there alongside 150,000 Palestinians. Armed with guns given to them by the army, the Jewish settlers of Hebron have always been among the most extreme, violent and abusive of all settler communities. They have routinely abused the city's Palestinian residents; beating them, hurling refuse at them, destroying their shops, chopping down their olive trees, poisoning their water wells, breaking into their homes and even killing them. They were able to do this not only because they were armed, but also because the army was on their side and when their provocations escalated the military would often attempt to calm down the situation by locking the Arabs up in their houses and imposing curfews on them.

Their open hostility to the Palestinians reached a bloody climax in February 1994, when a lone Jewish settler, Dr Baruch Goldstein, wearing army uniform and carrying a gun and hand grenades, entered the Ibrahimi mosque during Friday dawn prayers. Juwayyed Hasan el Jabari, aged thirty-one, was there on the day and recalls how 'A few seconds after we started the prayers, I heard the sound of a big explosion [of a hand grenade] which was followed by showers of gun shots . . .'[6] Opening fire, Goldstein mowed down twenty-nine Muslim worshipers and wounded 125. The Palestinian Nidal Maraca, aged fifteen and at the mosque with his parents and brothers, recalls how 'When I heard the gun shots, I was scared and I fell on the floor. I looked around and saw my brother, Kifah [aged eleven] bleeding. He suffered multiple wounds to the head and next . . . my father [was] bleeding too from his wounds . . . near the shelves where people put their shoes, I saw my classmate, Jabr Abu Hadeed . . . holding his waist . . . he was collapsing on the floor . . . later I realized that my brother died . . . On the next day I learnt that Jabr was dead too . . .'[7] Eventually, the Palestinians in the mosque overpowered Goldstein when he tried to reload his rifle and beat him to death with metal poles and a fire extinguisher. This event, which came to be known as the 'Hebron massacre', had a profoundly negative effect on the already tense relationship between settlers and Palestinians in Hebron.

The Oslo II Agreement signed a year after the Hebron massacre had a specific provision for Hebron: as part of the military redeployment in the West Bank and the Gaza Strip there should also be a withdrawal from Hebron; this was spelled out specifically in Article VII under 'Guidelines for Hebron'. There was also a clear schedule expressed in paragraph 1b of 'Guidelines for Hebron', where it was stated that the Hebron redeployment would be completed not later than six months after the signing of the Oslo II Agreement. However, as was often the case with Israeli–Palestinian deals, this expected withdrawal did not take place on time; while Rabin had been reluctant to handle this hot potato, his successor, Peres, sought to delay the matter until after the next general election. Peres had, in fact, thrown the ball into Arafat's court by saying that before Israel tackled Hebron, Arafat should first cancel the anti-Israeli clauses of the Palestinian Convent, as he had promised to do in the past.[8] Thus, when Netanyahu came to power, the issue of Hebron was still unresolved and by opening the Jerusalem tunnel and causing so much bloodshed, he gave Arafat the opportunity to reopen this unfinished business.

Tough negotiations followed which eventually produced, on 17 January 1997, 'The Hebron Protocol', or 'The Protocol Concerning the Redeployment in Hebron'. It set out the agreed arrangements regarding the military's withdrawal from 80 per cent of Hebron, stating that this had to be carried out and completed within ten days from the signing of the protocol. In the original Oslo II Agreement, paragraph 12 stated that Hebron would continue to be one undivided city, but the new Hebron Protocol effectively reversed this and partitioned the town. Two areas emerged: Area H-1, where the vast majority of people were Palestinian and where their police would take responsibility for internal security and public order; and Area H-2, a smaller district, where Israel would retain security control, comprising a number of Jewish settlement enclaves in downtown Hebron, the settlement of Kiryath Araba, which is just outside Hebron, and the areas surrounding these settlements deemed necessary for the free movement of the settlers and the army; within this area there were also 20,000 Palestinians. The Protocol also defined how joint Israeli–Palestinian mobile patrols would operate in areas of particular sensitivity, for instance in four Jewish holy sites located within the H-1 zone, and defined the number of Palestinian police and type of weapons they would carry.

In the negotiations Arafat insisted on an international presence in Hebron to monitor the implementation of the Protocol – and for good reason. Not only, as mentioned, were the settlers of Hebron notorious for their antagonistic behaviour, but the Goldstein massacre of Palestinians in 1994 left a legacy of mistrust and now Arafat wanted to ensure that an independent body kept an eye on the violent settlers of Hebron, rather than the Israeli military, which had failed to protect Palestinian civilians in the past.

With US pressure on his back, Netanyahu had little choice but to agree to foreign monitors, and an Agreement on the Temporary International Presence in the City of Hebron (TIPH) was signed on 21 January 1997. It authorized an international force of 180 observers from Norway, Italy, Denmark, Sweden, Switzerland and Turkey to come to Hebron to monitor and report on efforts to maintain normal life there.

The Hebron Protocol was significant as it showed that Likud, despite its strong opposition to the Israeli–Palestinian deals since 1993, was still willing, when in power, to implement them, albeit grudgingly, and to endorse effectively the Laborite notion of land for peace. The Hebron deal was, in fact, the first time that Likud had made a territorial concession in the occupied West Bank. It left the polemics of the past behind and affirmed the reality of the Oslo process.

Still, it was sad to see that at a time when cities across the world, from Berlin to Nicosia, were striving to cancel partitions and pull down separation lines, in Hebron a new division was being established, turning the city into a microcosm of the continuing Israeli–Palestinian conflict.

HAR HOMA

Any hopes that Netanyahu might take advantage of the momentum gained by the Hebron deal to continue the process of ending the occupation and striking peace deals with the Palestinians were soon dashed. Netanyahu, as a diplomat once observed, was often like a drunk lurching from lamppost to lamppost and now the next lamppost turned out to be Har Homa, a spot on the south-west border of Palestinian East Jerusalem where, on 28 February 1997, Netanyahu approved the building of 6,500 Jewish housing units on land that was expropriated from its Palestinian owners.[9] He sought to form a ring of large Jewish settlements around East Jerusalem that would effectively detach it from the West Bank – Har Homa would block routes to Bethlehem and Beit Sahour to the south.

Predictably, these new settlements caused an uproar among the Palestinians and riots soon broke out. A month later, when Arafat visited the White House, Netanyahu's Har Homa project was top of his agenda and he urged President Clinton to demand that, at least, the prime minister delay the implementation of the controversial project, but to no avail. Netanyahu proceeded anyway and all Washington did was to dispatch the US ambassador in Israel, Martin Indyk, to deliver a message to the prime minister that the United States regarded the building of the new neighbourhood as 'a step that undermines everything that we are trying to do'.[10]

Jordan's King Hussein was furious at the prime minister's approach – the continued building of settlements and the general violence and lack of respect towards the Palestinians. Jordan, we should recall, had signed a peace treaty with Israel in October 1994, ushering in a new era of peaceful relations, in part, at least, with the expectation that the Oslo process with the Palestinians would continue apace. At the time, in a symbolic gesture of good will, the king's partner for peace, Rabin, allowed Hussein – an amateur pilot – to fly his own aeroplane to Israel in what came to be known as the 'First Flight of Peace'; Rabin even dispatched jets to escort the king's flight when it entered Israel's air space. Now, however, with relations between Israelis and Palestinians at such a low ebb, the king sat down to write a letter to Netanyahu 'for posterity . . . in the face of the unknown'.[11] Here, in full, is the astonishing document:

Amman, March 9 1997

Prime Minister,

My distress is genuine and deep over the accumulating tragic actions which you have initiated at the head of the government of Israel, making peace – the worthiest objective of my life – appear more and more like a distant elusive mirage. I could remain aloof if the very lives of all Arabs and Israelis and their future were not fast sliding towards an abyss of bloodshed and disaster, brought about by fear and despair. I frankly cannot accept your repeated excuse of having to act the way you do under great duress and pressure. I cannot believe that the people of Israel seek bloodshed and disaster and oppose peace. Nor can I believe that the most constitutionally powerful PM in Israel's history would act on other than his total convictions. The saddest reality that has been dawning on me is that I do not find you by my side in working to fulfil God's will for the final reconciliation of all the descendants of the children of Abraham. Your course of actions seems bent on destroying all I believe in or have striven to achieve with the Hashemite family since Faisal the First and Abdullah to the present times. You cannot send me assurances that you would not sanction any further construction of settlements and tell me of your decision to construct two roads to help all concerned – Israelis and Palestinians alike and then renege on your commitment . . .

Mr PM, if it is your intention to manoeuvre our Palestinian brethren into inevitable violent resistance, then order your bulldozers into the proposed settlement [of Har Homa] site without doing much which is needed in recognition of Palestinian and Arab sensitivity, anger and despair . . . [or] order the young Israeli members of your powerful armed forces surrounding Palestinian towns to commit wanton murder and mayhem, possibly resulting in creating yet a fresh exodus of hapless Palestinians from their, and their ancestors', homeland and bury the peace process for all time . . . Why the apparent continued deliberate humiliation of your so-called Palestinian partners? Can any worthwhile relationship thrive in the absence of mutual respect and trust? Why are Palestinians still confirming that their agricultural produces still rot awaiting entry into Israel and export? Why the delay when it is known that unless work is authorized to commence on the Gaza port, before the end of this month, the complete project would suffer a year's delay? Finally, the Gaza Airport – all of us have addressed the subject numerous times with a view to having a legitimate Palestinian need met and to giving their leaders and people their own free access to the world rather than their present confinement and need to exit and return

*through other sovereign territories. I had requested permission and
intended to fly to President Arafat myself, in Jordan's official State
Tristar, to the Palestinian airport of Gaza as I had requested earlier . . .
to fly by a fixed-wing aircraft accepting your refusal then only because
there were far more important issues at hand.*

*I anticipated your positive response this time. I believed it would
have helped improve the atmosphere considerably but, alas, it was not
to be. Now, suppose I had taken off nonetheless for Gaza, in the full
right of a friend, then would you have ordered my fellow pilots in the
Israeli Air Force – those who escorted me on the same aircraft over
Israel in what became known as the First Flight of Peace – it seems so
long ago – to prevent me forcibly from landing or worse? You will
never know how close you came to having to make a decision on the
subject had I, on this occasion, not planned to carry guests back
home. How can I work with you as a partner and true friend in this
confused and confusing atmosphere when I sense an intent to destroy
all I worked to build between our peoples and states. Stubbornness
over real issues is one thing, but for its own sake, I wonder. In any
event I have discovered that you have your own mindset and are in no
need of any advice from a friend.*

*I deeply regret having to write to you this personal message but it is
my sense of responsibility and concern which has prompted me for
posterity to do so in the face of the unknown.*
Sincerely
[Signed King Hussein]

This heartfelt letter demonstrates just how disappointed the king had
become with Netanyahu. Perhaps the king was also looking into the
future, hoping that historians would publish this letter, as some have
already done, to show history that the king of Jordan did his best to
help the Palestinian cause.

ESCALATION

By July 1997, President Clinton had concluded that if he failed to rein
in Netanyahu's settlement building and Arafat's propensity to wriggle

out of his previous commitments on halting attacks and incitement against Israel, then the entire Oslo enterprise might well unravel. He dispatched his Middle East emissary, Dennis Ross, to Israel with a personal, emphatic letter to the prime minister, urging him to help revive the broken negotiating process. Clinton explained that Ross was in Israel discreetly and emphasized that he felt that this was a particularly dangerous juncture.

As polite as this letter was, however, it also signified a new American initiative, which Ross went on to present to the prime minister. At the heart of it was the idea that Israel should freeze construction of new settlements at Har Homa and elsewhere, which was like a red rag to a bull for the Palestinians, and stick to expanding only existing settlements; Israel should also rebuild security cooperation with the Palestinians, and make more troop withdrawals from the West Bank as envisaged in the Oslo II Agreement between the parties. The Palestinians, in return, would have to improve their security performance and both put a stop to attacks on Israel and desist from inciting such attacks.

Netanyahu resisted Clinton's programme, as he felt that he was being asked for more concessions than Arafat. He sent Ross back to Washington with a message to the president that Israel could not accept the new US initiative as it was, but 'if you want we will agree to further talks'.[12] Netanyahu then dispatched his government secretary, Dan Naveh, to Washington for further discussions on the initiative with Dennis Ross. But it was too little and too late as by now – deeply resentful of Israeli tactics, particularly the continued expropriation of Palestinian land and the building of settlements – the Palestinians resorted to violence. On 30 July 1997, two suicide bombers, members of the Islamist movement Hamas, explosives strapped to their bodies, blew themselves up in the heart of Jerusalem, killing sixteen and injuring 200; it was a devastating attack and the first for a year. It also killed the new Clinton initiative.

The prime minister now led his cabinet in a decision to extend the war on Palestinian militants beyond the occupied territories as a response to the Jerusalem bombing. They decided that Mossad would assassinate Khaled Mashal, head of the Political Department of Hamas in Jordan. Mashal was almost unknown to the wider world, but intelligence showed that he was instrumental in directing Hamas activities in the occupied territories and thus, in Israeli eyes, a legitimate target for an assassination.

The director of Mossad, Dany Yatom, gave the planning of the operation to Haim Ha'Keini, who headed the organization's Caesarea unit, under which was the Kidon division, the unit charged with carrying out assassinations.[13]

Operating in Amman, however, carried the risk of damaging the delicate relations between Israel and Jordan if anything went wrong. This is why Haim Ha'Keini opted for a 'silent' operation, which meant that rather than using guns or explosives to kill Mashal, the hit team would use 'Almog', the code name given to a lethal substance so deadly that a few drops in contact with the target's skin would kill him. Ha'Keini's assumption was that a successful execution of the assassination using poison would leave no traces that could incriminate Israel directly, as the weapon had no immediately evident effect upon the target.

On 25 September, Ha'Keini's two hitmen were waiting for Mashal to get to his office in Amman and when he showed up they approached him from behind and tried to spray him with the lethal poison. They partly succeeded, but Mashal managed to run away from his assailants and the two of them were apprehended; a few other Mossad combatants also involved in the operation took refuge in the Israeli embassy.[14]

King Hussein was livid, feeling completely betrayed by the Israelis.[15] What further upset him was that he had recently conveyed to Israel, through the Mossad representative in Amman, a proposal by Palestinian militant groups, including Hamas, to sign a thirty-year truce, a so-called 'hudna', with Israel, and halt all violence in the occupied territories. The king had not yet received any reaction to his proposal when the abortive Mossad attempt in his own capital city had shaken his trust.[16] The king now demanded that Israel should, at once, provide details of the poison used against Mashal and that an antidote be handed over to save his life, to which the Israelis, concerned that the crisis might lead to a further deterioration in relations with Jordan, agreed.[17] The king also insisted that Israel release from jail a number of Palestinian prisoners, including the founding leader of Hamas,

Sheikh Ahmed Yassin, and turn him over to Jordan; he would most probably be transferred subsequently to his home in the Gaza Strip, but it would be a coup for the king to be able to say *he* had secured the man's release. Netanyahu had little choice but to agree and following further negotiations, twelve days after the disastrous operation, a series of helicopters flew from Israel to Jordan and back, in one of them the released Mossad agents and in the other Sheikh Yassin and twenty prisoners just released from prison in Israel.

The Mashal affair had a direct effect on the occupied territories, as the released Sheikh Yassin, who eventually returned to Gaza as expected, became a focal point in the Hamas campaign against Israel for many years to come. As for Mashal, after surviving the attempt on his life he returned to his duties as an important Hamas operator – he remains so to this day.[18]

AN ISRAELI–PALESTINIAN COUP

Since the signing of the first Israeli–Palestinian Oslo deal in September 1993, the army had withdrawn from 27 per cent of West Bank and Gaza Strip occupied lands, transferring them to Arafat's Palestinian Authority. In these evacuated areas, mainly towns and cities across the West Bank and Gaza Strip, where no more Israeli troops patrolled the streets, Arafat's Palestinian Authority oversaw Palestinian daily life, providing such services as education, health care and tax collection. Arafat expected that by 1998 the army would withdraw from a further 13 per cent as part of what came to be known as the First and Second Further Redeployments. This would end Israeli occupation of over 40 per cent of the occupied Palestinian land, before moving to the Third Further Redeployment during which the army would withdraw from yet more land. But Netanyahu was reluctant to proceed with the redeployments, insisting that Arafat had yet to comply with what had been asked of him in previous agreements.

Meanwhile, Israeli opposition leaders such as Yossi Beilin, one of the architects of the original Oslo Accord, and others, regarded their prime minister, rather than Arafat, as the culprit in the stalemate and they therefore put their heads together with Palestinians, such as Saeb

Erekat, Abu Mazen, Hassan Asfour and Mohammed Dahlan, all young people close to Arafat and playing roles in the new Palestinian Authority, to try to twist Netanyahu's arm into proceeding with the expected withdrawals. Here was indeed a most extraordinary situation – important Israeli politicians colluding behind the back of their own leader with leading Palestinians to force the hand of Israel's prime minister. Meetings took place at the residence of Egypt's ambassador to Israel, Mohammed Bassiouni (which gave the group its name – the 'Bassiouni Forum'), and there a plan was hatched on how to persuade Netanyahu to honour previous agreements.

According to Beilin, in an interview with the author: 'We would usually get to the ambassador's house in the evening . . . there would be dinner . . . then we would talk.'[19] The Palestinian Erekat has described these meetings as 'collusion between me and members of the Israeli opposition . . . a cabal of me and my Israeli sympathizers' where, as he goes on to explain, 'We developed certain ideas about how to deal with Netanyahu and we contacted the Americans with it and gave them something.'[20] The US special envoy to the Middle East, Dennis Ross, as Beilin recalls, would 'often phone during the meetings . . . Sometimes the [US] ambassador would join these talks.' When the package was ready they gave it to the Americans and, Beilin remembers, it was they who then offered it to Netanyahu and Arafat, as 'an American idea'. It then became the basis for negotiations at a summit convened by President Clinton at the Aspen Institute in the Wye River Plantation, Maryland.[21]

The Wye summit opened on 15 October 1998 and by 23 October, after seemingly endless stalling points and crises, it produced the Wye River Memorandum, signed by both Netanyahu and Arafat. Aimed at facilitating the implementation of previous Israeli–Palestinian agreements and hence further Israeli withdrawals and Palestinian co-operation on security, the Wye River Memorandum called on Israel, among other things, to relinquish to the Palestinians 13 per cent of the West Bank land.[22] Also Netanyahu agreed to release 750 Palestinian prisoners, to provide the Palestinians with a licence for the operation of Gaza's air and sea ports, and to create a safe passage between the West Bank and the Gaza Strip, so that Palestinians could travel freely between the two parts of the Palestinian areas. In return, Arafat pledged to take concrete measures to prevent attacks on Israel, which had continued at a low level even after the signing of the Oslo deals, to collect illegal guns and to reduce the Palestinian police force numbers by 6,000 to 30,000, as over time it had grown bigger than originally agreed. Arafat also pledged, as he had done before but had not so far acted on, to nullify all the provisions of the Palestinian Covenant that were inconsistent with the PLO's commitment to recognize and live in peace side by side with Israel.[23]

Netanyahu hated the emerging agreement, as he felt that he was being asked to give tangibles – land and so on – in return for what he regarded as Arafat's empty words. But the prime minister could not simply defy the wish of the US to proceed; so at Wye he attempted to provoke the Palestinians into taking a hard line, which, in turn, would allow him not to accede to their demands and blame them for the failure of the summit. Erekat, the Palestinian lead negotiator at Wye, recalls how 'Netanyahu was looking for ways to make us say "no" to the proposal.'[24] But, thanks to the advice of the Israeli opposition leaders back in Israel, where they and the Palestinians had put together the very ideas now discussed at Wye, Erekat knew that by agreeing to everything in the proposed paper the Palestinians would win. For 'if [Netanyahu would] implement [the withdrawals] we're in business ... and if he fails to do so then he's out [as he will turn both the Americans and many in Israel against him]. So we were in a win-win situation.'

The plot hatched in Ambassador Bassiouni's residence worked; Netanyahu was trapped, and had little choice but to sign the Wye River Memorandum. Back home he had the right wing of his own party rising against him, as they felt he had betrayed them by agreeing to give up land from Eretz Yisrael. And when he tried to placate his supporters by backtracking on the deal, the left in Israel accused him of dragging his feet. Thus he managed to upset both his own party, in accepting the Wye Memorandum in the first place, and the left, when he attempted to slow down the process; as a result he found himself in deep political trouble.

The coup de grâce came on 4 January 1999, when left and right joined forces in the Knesset to produce an overwhelming majority of eighty-one in favour of dissolving itself and forcing a new general election. Therefore, ironically, Wye's greatest achievement was to bring about the demise of Netanyahu's government, which had proven such an obstacle to peace since Rabin's assassination.

10
Golan First, 1999–2000

General elections took place on 17 May 1999 which saw Ehud Barak, at the head of the centre-left Labor Party, defeat Netanyahu and his right-wing Likud coalition. A bright former army Chief of Staff, Barak could also be arrogant, unpleasant and dismissive, with a slight Machiavellian streak; and while his tenure as prime minister would turn out to be a short one, a mere twenty months, in retrospect it was a most important phase in moving the cause of peace forward and helping end the occupation. During Barak's time in office the gaps between Israelis and Arabs were significantly narrowed and conventions against discussing taboo issues were broken.

Barak made peacemaking the principal plank in his foreign policy, but for this he needed President Clinton's support, not only to help mediate between Israel and its foes, but also as the provider of diplomatic and financial clout, as only the US had the status to help push forward a bold process of negotiation and come up with the funds to bribe the various parties into compromise.

Time, however, was short: Clinton was in the last eighteen months of his final term in office and due to leave the White House in January 2001. In Washington, at the same time, Barak's election raised expectations and gave a new sense of urgency to the Democrat administration, as expressed in the briefing given by senior aides to the president on the eve of Barak's first official visit to the White House as prime minister. 'There is no time for the first Clinton–Barak summit "get acquainted" session,' the briefing goes:

> It must be a substantive strategy, agenda setting and ground rules defining session. What is not accomplished in the first year of this Clinton–Barak partnership through the summer of the year 2000 will

not be achieved. What is accomplished in the first year will . . . be historic for both leaders . . . Therefore the temptation to go slow and be
gentle with a new Israeli prime minister, especially a friendly one following a smashing victory over a hostile one [a reference to Netan-
yahu], must be resisted. Celebrate – yes, but then business, clear and
definite . . . Barak must be encouraged to share with the president
where he wants to go, when he wants to go there. Barak needs to
know clearly which variables to take into account or he will simply
ignore them until trouble arises. President Clinton will set the variable
list for Barak. . . [1]

Someone in Washington leaked this briefing to a certain Nimrod
Novik, a former Israeli diplomat who now worked with Barak as a
roving spy, so that the prime minister would know what to expect
when he faced the president.

They met on 15 July 1999 and Barak presented his peace strategy
to Clinton. He would put peace talks with the Palestinians on ice in
favour of negotiations with Syria; domestically, no Israeli prime minister could pay the price for peace on these two fronts simultaneously.

Like his predecessors – Rabin, Peres and Netanyahu – Barak believed
that ending the Golan occupation and striking a peace deal with Syria
should be given precedence because, as he saw it, the dispute with Syria,
mainly a conflict over the Golan Heights territory, would be simpler to
resolve than the complex and deep-rooted Israeli–Palestinian dispute.
Also, Syria posed a greater threat to Israel as, unlike the Palestinians, it
had a proper army and long-range missiles. The age and state of health
of the Syrian president, Hafez al-Assad, had also to be taken into consideration; by the time Barak became prime minister, Assad was known
to be gravely ill and it was clear that it would not be long before he died
and was replaced by a new leader, for whom it would most likely be
more difficult to contemplate a peace deal for some time. It therefore
made sense to embark first on peacemaking with Assad, as he had the
authority to make crucial decisions, especially one as momentous as
striking peace with Israel. All in all, Barak told Clinton, he believed that
a 'Syria-first' strategy could affect the entire regional dynamics – something that a Palestinian-first deal would not.

Clinton generally agreed with Barak's analysis of tackling Syria first
by negotiating the return of the occupied Golan to it in exchange for

peace and security for Israel, while temporarily putting the Palestinian negotiations on hold. However, he urged the prime minister to offer the Palestinians 'some sweeteners' (as he put it) in the meantime, so that their leader, Yasser Arafat, would not try to challenge the status quo once he realized that Barak was ignoring peace talks with him; indeed, while a Syria-first strategy was logical, it was, at the same time, an approach that was certain to upset the Palestinians.

After three years of 'hostile' Netanyahu, as he was regarded in Washington, President Clinton decided to reward Barak just for showing willingness to give peace talks new momentum, giving him a pledge in the form of a letter. In this secret letter Clinton wrote:

> As Israel prepares to renew its efforts to attain a comprehensive peace in the Middle East and recognizing the risks Israel faces and undertakes as it moves ahead in this direction, I wish to reassure you:
>
> Of the unshakable US commitment to Israel's security and to the maintenance of its [weapons] qualitative edge . . . Of the US determination to minimize the risks and costs Israel confronts as it pursues peace and to provide Israel with long term and enduring diplomatic, economic, security and technological backing . . . Of the US commitment . . . to work closely with Israel to curtail the proliferation of weapons of mass destruction and ballistic missiles threatening Israel and . . . to consult closely with Israel regarding arms control matters in order to ensure that US and others' arms control initiatives and policies do not detract from Israel's deterrence and security . . .[2]

The last paragraph, of course, hints at not meddling with Israel's nuclear capability, or allowing others to do so.

REVIVING TALKS WITH SYRIA

Back in Israel the prime minister started pulling all the strings he could to revive peace talks with Syria. He asked Jordan's King Abdullah to act as interlocutor and to try to arrange a meeting with Assad, giving him a personal message to deliver which stated: 'I'm willing to go all the way to make peace . . .'[3] The young king of Jordan, who came to the throne following the death of his father, King Hussein, in 1999, was keen to help, as peace between Israel and Syria would do much to strengthen the peace between Jordan and Israel which was signed in 1994.

On 27 July, Abdullah reported back that, while Assad did indeed acknowledge that Barak was committed to the peace process, he would not meet him at this stage; this was not much of a surprise given that theatrical moves had never been President Assad's style. Assad's message, through the king, also made it clear that, while it would be possible to conclude a peace deal 'in 4 months', as Assad put it, in any future negotiations Syria would insist on its fundamental demand: to get back all the Golan Heights, down to the 4 June 1967 line.

For Assad, it is worth mentioning, the most important element in any peace deal with Israel was the *depth* of the Israeli withdrawal from the occupied Golan. He insisted on *full* Israeli pull-out from *all* the land which was under Syrian control before the Israelis invaded in 1967, namely the entire Golan mountains and down to what Assad called 'the 4 June 1967 line', running along, and indeed touching, the Sea of Galilee (or 'the lake', as Assad called it), in its north-eastern sector, thus allowing Syria access to the waters of the lake. Israel has always been reluctant to see the Syrians sit on the water, as they did before 1967, as the Sea of Galilee provides Israel with 35–40 per cent of its fresh-water needs. And yet, there was one Israeli prime minister – Yitzhak Rabin – who did let Assad understand that Syria would, after all, get back the entire Golan down to the water line if Israel's needs, mainly security ones, were met. This happened in July 1994 when, following a meeting with Rabin in Jerusalem, the American Secretary of State, Warren Christopher, travelled to Damascus to relay an important message to Assad: 'I'm just back from Israel,' he said, 'and I can tell you that at the end of the day . . . the United States understand that . . . full Israeli withdrawal [from the Golan] . . . would be to the June 4, 1967 line . . .'⁴ This Israeli pledge, which came to be known as the 'deposit' because it was given just indirectly to Assad – 'deposited' with the Americans – surprised Assad so much that he hastened to ask Christopher: 'Does Rabin mean the withdrawal will include all the land that was under Syrian sovereignty at June 4 1967?', to which Christopher replied: 'Yes.'

This, at the time, was regarded as an extraordinary breakthrough in Israeli–Syrian relations and their efforts to end the Golan occupation and secure peace, as it gave the Syrians what they were really after. While at the time it led to some low-level negotiations, no major break-throughs actually took place, neither during the remaining tenure of Rabin, nor during the premierships of his successors Peres and Netan-yahu. The main reason for the lack of progress was that during the actual talks with the Syrians, the Israelis were far less explicit in their promises that they would indeed fully withdraw from the Golan as the Syrians had understood from Christopher back in July 1994.[5]

Now, some five years after Rabin's pledge via the Americans to Assad, Barak again sought American assistance in reviving peace talks with Assad. He turned to Clinton, asking him to contact Assad and try to arrange secret negotiations between an Israeli and a Syrian representa-tive to be chaired by Clinton's special Middle East envoy, Dennis Ross. The prime minister urged Clinton to reassure Assad that Barak respected him, and that the Rabin 'deposit' – the pledge of the late prime minister on a full Israeli withdrawal from the Golan mountains down to the 4 June 1967 line – was still there, and that Barak had no intention of withdrawing it, though he would not repeat it again explicitly. Always keen to help, Clinton phoned Assad to urge him to agree to renew peace talks with Israel. Here is what Clinton said to Assad in a telephone conversation secretly taped by Israeli secret agents:

> Your gaps are not significant ... yes, what is clear to me is that he [Barak] knows [the details of] what Rabin gave [namely the 'deposit' that Israel will withdraw fully from the Golan] and he is not asking it back ... He believes you are a man of honour ... he is much more interested in proceeding on the Syrian track and do it before he does the territorial moves with the Palestinians ... I know he is not playing games because he really believes that strategically it is important to do [Syria-first].[6]

Assad accepted Clinton's advice and agreed to send Riad Daoudi, a lawyer serving in the Syrian Foreign Ministry, to meet with Barak's man, the former General Uri Saguie, in Switzerland on 27 August to renew peace negotiations. Not much, however, came of their talks as the Syrian, acting on the instructions of his direct boss in Damascus, the foreign minister, Shara, insisted that Saguie should explicitly confirm the late Rabin's pledge on full Israeli withdrawal down to the waters of the Sea of Galilee, something the Israeli was reluctant to do. Daoudi phoned Damascus to report to Shara on the situation and given below is their conversation as secretly recorded by Israeli agents:

> **Daoudi:** Sir, the situation now . . . is a bit tense. He has expressed his views regarding their needs. I noticed that he said that his boss [Barak] is aware of the existence of the [Rabin] Deposit [to withdraw fully to the 4 June 1967 line]. He's not asking to withdraw it . . . [he said] that he can't in any way declare anything else [namely be explicit about an Israeli pledge to fully pull out from the Golan down to the water].
>
> **Shara:** Carry on insisting . . .
>
> **Daoudi:** I really insist . . .
>
> **Shara:** Yes, carry on insisting . . .
>
> **Daoudi:** He said to me that I haven't uttered even one word since the morning . . . I said that I've come to listen to him to see where they are and then we'll see.
>
> **Shara:** Yes, good. We'll talk tomorrow.
>
> **Daoudi:** Inshallah.

*

Lack of progress, however, would not deter Barak, who urged President Clinton to keep up the pressure on Assad and persuade him to upgrade the talks so that Barak himself (he would not trust any representative to do it as well as him) could negotiate with a top Syrian official. Clinton, in response, dispatched his Secretary of State, Madeleine Albright, to Damascus to see President Assad in person and Clinton phoned Assad on 2 September, just ahead of her arrival there, to bolster her mission. The following quotes from the transcript of their conversation, secretly recorded by Israeli agents (although Assad himself cannot be heard), shows that the most important matter for Assad remained, as before, an explicit promise, in fact a reconfirmation of the Rabin promise (his 'deposit') that Israel would fully withdrawal from all the Golan down to the 4 June 1967 line:

> **Clinton:** Secretary Albright will meet you on Saturday. I've asked her to agree with you some wordings so that we could progress [with peace talks].
>
> **Assad:** [It seems that Assad mentions the 4 June 1967 line.]

Clinton: I want to explain why Barak is not interested in explicitly mentioning 4 June [line touching the water]. . . can you remember that he had promised to bring any agreement [signed with Syria] to a referendum in Israel? He's afraid . . .

Assad: [. . .]

Clinton: Mr President let me try and finish . . . he's afraid that if he mentions explicitly the 4 June line the matter will be leaked – and it would not be your fault Mr. President, but because in Israel the nature of everything is to be leaked . . . he's afraid that over a period of time, the public in Israel, before its vote [in a referendum] will only hear about 4 June without understanding whether there was a [Syrian] response to [Israel's] security interests . . . or to any other issue . . .[7]

Twelve days later, Dennis Ross, who accompanied the Secretary of State to Damascus, reported to Barak on the visit, including on Assad's state of health, which concerned them all, as it was important to conclude a deal with Syria before Assad died. Ross said that physically President Assad 'looks not bad . . . strong hand shake', but 'mentally [he is not as] sharp as he used to be . . . in parts of the conversation he was detached and he couldn't remember names . . .'[8] Ross added: 'I don't think we've got lots of time [before he dies].' The good news, as Ross now reported, was that Assad had agreed the resumption of low-key peace talks between Israel and Syria in Bethesda, Maryland, to start on 24 September, leading later to upgraded talks between the Syrian foreign minister and the Israeli prime minister in the US.

When Barak and Shara finally met in Washington on 15 December it became apparent that Barak, who pushed hard to have the meeting in the first place, was now backtracking and attempting to slow the process down. Barak, perhaps more than any Israeli prime minister before him, was an obsessive reader of opinion polls, which now revealed that there was little enthusiasm among Israelis for any withdrawal from the Golan Heights, let alone to allow Syria access as previously to the waters of the Sea of Galilee. The opinion of many Israelis was that on the Syrian front Israel should not hurry. For why should Israel consider returning the Golan when things with Syria had seemingly been so tranquil for so many years? Why not just wait for Syria – and indeed the world – to get used to the idea that the Golan belongs to Israel?

The prime minister, however, who saw the wider strategic benefits that a proper peace with Syria would bring, nonetheless felt that he must try to impress upon his public that he was fighting hard and not giving in easily on the Golan. So from the moment he landed for the Washington talks he looked for opportunities to show Israelis that he was fighting for their interests; and the opportunity to stall, and thus to demonstrate that the negotiations were hard, was soon given to him on a silver platter by the Syrian foreign minister himself.

Shara, on the first day of the summit, delivered a bold speech in which he criticized Israel, at some length, for the Golan occupation: his words flew in the face of a request from Clinton that his and Barak's speeches remain 'brief and positive'. Now, jumping on the opportunity to stall, Barak told Clinton, straight after Shara's speech that, given the Syrian's criticism, the president could not possibly expect Barak to move fast or make public concessions. Clinton, who himself was cross with Shara ('Shara has screwed us,' he said to Barak), agreed and was sympathetic to Barak's point of view. He even told the prime minister, quite astonishingly given that one should have expected him to act as an objective facilitator, 'I think that the most important thing for you is the Sea of Galilee. If I were in your place I would be concerned that someone [a reference to Syria] could try to poison the water of the Sea of Galilee.'[9] Clinton, as the transcript of this conversation with the prime minister shows, was condescending towards the Syrians, boasting to the prime minister: 'See how he [Shara] came to the talks . . . I did not even have to [put too much pressure on Assad] . . .'

Overall, with Barak backtracking and stalling, these first ever high-level Israeli–Syrian talks failed to lead to any significant breakthrough. And yet again, it was Barak who pressed Clinton to resume talks with the Syrians 'as quickly as possible in order not to lose the momentum'. Clinton agreed and it was decided that another round of talks would start on 3 January 2000 at a location yet to be chosen.

ASSAD'S GESTURE

Barak also urged Clinton to persuade Assad to make a gesture of goodwill in order to impress upon the Israeli public that the Syrians were not the devils that they were depicted to be in the Israeli press. More specifically, that Assad should allow the bodies of three Israeli soldiers, missing in action since the 1982 war in Lebanon, to be recovered and return them to Israel for proper burial.

In spite of the insistence by their families that the missing soldiers were still alive, the prime minister knew from intelligence reports that they were not. His intelligence was based, among other things, on information gathered by the Italian secret service from one of their most reliable informers, the Palestinian mayor of a West Bank town, and passed on to the Israeli security services. The mayor informed the Italians, and this was corroborated by other sources too, that the three bodies had been moved from Lebanon to Syria, some time between 1984 and 1987, and buried there. This information then led Israeli agents to three graves in a cemetery in Damascus, where, in row number 10 and adjacent to a road, there were four unmarked graves, three of whom were presumed to be the missing Israelis. Israel's agents in Syria would keep an eye on the graves and an American satellite would take an image of them once a month, delivering it to Israel. Given this information, Barak believed that President Assad could no longer hide behind the excuse that he did not know where the three were buried.

Clinton phoned Assad to discuss the matter, as this could help Barak with his public, and Assad approved an American team, which would include a rabbi, to come to Damascus to remove the bodies of the three dead soldiers. It was, however, a huge disappointment to the prime minister, when, following seven and a half hours of digging, three bodies were indeed recovered, but their age, height and DNA failed to match those of the missing in action; the intelligence, as intelligence often is, was flawed.

A DISASTROUS ENDGAME

Barak and the Syrian foreign minister met again, this time in Shepherdstown, West Virginia, where Clinton soon found out that, yet again, Barak, the main driving force behind the resumption of talks with Syria, was not willing to play ball and was slowing down the pace of talks on purpose. It was again due to the lack of public support in Israel for a compromise with Syria and to Barak's wish to impress on his people that negotiations were difficult, and that he was fighting long and hard for Israel's interests. However, by playing this stalling game, Barak offended not only the Syrians but also the Americans. Robert Malley of the American team recalls how

> Clinton gathered [the American team] around a table with his head a little bit down and he said: 'Guys, we've got a problem . . . Barak is telling me that he can't move forward here . . . because he's facing problems at home and if he reaches a deal too quickly, the Israeli people are gonna think that he gave in too soon and that he didn't put up a fight. He needs the appearance of a fight, he needs to have this dragged out longer, he needs to slow walk it . . .'[10]

A frustrated Secretary of State Albright lashed at Barak, telling him:

> Very frankly . . . in all our history we haven't had so many telephone conversations, the vast majority of which were on your initiative, and in these conversations you said that it was very important to advance on the Syrian track . . . and we took it very seriously . . . But you surprised us . . . because you have made the decision not to progress fast . . . nothing has happened from your side . . . you have not got a better friend than the US and you have no better friend than Clinton and you have played with his credibility . . . they [the Syrians] have been flexible . . . and we are concerned.[11]

*

Not much came of the Shepherdstown talks and yet, despite Barak's disappointing tactics, Clinton agreed to the prime minister's request to try to organize an endgame summit and to bring to it the Syrian president himself. What Barak proposed was that, as Assad would not meet Barak, Clinton should get Assad on an American cruiser in the Mediterranean, where he would present Israel's final peace proposal and then complete the endgame with Assad. Barak even proposed that he could parachute in and join the endgame meeting whenever Clinton felt it was appropriate.

It was agreed, upon Barak's insistence, that, as accuracy was paramount, President Clinton should *read* from a pre-prepared presentation the Israeli proposals. But even at this advanced stage the prime minister still kept his real rock-bottom line close to his chest, citing concerns that they might be leaked ahead of the summit. Barak promised Clinton that he would phone him on the very day of the summit, just before Clinton entered the meeting with Assad, to reveal the limit beyond which Israel would not negotiate.

While Israeli and American aides kept working on the text Clinton would read to Assad in their summit, Barak, on 2 March, phoned Clinton to say that the president must 'personally' present the Israeli offer to Assad, so it will raise the probability of getting a positive response, as 'this is the only way to break the deadlock'.[12] Clinton, however, wishing to test the water with Assad before jumping into it himself, had already – without consulting the prime minister – asked the Saudi ambassador in Washington, Prince Bandar, a close ally of American presidents before and after Clinton, to run Barak's ideas past the Syrian leader informally. Israeli spies, however, a strong presence in Washington and, indeed, in Damascus, had found out about Clinton's Saudi back channel, so now the prime minister surprised Clinton by saying: 'I've learned from intelligence that you intend to give Israel's needs to Syria through the Saudis . . . this is a mistake.' Caught red-handed, a taken-aback Clinton replied blustering, '. . . I gave Bandar nothing substantial . . . don't give it another thought . . .' At the same time Clinton was also concerned with the Palestinian front, where Arafat was showing signs of impatience, and he urged Barak to give Arafat something to assuage him. Clinton said to the prime minister: 'It's very important that you and Arafat agree to where we're heading . . . and before I meet Assad, otherwise it will cause you troubles. I was surprised at the extent to which the Palestinians are worried and concerned that you and I are neglecting them because we are going on Assad . . . so if you could . . . bring Arafat to say that we are in a good shape.' Reluctantly Barak promised to do so, not before, however, commenting that 'Arafat is like a crocodile . . . he eats and eats and still wants more.' Like his predecessors, Barak did not trust Arafat, whom he regarded as shifty, always attempting to squeeze more and more concessions from Israel while giving very little in return. However, since he needed Clinton's help in dragging Assad to a summit, Barak proceeded to negotiate with Arafat a staggered transfer of control over three Palestinian villages near Jerusalem; these were important to Arafat, as it would extend his authority right up to the gates of Jerusalem. The pair agreed that on 23 April Arafat would get two of the three villages, and on 23 May the third. With that under his belt, Arafat, as Barak rightly predicted, did indeed ask for more. So President Clinton phoned Barak again, on 7 March, to thank him but also to ask him to release some Palestinian prisoners kept in Israeli jails.[13] Annoyed, the prime minister said: 'I'll do my best but I would like to suggest that we agree that it should not be a precondition for your talks with Assad'. Realizing that he had pressed Barak as far as he would go for now on the Palestinian front, Clinton hastened to add: 'I'll phone Assad as soon as possible and come back to you the moment I have an answer.'

By 10 March 2000, the text Clinton would read to President Assad in their forthcoming summit was ready. This is a most important text as it is the last and most comprehensive Israeli offer which has ever been made to the Syrians to date. Here is how Clinton would open the meeting:

Mr President, I invited you to this meeting because I believe we have reached a moment of truth in the effort to achieve a comprehensive peace between Israel and Syria . . . You know that I have been working on this since I first came into office, seven years ago . . . I am now in the last year of my Presidency. I have a lot of things I would like to finish in that time. One of them is a Syria–Israel peace. A peace of the brave that when implemented will end the Arab–Israeli conflict and provide a better future for Arabs and Israelis alike. A peace that will open the way to a new era in US–Syrian relations from which both sides would gain a great deal. A peace that will help ensure a stable environment for Syria, one in which your proud legacy will be carried into future generations . . . But I don't have time to waste. Either we are able to overcome the differences now and achieve an agreement, or it will have to be left for another president and another time. You have told us repeatedly that you want to cut to the heart of the matter, put all the cards on the table and finish the negotiations. PM Barak has exactly the same desire. But to do that you both need to know whether your needs will be met. I have emphasized to Barak, and he has agreed, that the peace must be an honourable one – a peace that fully respects your dignity and secures the vital interests of Syria just as it secures the vital interests of Israel. With all these considerations in mind, I have been working hard with PM Barak since we last talked. I have asked him to detail for me what he can do to address your needs and what he feels he must have on his needs in order to do that . . . On my urging, he has limited his requirements to his vital needs. He has gone as far as he feels he can to meet your needs, and he has done his best to take into account your sensitivities. I believe the differences are quite narrow. Historians looking back at this situation would not be able to explain why these gaps were not bridged, except by a failure of courage and statesmanship. So what I would like to do today is outline for you my impressions of what Barak can do to respond to your fundamental needs and what he needs you to do to respond to his fundamental needs . . . If you can't respond to his fundamental needs, I will respect your position but you will need to understand that I will have taken it as far as I can.[14]

From this general opening Clinton would then, as the script prepared for him went, turn to the most important item for Assad, namely, the route of the future border between Israel and Syria, which he wished to be the 4 June 1967 line, touching physically the waters of the Sea of Galilee around the north-eastern section of the lake, allowing the Syrians direct access to it:

> 1. The Border: My first impression is that Barak is prepared for a full withdrawal to a commonly agreed border based on the June 4, 1967 line . . . Barak feels that Israeli sovereignty over the lake . . . [is an] essential element in any peace agreement with Syria. In this regard, he must have a strip of some 500 metres around the north-eastern side of the lake . . .[15]

On 17 March, President Clinton phoned Barak to report that the summit with Assad was arranged for 26 March in Geneva. They decided to speak again on the day of the summit, so that Barak could provide Clinton with his rock-bottom red lines just before Clinton walked into the meeting with Assad. Clinton was expecting that the 500-metre figure given for the strip of land around the north-eastern side of the lake that Barak wished to retain would be cut down dramatically, so that he could go into the summit with Assad with a realistic chance of success.

The scene was now set for a historic summit, with success hinging on Barak making a realistic offer. At 13.10 on the day of the summit, he phoned Clinton at the Intercontinental Hotel in Geneva and talked to him on a secure line to relay his final offer and ensure the president approached the meeting with Assad in the right way. The transcript of their telephone conversation shows that the prime minister was nervous and Clinton impatient.[16] Barak urged Clinton that his meeting with Assad should be in four eyes – only the two presidents and perhaps an interpreter for Assad because, as Barak put it, 'a leader like Assad would not be able to listen to it in the presence of strangers and this will reduce, quite dramatically, his willingness [to compromise]'. Clinton said: 'I'll do my best . . . I've gone through the script.' The prime minister said that Assad 'should know the consequences if such a thing fails to materialize. He must realize that he will remain on his own . . . the Golan in our hands for another thirty years . . . he should see this alternative . . .' Clinton replied: 'I'll do a good job.'

Now, however, Clinton wanted to get to the crux of the matter and hear how large a strip of land the prime minister was going to insist on keeping around the north-eastern side of the Sea of Galilee. Barak's response did not start well. He explained to Clinton that his pollster was telling him that there was still little support in Israel for a deal with Syria, particularly any that gave the Syrians access to the waters of the Sea of Galilee, '. . . and therefore [the strip]. . . could go down from 500 to 400 metres . . . This is a make or break . . . if he fails to agree to 500 metres or a minimum of 400 . . .'

This was a terrible blow for Clinton. Barak had once again failed to live up to his talk; failed to deliver the promised compromise. Clinton knew he now faced very little chance of success with Assad, who was still expecting a future border which *was* the 4 June 1967 line, where Syria sat *physically* by the waters of the lake, not 400 or 500 metres away. National Security Advisor Sandy Berger recalls: 'The President was quite upset that we had gotten Assad to this meeting based upon the impression that we were going to make a serious new offer.'[17] Devastated, Clinton pleaded with Barak: 'In the past we talked about

300 metres.[18] Do you think it can't pass in polls?' Barak replied: 'I have checked and under 400 [metres] it is a problem.'

The summit started well enough. Assad's interpreter remembers: 'At the beginning of the meeting President Clinton gave a present to President Assad, and it was a tie with a lion on it, and lion, of course, in Arabic means Assad. So Assad found that quite entertaining. As Secretary Madeleine [Albright] is wearing a lion brooch and President Clinton brings a lion tie, President Assad was quite entertained and he took the gift gratefully.'[19]

But, in spite of this positive atmosphere, the summit was doomed. Indeed, when Assad heard that Barak's 'full' withdrawal would *not* be to the 4 June 1967 line as he expected and as had been promised to him by Rabin back in 1994 but, instead, a border which would be 'commonly agreed' and 'based' on the June 1967 line – which had become Israeli code for away from the water line – he was taken aback. His interpreter, Bouthania Shaaban, recalls what happened next: 'President Assad said to me: "Ask him what is this 'commonly agreed border' . . . what is this phrase? Let him say that again!"' When President Clinton repeated the phrase Assad turned to Shaaban and said: 'Tell him I'm not interested.'[20]

It was a disastrous diplomatic failure.

After the meeting Clinton phoned Barak. 'I have done my best,' he said, adding: 'He is not willing to give up on the water. He wants to get back to the water. I have explained to him the consequences . . . It is clear to me that he is not willing to compromise on the water . . . He can't explain to the Syrians why he failed to bring them [all] the land . . .'[21] The prime minister replied, stating the obvious: 'If he isn't willing to be flexible on the strip then a deal is not possible.'

In retrospect, the failure of Israel and Syria to reach peace during this period on the basis of a full Israeli withdrawal from the occupied Golan was a missed opportunity and, clearly, the fault lay with Barak. He hesitated, fearing that his public would not support him, and squandered the opportunity. His offer to Assad, through Clinton in Geneva, in March 2000, was too little and much too late. Too little, because he was offering the Syrian less than what the late prime minister, Yitzhak Rabin, had proposed before, namely a full Israeli withdrawal from the Golan Heights and a restoration of the pre-1967 situation, whereby Syria could access the Sea of Galilee. And it was too late, because it seems that by the time Clinton met President Assad in Geneva with the Israeli offer, a very ill Assad was more concerned with the transfer of power to his son than getting back his lost land; Assad would die less than three months later.

II

Camp David II, 2000

Following the collapse of the Geneva summit between Presidents Clinton and Assad, Barak turned his attention from his now defunct 'Syria-first' programme back to the Palestinian track. By shifting back to negotiations with Arafat, Barak intended to drastically alter the entire strategy Israel had employed so far with the Palestinians.

Barak had strongly objected, since its inception in 1993, to the Oslo peace process, which envisaged a gradual transfer of land from Israeli to Palestinian hands, while deferring negotiations on the 'core issues' of the conflict – the most difficult ones, such as the fate of holy Jerusalem – to the very end of the process. Indeed, the architects of the Oslo process had congratulated themselves on its gradualism, which was intended to enable Israelis and Palestinians to gain confidence and build trust before turning to deal with the big, complex matters of their conflict. But Barak thought differently. He felt that delaying talks on the greater, contentious problems until the end of the negotiations would leave the entire peace process hostage to extremists, on both sides, who would try to change realities on the ground in their favour before the final stage was reached. He also thought that Oslo's strategy of staged transfers of land to the Palestinians would harm Israel's interests, as by the time Israel came to do the final deal on the thorniest issues, it would have few assets at its disposal to use as leverage on the Palestinians to get them to compromise. Also, the gradual transfer of land, Barak thought, would endanger the Jewish settlements on the ground – the fate of which, according to the original Oslo Accords, would be discussed at the end of the negotiations, leaving them scattered like isolated islands on the West Bank, surrounded by Palestinians.

So instead of deferral of the core issues and gradualism, the prime minister sought to jump straight to the end of the process, sort out the difficult core issues while Israel still held most of the land, get Arafat to declare, in no uncertain terms, that his conflict with Israel was over and he had no more claims, and with that transfer to him, in a single stroke, the occupied lands on which he could establish his Palestine.

But it would by no means be an easy matter: Arafat, following precisely the same reasoning as Barak, would naturally prefer to stick to the process agreed at Oslo. Furthermore, Barak's new strategy would require renegotiating previous Israeli–Palestinian agreements, not least the Wye memorandum which Arafat had signed with Barak's predecessor, Netanyahu, back in 1998. That agreement had committed Israel to continue to transfer lands to the Palestinians, lands which Arafat sought to get without delay.

THE ROAD TO A SUMMIT

On 27 July, soon after his 1999 election victory, Barak had met Arafat to try to persuade him to go along with his new strategy. Ahead of their meeting, Barak's man, Nimrod Novik, who roamed the world on his behalf on a variety of special missions as his secret investigator, held a five-hour secret meeting with Arafat's chief negotiator, Saeb Erekat, in Washington to extract from him tips on how best to handle Arafat. Novik then faxed the prime minister to say that

> In order to put Arafat in the right frame of mind [Erekat's] suggestion is that you should include some of the following elements in your words: 'you're my partner; thanks to you the process has survived'; 'your people have suffered very much and only now start to recover'; 'I want to work with you together, hand in hand, for the common strategic aim ... Let be there no doubt: I intend to implement ... [previous] commitments.' [1]

When Barak and Arafat finally met at Erez, the main crossing between Israel and the Gaza Strip, they started with a casual conversation about King Hassan of Morocco, who had recently died. Arafat said: 'Hassan used to call me "my cousin" and I would call him "my cousin".'² Barak, trying to lead the conversation in a different direction, said about King Hassan, who played a leading role in facilitating the Israeli–Egyptian peace treaty in the late 1970s: 'It's very exciting to see how leaders like Hassan and others who dedicated themselves to peace became great world leaders.'

Barak then explained that he wished to see 'certain modifications' to the Wye agreement and defer implementation of it, namely the transfer of land promised by his predecessor, until after they had sorted out all the remaining issues of the Israeli–Palestinian conflict. But Arafat would not accept that: 'We expect to end this stage of Wye,' he said, by which he meant that first Barak should transfer to him the promised lands, 'and only *after* that we'll talk about a permanent settlement [of the conflict].' This Barak rejected: 'I understand your answer,' he said, 'and I'm still asking you to reconsider [your position] . . . If we do Wye first . . . then we create a problem that will hurt the chances of achieving a permanent settlement . . .' Reluctantly, Arafat acquiesced. He knew that should he keep insisting on Wye, then the prime minister would put up obstacles at a later stage by implementing the previous intermediate Oslo agreements according to the minimum possible interpretation. It is worth noting here that the language used in the previous intermediate Oslo agreements often refers to the need for an Israeli withdrawal from lands, 'except from specific military bases and areas whose status will be decided in the permanent agreement', and this phrase, Arafat acknowledged, was open to various interpretations; after all, what *is* the size of 'military bases' and how big are 'areas'?

Having his arm twisted, Arafat attempted, at least, to improve the atmosphere. 'We have started with the late Rabin and continue with Barak,' he said. The prime minister, delighted as he felt he had managed to persuade Arafat to go along with his new strategy, replied alluding to previous Middle Eastern peacemakers: 'I feel that [the late] Yitzhak Rabin, [the late King] Hassan [of Morocco] and [the late King] Hussein [of Jordan] are all watching us from the sky . . . and expect us to find a way to end the conflict.'

Subsequently the two sides embarked on negotiations to amend the Wye memorandum and, on 4 September 1999, Arafat and Barak got together to sign the new deal at Sharm el Sheikh in Egypt. The 'Sharm Memorandum' delayed further Israeli withdrawal from the West Bank which, if it had happened as Arafat had wanted and as had been promised to him in the past, would have seen the Israeli army withdrawing from most of the West Bank, leaving it in Palestinian hands. They set a new timetable and important deadline: a final deal would be signed between them by 13 September 2000.

Putting Arafat in a cage

Nothing, however, came of the talks Barak and Arafat initiated in Sharm back in September 1999: the agreed deadlines came and went, while Barak was trying to clinch a deal, as shown in the previous chapter, with 'the other woman', as the Palestinians referred to Syria. And in the meantime, on the ground in the occupied territories, even with Arafat in control of most of the population of the Palestinian cities, refugee camps and villages, the occupation continued, as the roads between Palestinian urban centres were mostly under army control and army checkpoints, armed settlers and closures still restricted the Palestinian people's freedom and caused them daily humiliations.

Now, however, following the failed Clinton–Assad summit, Barak wished to 'lock' Arafat into agreeing to a make-or-break conference and go for the complete agreement in one go. A summit with him, Barak insisted, would be the only way to get Arafat, whom Barak considered to be always slippery and hard to pin down, to make stark decisions. Should Arafat prove willing to compromise on the big issues, then there would be an Israeli–Palestinian deal to end the Israeli occupation of the West Bank and Gaza Strip and allow Arafat to establish a Palestinian state there. But should Arafat refuse to play ball and compromise, then Barak, as he put it, would 'unmask' Arafat's perfidy by exposing him to the entire world as not interested in peace. It was Barak's typical all-or-nothing approach.

The prime minister, of course, could not simply 'lock' Arafat into a peace summit by himself since for that he would need America's power and influence. Clinton, always willing to help, promised Barak that in his upcoming meeting with Arafat in the White House, on

15 June, he would raise the idea of a summit and see what the Palestinian leader thought of it.

A few days later, and ahead of his meeting with Arafat, Clinton phoned the prime minister to urge him to release Palestinian prisoners held in Israel, as a gesture of goodwill that could help Clinton gauge Arafat's willingness to go for a summit; Palestinian prisoners in Israeli jails is a sensitive issue in Palestinian society, their release always a priority. In response, Barak released just three out of 1,860 Palestinians imprisoned in Israel – almost worse than releasing none at all, and a humiliating insult to Arafat. No wonder then that Clinton's meeting with Arafat went badly: Clinton reported afterwards to Barak that he had found a very suspicious Arafat, complaining that what the prime minister sought was to trap him into coming to a summit, at the end of which Clinton would blame him for its inevitable failure. Clinton explained that he had promised Arafat that should he call a summit and it failed, under no circumstances would he place the blame on Arafat, and that, in the meantime, he would support the Palestinian call for further Israeli withdrawals from occupied lands as agreed in previous deals.

On the day Clinton saw Arafat in Washington, the prime minister held a meeting with his advisers in his Tel Aviv office, where the view among participants was that Arafat would not compromise at a summit and a failure of such a high-profile meeting might, in turn, lead to bloodshed in the occupied territories – to a second *intifada*.

General Amos Malka, the Director of Military Intelligence, said, as quotations from a secret transcript of the meeting published here for the first time show, that after a failed summit, 'what [Arafat] will look for is . . . an event which could bring together emotions . . . such [an event] that could bring about an explosion . . .'[3] The only way to avoid this explosion of Palestinian violence, General Malka went on to say to Barak, is to fully accept Palestinian demands. This, as the general continued, would have to be 'a total Israeli capitulation on Jerusalem, refugees and borders . . .' What Malka was getting at was that because Israel could *not* provide Arafat with these concessions, perhaps it would be wiser *not* to convene a summit at all.

But in spite of the growing evidence and expert opinion that a failed summit might lead to an open confrontation with the Palestinians, the prime minister was adamant that he would go ahead. To those who doubted his strategy, he said: 'It's important to try and exhaust the chance of getting to a deal . . . without giving up on the vital interests of the State of Israel. At the same time, we should be prepared for a situation where we fail to reach an agreement [and find ourselves facing] violence and, at a certain stage, full blown terror.' He was well aware, then, that his was a high-risk strategy.

Back in Washington the president and his advisers were torn as to whether they should bow to Barak's relentless nagging and call a summit with Arafat. The failure of the Clinton–Assad summit at Geneva in March was still fresh in their minds and Clinton's advisers had no appetite to expose their president to yet another potentially humiliating diplomatic disaster. The Geneva failure also made reaching an Israeli–Palestinian deal even harder: had an Israeli–Syrian deal been achieved then an agreement between Israel and Lebanon was expected to follow suit, as Syria, so influential in Lebanon, would have pressed it to sign with Israel. In such circumstances there would have been intense pressure on Arafat to settle for what he could get from Israel. But with the collapse of talks between Syria and Israel, it was apparent that Arafat, now regarding himself as the only game in town, and knowing just how important it was for Clinton and Barak to demonstrate success in peacemaking, would drive up his price for peace with Israel. And, although so far undecided, Clinton instructed his aides to check the proposition of a summit between Barak and Arafat and to begin preparing the ground work for the possibility.

At the same time Barak pulled as many strings as he could to put pressure on Arafat to come to a summit. He summoned Egypt's ambassador in Israel, Mohammed Bassiouni, asking him to carry a message to President Hosni Mubarak asking him to use all his influence to get Arafat to agree to a summit with Barak. On his return to Israel, on 23 June, Bassiouni reported that Mubarak liked the idea of a summit and had commented that 'the Clinton–Barak combination is a fantastic opportunity which must not be missed', and that 'it's a moment of truth'.[4] Bassiouni also reported that Mubarak, who had more influence on Arafat than any other Arab leader, had then and there picked up the phone and 'ordered Arafat' to get to Egypt to discuss the idea of a summit.

In the meantime, the prime minister received a secret report from his Foreign Ministry. Entitled 'Arafat's Positions', it summarized what 'a foreign official', who saw Arafat in Nablus, on 25 June, reported discreetly to the Israelis. This secret document is significant as it sheds some light on Arafat's state of mind and what he really felt about the idea of a summit with Barak. According to the report:

> Arafat says that the planned summit is an Israeli–American trap and they want to take advantage of the fact that his English is poor, he's tired and physically frail, all in order to extract from him, in a four-eyes-meeting, more concessions . . . Arafat said that Barak attempts to put him into 'the cage of end of the Israeli–Palestinian conflict', but he would not go into this cage before all his demands from Israel were fulfilled . . .[5]

On 27 June Secretary of State Albright visited Arafat in Ramallah and then proceeded to Jerusalem to see the prime minister. Albright inquired whether Barak would accept Arafat's request to hold two weeks of low-level preparatory talks between Israeli and Palestinian negotiators to narrow the remaining gaps before the summit. But Barak would not have this, saying that he knew the pattern of such talks: Israel would raise ideas while the Palestinians would 'reject them and ask us to give them more'.[6] Albright returned to Ramallah to apply more pressure on Arafat and, on the next day, reported to the prime minister that while Arafat had agreed in principle to go to a summit, he would still insist on pre-summit talks lasting two weeks before the meeting itself.

It is important to note here that at this point in time – June 2000 – Arafat controlled only 42 per cent of the occupied territories; 14 per cent was under his direct and full control and 28 per cent came under shared control with the Israelis, with the latter being responsible for security issues. In these areas Arafat was responsible for running Palestinian affairs and providing the Palestinian inhabitants with all services: from health and education to transport, urban planning and communications, tax collection and so on. His interpretation of the Oslo agreements – although this was rejected by the

Israelis – had always been that *before* final status talks took place (like the ones Barak was now proposing) more than 90 per cent of occupied land should come under his full control. This is why, now, Arafat insisted on pre-summit negotiations: to see if he could wrest from the Israelis this land *before* his summit with Barak. But the prime minister, whose strategy remained to preserve his assets for the moment of truth – to hang on to as much land as he could until all the other issues had been sorted out – would not agree to any pre-summit negotiations.

Words of war

Around this time intelligence reports from the occupied territories were ominous, indicating that Palestinians, expecting an imminent collapse of the peace talks, were preparing for an all-out war against Israel, with Arafat's full knowledge and even encouragement. According to these reports, based mainly on listening devices, on 29 June Haj Ismail, a leading Palestinian militant, met his officers and warned them of the likely collapse of the peace talks, after which 'the Palestinian forces will confront the IDF and the settlements'.[7] Ismail instructed his men 'to start intensive and substantial training of the forces to [prepare them for] the confrontation'. When Ismail finished his briefing, the intelligence report indicates, the participants met Arafat in person, who told them: 'The Palestinian Authority is confronted by a strong and dangerous Israel headed by a prime minister who isn't interested in real peace. Therefore . . . in spite of the many talks, there will be no peace agreement between the Palestinian Authority and Israel . . .' Arafat called on his audience to follow Ismail's instructions and prepare for a battle with Israel.

This recorded information would be used later by the Israelis to claim that, all along, the Palestinians were intent on war rather than peace. But it also calls into question the motivation of Barak, who decided to proceed with preparations for a summit in spite of this and other clear indications that a failure there would lead to clashes. That he did so is extraordinary as it shows that he was a reckless gambler; that President Clinton was still willing to follow Barak even in the wake of the Shepherdstown Conference and the Geneva debacle, where the prime minister had let him down so badly, suggests that he too was something of a risk-taker.

On 4 July, Clinton phoned Barak to ask what 'sweeteners' the prime minister could offer Arafat to make Clinton's telephone conversation with the Palestinian leader, when he would formally invite him to a summit, run a bit smoother. Barak tried to be helpful, saying that Clinton could let Arafat know that as a reward for coming to a summit, he would release thirty-two Palestinian prisoners (a minuscule number given that 1,860 were held in Israeli prisons) once the summit started, and during its course he would consider limited compromises on Palestinian control over neighbourhoods in East Jerusalem. A short while later, the president got back to the prime minister to say that his conversation with Arafat went well enough, and that Arafat agreed to join the summit; not a big surprise given that Arafat did not want to be blamed for not cooperating with peace efforts. It was decided that the summit would be held at Camp David and would be preceded – and here the prime minister agreed to a little compromise – by two days of low-level talks between Israeli and Palestinian negotiators in an attempt to narrow gaps.

Barak gathered his government, on 9 July, to report that 'the US president has decided to convene a summit and yesterday, after midnight, I talked to him on the phone and I expressed our appreciation for his decision'.[8] He added: 'if – God forbid – we fail to reach an agreement then we'll find ourselves facing a new reality, which is much more difficult than we could imagine . . . but if we do manage to strike a deal, then we are going to change the map of the Middle East'. Again, it is extraordinary that Barak was fully aware of the dire consequences of a failed summit, yet was still willing to embark on this dangerous route. To encourage his ministers to approve his mission, Barak pledged that should he manage to strike a deal at the summit, then 'the nation, in a referendum, will [be asked to] approve it and I'm confident that if we get a deal [Israelis would approve it] by a landslide majority'. He explained that the idea was to reach an agreement that would bring about peace by means of a separation between Palestinians and Israelis, whereby, as he put it, 'We are here and they are there' – a two-state solution. The ministers approved.

When the meeting ended and most participants had dispersed, the prime minister stayed behind and was approached by the Director of Military Intelligence, Amos Malka. What General Malka said to the prime minister is, in hindsight, prophetic:

> You are going [to a summit in Camp David] and you'll return empty handed. Because according to our best available intelligence, Arafat was dragged to a summit [only] because of your and Clinton's pressure. He had no intention to go to a summit. He wanted to get to a summit only after he closed the territorial gap [with 90 per cent of land in his hands as he believed was promised to him in the past] . . . also he wants to go to a summit after a big release of prisoners [from Israeli jails].[9]

The prime minister ignored the warning.

FIASCO

Israelis, Palestinians and American negotiators got to Camp David – a place loaded with symbolism because of the Israeli–Egyptian peace treaty that was negotiated there in 1978 – on 10 July, but actual discussions started only on the next day. Following a first meeting with Arafat, Clinton reported to Barak: 'Arafat thinks that you and I will trick him . . . I said to Arafat, "I will not blame you even if the summit fails. . ."'[10] Barak did not trust Arafat any more than Arafat trusted him and warned Clinton that Arafat must realize that 'nothing is agreed until all is agreed'. If the parties failed to reach a deal, Barak warned, then all ideas raised at the summit would be 'null and void'. Barak – who dominated the conversation, as was his style, forgetting that he was representing the junior partner in the relationship – advised the president to present Arafat with a potential reward for cooperation, namely American financial support to the tune of $10bn–20bn to resettle Palestinian refugees, improve Palestinian infrastructure in the occupied territories, and revive their ailing economy. 'Arafat,' Barak said, 'must realize that he might miss a unique opportunity.' It was a while later, at the entrance to the Aspen cabin, where Clinton gathered everyone to officially launch the summit, that Arafat and Barak sparred over who would cross the threshold first. It was Arafat, helped by a push from Barak, under the eyes of a laughing Clinton. The photo of that moment became, perhaps, the most famous of the whole summit – a symbol, as it were, of things to come.

Killing the American strategy

With the opening niceties out of the way, the president sat with Barak, telling him: 'I've worked very hard to find a way to start the negotiations', and he went on to present his strategy to the conference.[11]

He proposed that rather than starting from scratch and going back to the very basics of the disagreements between the parties, they should take some foundations for granted; these were already summed up in a text Clinton brought with him to the meeting. Such an approach, he explained, could 'give momentum to the talks'. He proposed, for instance, that the discussion on the future Palestinian state's borders be based on the 1967 lines, namely the boundaries separating Israel proper from the West Bank and Gaza Strip before the war, as the Palestinians demanded. In order to accommodate Israel's needs, namely to include the big West Bank blocs of settlements where most Jewish settlers resided and which were adjacent to Israel, the western border of the future Palestinian state would be sufficiently modified to enable Israel to annex these blocs; Israel would then compensate the Palestinians for these modifications by giving them land elsewhere ('land swaps', as it would be called). On the eastern border of the future Palestinian state, along the River Jordan, Clinton continued, the Palestinians would get the sovereignty they sought, but in order to take on board Israel's security concerns, there would be arrangements on the ground to deal with the potential danger of a combined Arab attack coming from the east from across the River Jordan. As for the Palestinian refugees, Clinton went on to say, this problem would be dealt with by allowing a very limited return of refugees to Israel proper, so that the Palestinians' demand for a 'right of return' would be, at least symbolically, met. There would be an international mechanism to deal with the remaining refugees by helping them to rehabilitate and resettle either in the future Palestinian state or in third countries; Clinton mentioned a conversation he had had with Arafat in which the latter agreed to the Palestinian refugees residing in Lebanon to go to Canada rather than to Israel.[12] On Jerusalem, Clinton's text remained vague as this was the most sensitive issue of all and best left for a later stage in the summit, lest touching on it early on lead to a premature collapse of the talks.

The prime minister was not surprised by the American strategy, as reports from his spies in Washington had reached him just before he left for Camp David, giving him enough time to make up his mind about the US approach: he was not in favour. He explained to Clinton that starting the summit with a text laying out parameters, as the president now suggested, would limit Barak's ability to have the informal exchanges he needed, where he could establish whether Arafat really meant business at Camp David, or had only come to squeeze concessions from Israel. In other words, the prime minister sought to get to what Clinton had already put in his text through a process of negotiation with the Palestinians. Perhaps also, like in his previous talks with the Syrians, Barak wanted to play to his domestic audience in Israel, to give the impression that negotiations were difficult and that concessions were not granted easily; he wanted, as Clinton would later put it in his memoirs, 'to slow-walk things for a couple of days'.[13] But not wanting to be seen as rejecting the president's ideas outright, Barak told him that he would go along with an improved American text, in which Israeli and Palestinian positions were shown side by side, to be labelled 'I' and 'P' respectively, and the parties would take it from there.

Clinton, in a pattern that would repeat itself throughout the conference, backed off, promising to table a revised text in two days' time. Barak also insisted that the president should show him the new American draft *before* presenting it to Arafat, to which Clinton also had to agree, as he almost certainly knew of the secret letter his Secretary of State had deposited with Barak's predecessor back in 1998, whose contents still stood, in which Albright pledged to consult with Israel *first*. Here is her letter:

> *The Secretary of State, Washington,*
> *November 24 1998,*
> *Secret*

Dear Mr. Prime Minister,
  Recognizing the desirability of avoiding putting forward proposals

that Israel would consider unsatisfactory, the US will conduct a thorough consultation process with Israel in advance with respect to any ideas the US may wish to offer to the parties for their considera- tion. This would be particularly true with respect to security issues or territorial aspects related to security . . .
   Sincerely
   Madeleine K Albright[14]

This American pledge effectively gives Israel carte blanche to veto any American peace proposals and it was probably given out of convic- tion that, as the experienced American diplomat Aaron David Miller once put it, 'if you couldn't gain Israel's confidence, you had zero chance of erecting any kind of peace process'.[15] True, perhaps, but it did nothing to ease the Palestinian suspicion that the Americans, at Camp David as elsewhere, were not acting as impartial mediators and that the Israelis dictated the US position.

When finally the amended US text reached the Israelis they were surprised to see that the point in the paper on Jerusalem was not in an 'I' or a 'P' bracket; effectively implying that the parties already agreed that there could be two capitals in the existing municipality of Jerusalem and the city be shared with the Palestinians. The prime minister dispatched his aide, Dany Yatom, to protest to the White House; when Yatom returned he reported that the Americans claimed it was 'an innocent mistake', and they had changed the text on the spot, adding the word 'expanded' before 'Jerusalem'. This implied that any division of Jerusalem would only take place *after* the expansion of Jerusalem's municipal boundaries to include more West Bank Palestinian areas, allowing the Israelis to offer a piece of the new, enlarged city, say around the suburb of Abu Dis, to Arafat to turn into his capital.

   The Palestinians were not happy with the document either. The chief Palestinian negotiator, Saeb Erekat, recalls: 'When I translated [to Arafat] what it said about Jerusalem . . . he was extremely upset . . . Arafat took the paper out of my hand, threw it in the air and said: "This is a non-starter."'[16] What upset the Palestinians so much was that they could detect Israeli fingertips on the draft; of course they could, as the word 'expanded' was added in a sloppy way by hand and the Palestinians rightly guessed that this was an Israeli idea.

When later the prime minister sat on Aspen's balcony with President Clinton he raised the issue of Jerusalem in the American text, implying that it was not an innocent mistake: 'I'm very disappointed with the content [of the American draft] and also with us as human beings and us as leaders,' he began.[17] 'We've talked so many times and the basic understanding between us had been that you don't surprise [us]. And I must tell you that I feel surprised . . . I want to ask you that this will not happen again . . .' These were harsh words, and that President Clinton went on to apologize shows the extent to which the prime minister was actually controlling the running of the conference. 'What happened yesterday,' Clinton said apologetically, 'was my mistake . . . they [the US team] rushed it because of the time pressure.' Taking advantage of the president's embarrassment and keen on killing the US text as a basis for negotiations, as he did not want anything on paper before establishing whether he could reach peace with Arafat, the prime minister said: 'perhaps it would be better if we started with no document at all . . . You, the Americans, should say that the draft is off the table and we should start our discussions without a draft.' Still reeling from the prime minister's assault Clinton, once again, caved in to Barak's demand. 'We agree,' he said, 'the paper no longer exists.'

This, perhaps, was Clinton's biggest mistake in this summit. His eagerness to please and inability to stand his ground, particularly with Barak, turned out to be a serious liability in a summit where only hard pressure on the Palestinians *and* the Israelis could have led to success. What was needed from the American president was not empathy but unsentimental toughness and leadership, which it seems in this instance Clinton lacked. Clinton would later describe Barak in his memoirs as a 'brilliant Renaissance man', and it may be that it was his admiration for him that made Clinton so flexible with the prime minister.[18]

Now, with the American written text off the table, the parties were instructed that henceforth all discussions would be purely oral. Negotiations, it was decided, would take place in four groups where the core issues of the conflict would be tackled, namely: borders and settlements; refugees; security; and, most crucially, Jerusalem. But with no text to guide the negotiations, the conference was in total disarray and the Americans lost any semblance of control over it.

A pressure cooker

On the fourth day of the summit, the president called a three-way meeting with Arafat and Barak at Aspen. The following are quotes from the transcript of their conversation:

> **Clinton:** There is a lot to do . . . and if we don't accelerate . . . we will not finish . . . we have a time problem . . . you're both wise and brave . . .
>
> **Arafat:** Your words give us a big momentum to move forward . . . I promise you in Barak's name and mine that we'll follow your instructions to the letter.
>
> **Barak:** I feel the spirit of [the late] Rabin [asking us] to push ahead . . . to put an end to war.
>
> **Clinton:** As if he's smiling on us.
>
> **Barak:** Together with [the late] Sadat and Begin.
>
> **Clinton:** All of them are saying to us 'to work comrades'.[19]

The next day, Saturday, 15 July, Dennis Ross of the American team came to see the prime minister to say that in the four discussion groups there was no progress and 'if things do not change today then it's hopeless . . . We need something on paper . . . written and agreed . . . *I don't get why you rejected our first paper* . . . I need to get your red lines.'[20] Barak replied:

> The Palestinians are not moving and you're now asking for my red lines . . . that I will give even more concessions while they don't move. If they don't move there won't be an agreement. If the chairman is not made to realize that if he fails to make decisions he [will never become] the president of the Palestinian state, [but] be thrown back . . . he will not move . . . my feeling is that you've failed to create in Arafat the sense that he would lose a lot should he fail to move.

*

To get things moving, President Clinton tried a new tack, setting up an alternate set of talks where two people from each side would negotiate without any boundaries to their discussion. Locked away, they would try to forge the contours of an agreement, but – and this was key – there would be total deniability of anything suggested there should either Arafat or Barak feel their people had gone too far. At the end of the exercise the negotiators would report directly to President Clinton and their respective leaders.

Barak dispatched a minister, Shlomo Ben-Ami, and aide, Gilead Sher, to represent him; while Arafat summoned his delegates Saeb Erekat and Mohammed Dahlan from the Camp David cinema, instructing them to 'use your brains'. Erekat recalls what Arafat did before they left for the night negotiations: 'He grabbed me and said, "Saeb, the most important thing for me is Jerusalem – the Haram."'[21]

It was a tough night of negotiations; a range of issues were discussed, from borders of the future Palestinian state, through the fate of settlements on the occupied territories, to Jerusalem, and emotions ran high. At one point, when they were discussing compensation for Palestinian refugees, the Israeli negotiators insisted that Jewish refugees who left Arab countries in 1948, emigrating to the newly established Israel, should also be compensated. But for Erekat this was too much. 'No, sir,' he shouted at Sher:

> You are not going to be compensated for your years of occupation. We will demand compensation for every day of your occupation, if you're going to go down this line. Somebody who has occupied me for thirty-five years and then comes to ask me for compensation? You took my childhood. I was twelve years old when your occupation came to my home town, Jericho. I was never again the same person. You have denied me the right to live normally. And now you want compensation for this. I will calculate every hour, and find every legal way to make you pay for every damn hour, killing, bulldozing of homes, confiscating of land, closing schools, deporting, wounding, killing . . .[22]

After a night of talks, the Israelis, on the next day, reported to the prime minister. It emerged that they had proposed to their Palestinian counterparts an Israeli withdrawal from 89.5 per cent of West Bank land, letting them set up their own state there and on the entire Gaza Strip, one third of which was still under Israeli occupation. The Israelis also offered Palestinian sovereignty in several outer neighbourhoods of East Jerusalem, and a link ('safe passage') between the Gaza Strip and the West Bank, so that people and goods could travel between the two parts of Palestine, among other concessions. The Palestinians, in turn, agreed to concede Israeli sovereignty over all the Jewish settlements that had been built on occupied territory in east Jerusalem since 1967, and they also recognized Israel's sovereignty over the Wailing Wall, holy to Jews and part of the Western Wall in Jerusalem.

Upon hearing his people's offers, the prime minister did not fall off his chair, but he did ask his two negotiators that, in their report to President Clinton, they should say that Barak 'can't live with the proposal . . .'[23] He was not impressed, or at least this is the impression he sought to leave, with the concessions made by the Palestinians. Indeed, as soon as his delegates left to report to Clinton, Barak sat down to write him a letter: 'I took the report of Shlomo Ben-Ami and Gilead Sher of last night's discussion very badly,' he wrote. 'This is not negotiation. This is a manipulative attempt to pull us to a position we will never be able to accept, without the Palestinians moving one inch . . . I do not intend to allow the Israeli state to fall apart physically or morally . . . I will not allow it to happen.'[24] He then went on to explain how he thought things could proceed better, namely: 'only a sharp shaking of Arafat by the president will give the process a chance . . . Only if Arafat comes to understand that this is the moment of truth will he move. He has to see that he has a chance to achieve an independent Palestinian state . . . or the alternative of a tragedy . . .' In the words of Martin Indyk of the American team, who saw Barak's letter to Clinton, what the prime minister wanted to see was the summit turning into a pressure cooker and he expected President Clinton to throw Arafat into the pot and turn up the heat.[25]

On Sunday, 16 July (the sixth day of the summit), President Clinton came to Barak's cabin to report on a crucial conversation he had had with Arafat. It seems he had adopted the prime minister's advice to put pressure on the Palestinian leader: 'I had the toughest meeting I ever had with Arafat,' the president reported and went on to describe what he had said to him:

> You've got to decide . . . you keep telling me stories all the time . . . You can't expect more concessions from Barak . . . if you don't propose

anything then let's stop now . . . The Israelis have been logical and you were not . . . you will have no state . . . I expect you to come up and present me with offers . . . you were not negotiating in good faith . . . Israel came here in good faith and you not . . . you are going to lose what is in reach . . .[26]

Arafat, as Clinton described him, 'was shaking and he apologized . . . he has no one to consult with. He said to me: "you're actually my psychologist . . ." I was very tough on him . . . [I said to Arafat] "So far this is bullshit . . . bullshit . . . this is crazy."' The prime minister replied, no doubt exaggerating a bit: 'I have seen battles and dangers in my life, but this morning was perhaps the toughest day of my life . . .' and then, being a bit economical with the truth, he added: 'Shlomo [Ben-Ami] and Gilead [Sher] overnight went beyond what I could live with . . . if with this offer made to him Arafat can't move, then we have to prepare for war . . . And I beg you, don't call me if he proposes something funny . . . You pledged not to blame him [should the summit fail but only] on the basis that he negotiates in good faith . . .'

Here, quite clearly, the prime minister was starting to prepare the ground for blaming Arafat for the summit's failure; it is important, though, to note that the record clearly shows that what Clinton promised Arafat before the summit was not to blame him should the summit fail, *not linking it in any way*, as Barak was now doing, to the question of whether Arafat negotiated in good faith or not. Clinton now said that he had asked Arafat to respond to the offers made to him by Barak's people during the unofficial night talks, adding: 'OK, I'm going to dine with [my daughter] Chelsea . . . If he comes with something ridiculous . . . I'll kick him out.'

Later, the president reported Arafat's response to Barak: 'He will come very close to meeting your territorial needs,' Clinton said, 'which I take it will be somewhere between 8 and 10 per cent [to be annexed by Israel in order to accommodate the big blocs of settlements].'[27] Clinton's assertion is questionable: the 'somewhere between 8 and 10 per cent' of the West Bank to be annexed by Israel which Clinton seems to suggest that Arafat agreed to is far more than the Palestinians had ever indicated they would accept in the past – it would be a major breakthrough if it were true – but was this just Clinton's *interpreta-*

tion of Arafat, putting a positive spin on his words in order to keep Barak negotiating? Clinton added that Arafat 'wanted a swap' to compensate him for the land Israel would annex, 'but only a symbolic one'.

Having achieved what now seemed to be a breakthrough on territorial issues, it became apparent that the parties would have to tackle the most contentious issue of all.

Jerusalem

On the summit's seventh day (17 July) the city which Israelis and Palestinians sought as their capital moved centre stage. While both parties felt – though they were reluctant to spell it out publicly – that there could be some give-and-take in Jerusalem, on one location both sides felt very strongly that they could not possibly compromise: the heart of Jerusalem's Old City, the Jewish Temple Mount and the Muslim Haram al-Sharif. The latter compound is physically located directly on top of the Temple Mount and both Israelis and Palestinians sought not only physical control of the place, but also to be legally regarded as the sovereign there.

Now, in Camp David, siding with the Israelis, President Clinton said to the prime minister: 'I accept your sovereignty on Temple Mount', by which he meant the entire site, including the Haram. But he went on to explain that 'the best way to move Arafat is for me to be able to draw for him a picture that looks good [on Jerusalem], without damaging your sovereignty'.[28] Clinton now wanted to see if Barak could come up with an offer on Jerusalem that could satisfy Arafat and bring the conference to a successful end. In a late-night face-to-face meeting with Clinton, Barak gave him the go-ahead to try to find a solution that, as he put it, 'I could live with'. This was to be an *Ameri-can* proposal to Arafat – not Barak's; the president would tell Arafat that he would try to get Barak to agree to it. After the meeting, back in his cabin the prime minister reported to his Chief of Staff, Dany Yatom, on the offer and Yatom took notes for the record. It emerges from this record that, in exchange for his willingness to allow Clinton to offer Arafat something Barak 'could live with' in Jerusalem, the prime minister had asked for quite a lot in terms of American military aid: '[I've asked] for the supply of F-22 [fighter jets],' Barak dictated, 'Tomahawk [missiles] . . . a Defence pact [between Israel and the US] which would cover a non-conventional missile attack and a full conventional attack . . . [i.e. a non-conventional weapon attack on Israel would be met with an equivalent attack by the US] . . .' Lastly, Barak dictated to Yatom: 'I said to him that they must not yet touch our non-conventional capabilities . . .'[29] The latter, of course, is a reference to Israel's nuclear capability.

It soon became apparent, however, that Clinton had made no progress with Arafat. The Palestinian leader said he would only agree to a deal that gave him full sovereignty over all of Arab East Jerusalem, including Haram al-Sharif/Temple Mount, which Clinton knew the prime minister would not accept. Increasingly desperate, Clinton told Barak that the only course of action left was to end the summit. Barak asked the president for some time to consider his next move.

Trapping Arafat?

When Barak and Clinton met again at Barak's cabin, they dismissed their note takers so there would be no record of the conversation and Barak told Clinton that he would now give him a far-reaching deposit, an offer the president should take to Arafat, though not as Barak's direct offer, rather as something Clinton thought he might just be able to extract from the prime minister, if he had Arafat's acceptance of the deal. At the heart of what Barak now proposed was the following: Israel would end its occupation of the Gaza Strip and West Bank but retain 9 per cent of the latter to accommodate its settlements, for which it would compensate Arafat by swapping him 1 per cent of Israeli land near the Gaza Strip for it. Israel would also give Arafat sovereignty over 85 per cent of the border with Jordan. In Jerusalem, seven out of the nine outer neighbourhoods would come under Palestinian sovereignty; in the inner neighbourhoods of Jerusalem the Palestinians would be in charge of urban planning; and in the Old City they would get sovereignty over the Muslim and Christian Quarters. On the Temple Mount/Haram, the UN Security Council would pass a resolution to hand it over for shared custodianship to Palestine,

Morocco and the Chair of the Jerusalem Committee (the higher Islamic commission in Jerusalem), but – crucially – Israel would maintain its sovereignty over the site and the Temple Mount which is buried under it. On security, the Palestinians would have to meet Israel's needs, including Israeli control over the Jordan Valley for up to twelve years after an agreement was signed, so Israel could defend itself against a potential attack from the likes of Iraq to the east, and block the smuggling of weapons into Palestinian areas from across the river. On refugees, there would be, as the prime minister put it, 'a satisfactory solution'. Barak then added that should Arafat reject this package, then he would regard Arafat for what he *really* was; as Barak put it: 'if he looks like a fanatic, walks like a fanatic, quacks like a fanatic then he probably *is* a fanatic'.

There is little doubt that in this plan Barak offered Arafat quite a lot in terms of land and other concessions, particularly on Jerusalem. United Jerusalem had become, in the years since its annexation in 1967, an essential part of the identity of the Jewish state and to divide its heart – the Old City – offering half of it to Arafat, was, as Martin Indyk of the US team rightly observed, 'an act either of extraordinary courage and statesmanship or of pure folly'.[30] Having said that, it is also important to note that Barak refrained from offering what for Arafat was *the* most important of all: sovereignty over the Haram al-Sharif.

Was this another Machiavellian trap laid by Barak to catch Arafat? Was it his estimation that Arafat would reject *any* offer put his way which did not include Palestinian sovereignty over the Haram – no matter how generous the other provisions – thus enabling the prime minister to demonstrate that he was willing to make major concessions, safe in the knowledge he would never actually have to follow through, and, what's more, could leave Camp David portraying Arafat as uninterested in peace? It is unlikely we shall ever know, but it was, nonetheless, a most dramatic moment at Camp David. Clinton's National Security Advisor, Sandy Berger, recalls that 'What Barak presented to the President was extraordinarily dramatic ... and the President came back to Aspen lodge, asked to see just Madeleine [Albright], Dennis [Ross], myself alone, sat down and said: "I think we now have something to work with."'[31]

Clinton asked for a face-to-face meeting with Arafat, with only Gamal Helal, a State Department interpreter, present to interpret the conversation; all other members of the American team retreated to the kitchen. Berger remembers how 'we all huddled behind the door, and alternatively one of us would go to the door to open it just a crack, peek through the window just a little bit so we could see what was going on'.[32] In the main room, Clinton presented the Barak offer to Arafat. Here is Berger again:

> Clinton was using the full range of the piano board on Arafat. Every key, every note, he was cajoling, he was persuading, he was in some cases intimating a bit. At one point he's leaning over Arafat. And Arafat listened mostly. I thought he looked like he was overwhelmed by this looming six-foot-four presence who was leaning, getting closer and closer and closer to his face as he was talking about this being an historic moment.

Arafat said he wanted some time to consider, and he would then get back with an answer. In the early hours of Wednesday, 19 July, Arafat finally dispatched the following letter:

> *Dear President Clinton*
>   *In the light of the importance of the discussion and the issues with which we are grappling, particularly the issue of Jerusalem . . . we are in the opinion that it is necessary to consult with the Palestinian leadership . . . We want to indicate our willingness to continue the negotiations in a place which you'll decide . . .*[33]

Clinton smelled a rat. He saw in Arafat's letter an attempt to 'pocket' Barak's proposals and then use them as opening positions in a further summit where more concessions would be demanded. Clinton also realized that should he allow Arafat off the hook now, and let him out of Camp David, he would lose all the advantages of the pressure cooker environment. He therefore demanded that Arafat should give him a straightforward answer – then and there. This answer, however, when it came, was a very clear 'No'. Upon hearing the news, the prime minister sent his own letter to Clinton:

Dear Mr President
  This letter is written to you with immense gratitude and deep
concern . . . Regretfully, I have learned early this morning that the
summit may be reaching a deadlock. It's our strong feeling that the
Palestinian side has not negotiated in good faith, nor did it seriously
move towards accommodating our concerns . . . Apparently, the
Palestinian leadership has at this point of time departed from its
declared commitment to end the conflict . . . the consequences of the
current situation may well cause deterioration in the region. We shall
do our best to avoid it . . .[34]

Barak ended his letter with a pledge to continue with the Oslo peace process ('I reaffirm our commitment to achieving negotiated solutions').

In a subsequent meeting with the prime minister, an obviously distressed Clinton thanked Barak for his letter, and told him he agreed with it. He added: 'I'll back you and protect you, I'm your guy . . . it's very upsetting . . . all the Arabs are the same . . . [they all try to] squeeze [you] . . .' The president went on to tell Barak how, when he criticized Arafat for not cooperating, Arafat then embarked on 'his little speech', by saying, 'I love you and thank you', so as to divert attention from the substance – his lack of cooperation in trying to find a solution to the conflict.[35]

A political crook

Thus far at the summit Barak had refused to meet Arafat face to face, but now Clinton suggested that they do so, adding that such a meeting would look good for Barak, who could not then be accused of not trying everything he could to achieve peace. Barak, however, was reluctant. 'We have been careful enough not to give him an American or an Israeli [written] paper so [he can't] go out with a record . . .' Barak said, adding: 'He needs a [face-to-face] meeting [with me] to have a record . . .' Clinton tried again, but Barak was unmovable.

Later, Clinton reported to Barak that he had talked to Egypt's President Hosni Mubarak and others, asking them to lend a hand in helping persuade Arafat to accept the offer put to him.[36] In hindsight, leaving Arab leaders – the Saudis, Jordanians and, particularly, the Egyptians, the unofficial patrons of the Palestinians – in the dark and not securing their support before and throughout the summit was a grave error; asking them to intervene now, when discussions were stymied and without them knowing the details and nuances, was hopeless. Indeed, Egypt's President Mubarak recalls how 'I got a call from the President of the United States, who tells me I've got to call Arafat and push him to take a compromise on Jerusalem. I asked him, "What are the terms" and the President said, "I can't tell you because I pledged not to reveal the details . . ." [so I said] "Thank you Mr President. There's nothing I can do for you."'[37] In fact, instead of pressing Arafat into accepting compromise, Arab leaders urged him to maintain his fortitude, especially on Jerusalem.

Clinton also reported to Barak that the Palestinians were 'scared to death', as he put it, that they would be blamed for the summit's collapse, and that they wished to stay on and continue the talks. Barak replied: 'We are grown-ups . . . not kids . . . what they did is bullshit . . . They have manipulated both of us.' Clinton described to Barak the situation in the Palestinian camp, where 'the problem is that their decisions are made by a committee . . . there are endless arguments there'. The president repeated his request for Barak to sit down with Arafat to try to sort things out directly, but again the prime minister turned it down: 'I'm not going to enter a room with a crook . . . he's a political crook . . .' Clinton: 'But you did not conduct any negotiations with him.' Barak: '*He* didn't conduct negotiations . . .' Clinton: 'Do you think it is the right thing to do not to look into his eyes?' Barak: 'I don't want to see him.' Clinton: 'Do you want to leave and kill it all?' Barak: 'I'm going to announce that we did not have a partner but a manipulator . . .'[38]

The collapse

Clinton had to leave for a long-planned Group of Eight summit in Okinawa, Japan, but he pressed Barak and Arafat to stay on at Camp David to continue the negotiations. Since neither Barak nor Arafat wanted to be regarded as the wreckers of the conference, they agreed to stay on and negotiate under the supervision of the Secretary of

State, Madeleine Albright, but with Clinton out in Japan they withdrew to their cabins and stopped negotiating.

Albright tried, at least, to improve the sour atmosphere at Camp David, so the prime minister was allowed a day trip out of the camp and taken to the Gettysburg battlefield. Of course, Arafat then had to be allowed to leave as well, so Albright invited him to her farm, located about twenty-five minutes away. She recalls:

> When we got there my two-year-old grandson had just woken up from a nap, and took one look at Arafat and screamed, and I thought this is the end of this. Then we sat by the swimming pool, and Arafat told stories ... that he liked *Tom and Jerry* cartoons, and he cheered my other grandson diving off the diving board, and he kissed my granddaughter, and then we have this completely lunatic picture of Arafat standing among all these people in their bathing suits, and he is in his uniform, it looks as though we had a cut-out figure that just joined us.[39]

Back in Camp David the delegates went ten-pin bowling in the camp's own bowling alley. *Gladiator* was shown in the cinema. They were all holidaying, waiting for the president to return.

Clinton got back from Japan on 23 July and sat with the prime minister. Now Barak emphasized that as much as he wanted to strike a deal and put an end to the Israeli–Palestinian conflict, 'we will not do it for any price'. He suggested that Clinton should go back to Arafat and ask for his reply to the proposals put to him before the president had left for Japan. Barak added:

> I can't go any further ... that's the maximum I can pass [in a referendum in Israel] ... it's not just a tactic but real ... it's a fair deal [for] the Palestinians ... Arafat must understand that it's now or never and that he will get over the weeks and months a logical state on 90 per cent of the land, viable borders, crossings to the different states ... he will get part of East Jerusalem ... It's a huge opportunity for him ... Now's the time for him to decide whether he wants to be head of state, or head of a gang ...[40]

Barak tried to reassure Clinton that the Arab world would support Arafat anyway, but Clinton disagreed. 'The Saudis,' he said, 'will cut

Arafat to pieces if he gives up sovereignty on the mosques [in Jerusalem].' Indeed, this reflects what Arafat, according to his colleague Akram Hanieh, told Clinton and his team:

> Jerusalem is not a Palestinian city only, it is an Arab, Islamic and Christian one. If I am going to take a decision on Jerusalem, I have to consult with the Sunnis and the Shiites and all Arab countries. I have to consult with many countries starting with Iran and Pakistan, passing by Indonesia and Bangladesh and ending with Nigeria. Do you expect that anybody would agree on giving up Jerusalem and the Aqsa mosque?[41]

Clinton said that should Arafat fail to cooperate and give a straight answer to the previous proposals put to him by Barak, then 'I'll blame him . . . I'll say that you've done what you could and he failed to respond appropriately . . . you've acted bravely. They failed to respond appropriately'. This quite clearly was a retrenchment from what Clinton had promised Arafat before the summit, namely that even if it failed he would not blame him.

By now the prime minister had stopped negotiating and started preparing for confrontation with the Palestinians, phoning the head of the Shabak in Israel, Avi Dichter, to warn him that 'We are probably going to have a failure . . . prepare yourself for a confrontation'; he sent a similar message to the army's Chief of Staff.

In the meantime, Clinton saw Arafat to inquire why he was still refusing to respond positively to the offer he had put to him before leaving for Japan, to which Arafat replied: 'Do you want to come to my funeral? I prefer to die than to agree to Israeli sovereignty on Haram. I'm not going to enter the history of Arabs and Muslims as a traitor . . . we'll liberate Jerusalem, perhaps not now, but in 100 years.'[42] Clinton snapped: 'Barak made concessions and you did not . . . we are talking about nations not religion. Have you ever dreamt of sovereignty over the Christian and Muslim Quarters [now offered by Barak] . . . and a Palestinian state?' But Arafat was completely immovable.

Later that night (24 July), in a last desperate effort, Clinton sat with Israeli and Palestinian negotiators. He offered the Palestinians sovereignty in the outer districts of Jerusalem; limited sovereignty in Jerusalem's inner neighbourhoods; sovereignty in the Muslim and

Christian Quarters of the Old City and something he thought would tempt Arafat, which he called 'custodial sovereignty', an unheard-of term in international law, over the Haram; he then sent the Palestinian representative in the meeting to Arafat to consider the new offer. The Palestinians reviewed the proposal but without full sovereignty over Jerusalem's Haram al-Sharif they felt they could not respond positively. At three in the morning Arafat dispatched his delegates Mohammed Dahlan and Saeb Erekat to deliver a letter to Clinton rejecting the proposal. As Dahlan recalls:

> It was raining, and we walked to President Clinton . . . Of course, President Clinton realized from the moment we walked in that we were carrying a rejection . . . from the way we looked . . . the way we entered, our performance, it was obvious, but it was a touching moment.[43]

At 3.15 in the morning, Clinton phoned the prime minister to say that Arafat had rejected the offer. A few hours later, the prime minister gathered his delegation at Dogwood cabin to announce the failure of the summit and to say that it seems that 'we've got no partner'.[44] He added: 'The real battle is now at home . . . For the time being Arafat doesn't have real readiness to end the conflict, but perhaps has another strategy . . . that he could get [what he wants] in a limited confrontation [with Israel . . .]'

Clinton and Albright came to Barak's cabin to discuss the statement the president would release to end the conference. Clinton said: 'I'll say that you've shown bravery and determination and that Arafat was mute . . . and that you were brilliant.'[45] Reflecting on the last two weeks at Camp David, Clinton said that the Palestinians 'came over with a strategy which was very bad . . . Arafat is seventy-two, he has only been a revolutionary leader, the people around him are old . . . Arafat is out of touch with the real world . . . he isn't living in the world we are living in. We all the time decide and check alternatives [but he doesn't . . .]'

After going over the statement, Barak told Clinton he accepted it, adding that, given Arafat's unwillingness to compromise, 'I'm not going to give him [more withdrawals from occupied lands]'. Clinton assured him he would support him. It was yet another retrenchment, since before the summit not only had Clinton promised not to blame Arafat if it failed, but also to continue with the transfer of land from Israeli to Palestinian hands as agreed in previous agreements. After the conference Barak would argue that 'by exposing Arafat as someone unwilling to compromise I was able to stop abruptly the transfer of land to him . . .'[46]

For all practical purposes the summit was over and the finger of blame was firmly directed at Arafat as the one who wrecked it.

The great American diplomat Henry Kissinger once observed that a negotiation can succeed only if the minimum terms of each side can be made to coincide.[47] At Camp David, Arafat's minimum was not reached and the offers made to him fell short of his requirements. True, Barak's offers were generous and far-reaching and he went further than any of his predecessors on everything from concessions on land to the fate of Jerusalem. But they were nowhere near what Arafat needed; for him the main issue was Jerusalem, where he felt that he was in no position to budge an inch over the holy sites as it affected the broader Muslim community, not only the Palestinians. Land mattered to him far less than emotional and Islamic values and, quite clearly, there was no way he could have signed off on any solution to Jerusalem which was less than full sovereignty over the Haram without Arab support, particularly from Saudi Arabia, Egypt and Jordan; this, however, was not forthcoming at the critical moment, and should have been something organized in advance by the US.

Could a face-to-face meeting between Arafat and the prime minister, which Barak steadfastly refused, have helped a deal to be reached? Even now it is not entirely clear whether such a meeting could have changed Arafat's position and saved the summit, as the main problem was that the gaps on the big issues – not only on Jerusalem, but also on the fate of the refugees, for example – were simply too large to be bridged. But it was unhelpful that Barak was never really capable of communicating with Arafat.

Despite the collapse of the Camp David summit, what happened there in the summer of 2000 will, no doubt, be regarded by future historians as a critical phase in resolving the Israeli–Palestinian conflict and ending the occupation, as it clarified the main issues, thus enabling the parties to digest the matters they would have to tackle in future negotiations.

A gathering storm

After the summit ended, the most immediate concern for both Barak and Arafat was to blame the other for its failure; this was essential in order to shore up domestic and international support. As Arafat was due to see President Jacques Chirac in Paris, on 29 July, to explain why he refused to accept the Camp David offers, the prime minister phoned Chirac the day before to get his side of the story in first and urge him to 'encourage Arafat to make the decisions that could enable us to reach a deal . . .'[48]

On the ground, in the meantime, a tense calm prevailed, but lines of communication remained open between Israeli, Palestinian and American diplomats to ensure that the big expected confrontation did not materialize. On 30 August, the prime minister met President Clinton's special emissary, Dennis Ross, along with Ambassador Indyk, Special Advisor Rob Malley and the US diplomat Gamal Helal, who had come to Israel to see how, if at all, the parties could resume peace talks. 'Do we have a partner [in Arafat],' Barak asked his guests, 'or are we dealing with someone who doesn't really want to have a deal?'[49] Gamal Helal, an Egyptian-born American and specialist at the State Department who also acted as President Clinton's interpreter at meetings with Arab leaders and who knew Arafat quite well, said: 'I don't really know . . . Arafat returned home from Camp David as a hero and this is how he feels . . . [he thinks he is] the defender of Jerusalem. Is he still in the same euphoria, or is he back to reality yet? I have no answer to that.'

On 6 September Barak talked with President Clinton on the phone, telling him: 'I have decided to give peace with Arafat another chance . . .'[50] Clinton was keen. He said that after Camp David 'Arafat visited thirty countries . . . maybe he prefers to tour the world like Moses . . .' and he wondered: 'how would he get a good deal if you and me are leaving [office]?' The president and Barak began thinking of ways to resume Israeli–Palestinian peace talks, perhaps in Washington, and their plan, developed in a subsequent series of lengthy phone calls, was to use the groundwork laid at Camp David to try to close the remaining gaps. Barak even suggested that he should sit down with Arafat – something he had so far been reluctant to do – in order to warm up their relationship and launch the new initiative; Clinton jumped at this suggestion, saying: 'I can't see how such a meeting with Arafat could hurt.'

Subsequently, on 25 September, exactly two months after the collapse of the Camp David summit, the prime minister dispatched a Black Hawk helicopter to Ramallah to collect Arafat and some of his colleagues and bring them for dinner at his home in Kochav Yair to try to mend broken fences. They had agreed in advance that, immediately after the meeting, they would dispatch their people for three days of peace talks in Washington. In their meeting Barak told Arafat: 'It's a moment of truth . . . we don't have a lot of time.'[51] Arafat said little, as he would usually do in meetings such as this, responding in his non-committal, mumbling style by saying: 'Yes, yes . . . very short time . . . things might happen.' But he did express his deep concern that should Ariel Sharon, leader of the right-wing opposition party Likud, embark on a visit to the sensitive Temple Mount in Jerusalem, as he had recently declared he would do, then this could spark a bloody confrontation. Such a visit was certain to anger Muslims, as the Jewish Temple is buried underground and a 'visit' to it effectively means a walk in the Haram al-Sharif compound, which contains a number of mosques, including the holy al-Aqsa. After the Camp David summit this area became a powder keg; after all, the summit itself collapsed over disagreements about who would control it.

12
Al-Aqsa *Intifada*, 2000–2001

Ariel Sharon's visit to the Temple Mount/Haram al-Sharif on 28 September 2000 turned out to be a watershed event in the history of the Palestinian occupied territories. The Likud leader arrived early in the morning under heavy police escort to protect him from possible assault by Palestinians, and toured the compound for half an hour. Haj Kamil, a Palestinian guard at the al-Aqsa mosque, recalls how Sharon was walking around the courts of the mosque 'very provocatively, humiliating the Palestinian people and the Muslim holy places . . . we started shouting, asking him to leave, "Get out of the mosque, the holy mosque, the al-Aqsa mosque . . ." [his guards] hit me with a stick . . .'[1] While during the visit there were only limited disturbances, for the remainder of the day there were sporadic outbreaks of Palestinian stone throwing at police in the vicinity of the site. These incidents, we now know, were the opening salvos of the second Palestinian *intifada*, or as it is better known in its religiously loaded name, the 'al-Aqsa *intifada*'.

The prime minister could have prevented Sharon from making his visit. Why Barak failed to do so, particularly after Arafat had warned him at their meeting of 25 September of the potentially dire consequences of such a provocative visit, is not entirely clear. In an interview with the author, Barak said that it was simply not in his power to stop anyone, including the leader of the opposition, from visiting the site, unless it posed a threat to national security. But of course it did just that, as the events that followed quickly made clear. As for Sharon, what he wished to achieve by visiting the site was to boost his support, particularly within his own Likud Party, where a younger, more eloquent political rival, Benjamin Netanyahu, was enjoying growing popularity. It was also Sharon's way of showing that he would not negotiate Jerusalem away, unlike the prime minister, who had put it on the negotiating table at the Camp David summit.

And thus, just like the first *intifada* in the Palestinian occupied territories, which had been sparked by a minor incident – a car crash – so the second *intifada* was ignited by this seemingly minor event, a visit by a politician to the Temple Mount in Jerusalem. Sharon's visit – as controversial as it was – was just a catalyst, however, rather than the underlying cause of the new Palestinian uprising. So what *was* the deeper cause of the new war?

Ted Gurr, a leading expert on conflict, notes that civil strife is often the result of a gap between what individuals believe they are entitled to and what they actually receive. This relative deprivation, he explains, often leads to 'discontent and anger, and that anger is a motivating state for which aggression is an inherently satisfying response'.[2] This, in essence, explains the cause of the second *intifada*, which emanated not from the individual behaviour of people like Sharon, Barak, Arafat or others, but rather from the disparity between what the Palestinians had been expecting from the peace process and what they actually got, which was failing to meet even their most basic needs.

Indeed, a close look shows that the peace process had brought the Palestinians very few gains; if anything, in fact, it had worsened the conditions under which they lived. When the Oslo process was launched in 1993, the Israeli settlers in the Gaza Strip numbered 3,000, and in the West Bank 117,000; while on the eve of Sharon's visit to Jerusalem, in 2000, there were 6,700 settlers in Gaza and 200,000 in the West Bank. This was a substantial increase and deeply upsetting for the Palestinians; after all, if the Oslo process was all about Israel relinquishing land for peace, then one would expect it to stop settling even more Jews and erecting new settlements on this land. The construction of new settlements also led to more inconveniences in the daily lives of Palestinians, as security measures were put in place to protect the settlers, and they exploited more resources, notably water, to serve their needs.[3] These frustrations among the Palestinians all added up to create a powder keg, waiting for just such a spark as Sharon's visit to the Temple Mount to set it off; chances are, had Sharon not made his trip, sooner or later some other event would have lit the fuse.

All hell breaks loose

While congratulating themselves that on the day of Sharon's visit there were few clashes, the Israelis were still apprehensive that on the next day, after the Friday prayers – always a sensitive time, as the muftis often used them to instil fervour in the crowds – Palestinians might riot. The prime minister contacted the US State Department, asking it to relay a message to Arafat that any protests would be disastrous, especially given the positive progress between Israeli and Palestinian negotiators in peace talks in Washington, which Arafat and Barak had initiated just three days earlier.

Of course, Arafat had only limited control over the protests and demonstrations; first, because most of the West Bank and the Gaza Strip was still under Israeli military control, and, second, not all Palestinians, particularly the Islamists, would listen to him anyway. But it has always been the Israeli practice to identify a single source of authority – in this case Arafat – and regard it as the one responsible for any violence or protest. The US Secretary of State, Madeleine Albright, spoke personally with Arafat, urging him to calm the streets, and while we do not know whether he took any measures, what we do know is that on Friday, 29 September, when the prayers were over at the Haram al-Sharif in Jerusalem, all hell broke loose.

From the Haram, Palestinians began hurling stones down at Jews in front of the Wailing Wall, which stands at the foot of the Haram compound, and as it was the eve of the Jewish New Year the plaza in front of the Wall was crowded with worshippers, who were now evacuated. Then serious clashes erupted in the Haram compound itself between the police, who had broken into the complex, and Palestinians, resulting in seven Palestinians deaths, and 200 more injured. Haj Kamil, a guard at the Haram, recalls 'shooting . . . people scared . . . terrified . . . women urinating in their pants . . . kids screaming and young men's blood all over the carpets . . . everybody was either lying on the ground, or behind the wall, or behind the trees . . .'[4] Riots continued the next day too and the army responded heavily, firing live rounds at the demonstrators, killing eight and injuring hundreds.

In a pattern which would continue throughout the second *intifada*, the number of casualties on the Palestinian side was much greater than on the Israeli. Unlike the first *intifada*, in which the army hesitated during the opening phases and, as a result, lost much of its effectiveness as a deterrent, this time round it reacted swiftly and forcefully from the outset. Although we tend now to differentiate the second *intifada* from the first as being the one in which the Palestinians resorted to guns, this was not at all the case during the conflict's opening phase, when, like the first *intifada*, it was an unarmed civil uprising. But the army, which had initially struggled to meet the first *intifada* with an appropriate level of response, knew it could only take advantage of its technological superiority over the Palestinians if the uprising became an armed struggle – to that extent, the army *wanted* it to be a more violent insurgency. In order to achieve this desired transformation, the army massively overreacted to the riots, trying to fan the flames by firing, during the *intifada*'s first month, a staggering 1.3 million bullets. Of course, these bullets were not directly meant to kill, although there were Palestinian casualties, but to create an atmosphere of war and to provoke the Palestinians into returning fire.[5] By reacting so forcefully, the army did indeed manage gradually to transform the Palestinian civilian uprising into an armed insurgency in which, on the Palestinian side, guns replaced stones, and on the Israeli the military abandoned the cudgels it had used to put down Palestinian resistance in the past and resorted, instead, to outright military means.

But even live bullets would not suppress the Palestinian riots, which spread from Jerusalem across all of the occupied territories. On 30 September, in the midst of disturbances in the Gaza Strip, a twelve-year-old Palestinian boy, Mohammed al-Dura, was pinned down with his father Jamal in crossfire between Palestinian snipers and Israeli troops, and was shot and killed. This scene could have been just another tragic killing of a young boy, sadly not uncommon during the first and second *intifada*s, but this one was captured on video by a cameraman from France 2 television and the graphic footage of Mohammed and his father crouching behind a cement-filled barrel in a fruitless effort to avoid being hit by the bullets was then broadcast over and over again on Palestinian television, fuelling the rapidly esca-lating war. Mohammed al-Dura became a martyr, a symbol of the Palestinian struggle against the occupation; subsequently, postage stamps bearing an image of the father and son were issued through-out the Arab world, and streets were named after the boy.

Emergency diplomacy

On the same day as al-Dura was shot, Terje Rød-Larsen, the UN emis-sary to the region, came to see the prime minister to report on a recent meeting he had held with Arafat, in which he had urged the Palestin-ian leader to stop the riots. As Larsen told Barak, 'I have known him for ten years and every time he should [make critical decisions] he instead veers to violence and bloodshed . . .'[6] Larsen proposed that the prime minister should allow the UN to intervene to pacify the situa-tion and renew the peace process, a request put to him by Arafat himself. Larsen explained the reasoning for a UN intervention over an American one: 'any American proposal is seen as an Israeli proposal. Arafat even said that Martin Indyk [the US ambassador to Israel] is an Israeli spy, so therefore the SG [Secretary General] could help.' But the prime minister would not allow a UN intervention – just as the Palestinians mistrusted the Americans, the Israelis mistrusted the UN, as, since the 1960s, in many of its forums the Arab bloc had an auto-matic majority, enabling Arab countries to pass anti-Israeli resolutions.

So it was left to the White House to deal with the crisis and, appalled by the violence, President Clinton convened an emergency meeting in Paris, summoning Barak and Arafat in an effort to put a lid on the bloodshed. It was agreed that the meeting would take place at the US Ambassador's Residence and be overseen by the Secretary of State, and while a deal to stop the fighting in the occupied territories would be negotiated and initialled in Paris, the parties would then move to Sharm el Sheikh, in Egypt, to sign it formally so that Egypt's President Mubarak, who had much influence over Arafat, would be involved in helping to implement it.

As it emerged, however, Arafat and Barak came to Paris with very different agendas: while Arafat insisted on an international investiga-tion into the causes of the outbreak of violence, which he wished to place on Israel's shoulders in the light of Sharon's controversial visit to the Haram, the prime minister objected vehemently to any international investigation and insisted, instead, on an immediate end to the Palestinian protests.

They met on 4 October: amid a charged atmosphere Madeleine Albright exerted enormous pressure, particularly on Barak to rein in the military. 'We must restore calm and embark on the road for peace,' she told him. Barak then insisted that Arafat should stop the demonstrations at once and that he 'must not be allowed to gain anything [through violence]'.[7] He added that he had 'unambiguous evidence', by which he meant secretly recorded conversations between Palestinian officials, showing that those leading the riots, mainly the Tanzim, a military arm affiliated with Arafat's Fatah movement, believed that Arafat wanted the riots to escalate. 'The Tanzim is out of control,' Barak said, 'Arafat is the head of a gang.' Unconvinced, Albright warned him: 'Sentiment is against you . . . We [the US] are on our own in supporting you . . . the atmosphere is against you.' President Jacques Chirac, in a meeting with the prime minister, added to the pressure on him by echoing Arafat's demands to launch an international inquiry into the events leading to the outbreak of violence. Israel's account of events, Chirac told Barak, 'doesn't correspond with the impression of any country in the world' and he went on to criticize the tough handling of the insurgency by the army: 'This morning sixty-four Palestinians are dead . . . 2,500 injured . . . you can't, Mr Prime Minister, explain this ratio . . . We can't make anyone believe that the Palestinians are the aggressors.'[8]

They settled down for a trilateral meeting, where Arafat and Barak personally headed their teams, with Albright leading the American. In spite of the tough exchanges, they gradually managed to produce a two-page draft of a ceasefire plan, which set out a timetable for the withdrawal of the army from Palestinian areas it had re-entered during the first days of the clashes, along with the specific measures Arafat should take to stop Palestinian demonstrations. Under intense American and Israeli pressure, Arafat gave up his demand for an international investigation, accepting instead a US-led fact-finding committee which would look into how the violence erupted, why it intensified, and what lessons both sides could draw from it to avoid any repetition of it in the future. But then came a development that unravelled much of what had been achieved in many hours of negotiations.

President Chirac insisted that the parties should report to him, as the host country, at the Elysée Palace before the deal was initialled. The Israelis and Americans were expecting a short visit purely for protocol, and were appalled to find Chirac had organized his own full-blown conference to which he had invited the UN Secretary General, Kofi Annan, and his Middle East emissary, Terje Rød-Larsen, along with the EU's foreign policy tsar, Javier Solana. Now Arafat saw a new opportunity to raise again the issue of an international inquiry and wriggle out of the agreement he had just come to under intense US and Israeli pressure. President Chirac, unaware of what had already been agreed, sided with Arafat, saying he was sure the EU would support such an inquiry, adding that it would be desirable for the UN Secretary General to define and organize it. Seeing that the French were on his side in accepting the idea of an international inquiry into the events Arafat, straight after the meeting, slipped into his hotel, refusing to join the parties to sign. The emergency summit collapsed and clashes in the occupied territories continued.

6 October was a particularly violent day when, at the end of the Friday prayers, Palestinians raised the PLO and Hamas flags on the Haram al-Sharif and hurled stones onto the plaza in front of the Wailing Wall where Jews gather to pray. From there fresh riots spilled into Jerusalem's Muslim Quarter in the Old City, and the police station at the Lions' Gate was torched. The prime minister issued an ultimatum to Arafat, saying that if the Palestinians did not behave themselves then he would instruct the army 'to use *all means* to stop the violence'.[9] Arafat tried to call Barak's bluff by publicly responding: 'This is another Barak statement and after it there will be another statement and another statement . . .'

By now, however, with or without the prime minister's ultimatum, the army was already putting enormous pressure on the Palestinians: cutting off towns and cities and turning them into isolated islands, imposing round-the-clock curfews, closing roads and making arrests. Perhaps the most devastating measure the military now employed against the Palestinians was deploying hundreds of checkpoints and roadblocks all over the West Bank and the Gaza Strip which it would not remove for weeks and months. Israeli soldiers would make no exceptions at these road-blocks, not even for the ill or injured. A study conducted by the World Health Organization found that sixty-one Palestinian women gave birth at Israeli army checkpoints between September 2000 and December 2004; thirty-six of the newborns died shortly after birth due to complications that could not be attended to in the mud and dirt on the roadsides. Sick and wounded people also died while queuing at army checkpoints to go to hospitals. A testimony of an Israeli soldier gives us a glimpse into the way troops functioned and the arbitrary decisions they made at army checkpoints during this period:

> On an average morning, when things are going quickly, people will wait four or five hours in line. In other places you can often wait from 4am to 2pm. The commander at the checkpoint can arbitrarily decide not to allow the passage of someone . . . the issue of passage of mer-chandise is also arbitrary: sometimes they are permitted to pass goods . . . and sometimes the commander decides not to let them through.[10]

Ten days in October

During the first *intifada*, Arab citizens of Israel had mostly taken only an indirect part in the insurgency: they donated blood, food and money to Palestinians in the occupied territories, but refrained from taking direct action against Israel. This time, however, Israel's Arab citizens, at that time comprising 17 per cent of the nation's total population, reacted differently. One of them, Mohaned Irbari from the town of Umm el Fahm, explains that he and his friends were appalled at fellow Palestinians being killed in clashes with police in Jerusalem, which led to 'lots of us coming out [onto the streets] . . . to throw stones at the soldiers and the police . . . we'd go backwards and forwards with the police, like cat and mouse'.[11] The police reacted brutally, and for the first time in the country's history they opened fire on their own citizens. When one of these Israeli-Arab rioters was killed, as Mohaned Irbari recalls, 'everyone was just standing there in shock. But there was also anger, and we started to move again against the police . . . we got really angry and started shouting: "Allahu Akbar! Allahu Akbar!" My head was spinning.' By the end of ten days of riots in Israel, thirteen Israeli-Arabs were dead, about 700 were wounded and hundreds more had been arrested.

These dramatic events poisoned Arab–Jewish relations within Israel, further exacerbating the Jewish–Arab divide; while Israeli-Arabs were upset with the police's heavy handling of the situation, Israeli-Jews, on the other hand, regarded the Israeli-Arabs' active participation in the al-Aqsa *intifada* as a betrayal. In opinion polls, 55 per cent of Israeli-Jews reported that their opinion of Israeli-Arabs had deteriorated as a result of their joining the Palestinian uprising. There were also renewed calls to physically remove Israeli-Arabs, an idea that had gathered pace over the years preceding the insurgency; in an opinion poll conducted in March 2002, 31 per cent of Israeli-Jews were in favour of forcibly transferring Israeli–Arabs out of the country, up from 24 per cent in 1991; 60 per cent said they favoured encouraging Arabs to emigrate voluntarily.[12]

It is worth noting, however, that like their indirect protests during the first *intifada*, demonstrations by Israeli-Arabs were not only in solidarity with their brethren under military occupation, but also an expression of their frustration with the historic prejudice against them within Israeli society. 'Our Arabs,' as Israeli-Jews would often refer to Arabs living in Israel proper, had always been treated as second-class citizens, routinely discriminated against, and with an average income the lowest of any ethnic group in the country. As Mohaned Irbari explains: 'It was not just Sharon going to al-Aqsa' that made him demonstrate and clash with the police, but also the discrimination he had suffered in Israel and the fact that 'I'd had enough of eating shit for all these years . . .' [13]

In retrospect, the October 2000 events signalled a new phase in Jewish–Arab relations in Israel, which, at the time of writing, is characterized by growing tensions between the two communities that are only likely to increase further in the coming years, perhaps even leading to an *intifada* between Israeli-Jews and Israeli-Arabs in Israel.[14]

A lynching in Ramallah

Back in the Palestinian occupied territories, on the West Bank, on 12 October, Palestinians murdered two Israeli reservists. This event turned out to be yet another milestone in the gruesome history of the second *intifada* in terms of its brutality, the Israeli response to it and the cycle of escalation it set in train.

The two reservists took a wrong turn en route to their army base and wandered into Palestinian Ramallah, which is the largest, most modern and most secular of the Palestinian cities. Amid the charged atmosphere, the soldiers were taken by Palestinian police into a nearby police station and, for a time, detained there. A mob soon descended on the police station and, while an Italian TV crew that happened to be in the area captured the unfolding drama on camera, rioters got into the police station and stabbed the Israelis, before one of the attackers appeared at the window showing his blood-soaked hands to the jubilant crowd. Moments later, the body of one of the reservists was thrown out of the first-floor window and smashed into the mob below, who then paraded the corpse through the streets of Ramallah; the raw hatred on display was harrowing in the extreme. Shown on television round the world and in Israel, the killing was a mirror image of the televised death of Mohammed al-Dura in Gaza which had served to harden Palestinian attitudes: likewise now, Israeli minds were galvanized, and vengeance was demanded.

At the Defence Ministry in Tel Aviv, the prime minister chaired a special emergency meeting, where it was unanimously agreed that a major retaliation was necessary, targeting Arafat's Palestinian Authority, which the Israelis held responsible for the lynching: they decided to use attack helicopters to hit back, the first time they had been used in the *intifada* and a major escalation of the war. Before going into action, Barak spoke to Egypt's President Mubarak to warn him of the imminent military strike; it was vital to keep Mubarak in the picture as Egypt was at peace with Israel and Mubarak himself was a leading figure in the Arab world, and the Palestinians' most important patron. 'There are pictures that can't be tolerated,' the prime minister said, adding, 'one of the bodies was dragged in the streets . . . like a dog'.[15]

Attack helicopters went into action, striking at the police station in Ramallah, where the lynching took place, destroying several police vehicles; they also hit the Voice of Palestine radio station, three transmitters and targets in the Gaza Strip. After the attack, the prime minister phoned President Clinton and urged him to isolate Arafat. 'The US position must be clear,' Barak said. 'The Palestinian side can't continue to enjoy [US] financial or any other aid . . . The US should seriously consider publicly blaming Arafat for causing irreparable damage to the peace process, instigating violence . . .'[16] Barak also expected Clinton to 'stand by Israel clearly and loudly', and help it diplomatically by 'conveying its concerns . . . to European countries in an effort to form as unified a policy as possible [against Arafat] . . .' The prime minister issued a warning to Clinton too: 'It would be a distortion of history if President Clinton's seven-year-long dedicated commitment to the peace process would be reduced to a legacy of a collapsed process caused by Arafat's incessant deceit.' Barak then sat down to write Clinton a formal letter. 'There is serious doubt,' he wrote, 'whether Chairman Arafat is still a genuine partner for peace. The events of the last week and today's lynching have caused a lot of us here in Israel to doubt this . . .'[17] The prime minister's mantra since Camp David that there was no partner for peace on the Palestinian side continued; it would reach its climax during the next Israeli administration.

Pressure was growing, in the meantime, on both Arafat and Barak to come to a summit in Sharm el Sheikh in Egypt to negotiate a truce and put an end to the violence in the occupied territories. President Mubarak phoned the prime minister to convince him to come. 'You're the strong one,' he said, 'be as patient as you can. I'll talk to him now . . . [The lynching] was a shock for all of us.' When President Clinton kept pressing the prime minister to join the summit Barak snapped: 'Seven years ago he [Arafat] was a terrorist . . . Untouchable . . . *you*'ve turned him into a welcome personality.'[18] Barak, however, confirmed that, after all, he would come to Egypt to join Arafat and others.[19]

Trying to sort it out in Sharm

They gathered in Sharm el Sheikh on 16 October, for what turned out to be the most intense international effort so far to stop the violence: Barak and Arafat, Presidents Clinton and Mubarak, the UN Secretary General, Kofi Annan, Jordan's King Abdullah II, and Javier Solana representing the European Union.

In the meetings, progress was slow and somewhat painful; the atmosphere tense and unpleasant. The host, President Mubarak, was particularly active and determined to succeed; referring to Ariel Sharon's visit to the Temple Mount, he complained: 'Sharon is the reason for all that mess'.[20]

With Arafat insisting on an international inquiry into why the *intifada* started, as he had in Paris a few days earlier, talks were stalled. Barak sat with the UN Secretary General and showed him the horrifying pictures of the lynched soldiers and told him: 'We won't accept any international investigation unless the source of authority is American.'[21] He reassured Annan that, 'We can let you inspect the report before it is made public . . . but we can't give a reward [to Arafat] by [agreeing] to an international inquiry.' Barak then met Jordan's King Abdullah II and showed him the pictures. The king replied: 'We want to get out of here with a positive declaration . . . There's an ugly mood in the Arab street.'[22] President Clinton eventually managed to cut a deal, but just before the parties were due to sign it, Arafat, as he had done in Paris, sneaked out of the room without signing. A desperate Clinton could only read out the agreed, but not signed, ceasefire document to the world's assembled media:

> Prime Minister Barak and Chairman Arafat have agreed . . . first, to issue public statements unequivocally calling for an end of violence. Second, the US will develop . . . a committee of fact finding on the events of the past several weeks . . . A final report shall be submitted under the auspices of the US President for publication. Third . . . the US would consult with parties . . . about how to move forward [with the peace process].[23]

On the ground, however, the Palestinian insurgency remained in full swing and the army's methods of suppressing it became ever more heavy-handed; although in Sharm the prime minister promised to withdraw his tanks from new areas they had invaded since the start of the uprising, on the ground the army remained in the same positions. In fact, in a meeting with his generals Barak instructed them to turn the screw even further – some of his instructions defied international law: 'to upset the Palestinian ability to broadcast TV and Radio . . . Cut off their electricity for six hours . . . Stop petrol [getting into Palestinian areas] . . . Stop buying their agricultural products.'[24] To his ministers the prime minister said: '[we should act] with open eyes, knowing that we aren't living in Western Europe or in North America . . . [the Middle East] is a very tough neighborhood'.[25]

Barak phoned Clinton on a daily basis urging him to shake up Arafat and pressure him to 'immediately stop the violence, the incitement . . .'[26] When Clinton got back to Barak after one of his conversations with Arafat, he described what he said to him: 'You know, we haven't brought an end to the violence and you haven't done some of the things you promised to do [at Sharm].' The president said he next went through the list of items the parties had agreed on in Sharm that Arafat had not yet done. But then, as Clinton reported to Barak, Arafat 'launched into a whole thing about how Barak was using excessive force and look at how many casualties the Palestinians had . . . and how they couldn't get food and they couldn't work and all that . . .' Clinton replied to Arafat, as he now described to Barak: 'Well, that may all be true, but you still have to enforce your end of the deal; unless there's an end to violence you're gonna have more trouble like that.'

With the uprising continuing, the prime minister kept urging his military generals to increase pressure on the Palestinians: 'to disturb the transfer of money . . . Petrol . . . Cement . . . Electricity [and] to . . . increase security checks [in checkpoints . . .]'[27] However, not all Barak's ministers thought that force could end the war with the Palestinians: Shimon Peres, the brains behind the Oslo agreements, urged Barak to allow him to see Arafat in Gaza to try to reach a deal to stop the clashes. Barak, sceptical as he had been so far, approved the meeting and Peres subsequently travelled to Gaza, where he sat with Arafat on 1 November. Arafat was in a black mood, blaming the prime minister for the army's actions:

> Heavy bombardments everywhere [in] Jericho, Ramallah, Nablus, Bethlehem . . . tomorrow [it was reported on Israeli radio] the air force would be used . . . New weapons would be used to hurt Palestinian leaders . . . [Barak] did not withdraw the tanks [as he agreed to do in Sharm]. You prevent the transfer of food . . . besiege [Palestinian] cities . . . more than 200 [Palestinians] were killed and 1,000 injured . . . we are doing our best to calm down the situation [but] you're using tanks, helicopters . . .[28]

One of Arafat's colleagues, also in the meeting, snapped: 'Get your tanks out, at once', adding, 'You're killing the people like cows . . . Withdraw your tanks . . .'[29]

On his return Peres reported to Barak on Arafat's many grievances – particularly Palestinian anger over the army's heavy hand and the use of tanks – but he also reported some success: he and Arafat had reached an understanding – a text which would be read on radio simultaneously by Barak and Arafat to restore calm. This is the text of the proposed announcement:

> The Israeli and Palestinian sides have agreed tonight to issue a joint call for the cessation of violence. I hereby call on all forces and parties to refrain from violence, incitement and the use of force, in order to restore peace and calm. . . . The sides share the hope for a future of stability, prosperity and peace, when two separate political entities will coexist side by side in good neighbourly relations. The sides undertake to exert every effort to realize this dream of the Peace of the Brave in dignity, fairness and mutual respect.[30]

At around 12.45 that afternoon, the prime minister was at a radio station in Tel Aviv, ready to deliver the agreed announcement at 14.00. But he then learnt that rather than Arafat reading the statement it would be one of his aides. This was clearly in breach of the understanding reached with Peres and would obviously significantly reduce the chance that Palestinian militants would take it seriously; as if to confirm Arafat's snub, soon after, at around 15.00, an explosion in Jerusalem killed two Israelis. The Arafat–Peres deal was dead in the water.

Assassinations

Later, France's President Chirac phoned Barak to express his condolences. 'I was shocked by the attack in Jerusalem today . . .' Chirac said, 'I condemned it. I have talked with Arafat this morning and I said to him decisively that he needed to go back to the negotiating table . . .'[31] Pressure to calm the situation also came from the US when, on 4 November, the US ambassador in Israel, Martin Indyk, saw the prime minister with a message from his president that the Arafat–Peres meeting should serve as a good beginning for a renewal of peace talks, and that the parties should give the peace process another chance. Indyk reported that Clinton had sent a message to the same effect to Arafat, urging him to arrest terrorists, stop firing at Israel and halt demonstrations and riots. Indyk urged Barak to try minimizing Palestinian casualties, as the large number of killed and injured on the Palestinian side was serving only to incite even more violence. Indeed, Barak was well aware that so many Palestinian casualties hurt Israel's image abroad and this was an important consideration in his decision to authorize a new policy to fight the insurgency: assassination.

The Israelis referred to this new policy in obfuscatory terms such as 'liquidation', 'targeted killing', 'pinpointing attackers' or 'neutralizing the organizers of attacks'. The first known target of this policy, since the outset of the al-Aqsa *intifada*, was the Palestinian activist Hussein Abayat, who was assassinated on 9 November 2000, at Beit Sahour near Bethlehem, by missiles fired at his car from Israeli attack helicopters.[32] Imad amil Fares, a resident of Beit Sahour, was an eye-witness to the killing:

> I suddenly heard an explosion. The windows of my house were broken and the shutters damaged. When I looked out I saw a grey Mitsubishi on fire and the burnt body of the driver [Abayat]. Two women were lying on the ground near the car and appeared to be critically injured. Their faces were black, completely burnt and still bleeding . . .[33]

More assassinations soon followed; but even this would not stop the insurgency.

Barak blamed Arafat for the escalation, insisting – and telling the world, and particularly Washington, so – that Israel had no partner for peace on the Palestinian side. His argument was strengthened by a report from a group of American senators, led by Danny Abram, a close ally of President Clinton and indeed Barak, who went to see Arafat in Ramallah and returned to Israel to report orally, and in writing, to the prime minister's head of Bureau, who summarized what they had told him as follows:

A report from Danny Abram (25 November)
   1. On Monday 22/11/00 Danny Abram, Wayn Evans, Senator

Torichli and member of Senate Hintzi met with Arafat. 2. The guests found Arafat as someone who lost his self control. Abrams reported that Arafat behaved strangely and even scared his guests by threatening their lives. 3. As a result of this meeting Abrams concluded that Arafat is no longer a partner [for peace].[34]

And yet, on 11 December, the prime minister spoke with Clinton on the phone and after updating him on the security situation ('a bad day after two relatively good days') he proceeded to say that he wished to give peace another chance and perhaps Clinton could encourage Arafat, 'for a last effort . . . to renew the negotiations'.[35] Clinton – always willing to sign up to Barak's ideas – replied: 'I've got another forty days [in office] and I'll do my best to help achieve peace . . .'[36]

Barak's was an odd and quite confusing approach: ever since the failed Camp David summit he had insisted that Arafat was no partner for peace, but at the same time he was urging Washington to try and resume talks with this 'non-partner' Arafat. It is possible, of course, that Barak felt he had to be seen to give negotiations a chance from time to time in order to placate international opinion, and that of some Israelis in his own left-of-centre Labor Party. Whatever the reason, President Clinton summoned Israeli and Palestinian negotiators, on 19 December, to Bolling Air Force Base, just outside Washington. On the basis of their talks and just before Christmas 2000 he invited them to the White House to present his own ideas for peace – his last effort before leaving the White House for good the following month.

Bill Clinton's last-ditch effort

What Clinton presented at the White House, which came to be known as the 'Clinton Parameters', were not the terms of a final deal, but guidelines for accelerated negotiations he hoped could be concluded in the coming weeks. These guidelines should then be followed by fast-track negotiations between the parties in an effort to conclude a peace package by 10 January 2001 – just before Clinton was due to leave office. As Barak was obsessed by the fear that Arafat would pocket any proposal to use later as an opening position to squeeze even more concessions from Israel, it was agreed, between Barak and Clinton, that the president would only read his thoughts to the parties, but not provide them with an official written document. It is likely, given the understanding between Israel and Washington, that Clinton had shown his parameters to the prime minister beforehand, though not to Arafat. Now, on the morning of Saturday, 23 December, at the White House, Clinton read his ideas out loud to Israeli and Palestinian negotiators as they took notes. He then gave the parties just a few days to respond with either a yes or a no. What Clinton proposed as a way to end the Israeli occupation and put the lid on the Palestinian–Israeli conflict was as follows.

On the territory Israel should transfer to the Palestinians, on which they could establish their state, Clinton suggested that the figure should be in the mid-90 per cents, from 94 to 96 per cent of the West Bank territory.[37] For the 4–6 per cent of West Bank land that Israel would annex in order to incorporate its big settlement blocs, where 80 per cent of its settlers lived (all isolated settlements would be dismantled), Clinton suggested Israel compensate the Palestinians by means of a land swap elsewhere. On Jerusalem, a main stumbling block in previous talks, Clinton proposed that 'The general principle is that [within the boundaries of current Jerusalem] Arab areas are Palestinian and Jewish ones are Israeli.' On the heart of the matter, namely the Temple Mount/Haram al-Sharif, the president basically proposed that the parties would share sovereignty over the area: there would be Palestinian sovereignty *over* the Haram and Israeli sovereignty just *under* it, where the ruins of the Jewish Temple are buried. Regarding refugees and the Palestinian claim to have a 'right of return' to the homes of their forefathers in Israel, Clinton proposed that the guiding principle should be that the Palestinian state would be the focal point for Palestinians who chose to return to the area without ruling out that Israel would accept some of these refugees.

A careful reading of the Clinton proposal shows that what he sought was to use the two main obstacles to an Israeli–Palestinian deal – namely the question of sovereignty over Haram al-Sharif/Temple Mount in Jerusalem and the Palestinian demand to have right of return to Israel proper – to cancel each other out. Thus, the Palestinians were offered sovereignty on Haram, which was an Israeli concession, and, in return, would be asked to give up their demand to have right of return to Israel. Finally, and critically, as far as Israel was concerned and upon which it insisted, Clinton said that the agreement would mark the end of the conflict and its implementation would put an end to all Palestinian claims upon Israel.

While the prime minister was working to convince his own ministers to accept the Clinton programme he also attempted to pile pressure on Arafat to do the same. He spoke with Egypt's president, suggesting that Mubarak should see Arafat and try to squeeze from him a positive response; he also asked Mubarak to urge him to reduce the level of rioting in the occupied territories, which could 'help me persuade the Israeli public to accept [Clinton's ideas]'.[38] The compromises asked of Israel, Barak told Mubarak, 'are very painful', but should Arafat give a straightforward yes to the Clinton ideas, then 'I'll do the same.' Barak finished his conversation with Mubarak by saying: 'I'm sitting here in the same chair [the slain prime minister] Rabin used to sit in, and he used to contact you whenever there was a crisis and I'm sure that you could help very much if you convinced Arafat to move forward.'

Israel's official acceptance of the Clinton Parameters was enshrined in a letter to the White House and also included a twenty-page-long document with Israel's reservations and comments.[39]

While Washington was awaiting Arafat's response, the army continued to trade blows with Palestinian insurgents back in the occupied territories. The appointment, in December 2000, of General Doron Almog, as Officer Commanding Southern Command, led to a massive military response to Palestinian insurgency in the Gaza Strip. Under his command, entire stretches of land were exposed: trees were uprooted and houses demolished, and large areas were turned into 'special security zones' – effectively killing zones. As the Palestinian insurgents found it increasingly difficult to grapple directly with the military in the occupied territories, they carried, instead, their war into Israeli cities: on 28 December a bomb exploded on a bus near Tel Aviv, wounding thirteen.

By the end of December 2000, three months into the al-Aqsa *intifada*, the toll, particularly on the Palestinian side, was heavy: 272 had been killed, compared with forty-one Israelis during the same period.

A missed opportunity

A day before President Clinton was due to meet Arafat in Washington to get the Palestinian response to his proposed peace programme, he reported to Barak on a telephone conversation he had had with the Palestinian leader in which 'Arafat had all sorts of comments' that made Clinton wonder whether Arafat would give, after all, a positive response to the Clinton Parameters.[40] The prime minister was sceptical: 'When I look at his behaviour and at intelligence reports I can see an attempt to drag his feet . . .' Barak said, adding:

> He feeds the violence . . . He tries to squeeze from you and from me the maximum . . . You, Mr President, must help present things as they are – which side was willing to go further, and which side fostered terrorism . . . Arafat can't continue to fool you and us . . .

On 3 January, Clinton phoned Barak to report on his meeting with Arafat, and tell him that Arafat had turned the proposal down. As he informed Barak, a deeply disappointed Clinton had said to the Palestinian leader: 'You know, they've always told me that you are someone who will wait until five minutes till twelve, but I'm afraid your watch is broken, Mr Chairman.'[41]

Indeed, there is little doubt that the verdict of history will show that here, in December 2000, Arafat missed an opportunity to have an independent Palestine with Arab East Jerusalem as its capital, including what eluded him at Camp David and what was offered to him now, namely Palestinian sovereignty over the Haram al-Sharif. So why did Arafat turn down this offer? Perhaps he thought that the incoming US president, George W. Bush, would be more generous than the Clinton administration, as the Palestinians regarded Clinton as much too close to the Israelis. Or he didn't want to have to stand before his people and tell them that, while he had secured sovereignty in Jerusalem, at the same time, he had also failed to gain for the Palestinians a right to return to old Palestine. For years he, and others, had promised the Palestinian refugees that they would one day be back in their old homes in what was now Israel. The Palestinian negotiator Abu Ala'a, a close ally of Arafat, once explained that

No single Palestinian ever abandoned the dream of return. That dream
. . . has been the driving force behind our lives, indeed it has been what
has kept us alive . . . The Palestinians in exile came to use various
phrases among themselves. They would greet each other with the
expression 'On our return'; they spoke constantly of 'Our homeland';
and on high days and holidays they would say, 'Our feast comes with
our return.'[42]

Arafat apparently could not bear to abandon this central element in
Palestinian identity and life; he decided instead to wait for a better
offer and to avoid making the hard decisions in favour of sticking to
the status quo. His close adviser, Mohammed Rashid, would later
admit that 'we have made a strategic mistake in not accepting the
Clinton proposals'.[43] At the time of writing, no offer better than the
Clinton Parameters has been officially offered to the Palestinians.

In the meantime, the prime minister's main concern was to keep Palestinian insurgency at bay in the run-up to Israel's general elections,
which were due in February 2001. He therefore allowed his negotiators to hold low-level peace negotiations in Taba, Egypt, as keeping
the dialogue going could do no harm in helping reduce the level of
violence.

At the same time, however, Barak instructed the military to use an
iron fist to deal with Palestinian militants by imposing curfews,
deploying even more checkpoints, controlling Palestinian movements
and accelerating the assassination of leading Palestinian activists: on
13 February, Maso'oud Ayyad, a fifty-year-old senior officer in Arafat's
presidential guard, known as Force 17 (*quwa sab'a 'asher*), was killed
when driving his car near the Jabalya refugee camp in the northern
Gaza Strip; it was hit by three missiles fired from Israeli helicopters.
Four bystanders, including a child, were wounded in the attack and
two people suffered from shock. The prime minister said that the
assassination was 'a clear message that anyone who intends to harm
Israelis will not escape and the long arm of the Israel Defense Forces
will find him and settle his score'.[44] This was a good statement for the
elections, but, in truth, the overall success of the assassination policy
in reducing Palestinian violence during the *intifada* has always been
unclear. And although Israel's Supreme Court ruled that assassina-

tions were legal, as long as the targets were actively engaged in fighting, or else worked as full-time militants, it led to some uneasiness among the Israeli public. On 19 February 2001, Dan Meridor, chairman of the Knesset Foreign and Defence Committee, dispatched a letter to the prime minister, advising him to reconsider the controversial policy. Here is the letter:

> *Top Secret*
> *Mr Prime Minister,*
> *I want to draw your attention to a dangerous development following what's regarded in the world . . . as 'a policy of assassinations'. The European Community turned to us in a request to stop this activity because this is 'a policy that goes against international law'. The US expressed its opposition to a policy of 'pinpointed operations' and even declared that it will delay the supply of telescopic sights to Israel . . . the changes the world has undergone in recent years which allow indicting on war crimes, should be taken into account in deciding on our policies . . .*[45]

The decision on whether to proceed with assassinations of Palestinian activists, however, and indeed all other policies to put down the Palestinian insurgency, would now be made by a new prime minister – the man who had sparked the uprising in the first place with his tour of the Temple Mount – Ariel Sharon.

13
Sharon and Arafat, 2001–2004

It is an irony that not long after his controversial visit to Haram al-Sharif/Temple Mount, Sharon defeated Barak in a landslide election victory, becoming Israel's prime minister in March 2001. Unlike his predecessor, who had sought sweeping peace deals to end the Israeli–Arab conflict and occupation, Sharon's goals were more modest: to end the Palestinian insurgency, restore stability, return to normalcy and – providing that the calm held – to negotiate a limited interim agreement with the Palestinians. Sharon had no desire to negotiate with Syria at all, feeling that the price for peace there – the return of the Golan – to be too high and that there was no urgency to do so as the Israeli–Syrian front had been quiet for many years.

A MOST BLOODY INSURGENCY

Sharon faced the wrath of the Palestinian insurgency almost at once. In March alone, the month he became prime minister, there were three suicide bombings in Israel, in which six Israelis were killed and scores injured. Outraged at the attacks, Sharon publicly blamed Arafat, as he would come to do often; his language was fiery enough for the new US president, George W. Bush, to become concerned that Sharon might kill the Palestinian leader, something that could set the Middle East alight. When, during this bloody March, the two leaders met in Washington, the president wanted to ensure that Sharon would not resort to such an extreme measure. The following exchange between the two, on 20 March, is a pledge by the prime minister not to do so:

President Bush: Do you really hate Arafat?

Prime Minister Sharon: Yes!

Bush: Do you intend to kill him?

Sharon: No!

Bush: Good![1]

Violence continued: on 18 May, in Netanya, northern Israel, a Palestinian suicide bomber blew himself up, killing five and wounding over 100. Sharply criticized in Israel for not doing enough to stop these attacks, Sharon dispatched F-16s to bomb Nablus and Ramallah; it was the first time warplanes had been used to strike the West Bank since the 1967 war.[2] But even air strikes would not stop suicide bombings as, by now, militant Palestinian organizations had developed the tactic into an effective tool to force Israel's hand.

It was a method aimed at addressing the enormous asymmetry of power between the Israeli military and the Palestinian. Sayeed Siyam, a Palestinian activist, explains: 'We in Hamas consider suicide attacks . . . to be the card that Palestinians can play to resist occupation . . . We do not own Apache helicopters . . . so we use our own methods.'[3] As precise, guided human missiles, suicide bombers inflicted heavy, mainly civilian, casualties on the Israelis, paralysed daily life and badly damaged morale in Israel. During the first two years of the al-Aqsa *intifada* the Palestinians sent out 145 suicide bombers.[4] And thus, while the symbol of the first *intifada* was Palestinian children throwing stones at the army, that of the al-Aqsa *intifada* became the suicide bomber.

On 20 May, an opportunity to calm the situation emerged with the publication of the Mitchell Report. The former American senator George J. Mitchell had chaired the commission of inquiry set up at the October 2000 summit meeting in Sharm el Sheikh – which had otherwise been something of a failure – following his successful mediation in the Northern Irish conflict. Mitchell's purview was to investigate the causes of the al-Aqsa *intifada*, to propose ways of ending it and to see how similar events could be averted in the future. In his report Mitchell proposed a series of concrete steps to be taken by both sides, beginning with a cessation of hostilities – critical if the parties were to move on to the next phases – and eventually leading up to a resumption of peace talks.

The prime minister responded swiftly by declaring, on 22 May, a unilateral ceasefire, pledging that the army would only shoot in self-defence; Sharon probably concluded that the Palestinians would proceed with their insurgency anyway, which would enable him to blame Arafat for the violence. Indeed, the Palestinian response was not encouraging; on 25 May, two suicide bombers blew themselves up, one at the Israeli town of Hadera, the other at a security outpost in the Gaza Strip, between them wounding sixty-five Israelis. Two days later, thirty Israelis were injured by a bomb in Jerusalem. It is hard to say why Arafat failed to embrace the ceasefire. Perhaps because he felt that he could not control most of the militants, particularly the Islamists of Hamas, many of whom rejected his leadership, or maybe because he knew that a ceasefire would not really stop the army from applying its iron fist in the occupied territories in the shape of curfews, checkpoints, embargos and other methods. Indeed, although officially embracing the Mitchell Report, at the same time Sharon also advised the army's Chief of Staff, General Shaul Mofaz, 'to strike at the Palestinians everywhere . . . simultaneously. The Palestinians should wake up every morning to find out that twelve of them are dead . . .'[5] Sharon made the war on Palestinian 'terrorism', as he referred to the insurgency, the military's top priority, telling Mofaz: 'That's your war . . . Your test is in victory over the Palestinians.'[6] Did Sharon, who was not lacking in war experience both as a former soldier (in each of Israel's wars from 1948 to 1973) and as defence minister during the invasion of Lebanon in 1982, really believe that the army could achieve a 'victory' over the insurgents in this way? Probably not, and by demanding the army kill scores of Palestinians he gave them a green light to act fiercely, which, he must have realized, would only feed the vicious circle of violence.

On 1 June, in a Tel Aviv nightclub, Said al-Hutri, a Hamas operative from Nablus, inflicted carnage by blowing himself up; he killed twenty-one and wounded more than eighty, most of them teenagers, in what was the worst ever suicide attack on Tel Aviv. For Sharon this was all Arafat's fault, for although most of the suicide bombings were carried out by Hamas and Islamic Jihad, rivals of Arafat's secular Palestinian Authority over whom he had little direct control, Sharon felt that Arafat was not doing enough to stop the attacks. There was, to be sure, a lot of bad blood between the pair, going back to the days of the 1982 Lebanon war, when as the architect of that war Sharon had besieged Arafat in Beirut and refrained from killing him only on clear US instructions. Now, on the night of the attack in Tel Aviv, the prime minister urged his cabinet, at an emergency session, to approve a plan to 'remove' Arafat – perhaps to expel him; Sharon, we should recall, had promised President George W. Bush in March not to kill Arafat. Apprehensive, however, that expulsion even if it were physically possible – Arafat was known always to carry a gun and might choose to go out fighting rather than let himself be arrested by Israeli troops – might be counterproductive, as it could turn Arafat into a martyr, the cabinet decided not to expel Arafat.

In the meantime, shocked by the bloodshed in Israel and the occupied territories, world leaders urged Arafat to reciprocate and join Sharon in accepting the ceasefire required by the Mitchell Report, which he finally did on 2 June. But this would not stop the *intifada*, and what, in particular, inflamed the situation was Israel's assassination policy, an inheritance from the previous Barak government, and one that put pressure on the militants to hit back in order to demonstrate their resilience. Thus, when on 31 July the army assassinated two senior Hamas activists in Nablus – Sheikhs Gamal Mansur and Gamal Salim – this, as expected, led to a retaliatory attack by Hamas, on 9 August, which was directed against the crowded Sbarro pizzeria in central Jerusalem; fifteen were killed and 130 wounded.

The Israelis then hit again, on 27 August, with a missile attack on the office of the Popular Front for the Liberation of Palestine (PFLP) in Ramallah, which killed its target – the 63-year-old Abu Ali Mustafa, the faction's head. This was a serious escalation of the conflict, as Mustafa was a political leader rather than a militant. The Palestinian Jibril Rajoub, a close associate of Arafat, recalls his shock upon hearing of the assassination: 'I could not move [it was like] I was paralysed [and I knew] that the assassination of Abu Ali Mustafa would have to provoke a huge Palestinian response.'[7] Indeed, by killing a political leader Sharon took his counter-insurgency tactics to a new level, effectively forcing the Palestinians to upgrade their attacks and target an Israeli political leader to show they could prevail. Their success came on 17 October, when at the Hyatt Hotel in Jerusalem two Palestinians assassinated Israel's tourism minister, Rehavham Ze'evi – one of Israel's most hardline politicians. His killing, so the Palestinians later stated, was their retaliation for Israel's assassination of their leader, Ali Mustafa.

The tit-for-tat continued for weeks and months and when, on 12 December, an attack on a bus near the Jewish settlement of Emanuel, on the West Bank, left ten dead and thirty wounded, it was for Sharon the last straw: he picked up the phone and ordered the military to bomb Arafat's headquarters in Gaza and destroy his entire helicopter fleet – a signal to the Palestinian leader that the noose was tightening and that the army was getting closer to him. Putting all the blame for the continuing violence on Arafat, Sharon declared: 'Chairman Arafat has made himself irrelevant . . . no contacts will be maintained with him.'[8]

But whether the prime minister liked it or not, Arafat remained the most relevant Palestinian leader in the occupied territories and at this stage he himself concluded that he should restrain the militants, perhaps if only to demonstrate his continued relevance. Thus, on 16 December, he called 'for a complete halt to all operations, especially suicidal operations'; his instruction had a strong effect, leading to an almost total end to attacks against Israel – including those of Hamas and Islamic Jihad.[9] For those who claimed that Arafat could – if he so wished – bring Palestinian violence under control, this was good proof. It seems that in spite of the growing influence of the Islamists, he was still – as the most famous Palestinian leader – able to maintain some authority even over them.

In the meantime, Israel continued to hunt down Palestinian militants. One of their prime targets was the 28-year-old Raid Karmi from the West Bank town of Tulkarm. According to the Chief of Staff, Shaul Mofaz, in an interview with the author, Karmi was 'a terrorist with blood on his hands . . . we had to either arrest him or kill him'; the latter being somewhat easier, the decision that was taken was to kill him.[10] Karmi was elusive and had already survived one attempt on his life. The defence minister, Ben Eliezer, explained to the author that Karmi 'used costumes, he moved from place to place . . . changed locations . . .' But the Israelis finally discovered a weakness; Karmi used to visit his mistress, the wife of a Palestinian official, almost every day before lunch. On the way back to his hideout Karmi would use the same route along a cemetery wall; knowing Karmi's routine would enable the army to kill him.

The Israelis, though, had a dilemma: since December 2001 a cease-fire, albeit a fragile one, was still holding and a high-profile assassination would certainly wreck it. Sharon, however, was keen on such special operations and so got his way in spite of some opposition within his cabinet. The green light to eliminate Karmi was given and, subsequently, a bomb was planted in the wall of the cemetery on Karmi's regular route; on 14 January 2002, as he walked past it, a powerful explosion killed him instantly. Abu Hamid, a colleague of Karmi, recalls how after the assassination they consulted and issued a response saying: 'The so-called ceasefire is cancelled, cancelled, cancelled . . . You [Israel] have opened hell on yourself. You will be burned by its fire.'[11]

The weeks after Karmi's assassination were bloody for both sides – twenty-eight Israelis and scores of Palestinians were killed in February alone, and one cannot help wonder why the Israelis felt that the killing of one person – even as dangerous as Karmi – was worth while in the certain knowledge that it would also kill a ceasefire. The army, of course, hit back following the instructions of the prime minister, who openly declared that 'The Palestinians must be hit and it must be very painful. We must cause them losses, victims . . .'[12]

The situation would soon get even worse in the form of a major retaliatory strike by Palestinian militants based in Karmi's home town of Tulkarm, one which would dramatically alter the course of the Israeli–Palestinian war.

DEFENSIVE SHIELD

Muhammad Abd al-Basset was a 25-year-old Palestinian who had been recruited into Hamas by Muammar Shahrouri under the auspices of Abbas al-Sayyid, the leader of Hamas in Tulkarm. With the Jewish festival of Passover approaching, Abd al-Basset met al-Sayyid and Shahrouri in the apartment of the latter's grandfather in the town to make the final preparations for his suicide-bombing mission. Abd al-Basset was an angry young man whose wish to travel to Jordan to marry his fiancée had been rejected by the Israelis; he was frustrated with the occupation and decided to become a suicide bomber.

The two recruiters videoed Abd al-Basset as he read his farewell statement in front of a Hamas flag and holding an M-16 assault rifle; his recording would later be distributed to publicize the mission all over Palestinian territories as part of Hamas's efforts to compete with the various other Palestinian militant factions, and demonstrate to their constituencies that they were fighting against the occupation. 'Our blood, Sharon,' Abd al-Basset read, 'isn't cheap and our homeland is not easily invaded and no one will protect you from our bodies' shrapnel . . .' When they finished with the recording, al-Sayyid equipped Abd al-Basset with a belt that contained 10 kg of explosives – the belt had earlier been delivered from Nablus, where Hamas engineers had manufactured it. The two then helped the bomber to dress. As Muammar Shahrouri recalls:

> Abd al-Basset bought the clothes himself – they had to fit properly. He bought a sweater, and he bought a wig, a blonde wig. He was a nice looking guy, and so the most appropriate thing for him was that we dress him like a woman . . . we shaved him, we gave him a haircut and he put on the wig, and we made him very pretty . . . and he was carrying a bag, and he had sunglasses . . . he looked like a foreign woman . . .'[13]

Shahrouri recalls what happened when preparations were completed:

> Abd al-Basset kept smiling . . . Abbas [al-Sayyid] said to Abd al-Basset: 'Today *inshallah* (God willing) you are going to become a *shahid*, and tomorrow . . . you will be in paradise . . . Abd al-Basset . . . was calling to God . . . he was asking forgiveness . . . he was reading the Koran a lot, he was praying, I prayed with him . . . and there was an air of freedom . . . of happiness in the room, because Abd al-Basset was going out, and he knew he wasn't going to just die, he was going out to get close to God, and that he was going to do in it the best way, the best way possible . . . Yeah, he was happy . . . Yeah, he had waited eight months for this moment . . .

Outside the house, Fathi Raja Ahmed Khatib was ready to drive Abd al-Basset to Israel, as he had an Israeli identity card that would allow them to cross easily from the West Bank into Israel. The role played by Israeli-Arabs to help Palestinians from the occupied territories to carry out attacks against Israel merits an independent study, and although only a minority of Israeli-Arabs actually crossed the line, it did much to cloud relations between them and the Jewish-Israeli community. When the bomber was ready to leave, as Muammar Shahrouri recalls:

> Abbas [al-Sayyid] said goodbye to him, and hugged him, and said to him 'we'll miss you', and me . . . I don't know exactly what I did . . . I felt hot . . . I showed him warmth, and I hugged him and I kissed him, and I said to him, 'You are going to paradise, and I hope to come some time.'

The driver and bomber departed Tulkarm at around two in the afternoon, on 27 March, and crossed into Israel, where they were looking for a gathering of troops, as their preference was to attack the military rather than civilians. 'We hardly talked,' recalls the driver, Fathi Khatib, 'he was just praying to God saying, "Let me be successful."'[14]

Failing to find a suitable military target, they then headed to the seaside town of Netanya, where Abd al-Basset walked into the Park Hotel, a place he knew as he had once had a job there. In the main dining hall, where guests were assembled around the Passover table, he detonated the explosive belt, instantly killing twenty-nine and wounding 150; it was the most devastating single suicide bombing since the outbreak of the al-Aqsa *intifada*.

Israel was shocked. Sharon gathered his ministers to approve what he thought should be the appropriate retaliation: an all-out attack on Arafat's Palestinian Authority on the West Bank. He wanted to see a complete reoccupation of Palestinian towns and cities and boots on the ground to tackle terrorist cells.

One item which led to a long discussion was what to do with Arafat himself. Some suggested expelling him but others, notably Shimon Peres of Labor, which was part of Sharon's coalition, objected as he felt that there was no point in expelling Arafat because Arafat outside could cause more damage to Israel than Arafat inside. On the outside, as Peres explained, Arafat would be seen, and appear to be persecuted, and the television would be all over him. In the cabinet meeting Peres said: 'I don't want another Jesus story on our backs.'

Another possibility discussed at this governmental gathering was to assassinate Arafat by, as it was put to the author by one of the participants in the cabinet meeting, 'starting [the operation] with a one-tonne bomb on [Arafat's] headquarters in Ramallah [as] the very first move'.[15] However, the US had vetoed the measure – the American ambassador in Israel, Dan Kurtzer, passed a letter to the prime minister making it absolutely clear to him that Israel must not touch Arafat. In the end the ministers decided to define Arafat as 'an enemy' and ordered the military to lay siege to his office in order to physically isolate him.

The die was cast: Operation Defensive Shield, a full-scale invasion of the West Bank, was sanctioned by the ministers. This would be a dramatic break from the Oslo agreements and would reverse the years of agreed gradual withdrawal and separation by bringing under direct military control West Bank territories that had already been transferred to Arafat.

In the meantime, in Arafat's headquarters in Ramallah, the *muqata*, they expected an attack, so Palestinian leaders from across the West Bank started gathering there, where they found Arafat, 'in his khaki fatigues . . . ready . . . very cautious . . . alert'.[16]

Devastation in Jenin

The West Bank invasion started on 29 March with troops rapidly closing in to attack Arafat's headquarters in Ramallah. It was particularly devastating: surrounded by tanks and troops the compound's perimeter walls were crushed and a tight siege imposed, with troops taking up positions close to Arafat's private office.

Over the next few days the army moved into several more West Bank towns: high on their list of priorities was Jenin, a town in the northern West Bank, which the Israelis dubbed 'the martyrs' capital' and from where twenty-eight suicide attacks had been launched between October 2000 and April 2002. Jenin's refugee camp was the second-largest on the West Bank, home to 14,000 refugees and a hotbed of Palestinian militancy.

The army entered this area on 3 April, but finding the Palestinians well prepared, and large sections of Jenin booby-trapped, they made slow progress. Troops avoided the camp's narrow alleyways and moved only after gigantic armoured bulldozers had flattened paths for them through Jenin's densely packed houses. An Israeli operator of one of the bulldozers recalls how

> For three days, I just destroyed and destroyed the whole area. Any house that they fired from came down. And to knock it down, I tore down some more. They were warned by loudspeakers to get out of the house before I came, but I gave no one a chance. I didn't wait . . . I would just ram the house with full power, to bring it down as fast as possible. I wanted to get to the other houses. To get as many as possible . . . I didn't give a damn about the Palestinians . . . I got a real kick out of every house that was demolished, because I knew that dying means nothing to them, while the loss of their house means more to them . . .[17]

By 15 April, the battle of Jenin was over. When the army finally allowed journalists and international observers into the town, they found colossal destruction, particularly in the centre of the refugee camp, where a large area had been flattened and 4,000 Palestinians made homeless. The smell of death was everywhere. Mohamad Abu Hamid, a militant Palestinian, remembers how 'You could see heaps [of bodies . . .] an arm here or a leg there . . . sticking out of the rubble.'[18] Some Palestinians were trapped under the rubble. Abu Hamid recalls how one Palestinian survived for eight days beneath it. Half his body had been burned and he was without food. The bulldozer had destroyed the house and he was left in a small space under the collapsed roof. As Abu Hamid describes: 'moving around he found a little jar of cheese, so he ate from that cheese and then he urinated in the little jar, and he had to drink his own urine to survive . . .'[19]

Such tales and horrific scenes had a strong impact on Palestinians, particularly on the younger generation, galvanizing them to join the militants ready to fight the occupation. A Palestinian leader named Hani al-Hassan saw the effect of the Jenin events on one Zakaria al-Zubaidi, who had seen his family's house demolished and his young sister killed. 'He came to me,' Hani al-Hassan recalls:

> and asked for compensation for the destroyed house. We gave him $2,500. First he bought a Kalashnikov for $1,500. And he used the rest

of the money to recruit other people. Since that time he is the strongest fighter against the Israelis. Sometimes he calls me and says: 'Hani, I killed another dog [an Israeli]. I need another ninety-nine in revenge for my little sister.' They made him mad.[20]

Shocked by the scenes, the UN Security Council, on 19 April, adopted Resolution 1405 (2002), which resolved 'to develop accurate information regarding recent events in the Jenin refugee camp through a fact-finding team'.[21] The UN Secretary General, Kofi Annan, established the fact-finding team, but Israel would not cooperate with the investigation, and put up obstacles, and it was never able to get off the ground.[22] It was one of many unsuccessful attempts by international agencies to investigate the alleged war crimes committed by the Israeli army in the occupied territories.

Back in Ramallah

Inside Arafat's besieged *muqata* the situation was worsening. 'It was horrible,' remembers Yasser Abed Rabbo, a close aide of Arafat, whom the Israelis let in and out of Arafat's headquarters:

> The smell! It was killing, killing. They had perhaps five or six toilets for three to four hundred people in there. And not always working. And often no water. And they had no underwear to change. I went into the *muqata* pretending I had documents, but really I had underwear from my home. This was the request of the people.[23]

An American diplomat who was allowed into Arafat's besieged headquarters to try to arrange a ceasefire described the situation inside:

> I looked through the passageways and there were all these people that looked like they hadn't eaten, obviously hadn't used the bathroom. As I made my way through and up the second floor I saw some of Arafat's staff there, and they looked really horrible ... unshaven, they had lost weight, really haggard, and I thought, God ...[24]

*

The Israeli onslaughts in 2001 and, particularly, Defensive Shield in 2002 had a particularly devastating impact on schoolchildren, as we can learn from the following findings:

The past academic year was particularly traumatic as spiralling poverty gripped the [Palestinian] nation, and as environmental and infrastructural destruction, residential and institutional demolition, death, injury, disability, and the arrest of loved ones . . . became the new and only way of life . . . The school system was not spared this destruction. By the end of the 2001–2002 school year . . . 216 students were killed, 2,514 injured and 164 arrested, 17 teachers and staff . . . were killed and 71 were arrested, 1,289 schools were closed for at least three consecutive weeks during the Israeli invasion between March 29 [2002] and the end of the school year. Approximately 59 per cent of school children and 3,000 employees in the education sector were prevented from reaching their schools . . . the scheduled examinations were disrupted by military operations . . . Most of these children . . . spent their 'summer break' imprisoned at home under strict military curfews . . . the Israeli onslaught . . . has had a deep negative influence on children's ability to learn, their sense of security, their mental health, their dignity, and indeed, their consciousness. These children have been violated in every way, and are growing up being dominated by a sense of hate, a sense that can only predispose them to what is called 'a tendency toward violent behaviour' . . . in the Palestinian case, the construction of violence begins and ends with Israeli military occupation.[25]

On 2 May, responding to American pressure, Sharon ordered an end to Defensive Shield, but the army would stay on in the region, transforming West Bank cities, towns and villages into restricted military zones, where residents were often held under sustained curfews for days on end while troops would move from house to house to make arrests. It was one of the most traumatic periods in the history of the Palestinian occupied territories.

WAR CRIMES IN GAZA?

Defensive Shield reduced, but overall fell short of stopping, the Palestinian insurgency. This was brought into stark relief on 5 June, when a car packed with explosives detonated in northern Israel, killing sixteen and wounding fifty. Then, on 16 July, Palestinian militants ambushed a Jewish bus near the West Bank settlement of Emanuel, killing nine and wounding eighteen, and on the next day two suicide bombers killed five and injured forty in Tel Aviv.

Many of these attacks originated from within Hamas, the Islamic movement which was quite strong in the Gaza Strip, and as it objected to the peace process with the Israelis it felt fewer obligations and was thus more aggressive towards the occupation. While Sharon continued to regard Arafat as the main culprit, he also instructed the military to go after a significant target – Salah Shehadeh, one of the founders of Hamas and commander of its military wing in the Gaza Strip. Subsequently, on 17 July, a meeting took place at the office of the army's Chief of Staff, Moshe Yaalon, to discuss plans to assassinate Shehadeh by an attack from the air. The air force representative at this meeting, Eliezer Shkedi, presented the military plan and estimated that a bomb smaller than a ton would not necessarily kill Shehadeh, as the attack was aimed to strike while he was known to be inside a specific building. In an interview with the author, the defence minister, Ben Eliezer, explained: 'A one-ton bomb has an element of certainty. You can be sure it takes a person out, for sure . . . and here [Shehadeh] justified use of a bomb of this kind.'[26] Indeed, a one-ton bomb of the sort Israel stocked at that time, and which is often referred to as a Mark 84 general-purpose bomb, is so powerful that it is capable of making a crater fifteen metres wide and eleven metres deep and penetrating more than three metres of concrete. This is why Shkedi pointed out that, if dropped, the bomb would cause colossal damage to the huts close to the scene. 'These shanties of tin,' he predicted, 'will not be there after this incident . . . what would happen to the people inside them? In my view there's a chance . . . that they will be killed . . .'[27] But the IDF's Chief of Staff ordered that the operation proceed anyway, and on 22 July an Israeli F-16 delivered the Mark 84 on target. However, when this massive one-ton bomb was dropped on the apartment block in Gaza City, it caused collateral damage, killing, in addition to Shehadeh, fourteen innocent people, including his daughter and wife ('his wife we knew,' Ben Eliezer told the author, 'was also a terrorist').[28] There was no remorse from the Chief of the Air Force, General Dan Halutz, who congratulated the crew of the plane that had dropped the bomb, telling them: 'Guys, you can sleep well at night . . . I do . . . Your execution was perfect . . . Perfect.'[29]

It should be left for experts on international law to decide whether this operation constitutes a war crime, but there is little doubt that the decision to drop such a big bomb in a densely populated area casts serious doubts on the judgement of those who took it.

A ROADMAP

In the meantime, on the diplomatic level, Sharon and his team of advisers managed to persuade the Bush administration that the continuing violence was all Yasser Arafat's fault. The fact that the main weapon Palestinian insurgents used against Israel at that time was suicide bombings – a method which, since the 9/11 attack on the US, which killed close to 3,000 Americans, struck a deeper chord – provided the prime minister with a powerful argument against Arafat.

The climax of Sharon's success in turning the US administration against Arafat came shortly after Defensive Shield when, on 24 June 2002, President Bush went public to put forward his vision of a two-state solution in which a secure Israel would live alongside a viable, democratic Palestine, but he made it conditional – and this was Sharon's idea – on the Palestinians choosing a new leadership. 'Peace,' Bush declared, 'requires a new and different Palestinian leadership', and he went on to call on the Palestinian people to elect new leaders who were not 'compromised by terror'. In his memoirs Bush wrote: 'By the spring of 2002, I had concluded that peace would not be possible with Arafat in power . . .'[30]

This was an extraordinary intervention in Palestinian internal affairs which deeply shocked many Palestinians. In this case, in the words of a US official, Doug Feith, who was involved in the process that led to Bush's declaration: 'The president took the horse [Arafat], this old nag, and shot it in the head and said we don't want this goddamn Arafat, PLO, antidemocratic, violent, terroristic, receiving arms from Iran nag. Screw it. Bang.'[31] Bush's vision of a two-state solution, along with the request to the Palestinian people that they remove Arafat, was an important step in the realization of what came to be known as the 'roadmap' – a new way forward to end the Israeli occupation and to resolve the Israeli–Palestinian conflict.

*

It is little known that Jordan played a leading role in initiating this new programme, but Jordan certainly had good reason to do so, as it had a Palestinian refugee population of 1.7 million, highly sensitive to the situation in the occupied territories.[32] Thus, after President Bush made his 24 June speech advocating a two-state solution to the Israeli–Palestinian conflict, Jordan's King Abdullah II concluded that while Bush laid down a vision, the vision in itself would not do much if it were not followed by practical steps.[33] The king, due to visit Washington, was determined to press President Bush to come up with an action plan to turn his vision of a Palestinian state into a reality.

At the White House, on 1 August 2002, the king said to the president: 'We need a roadmap on how we're going to get from where we are now to realizing the vision that you, the president, have laid out . . .'[34] The king added, as the Secretary of State, Colin Powell, who was present in the meeting recalls, that 'it's one thing to have a speech and vision, but you're not laying out *how* you get there . . . You have to have a path . . .'[35] The president agreed to take the extra steps to realize his vision and instructed his officials to start drafting such a plan. It was to lay out the actions that Israelis and Palestinians would take to turn Bush's vision of a two-state solution into reality, and establish a viable Palestinian state living side by side with Israel.

The roadmap was to be released by the end of 2002 under the auspices of the Quartet – Russia, the UN, the European Union as well as America, all notionally at least equal partners in the venture. The emerging roadmap had three phases. Phase I required the Palestinians to undertake an unconditional cessation of violence, while at the same time Israel was required to freeze all settlement activity and dismantle settlement outposts erected since March 2001. During this phase, the Palestinians should also undertake comprehensive political reform by appointing a prime minister, drafting a constitution and holding democratic elections – this was all meant to sideline Arafat, whom President Bush wanted the Palestinians to get rid of. In Phase II, an independent Palestinian state with provisional borders would be created by December 2003. In Phase III, a final peace treaty would be signed some time during the year 2005 which would resolve borders and the status of Jerusalem, refugees and the settlements. Then there would be a conference and all the Arab states would sign peace treaties with Israel and, with that done, the Arab–Israeli conflict would be over.[36]

Arafat, however, had held the reins for the Palestinian people for so long that getting him to give up *any* of his authority to a new 'empowered' prime minister – as now required by Bush before he would allow the roadmap to go ahead – took much persuasion – both by international emissaries and by his own people. Isolated, he had little choice; to convince him he was promised that he would be the one to choose the prime minister and have the power to dismiss him. On 7 March 2003, he finally relented and publicly invited Abu Mazen, a moderate and critic of the violent *intifada*, to become the first Palestinian prime minister. On 30 April, a few hours after Abu Mazen and his new cabinet were sworn in, the Quartet released the roadmap.

To implement the roadmap, President Bush dispatched a veteran Foreign Service officer by the name of John Wolf to the Middle East. One of Wolf's aims was to reach an agreement on the transfer of responsibility for security from Israel to the Palestinian Authority in the Gaza Strip and the Bethlehem area, the latter still under Israeli control since Defensive Shield. This was intended to be the first step in the Israeli withdrawal from areas reoccupied during the al-Aqsa *intifada* – as long as the Palestinians could prove they were able to maintain security and curb attacks from the transferred lands. This would then achieve two of the requirements of the first phase of the roadmap – Israeli withdrawal and Palestinian clampdown on terror.

On 27 June, Wolf managed to have Israelis and Palestinians agree on a deal which they called 'The Gaza Agreement' and this led, the next day, to the Gaza Strip and Bethlehem areas coming under Palestinian control. What's more, the new Palestinian prime minister, Abu Mazen, also managed to persuade the militants to agree to suspend their military operations against Israel, for an initial period of three months. Given the circumstances these were incredible achievements, the results of which were felt almost immediately both in Israel, where suicide bombings stopped, and in the Gaza Strip, where life returned to some level of normality. According to Wolf:

> Tensions were reduced ... quality of life in Gaza and metropolitan Israel went up sharply. The Gaza Agreement enabled Palestinians to

move freely, people could go to the beach. We had an informal indica-
tor . . . how late are the stores open [in the occupied territories] – and
stores which had hardly been open at all were staying open until ten or
eleven at night . . . So this was a moment of opportunity . . .[37]

For his hard work in implementing the roadmap, the Palestinian
prime minister, Abu Mazen, was rewarded with an invitation to the
White House, something which had been denied to Arafat since
George W. Bush had been president.

ARIEL SHARON'S WALL

Abu Mazen arrived in Washington, on 25 July, with one aim in mind
– to persuade the president to condemn Israel's 'Security Fence', which
the Palestinians referred to as 'The Wall'. This was a network of concrete walls, electronic fences, ditches and guard towers which stretched
across the West Bank and was still in the process of being built by the
Israelis. The barrier was aimed at stopping suicide bombers from
crossing into Israel and the Israelis went out of their way to emphasize that it was no more than a security measure. The Palestinians,
however, believed that the Israelis intended to use it as a de facto
political border between Israel and the West Bank – which would
represent an annexation of Palestinian territory, as the barrier's route
cut into the West Bank, rather than running along the so-called Green
Line, the original boundary separating the West Bank and Israel
proper before the 1967 war.

Now, inside the Oval Office, Abu Mazen spread a big map on the
table in front of the president, showing how the Israeli barrier, built
deep in the West Bank, deviated significantly from the Green Line.
This was not only a land grab, but was already causing immense misery to West Bankers, as it cut off farmers from their lands, patients
from hospitals and children from schools. Bush glanced at the map
and told him: 'With a wall like this, with a map like this, we can never
have a viable Palestinian state.'[38] At the press conference in the Rose
Garden afterwards, the president said: 'I think the wall is a problem
. . . it is very difficult to develop confidence between the Palestinians
and the Israelis with a wall snaking through the West Bank.'[39]

Four days later, it was the turn of the Israeli prime minister, Ariel Sharon, to visit the White House, and after Abu Mazen's presentation his Security Fence was top of the president's agenda. But the prime minister was immovable, arguing that it was necessary for Israel's security – the numbers spoke for themselves, the barrier was stopping suicide bombers from crossing into Israel. And although Bush had been quite enraged about it in his talk with the Palestinian prime minister just a few days before, now he would not press Sharon on the matter, just saying: 'I would hope that in the long term, a fence would be irrelevant.'[40] The Secretary of State, Colin Powell, explains the president's thinking: 'It's hard to argue when you're under attack that you shouldn't protect yourself, and if one way to protect yourself is with a fence, that's fine ... [Sharon's] counterargument was a fence can go up, a fence can come down, so we're not making a final judgment as to where the line will be.'[41] President Bush accepted the argument; he already had a strong orientation towards Israel – an inclination to see things Israel's way – that only became stronger after 9/11; this outlook can be seen in his memoirs, where he writes: 'I was struck by Israel's vulnerability in a hostile neighborhood ... I came away convinced that we had a responsibility to keep the relationships strong ...'[42]

The International Court of Justice was less willing to compromise with the Israelis. In a 2004 Advisory Opinion, the court criticized the building of the wall as it 'impedes the liberty of movement of the inhabitants of the occupied Palestinian territory ... [as it does] their right to work, to health, to education and to an adequate standard of living ...' The court concluded that 'Israel accordingly has the obligation to cease forthwith the works of construction of the wall ... [Israel has the obligation] to return the land, orchards, olive groves and other immovable property seized from any natural or legal person for purposes of construction of the wall ...'[43]

BACK TO THE VICIOUS CIRCLE OF VIOLENCE

On 14 August, in spite of the ceasefire between Israel and the Palestinians, which was holding up quite well, the Israelis assassinated

Mohammed Seder, the head of Islamic Jihad's armed wing in Hebron; he had long been on the Israeli wanted list. According to the defence minister's Military Secretary, Mike Herzog: 'We knew Seder was planning an attack. So we sent our special forces to arrest him and in the exchange of fire he was killed. He was a bad man.'[44] Whether Mohammed Seder was actually planning attacks on Israel and whether, when the army came to arrest him, as the Military Secretary claims, he was killed in 'an exchange of fire' or was actually assassinated will probably never be known. But now, the Palestinian prime minister had a serious problem on his hands: how to prevent a Palestinian retaliation and a return to the vicious circle of attack and counterattack. Although the assassinated Seder was from Islamic Jihad, it was Hamas that was planning revenge.

On 19 August, Majd Zaatri, a painter from Gaza and member of Hamas, collected the 29-year-old Raed Abdel Hamid and drove him to the centre of Jerusalem, where Hamid was to blow himself up. Zaatri recalls how 'The bomber was dressed up [as an orthodox Jew] in a white shirt and black pants [and I] put a hat on him . . .'[45] In the car, on the way to downtown Jerusalem, Zaatri explained to Raed Abdel Hamid how to operate the explosive belt: 'I showed him the switch to cause the explosion. And I showed him how not to mess it up . . . that he shouldn't put on the belt backwards . . . I showed him how to put it on so the switch would be on the outside . . .' The would-be bomber was in good spirits, as Zaatri remembers: 'He was happy. He was laughing . . . he was a guy who had finished university. He wasn't a young kid. He had studied in Amman . . . He's got two sons and there was a third on the way.' They stopped at a bus stop in a Jewish religious neighbourhood in Jerusalem, where the bomber got out of the car. 'I said to him, "God be with you,"' Zaatri recalls. '"Goodbye and see you in paradise."'

The suicide bomber set off his device on a bus, causing a massive explosion which killed twenty-three – seven of them children and infants – and injured over 100 people. The Israeli retaliation came two days later, on 21 August, when the army launched a helicopter strike in Gaza, killing a Hamas official, Ismail Abu Shanab. And although it was Israel that had wrecked the ceasefire, there was no American rebuke for its acts; a White House spokesman, Scott

McClellan, said: 'Israel has a right to defend herself'. Hamas and Islamic Jihad called off their ceasefire and the *intifada* started once again.

It was around this time that Israeli intelligence gathered that the founder and spiritual leader of Hamas, Sheikh Ahmed Yassin, would attend a meeting in Gaza, on 6 September, with the entire Hamas leadership. This seemed to be a unique opportunity to assassinate the entire top tranche of Hamas in one go and cause serious damage to the organization as a whole. An air force jet dropped a 500-kilo bomb on the building where the meeting was taking place. But the Israeli intelligence was flawed: while they expected the meeting to take place on the third floor, instead the leaders met on the ground floor – perhaps because Sheikh Yassin was wheelchair-bound – and thus, while the third floor was completely destroyed by the bomb, the Sheikh and the other Hamas leaders on the ground floor were unharmed. Sheikh Yassin's son, who was with him at the time, remembers: 'We heard the explosion over our heads . . . [one of the participants] Ismail Hanieh said in his typically quiet way, "We have been bombed, Sheikh, we've got to leave the house quickly." Yassin asked: "Are you sure that it's our house?" "Yes," said Hanieh, "quick, quick."'[46] Then Hanieh held Yassin by his legs, his son took his arms and they rushed out of the house.

The Israelis, nonetheless, continued to hunt down the militants, which fuelled the vicious circle of tit-for-tat even further: on 7 September, a helicopter gunship hit the house of a Hamas member, Abdul Salem Abu Musa, in the southern Gaza Strip, injuring at least twelve people. The Palestinians responded two days later by carrying out two separate suicide attacks that left fifteen people dead and scores wounded in Tel Aviv and Jerusalem. Israel struck again, on 10 September, firing missiles at the Gaza City home of Mohamoud Zahar, a senior Hamas member, killing his son and a bodyguard and leaving twenty-five innocent people wounded; Zahar himself escaped with minor injuries.

Ariel Sharon, as before, blamed Arafat for the escalation, calling him, on 11 September, a 'complete obstacle to peace' and leading his cabinet in a decision to 'remove this obstacle in the manner and time of our choosing'.[47] He was now, no doubt, and in spite of his pledge to President Bush, starting to prepare the ground for Arafat's possible assassination.

14
Unilateralism and Its Rewards,
2004–2007

Against the background of the continued bloody war between Israelis and Palestinians, a new thinking had gradually taken root in Israel. At its heart was a shift from negotiating the end of the conflict with the Palestinians to, instead, taking unilateral steps aimed at physically separating from them, and ending the occupation in specific locations. This thinking reached its climax during Sharon's tenure as prime minister, as he led a unilateral pull-out of troops and settlements from the Gaza Strip, and symbolically from four West Bank settlements. It was, without doubt, a daring move given that even the previous leftist governments had been reluctant to evacuate occupied lands and dismantle settlements before a final status agreement with the Palestinians had been reached. The slain prime minister, Yitzhak Rabin, once said that he would have liked to see Gaza sink in the sea, but even he – the architect of the Oslo agreements with the Palestinians – would not evacuate any of its settlements before the conclusion of negotiations.

A unilateral withdrawal from occupied Palestinian lands was not Sharon's brainchild, but that of Barak, who, following the collapse of the Camp David summit, declared that there was no Palestinian partner for peace and that Israel – even unilaterally – must create a situation whereby, as he often put it, 'we are here and they are there'. Sharon, who defeated Barak in the general election, was attracted by his predecessor's idea of unilateral disengagement, as he lacked any faith in the Palestinians to negotiate a deal. But unlike Barak, whose main focus of attention was on a separation from the Palestinians on the West Bank, Sharon first sought a separation from the Gaza Strip, which he regarded as an albatross around Israel's neck.

He calculated that by setting up a new agenda, at the heart of which was an Israeli withdrawal from the occupied Gaza Strip, which he would depict as ultimately serving the peace process, he could receive new support both internationally and domestically; in the meantime, the Palestinians would have to struggle to bring some order to the miserable enclave that Israel would leave behind. More importantly, a withdrawal would be so unexpected – nothing short of revolutionary coming from the hardline Sharon – that it would derail the Quartet, the joint diplomatic initiative of the US, EU, Russia and the UN, from pushing ahead with the aforementioned roadmap; Sharon loathed the roadmap, as it would require him to compromise on issues of great sensitivity, including ownership of East Jerusalem, control of the Jewish settlements in the West Bank and, most threatening of all, the claims of 4.8 million Palestinian refugees to return to Israel.

Preparing the ground

The driving force behind the emerging plan to disengage unilaterally from the Gaza Strip was Sharon's key political and foreign policy adviser, Dov Weisglass. He brought the idea before a small forum of advisers that would often meet in the kitchen of the prime minister's Sycamore Ranch on Friday mornings or Saturday nights. It is difficult to accurately reconstruct the discussions there as no transcripts ever emerged from this forum, and only a few of the meetings even appeared on the official schedule of the Prime Minister's Office, and when they did they came under the code name 'Private Meira', after Meira Katriel, the staffer who coordinated the meetings. What we do know, however, is that by September/October 2003, as the prime minister's popularity was in decline, following allegations of corruption against him and his sons and what seemed to be a never-ending bloody war with the Palestinians, Sharon decided to go ahead with the unilateral disengagement plan. First, however, he would try his idea on the Americans.

At a meeting in Rome, on 19 November 2003, Sharon told Elliot Abrams, the US official responsible for the Israeli–Palestinian portfolio within the White House National Security Council, that he was considering an Israeli withdrawal from the Gaza Strip. Although knowing quite well that such a plan was sure to derail any other planned negotiated settlement for the occupied territories, Sharon went out of his way to emphasize that a pull-out from the Strip, of the sort he proposed, would not, in any way, contradict the roadmap, and he pledged that Israel was still committed to the Quartet's plan. The Rome meeting marked the first time Sharon revealed his thoughts about a unilateral pull-out from the Gaza Strip outside his intimate circle.

Sharon then set out to prepare the Israeli public for the unilateral withdrawal from the Gaza Strip, asking his speech writer to insert into his speeches the idea that while Israel continued to implement the roadmap, it was not excluding unilateral steps to end the occupation. Then, at a conference in Herzliya, northern Israel, on 18 December, Sharon openly presented his 'Disengagement Plan'; the original name, the 'Separation Plan' was dropped, as the word 'separation' evoked apartheid, and the word 'withdrawal' was still taboo in Israel, so it was assumed that 'disengagement' would work better with the public.

'Like all Israeli citizens, I yearn for peace,' Sharon announced; however, 'if the Palestinians do not make a similar effort toward a solution of the conflict – I do not intend to wait for them indefinitely'.[1] He added – no doubt for the benefit of his international audience – that the roadmap was the 'best way to achieve true peace', but 'the terrorist organizations joined with Yasser Arafat and sabotaged the process with a series of the most brutal terror attacks we have ever known . . .' He warned that if the Palestinians continued to disregard their part in implementing the roadmap – should they fail to curb attacks on Israel – 'then Israel will initiate the unilateral security step of disengagement from the Palestinians . . . fully coordinated with the United States'.

Sharon then proceeded to explain how his plan would work: he would remove all twenty-one Jewish settlements from the Gaza Strip, relocating their 8,600 settlers into Israel, and redeploy the army on the Israeli side of the fence with the Gaza Strip. But he also emphasized, and here was the tricky bit, that at the same time Israel would strengthen its control 'over those same areas in the Land of Israel [namely, on the West Bank] which will constitute an inseparable part of the State of Israel in any future agreement'. It was, in other words, a plan aimed at trading off the Gaza Strip – a 'nest of snakes' as the defence minister, Moshe Dayan, described it as far back as 1967 – for the West Bank, the cradle of Jewish history.

Leaving the Israeli public, and indeed the world, to digest his bold idea, Sharon proceeded, in the meantime, to decimate the Gaza Strip's militants. It was particularly important to produce a victory over Hamas and other militants opposing Israel in order to prevent a situation where they could claim that their pressure had brought about the Israeli withdrawal. Subsequently, collaborators in the streets of the Gaza Strip kept the Israelis informed of the whereabouts of various militants, whom the army then proceeded to eliminate one by one. The most senior Palestinian on Israel's assassination list was the elderly quadriplegic and spiritual leader of Hamas, Sheikh Yassin, who, as we have seen, had already survived an attempt on his life. Sharon nicknamed him the 'Squeaking Dog', on account of his thin, high voice, and wanted him dead. But since the last attempt on his life the Sheikh was more careful in his movements and the Israelis needed some patience before they could get him. 'There were several nights during which we followed him,' the defence minister, Shaul Mofaz, recalls in an interview with the author, 'and I would wait . . . until around one or two [in the morning] to know if there was a chance [to assassinate him].'[2]

On 21 March 2004, in spite of Israeli helicopters hovering over his house, the sheikh decided that he would pray in the mosque, where he went accompanied by his son, Abed el Amid Yassin, and some bodyguards. While at the mosque they identified more Israeli activities in the air and Abed el Amid said to his father: 'Dad, we must not leave here, let's stay in the mosque, they will not attack a mosque. Let's stay here and hide.'[3] But at 4.45 in the morning, as Yassin's son recalls: 'We decided to go home after the morning prayers because the Sheikh was tired . . . he slept on a mattress in the mosque after taking his medication. We could not hear the helicopters and everyone was sure that the danger had gone . . .' They left the mosque running – two of Yassin's bodyguards pushing the wheelchair and shouting to each other 'Igri, igri [run, run]' and 'Allah akbar [God is great].' They were struck by three missiles and the sheikh and his entourage were killed; his son survived.

Twenty-six days after Yassin's assassination, his replacement, Abdel Aziz Rantissi, was also killed after a missile attack on the car in which he was travelling, disguised as an old man. Following this assassination Hamas capitulated. They sent a message through the Egyptian intelligence minister, Omar Suleiman, to Sharon, stating that if Israel stopped the assassinations, Hamas would stop the suicide attacks. Sharon agreed and the truce stuck; for a long period there were no suicide attacks against Israel.[4]

Sharon's reward

The prime minister would not discuss his plan to disengage from Palestinian areas with the Palestinians, but he still thought that the US ought to reward him for his readiness to pull out from occupied lands, which, as he saw it, was a step in the right direction to realize George W. Bush's 24 June 2002 programme, in which he laid out his vision of two states living side by side.

Sharon sought to get a written guarantee from Washington on two critical issues in particular – Israeli West Bank settlements and Palestinian refugees. He wanted the US to officially agree that the final border between Israel and any future Palestinian state would diverge from the Green Line that separated Israel from the West Bank until the 1967 war and, instead, run *inside* the West Bank, so that Israel could annex its big blocs of Jewish settlements adjacent to the line. He also wanted written US recognition that, in any final settlement between Israel and the Palestinians, none of the millions of Palestinian refugees would be allowed to return to the homes of their forefathers in Israel – that the so-called 'right of return' (what Israel calls Palestinian '*claims* of return') would not apply. For Washington, however, publicly to throw its lot behind Israel and support the annexation of West Bank land and closing the door on the right of return of the Palestinian diaspora would be a red rag to the Arab world. American diplomats, therefore, set out to Amman, Jordan, to test the water on their close Arab ally. The vast majority of the population in Jordan are Palestinians and thus the king wanted to be consulted on any programme; if the Palestinians were not happy with the result they may have directed their anger at him.

In Jordan, on 31 March, American officials presented to the Jordanian foreign minister, Marwan Muasher, Sharon's unilateral withdrawal idea and the reward he was expecting from the US. Muasher, however, was appalled: Jordan, he said, could only agree to 'minor changes to the 1967 borders' and, as for abolishing the Palestinian right of return, he told his guests: 'no Arab state is going to accept this'.⁵ The Jordanians were also concerned that Sharon only intended to disengage from the overpopulated Gaza Strip, but not from the West Bank. This latter point, in particular, had not been overlooked by the American diplomats, who then proceeded to press Sharon to demonstrate – even if only symbolically – that this was not his intention. Secretary of State Powell remembers what he said to the prime minister: 'You've got to do something in the West Bank as well. It's gotta be seen as part of a comprehensive approach to the problem and not just [a withdrawal from the Gaza Strip].'⁶

Finally, Sharon conceded, pledging that, in addition to the Gaza Strip, Israel would also evacuate four small West Bank settlements. This, for Jordan, was a step in the right direction, but, still concerned about the sort of concessions the US president might offer to Sharon, King Abdullah II sent Bush a letter on 8 April:

> I'm writing to share with you some of Jordan's thoughts ... I fear the concessions asked for by Israel [as a reward for the Gaza disengagement] will undermine both our efforts. In particular we hope that no concessions on borders will be given that would suggest any major deviations from [the] 1967 [border]. The solution to the [Palestinian] refugee issue should also leave the door open for an agreed solution by both sides ...⁷

Despite the concerns raised by King Abdullah II, the Bush administration remained determined to go along with Sharon's plan. Sharon was due to visit Washington on 14 April, and he wanted to make absolutely sure he was going to receive the written guarantees he wanted, which he knew would enable him to sell his unilateral withdrawal more easily to the Israeli public, and would of course also help Israel in future negotiations with the Palestinians. Therefore, ahead of his arrival, Sharon dispatched emissaries to thrash out with American officials the final details of the US guarantee.

The Israeli negotiators insisted that the American pledge should specify – in writing and by name – each and every West Bank settlement east of the 1967 line that Israel would be allowed to keep in any future agreement with the Palestinians. The Americans, however, baulked at this – they knew accepting this demand would enrage the Arab world. Instead, they came up with a masterpiece of ambiguity: 'In light of new realities on the ground, including already existing major Israeli population centres, it is unrealistic to expect . . . a full and complete [Israeli] return to the [1967 border].'[8] This could guarantee the Israelis got to keep the big blocs of settlements ('new realities on the ground') but did so in language sufficiently vague to allow the Americans to defend themselves from Arab criticism.

On the Palestinian demand to have a 'right of return' to Israel proper, the Israeli negotiators demanded that the Americans guarantee that Palestinian refugees would be settled in the future Palestinian state and 'not in Israel'. The Americans, however, would not accept this wording, preferring, instead, to adhere to a positive formula: that the refugees will be absorbed in the future Palestinian state, with no mention of Israel at all. When Sharon's negotiators insisted on the words 'not in Israel', the Americans came up with a new formula: the Palestinian refugees would be absorbed in the future Palestinian state 'rather than in Israel'. The Israelis were satisfied; they had achieved their aims on both borders and refugees as a reward for their willingness to get out of the Gaza Strip and, symbolically, from four small West Bank settlements.

At the press conference following their summit, George W. Bush described what the prime minister had promised to do, namely to remove all settlements from the Gaza Strip, and certain military installations and settlements from the West Bank. As for the reward, as the president then put it: 'in an exchange of letters today and in a statement I will release later today, I'm repeating to the prime minister my commitment to Israel's security . . . the realities on the ground [a reference to the big blocs of settlements on the West Bank] have changed greatly over the last several decades, and any final settlement must take into account those realities . . .' And the Palestinian refugees will be absorbed in the future Palestinian state 'rather than in Israel'.⁹

It was a remarkable victory for Sharon. President Bush, leader of the most powerful country in the world, had moved even closer to Israel's position, declaring that two dearly held principles of the Palestinian people – Israeli withdrawal to the 1967 borders and the right of return of the Palestinian diaspora to their old Palestine – were null and void. It is not entirely clear whether the president had any real sense of the significance of what he was endorsing, but the rules of the peace process had been rewritten – at least for the time being.

POISONING ARAFAT?

In the meantime, Sharon continued to eliminate his foes in the occupied territories to ensure that when Israel evacuated the Gaza Strip they would not claim that the Israelis had left because of Palestinian pressure on them. Sharon focused, primarily, on Hamas and Islamic Jihad militants, but the Palestinian Authority chairman, Arafat, seemed also to be on his hitlist – despite the prime minister's promise to George W. Bush, in March 2001, not to harm him.

The language Sharon used in reference to Arafat seemed to indicate that, indeed, the Palestinian leader was facing real danger, and the few visitors he still received at the *muqata*, his headquarters in Ramallah, warned him that he was likely to be taken out by the Israelis. Alastair Crooke, a former British MI6 officer and later a diplomat working for the EU, recalls his last conversation with Arafat: 'You know,' he said to Arafat, 'if there is another big [Israeli] attack, I think they will kill you. There are no red lights.' To which Arafat replied according to Crooke: 'Alastair, there are *green* lights. This is more serious than [Sharon's 1982 siege on me in] Beirut.'¹⁰

Critically, during Sharon's aforementioned 14 April 2004 visit to Washington to receive the American written guarantees on refugees and borders, he also managed to extricate himself from his March 2001 pledge to the American president not to hurt Arafat. In their April talks at the White House, when Bush advised Sharon to leave the destiny of Arafat in the hands of divine providence, the prime minister hastened to reply that 'providence sometimes needs a helping hand'.[11] Indeed, a confirmation that Sharon no longer regarded himself as committed not to kill Arafat was given when a short time after returning from Washington he said in a television interview: 'I am released from this commitment . . . I released myself from this commitment regarding Arafat.'[12] And it seems that, unlike in March 2001, now, in 2004, President Bush no longer insisted on a clear pledge from Sharon not to hurt Arafat, effectively giving the prime minister if not a green light to proceed with the killing, then at least an amber.

Throughout 2004 Arafat's physical condition deteriorated. One of his aides, Bassam Abu Sharif, describes how Arafat 'was losing weight, his skin was very pale, almost transparent, and his energy levels had dropped significantly. His breath smelled strange and it had nothing to do with onion or garlic.'[13] Others also recognized a massive change in Arafat's state of health. His associate Mohammed Rashid recalls a visit to Arafat's and how 'When Arafat saw me he smiled, and he waved me to come in, but he was frail, he was weak, I leaned to him, I kissed him, and he said, "Stay away, I don't want to contaminate you."'[14]

By the summer Arafat was gravely ill but still refusing to be evacuated to hospital lest Sharon would not allow him to return to Ramallah. Finally, when his health deteriorated dramatically, he had no other option but to agree to be evacuated. On 29 October, a Jordanian helicopter carried Arafat from Ramallah to Amman, where a French plane was waiting to fly him to France. Arafat's associate Nabil Shaath saw Arafat just before he embarked on the plane to France and remembers:

> I rushed over to greet him. We walked together about fifty metres to the French plane. I was on his right side supporting him a little, but he was walking and talking. He said: '[My Dr] Hissam says I'll be fine, because Hissam himself had had similar symptoms as me and he's fine and well . . . I'll be fine. And Dr Chirac [as Arafat called the French president) will look after me. He cares for me . . .'[15]

But this was not to be. In the Percy Military Hospital in Chamart, near Paris, on 11 November 2004, Arafat died, aged seventy-five. The cause of his death remained shrouded in mystery and speculation is rife that he was poisoned by the Israelis.

While we do not have the smoking gun to show that Israel killed Arafat, the weight of evidence is such that one should not exclude this possibility. The fact that, as far back as March 2001, President Bush felt it necessary to extract a pledge from Sharon not to harm Arafat shows that the Americans suspected that that was precisely what the Israelis might indeed do. In subsequent months, Sharon spoke openly about the need to 'remove' Arafat, though it would be fair to add that he never explained what he actually meant by the word 'remove' in this context – whether physically or merely politically.

A clear indication that the Israelis did intend to kill Arafat can be found in the following 'Top Secret' document; in a report dated 15 October 2000 – a few months before even Sharon came to power – the Shabak, Israel's General Security Service, wrote:

> Following the violent events in the territories the question arises again as to whether Arafat is a factor helping to sort out the historical conflict between Israel and the Palestinian nation, or whether we are dealing with a leader who[se] ... policies and actions lead to a serious threat to Israel's security.

After going through 'why Arafat is necessary', and then 'why Arafat is not necessary', the document says that 'the damage [Arafat] causes is bigger than his benefits . . .' And the subsequent conclusion is straightforward: '7. Arafat, the person, is a serious threat to the security of the state. *His disappearance outweighs the benefits of his continuing existence.*'[16] And yet, even this Shabak 'Top Secret' report does not provide us with enough evidence of assassination and we will probably have to wait for more information to ascertain what really killed Arafat.

A missed opportunity

Arafat's death turned into another huge missed opportunity, as with a new moderate Palestinian leader – the former prime minister Abu Mazen – elected president, in January 2005, the US could have pushed hard to renew the Israeli–Palestinian peace process. But, as the American diplomat Aaron David Miller observes, 'instead of working hard to empower Abu Mazen and push a political process, the administration allowed the situation to drift'.[17] Perhaps it was because of President Bush's reluctance to push Sharon, or his gut feeling that it would be better to stay out of the Israeli–Palestinian mess altogether. Or maybe, at this juncture, the US administration felt that rather than pushing for a full-fledged Israeli–Palestinian deal, it would be better to help Sharon get out of the Gaza Strip unilaterally and thus set an important precedent in the withdrawal of Israeli military forces and settlers from occupied Palestinian lands.

A UNILATERAL WITHDRAWAL – BUT NO END TO THE OCCUPATION

At midnight on 14 August 2005, a curfew was placed on the entire Gaza Strip and troops and policemen moved from house to house in the Jewish sectors, handing out eviction warnings to the settlers in the Strip which called on them to leave or face forcible removal; eviction warnings were also handed to the 680 settlers in the four West Bank settlements earmarked for demolition. Three days later, the evacuation began. The operation consisted of four phases: the physical removal of the settlers who stayed on despite earlier calls on them to leave; evacuation of their belongings; destruction of empty structures; and, finally, a withdrawal of the military.

In spite of some dramatic scenes in which the army had to drag settlers out of their houses, the withdrawal proceeded faster than expected and on 11 September, in the headquarters of the Gaza Division, the flag was lowered for the last time and the army departed, thus bringing to an end thirty-eight years of military occupation in the Gaza Strip. All in all, some 2,530 houses were demolished. At the same time, the disengagement from four West Bank settlements took place, which, as early as 23 August, had ended and the settlers' 270 houses were demolished.

Sharon's unilateral disengagement turned out to be a mixed bag for Israel, and, indeed, for the Palestinians too. The most immediate and short-term outcome was an unparalleled round of applause from a usually sceptical international community, which seemed willing to accept Sharon's line that his withdrawal would ultimately promote a two-state solution. Sharon's bold move clearly relieved pressure on Israel and, as he expected, though never actually admitted in public, it undermined the Quartet's roadmap that had up till the evacuation been at the heart of the peace process, and which could have forced Israel to compromise on issues of great sensitivity. Sharon's right-hand man, Dov Weisglass, the brains behind the Disengagement Plan, alluded to the merit of unilateral disengagement as a way of pushing aside the less favoured roadmap when, in a frank interview, he said that disengagement would act as 'formaldehyde' on the roadmap. He explained:

> The significance [of the unilateral withdrawal] is the freezing of the political process. And when you freeze that process you prevent the establishment of a Palestinian state and you prevent a discussion about the refugees, the borders, and Jerusalem [all of which are at the heart of the roadmap]. Effectively, this whole package that is called the Palestine state, with all that it entails, has been removed from our agenda . . . and all this with authority and permission. All with a [US] presidential blessing . . . and we taught the world . . . that there is no one to talk to [on the Palestinian side]. And we received a no-one-to-talk-to certificate. It a certificate that says: 1. There's no one to talk to . . . 2. As long as there's no one to talk to the geographic status quo remains intact. 3. The certificate will be revoked only when this-and-this happens – when Palestine becomes Finland. 4. See you then and Shalom.[18]

*

On the ground, however, it soon became apparent that what, at first, had seemed to be the end of occupation was for the most part a mere illusion. On the West Bank, while the settlers were indeed removed from their four settlements and their houses demolished, the army continued to maintain control of the land, forbidding Palestinians access to it; it was therefore emptied but not handed over to the Palestinians. In the Gaza Strip, in the meantime, rather than an end of occupation, Sharon's disengagement exercise turned out to be more of a reorganization of the way the occupying forces operated, as Israel continued to maintain effective and exclusive, albeit remote, control of the evacuated area. Perhaps most notable was the continued Israeli control of the Gaza Strip's airspace – just as it had exercised control since 1967. This enabled the military to monitor Palestinian actions on the ground, attack suspects from the air, and interfere with radio and TV broadcasts.

Israel's exclusive control of Gaza's airspace also prevented the Palestinians from operating an airport which could have allowed them freedom of movement to and from Gaza and to carry out foreign trade. The 1993 Oslo Accord, it is worth mentioning, gave Israel full control over the Strip's airspace, but also established that the Palestinians could build an airport there. Gaza Airport was duly built and opened in 1998, providing a limited number of weekly flights to various Arab countries. However, on 8 October 2000, soon after the outbreak of the second *intifada*, Israel closed down the airport, later bombed its runways, and then turned it into a military base. When, after the Israeli disengagement was completed, the Palestinians regained control of their airport they found that not only were the runways totally destroyed, but that Israeli troops had also vandalized and destroyed many of the airport's buildings. Israel, after its unilateral move, officially recognized the importance of the airport to Gaza but, at the time of writing, and nine years since the disengagement, it has still not allowed it to be reopened.

Israel's continued control of the Gaza Strip is also manifested through its control of Gaza's territorial waters. In the Oslo II agreement, signed between Israel and the PLO in September 1995, Israel agreed to allow fishing boats from the Gaza Strip to sail some twenty nautical miles (about thirty-seven kilometres) out from the coastline (except for a few specific areas, to which they were prohibited entry). In practice, however, Israel denied permits to many applicants, and only allowed fishing up to a distance of no more than twelve nautical miles (twenty-two kilometres); at times Israeli patrol boats even fired at Palestinian boats that exceeded that distance. Following the disengagement from the Gaza Strip, Israel reduced the fishing area yet further. As a result, the fishing sector in Gaza, which provides a livelihood to many families and is an important source of food for residents, suffered a severe blow.

Also in the Oslo agreements, Israel agreed to allow the Palestinians to build and operate a seaport in Gaza, which could have drastically improved the Gazan economy. In the summer of 2000, infrastructural work for the port began, but in October of that year, following the outbreak of the second *intifada*, Israel bombed the seaport construction site. As a result, the donor countries ceased funding the project, and no work has been done on the seaport since then. After the 2005 disengagement from the Strip, Israel pledged it would allow renewal of the construction work, and in order to assure that foreign donors and investors invest in the project Israel also promised that it would not strike the port again. At the time of writing, however, the Israelis continue to stall the project.

In addition to their full control of Gaza's airspace and territorial waters, the Israelis, even after their disengagement from the Gaza Strip, continue to determine the flow of trade in and out of the Strip thorough their control of all of the commercial crossing points into the area; travel between the Gaza Strip and West Bank remains dependent solely on Israel's discretion and changing moods.

In other words, even after the Israeli departure from the Gaza Strip in 2005, Israel continues to control the area from air, sea and land, in addition to providing Gaza – and thus indirectly controlling it – with water for drinking and agriculture, communications, fuel, electricity and sewage networks. No wonder, then, that the Israeli insistence that their occupation of the Gaza Strip is over following their disengagement, and that, therefore, they are no longer legally responsible for the area, comes under severe criticism internationally as a reductionist interpretation of international law. Linking, as the Israelis do, occupation to *physical presence* is to ignore an important tenet of international law, which regards any form of *effective control* over an area – as the Israelis clearly continue to maintain in the Gaza Strip – as a feature of military occupation. Put differently, the general view – and that of international law – is that even after the 2005 disengagement the Gaza Strip remains a land occupied by Israel.

What, however, their physical absence from the Strip did prevent the Israelis from doing was to keep an eye on the militants there, who, after the Israeli evacuation, were freer than before to take control of the area.

We should recall that before the withdrawal the military attempted to weaken the militants by assassinating their leaders; but they underestimated the militants' remarkable resilience and ability to continue functioning even once the top brass was dead. In fact, a close look shows that the Gazan militants' performance before, during and after the Israeli disengagement was exemplary. They fired seventeen rockets from the Strip into Israel in June 2005, and twenty-eight in July, but in August, the month of the Israeli planned disengagement, they limited their firing – six missiles only – in order not to provoke an Israeli backlash that might prompt a change of heart. But in September, just after the Israelis completed their withdrawal, the militants launched twenty-nine rockets into Israel and went on to declare that the Israeli withdrawal was due to their resistance, a claim which was accepted by many Palestinians.[19]

In the absence of the Israelis, the Gazan militants also armed themselves as never before and managed to bring many Gazans on to their side. Indeed, with Arafat dead and the Israelis failing to strengthen his successors, the Palestinian Authority was in no position to establish order in the Gaza Strip in the wake of the Israeli withdrawal and this vacuum was soon filled by the militants. The deteriorating economic situation in Gaza, where the number of people classified as impoverished rose from 30 per cent in 2000 to 65–70 per cent by 2005, also contributed to the flocking of ordinary Palestinians to Hamas's side, Hamas being widely regarded as less corrupt than Fatah.

It should not have been surprising, in these circumstances, that when President George W. Bush, in pursuit of his vision of a democratic Palestine, insisted that the Palestinians undertake an election in January 2006, Hamas won control of the parliament, enabling it to set up a government in the Gaza Strip. On 15 June 2007, in Gaza, its gunmen defeated the pro-Fatah police and, for the first time, took full control of the Strip.

Thus Israel's unilateral withdrawal from the Gaza Strip opened a new phase in the Israeli–Palestinian relationship that saw the gradual weakening of the secular Palestinian leadership and the strengthening of more radical elements, especially in Gaza, which militants used as a launchpad to fire rockets and missiles into Israel. This, in turn, led to a heated debate in Israel regarding the merits of unilateral disengagements and whether, after all, it was in Israel's interests to evacuate occupied lands without leaving the keys to someone else.

Into a Fifth Decade of Occupation

The chronicle, thus far, of Israel's occupation of the lands it gained in its stunning victory in the Six Day War of 1967 is as follows: in the first decade after 1967, Israel found it difficult to decide what to do with the vast tracts of land it had unexpectedly captured from Egypt, Jordan and Syria. It had no organized plan and could not make up its mind as to which parts of the occupied territories to keep and which to return, but its instinct was to sit and wait, generally preferring to keep the land and forgo peace with her neighbours. Any considera- tion there was of returning some of the occupied lands – mainly the Sinai to Egypt and the Golan to Syria – emerged only as a tactical device to enable Israel to cling to the West Bank, the cradle of Jewish history, and to the Gaza Strip, which, for strategic reasons, Israel sought to keep. But, in the absence of any serious international pres- sure, even these peripheral thoughts disappeared. Ministers did not heed warnings that time was short and the opportunity to strike a deal, particularly with the Palestinians, could be lost for a generation or more if they did not act swiftly: in hindsight, it seems safe to argue that Israel missed a unique opportunity to strike peace deals with its neighbours during this first decade of occupation.

In the second decade, from 1977 to 1987, Israel, at last, decided what it wanted to do: after the 1977 electoral upheaval which saw the right-wing Likud Party come to power for the first time in Israel's history, the new prime minister, Menachem Begin, embarked on a grand plan to make the occupation irreversible, at the heart of which was the con- struction of Jewish settlements in the occupied territories, particularly on the West Bank and in the Gaza Strip. The Begin-led government did, after some international pressure, sparked by President Sadat's bold and public offer to conclude a deal, and with an unprecedented promise of economic and security aid from America, end the occupation of the Sinai. But Begin was determined to keep the Palestinian occupied territories – the West Bank and the Gaza Strip – for good, and the Golan Heights, which Israel officially annexed, for the time being at least. Oblivious to history and reality, Israel tried to consolidate its control over these occupied lands by employing anachronistic and illegitimate colonialist methods, notably the building of settlements in defiance of international law.

In the next two decades of the occupation, from 1987 to 2007, Israel finally began to sober up, not least in the face of the first *intifada* in 1987, which compelled a growing number of Israelis to realize that the occupation project was doomed. In 1991, a new peace initiative got underway with the Madrid Conference, aimed at bringing peace in return for land and an end to occupation. But this peace process was not rigorous enough and Israel failed to show magnanimity. The Palestinians, who by recognizing Israel's right to exist, in 1988, effectively gave up on their claim to 78 per cent of old Palestine, were determined not to allow the Israelis to eat into the remaining 22 per cent, and were, therefore, reluctant to compromise further during the peace negotiations. And in their frustration, on the ground, they fought against the occupation, as was their legitimate right, and perhaps the logical course given the lesson of history that Israel only gives in when under pressure.

Gradually, during the peace process, the Israelis came to realize that the price for peace would be high: that Syria would insist on a full withdrawal from the occupied Golan Heights and that the Palestinians would want an equitable deal. Unwilling to pay this price, the Israelis, in a process that would reach its climax during Sharon's tenure as prime minister, from 2001 to 2006, put peace with Syria on hold and unilaterally pulled out from the Gaza Strip, in truth a thorn in Israel's side, which let them cling on to the West Bank and its resources while avoiding the bigger issues of the occupation. However, Israel's short love affair with unilateralism came to an end after it was seen to lead to the ascent of Hamas in Gaza, which went on to attack Israel with rockets from the Strip.

Growing competition and divisions between Hamas in the Gaza

Strip and the more secular Palestinian regime on the West Bank over recent years play straight into Israel's hands, as the Israeli government justifies its reluctance to move ahead with the peace process by the fact that the Palestinians are just too divided and Hamas fails to recognize Israel's right to exist. And the so-called Arab Spring, and the disintegration of the Bashar Assad regime, removes, at least for now, any chance of talks between Israel and Syria to end the Golan occupation.

So where does this leave us and what is in store for the fifth decade of Israeli occupation, already well underway?

Clearly, the option of the first decade – sticking to the status quo – is no longer available, and the alternative of the second – building settlements in an attempt physically to swallow the occupied territories into Israel – was never realistic. The strategy of the fourth decade – unilateralism – has lost all support within Israel, which brings us back to the strategy of the early 1990s, namely an attempt to end the occupation through peace negotiations with Palestinians and Arabs. But for peace negotiations to resume in a meaningful way the international community, and particularly the US, will have to be tough with Israel and when necessary bribe it into compromise. If the past four decades have proved anything, it is that the Israelis will not give up the occupied territories easily.

I have little doubt that the occupation will come to an end at some point in the future, as all wars and conflicts do. In 1967, no one would have thought that Israel, Egypt and Jordan would have signed full peace treaties and, now, it is safe to expect similar agreements to be signed, at some point, between Israel and the Palestinians and between Israel and Syria and Lebanon. But given the depth of the bad blood between the parties, particularly the Israelis and Palestinians, and the current revolutions in the Middle East, which distract from the conflict with Israel, it could take many generations before a true reconciliation takes hold. What is clear is that Israel's attempt to swallow the occupied territories over the last four decades of occupation has failed.

I believe that the verdict of history will regard the four decades of occupation described in this book as a black mark in Israeli and, indeed, Jewish history. This was a period in which Israel, helped by the Jewish diaspora, particularly in America, proved that even nations which have suffered unspeakable tragedies of their own can act in similarly cruel ways when in power themselves. Back in 1967, the defence minister at the time, Moshe Dayan, observed that if he had to choose to be occupied by any force from among the nations of the world, he doubted he would choose Israel. He was right; looking back it is clear that Israel was – and in the time of writing is still – a heavy-handed and brutal occupier. While other colonialists, like the British in India and others, learnt the value of co-opting local elites, of building schools, universities and other public amenities for the colonized, Israel, by contrast, never really thought it had any duty to help or protect the people under its control or to improve the quality of their lives, regarding them, at most, as a captive market and ready source of cheap labour. But by forcing them to live in squalor and without hope, Israel hardened those under its power, making them more determined to put an end to the occupation, by violent means if necessary, and live a life of dignity and freedom.

Select Bibliography

Abbas, Mahmoud, *Through Secret Channels*, Reading: Garnet, 1995

Abu Sharif, Bassam, *Arafat and the Dream of Palestine: An Insider's Account*, London: Palgrave Macmillan, 2009

Abuelaish, Izzeldin, *I Shall Not Hate: A Gaza Doctor's Journey on the Road to Peace and Human Dignity*, London: Bloomsbury, 2011

Aburish, Said, *Arafat: From Defender to Dictator*, London: Bloomsbury, 1998

Albright, Madeleine, *Madam Secretary: A Memoir*, London: Macmillan, 2003

Arens, Moshe, *Broken Covenant: American Foreign Policy and the Crisis between the US and Israel*, New York: Simon and Schuster, 1995

Arieli, Shaul and Michael Sfard, *Choma u'mechdal (The Wall of Folly)*, Tel Aviv: Yediot Aharonot, 2008 (in Hebrew)

Ashrawi, Hanan, *This Side of Peace: A Personal Account*, New York: Simon and Schuster, 1995

Baker III, James A., *The Politics of Diplomacy: Revolution, War and Peace 1989–1992*, New York: Putnam's, 1995

Beilin, Yossi, *Touching Peace: From the Oslo Accord to a Final Agreement*, London: Weidenfeld & Nicolson, 1999

—, *The Path to Geneva: The Quest for a Permanent Agreement, 1996–2004*, New York: RDV/Akashic, 2004

Ben-Ami, Shlomo, *Scars of War, Wounds of Peace: The Arab–Israeli Tragedy*, London: Weidenfeld & Nicolson, 2005

Ben-Elissar, Eliahu, *Lo od milhama (No More War)*, Jerusalem: Maariv, 1995 (in Hebrew)

Boutros-Ghali, Boutros, *Egypt's Road to Jerusalem: A Diplomat's Story of the Struggle for Peace in the Middle East*, New York: Random House, 1997

Bowen, Jeremy, *Six Days: How the 1967 War Shaped the Middle East*, London: Simon and Schuster, 2003

Breger, Marshall and Ora Ahimeir, (eds.), *Jerusalem: A City and Its Future*, Syracuse, NY: Syracuse University Press, 2002

Bregman, Ahron, *A History of Israel*, London: Palgrave Macmillan, 2000

—, *Elusive Peace: How the Holy Land Defeated America*, London: Penguin, 2005

—, *Israel's Wars: A History since 1947*, London: Routledge, 2010

Bregman Ahron and Jihan el-Tahri, *The Fifty Years War: Israel and the Arabs*, London: Penguin Books/BBC Books, 1998

Brzezinski, Zbigniew, *Power and Principle: Memoirs of the National Security Advisor 1977–1981*, New York: Farrar, Straus and Giroux, 1983

Bush, George W., *Decision Points*, London: Virgin, 2010

Carter, Jimmy, *Keeping Faith: Memoirs of a President*, London: Collins, 1982

Cheshin, Amir, Bill Hutman and Avi Melamed, *Separate and Unequal: The Inside Story of Israeli Rule in East Jerusalem*, Cambridge, Mass.: Harvard University Press, 1999

Clinton, Bill, *My Life*, London: Hutchinson, 2004

Cobban, Helena, *The Palestinian Liberation Organisation: People, Power, and Politics*, Cambridge: Cambridge University Press, 1984

Corbin, J., *Gaza First: The Secret Norway Channel to Peace between Israel and the PLO*, London: Bloomsbury, 1994

Dan, Uri, *Mivtzha Gomeh (Operation Bulrush)*, Tel Aviv: Maariv, 1981 (in Hebrew)

Dayan, Moshe, *Diary of the Sinai Campaign*, London: Sphere Books, 1967

—, *Avnei Derekh: otobiographia (Milestone: An Autobiography)*, Tel Aviv: Yediot Aharonot, 1976 (in Hebrew)

—, *Story of My Life*, London: Sphere Books, 1976

—, *Breakthrough: A Personal Account of the Egypt–Israel Peace Negotiations*, London: Weidenfeld & Nicolson, 1981

Drucker, Raviv, *Harakiri: Ehud Barak be'mivchan ha'tozaha (Harakiri. Ehud Barak: The Failure)*, Tel Aviv: Yediot Aharonot, 2002 (in Hebrew)

Drucker, Raviv and Ofer Shelah, *Bumerang: kishalon ha'manhigut ba'intifada ha'shniya (Boomerang)*, Tel Aviv: Keter, 2005 (in Hebrew)

Dumper, Michael, *The Politics of Jerusalem since 1967*, New York: Columbia University Press, 1997

Eban, Abba, *An Autobiography*, London: Weidenfeld & Nicolson, 1978

—, *Personal Witness: Israel through My Eyes*, New York: Putnam's, 1992

Efrat, Elisha, *Geographya shel kibosh (Geography of Occupation: Judea, Samaria and the Gaza Strip)*, Jerusalem: Carmel Press, 2002 (in Hebrew)

Eldar, Akiva and Idith Zertal, *Adonei ha'aretz: hamitnahalim umedinat yisrael, 1967–2004 (Lords of the Land: The Settlers and the State of Israel, 1967–2004)*, Kinneret: Zmora-Bitan, 2004 (in Hebrew)

Enderlin, Charles, *The Lost Years: Radical Islam, Intifada, and Wars in the Middle East 2001–2006*, New York: Other Press, 2007

Fahmy, Ismail, *Negotiating for Peace in the Middle East*, Baltimore, Md: Johns Hopkins University Press, 1983

Farid, Abdel Majid, *Nasser: The Final Years*, Reading: Ithaca Press, 1994

Finkelstein, G. Norman, *The Rise and Fall of Palestine: A Personal Account of the Intifada Years*, Minneapolis, Minn.: University of Minnesota Press, 1996

Finklestone, Joseph, *Anwar Sadat: Visionary Who Dared*, London: Routledge, 1996

Fisk, Robert, *The Great War for Civilisation: The Conquest of the Middle East*, London: Fourth Estate, 2005

Freedman, Lawrence, *A Choice of Enemies*, London: Weidenfeld & Nicolson, 2008

Gazit, Shlomo, *The Carrot and the Stick: Israel's Policy in Judea and Samaria, 1967–68*, Washington DC: B'nai B'rith Books, 1995

—, *Trapped Fools: Thirty Years of Israeli Policy in the Territories*, London: Routledge, 2003

Golan, Galia, *Israel and Palestine: Peace Plans and Proposals from Oslo to Disengagement*, Princeton, NJ: Princeton University Press, 2007

Golan, Matti, *The Secret Conversations of Henry Kissinger: Step-by-Step Diplomacy in the Middle East*, New York: Quadrangle/*The New York Times*, 1976

—, *Shimon Peres: A Biography*, London: Weidenfeld & Nicolson, 1982

Gorenberg, Gershom, *The Accidental Empire: Israel and the Birth of the Settlements, 1967–1977*, New York: Henry Holt & Company, 2006

Grossman, David. *The Yellow Wind*, London: Jonathan Cape, 1988

Halevy, Efraim, *Man in the Shadows: Inside the Middle East Crisis with the Man Who Led the Mossad*, London: Weidenfeld & Nicolson, 2006

Haloutz, Danni, *Begovah ha'einayim (Straightforward)*, Tel Aviv: Yediot Aharonot, 2010 (in Hebrew)

Hart, Alan, *Arafat: A Political Biography*, London: Sidgwick & Jackson, 1994

Hefez, Nir and Gadi Bloom, *Ha'roeh: sipur chayav shel Ariel Sharon (The Shepherd: The Life Story of Ariel Sharon)*, Tel Aviv: Yediot Aharonot, 2005 (in Hebrew)

Herzog, Chaim, *The Arab–Israeli Wars: War and Peace in the Middle East*, New York: Vintage Books, 1982

Hirst, David, *The Gun and the Olive Branch: The Roots of Violence in the Middle East*, London: Faber & Faber, 1977

Hirst, David and Irene Beeson, *Sadat*, London: Faber & Faber, 1981

Hroub, K., *Hamas: Political Thought and Practice*, Beirut: Institute for Palestine Studies, 2000

Hunter, Robert, *The Palestinian Uprising*, Berkeley, Calif.: University of California Press, 1993

Indyk, Martin, *Innocent Abroad: An Intimate Account of American Peace Diplomacy in the Middle East*, New York: Simon and Schuster, 2009

Khalidi, Rashid, *The Iron Cage: The Story of the Palestinian Struggle for Statehood*, Oxford: Oxford University Press, 2009

Kimmerling, Baruch and Joel Migdal, *The Palestinian People: A History*, Cambridge, Mass.: Harvard University Press, 2003

Kissinger, Henry, *White House Years*, Boston: Little Brown, 1979

—, *Years of Upheaval, 1973–1977*, London: Michael Joseph, 1982

Kliot, Nurit and Shemuel Albeck, *Sinai: anatomia shel prida* (*Sinai: Anatomy of a Settlement's Evacuation*), Tel Aviv: Defence Ministry Press, 1996

Laqueur, Walter and Barry Rubin (eds.), *The Israel–Arab Reader: A Documentary History of the Middle East Conflict*, 6th edn, London: Penguin Books, 2001

Lochery, Neil, *The Difficult Road to Peace: Netanyahu, Israel and the Middle East Peace Process*, Reading: Ithaca Press, 1999

Lunt, James, *Hussein of Jordan*, London: Fontana/Collins, 1990

Makdisi, Saree, *Palestine Inside Out: An Everyday Occupation*, New York: W. W. Norton, 2010

Makovsky, David, *Making Peace with the PLO: The Rabin Government's Road to the Oslo Accord*, Boulder, Colo.: Westview Press, 1996

Ma'oz, Moshe, *Palestinian Leadership on the West Bank: The Changing Role of Arab Mayors under Jordan and Israel*, London: Frank Cass, 1984

Markus, Yoel, *Camp David: ha'petach le'shalom* (*Camp David: The Road for Peace*), Tel Aviv, 1979 (in Hebrew)

Miller, D. Aaron, *The Much Too Promised Land: America's Elusive Search for Arab–Israeli Peace*, New York: Bantam Books, 2009

Milton-Edwards, Beverley, *Islamic Politics in Palestine*, London: I. B. Tauris, 1996

Morris, Benny, *Righteous Victims: A History of the Zionist–Arab Conflict, 1981–1999*, London: John Murray, 1999

Naor, Arye, *Begin ba'shilton: edut ishit* (*Begin in Power: A Personal Testimony*), Tel Aviv: Yediot Aharonot, 1993 (in Hebrew)

Naveh, Dan, *Sodot memshala* (*Executive Secrets*), Tel Aviv: Yediot Aharonot, 1999 (in Hebrew)

Neve, Gordon, *Israel's Occupation*, Berkeley, Calif.: University of California Press, 2008

Newman, David (ed.), *The Impact of Gush Emunim*, London: Croom Helm, 1985

Noor, Queen, *Leap of Faith: Memoirs of an Unexpected Life*, London: Weidenfeld & Nicolson, 2003

Nusseibeh, Sari, *Once upon a Country: A Palestinian Life*, London: Picador, 2008

Oren, Michael B., *Six Days of War: June 1967 and the Making of the Modern Middle East*, London: Penguin Books, 2003

Ovendale, Ritchie, *The Origins of the Arab–Israeli Wars*, London: Longman, 1992

Pappe, Ilan, *The Ethnic Cleansing of Palestine*, Oxford: Oneworld Publications, 2007

Pedatzur, Reuven, *Nitzhon ha'mevukhah* (*The Triumph of Embarrassment: Israel and the Territories after the Six-Day War*), Tel Aviv: Bitan/Yad Tabenkin, 1996 (in Hebrew)

Peres, Shimon, *The New Middle East*, New York: Henry Holt, 1993

—, *Battling for Peace: Memoirs*, London: Weidenfeld & Nicolson, 1995

Peretz, Don, *Intifada: The Palestinian Uprising*, Boulder, Colo.: Westview Press, 1990

Quandt, William B., *Peace Process: American Diplomacy and the Arab–Israeli Conflict since 1967*, Berkeley, Calif.: University of California Press, 2001

Qurie, Ahmed (Abu Ala'a), *From Oslo to Jerusalem: The Palestinian Story of the Secret Negotiations*, London: I. B. Tauris, 2008

Rabin, Yitzhak, *Pinkas sherut* (*The Rabin Memoirs*), Tel Aviv: Sifriat Ma'ariv, 1979 (in Hebrew)

—, *The Rabin Memoirs*, London: Weidenfeld & Nicolson, 1979

Rabinovich, Itamar, *The Brink of Peace: The Israeli–Syrian Negotiations*, Princeton, NJ: Princeton University Press, 1998

—, *Waging Peace: Israel and the Arabs at the End of the Century*, New York: Farrar, Straus and Giroux, 1999

Rafael, Gideon, *Destination Peace: Three Decades of Israeli Foreign Policy*, New York: Stein & Day, 1981

Raz, Avi, *The Bride and the Dowry: Israel, Jordan and the Palestinians in the Aftermath of the June 1967 War*, New Haven, Conn.: Yale University Press, 2012

Riad, Mahmoud, *The Struggle for Peace in the Middle East*, London: Quartet, 1981

Ross, Dennis, *The Missing Peace: The Inside Story of the Fight for Middle East Peace*, New York: Farrar, Straus and Giroux, 2004

Rubinstein, Danny, *Mi lashem elai: gush emunim* (*On the Lord's Side: Gush Emunim*), Tel Aviv: Ha'kibbutz Ha'me'uhad, 1982 (in Hebrew)

Sadat, Anwar, *In Search of Identity*, New York: Harper & Row, 1977

Said, Edward, *The Politics of Dispossession: The Struggle for Palestinian Self-Determination, 1969–1994*, London: Chatto & Windus, 1994

—, *Peace and Its Discontents: Gaza–Jericho, 1993–1995*, London: Vintage, 1995

Savir, Uri, *The Process: 1,100 Days That Changed the Middle East*, New York: Random House, 1998

Sayigh, Yezid, *Armed Struggle and the Search for State: The Palestinian National Movement 1949–1993*, Oxford: Clarendon Press, 1997

Schiff, Ze'ev and Ehud Ya'ari, *Intifada. The Palestinian Uprising: Israel's Third Front*, New York: Simon and Schuster, 1990

Seale, Patrick, *Asad: The Struggle for the Middle East*, Berkeley, Calif.: University of California Press, 1988

Segev, Tom, *1967: Israel, the War and the Year That Transformed the Middle East*, London: Abacus, 2007

Shamir, Yitzhak, *Summing Up: An Autobiography*, London: Weidenfeld & Nicolson, 1994

Sharon, Ariel, *Warrior: The Autobiography of Ariel Sharon*, London: Macdonald, 1989

Sher, Gilead, *The Israeli–Palestinian Peace Negotiations, 1999–2001*, Abingdon: Routledge, 2006

Shlaim, Avi, *Lion of Jordan: The Life of King Hussein in War and Peace*, London: Penguin Books, 2008

—, *Israel and Palestine: Reappraisals, Revisions, Refutations*, London: Verso, 2009

Shultz, George P., *Turmoil and Triumph: My Years as Secretary of State*, New York: Scribner's, 1993

Smith, D. Charles, *Palestine and the Arab–Israeli Conflict: A History with Documents*, 5th edn, London: Palgrave Macmillan, 2004

Snow, Peter, *Hussein: A Biography*, London: Barrie & Jenkins, 1972

Sprinzak, Ehud, *The Ascendance of Israel's Radical Right*, Oxford: Oxford University Press, 1991

Tessler, M., *A History of the Israeli–Palestinian Conflict*, Bloomington and Indianapolis, Ind.: Indiana University Press, 1994

Teveth, Shabtai, *The Cursed Blessing: The Story of Israel's Occupation of the West Bank*, London: Weidenfeld & Nicolson, 1969

—, *Moshe Dayan: The Soldier, the Man, the Legend*, London: Quartet, 1974

Van Creveld, Martin, *Moshe Dayan*, London: Weidenfeld & Nicolson, 2004

Wasserstein, Bernard, *Divided Jerusalem: The Struggle for the Holy City*, New Haven, Conn.: Yale University Press, 2001

Weizman, Eyal, *Hollow Land: Israel's Architecture of Occupation*, London: Verso, 2007

Weizman, Ezer, *The Battle for Peace*, London: Bantam Books, 1981

Wingfield, Martin, *Golan Heights: Occupation and Resistance*, Washington, DC: ADC Research Institute, 2010

Ya'alon, Moshe, *Derech arukah ketzara* (*The Longer Shorter Way*), Tel Aviv: Yediot Aharonot, 2008 (in Hebrew)

Yatom, Dany, *Shutaf sod* (*The Confidant: From Sayeret Matkal to the Mossad*), Tel Aviv: Yediot Aharonot, 2009 (in Hebrew)

Zak, Moshe, *Hussein oseh shalom* (*King Hussein Makes Peace*), Ramat Gan: Bar Ilan University, 1996 (in Hebrew)

Notes

A PERSONAL NOTE

1. Eyal Erlich interviewing Ahron Bregman, *Ha'aretz* supplement, 21 February 1988 (in Hebrew).
2. Linda Grant, *Still Here*, London: Abacus, 2002.

INTRODUCTION

1. On the 1967 war see, for instance, Ahron Bregman and Jihan el-Tahri, *The Fifty Years War: Israel and the Arabs*, London: Penguin Books/BBC Books, 1998, part 2, 60–99; Michael B. Oren, *Six Days of War: June 1967 and the Making of the Modern Middle East*, London: Penguin Books, 2003.
2. 'Military Governors were Appointed to the West Bank, Gaza and the Sinai', *Maariv*, 8 June 1967 (in Hebrew).
3. Avi Shlaim, *Israel and Palestine: Reappraisals, Revisions, Refutations*, London: Verso, 2009, 32.
4. E. C. Hodgkin, 'Grim Reports of Repression in Israeli-Occupied Lands', *The Times*, 28 October 1969.
5. Figures are from Baruch Kimmerling and Joel Migdal, *The Palestinian People: A History*, Cambridge, Mass.: Harvard University Press, 2003, 297.
6. Gordon Neve, *Israel's Occupation*, Berkeley, Calif.: University of California Press, 2008, xvii; for number of Israeli casualties see www.mfa.gov.il/ MFA/Terrorism.
7. James Joll, *Europe Since 1870*, London: Penguin Books, 1990, viii.
8. On this so-called 'matrix of control', see Jeff Halper, 'The 94 Percent Solution: A Matrix of Control', *Middle East Report*, No. 216, Fall 2000.
9. Shlomo Gazit, *The Carrot and the Stick: Israel's Policy in Judea and Samaria, 1967–68*, (henceforth: *Carrot and the Stick*), Washington DC: B'nai B'rith Books, 1995, 120.

10. Ahron Bregman in conversation with Miriam Eshkol, London, 29 October 1999.

11. Yuval Elizur, 'New Horizons – Also to the Economy', *Maariv*, 13 June 1967 (in Hebrew); about objections to the return of Jerusalem see a letter from US President Johnson's envoy, Harry C. McPherson, to the president, 11 June 1967, *Foreign Relations of the United States (FRUS)*, 1964–1968, Vol. 19, Doc. 263.

12. Philip Ben, 'Senator Kennedy in New York: "The Arabs must recognise Israel without any preconditions"', *Maariv*, 12 June 1967 (in Hebrew).

13. Shaul Ben Haim, 'Richard Nixon: "Within 4–6 months the Arabs would agree to talks with Israel"', *Maariv*, 25 June 1967 (in Hebrew).

A NOTE ON OCCUPATION

1. Regulations Concerning the Laws and Customs of War on Land, The Hague, 18 October 1907; and Fourth Convention Relative to the Protection of Civilian Persons in Time of War, Geneva, 12 August 1949, both in www.icrc.org.

2. As cited in Robbie Sabel, *The ICJ Opinion on the Separation Barrier: Designating the Entire West Bank as 'Palestinian territory'*, Jerusalem: Center for Public Affairs, 2005 (my emphasis).

3. On this, see Meir Shamgar, 'The Observance of International Law in the Administered Territories', *Israel Yearbook on Human Rights I* (1971), 262–77; also in Meir Shamgar (ed.), *Military Government in the Territories Administered by Israel, 1967–1980: The Legal Aspects*, Vol. I, 1982, 13–59; also, Yehuda Blum, 'The Missing Reversioner: Reflections on the Status of Judea and Samaria', *Israel Law Review*, 3, 1968, 279–301; also, Stephen M. Boyd, 'The Applicability of International Law to the Occupied Territories', *Israel Yearbook on Human Rights, I*, 1971, 258–61.

4. 'Settlement in the Administered Territories, Meron Memorandum', 14 September 1967, in Iain Scobbie with Sarah Hibbin, *The Israel–Palestine Conflict in International Law: Territorial Issues*, The US/Middle East Project, 2009, 103–4. Original source: Israel State Archives, 153.8/7921/3A. Legal opinion numbered as document 289-91.

5. General Assembly Resolution 2252 (ES-V), 4 July 1967; see also UN 35/122A, 11 December 1980, in *Yearbook of the United Nations*, 34 (1980), 430.

6. 'Separate Opinion in the Matter of Legal Consequences of the Construction of a Wall in the Occupied Palestinian Territory, ICJ Reports' (2004), http://www.icj-cij.org/odcket/files/131/1689.pdf.

1 West Bank and Jerusalem

1. This was UN Resolution 181, 29 November 1947.
2. Albion Ross, 'Amman Parliament Vote United Arab Palestine and Trans Jordan', *The New York Times*, 25 April 1950. See also Naseer Aruri (ed.), *Occupation: Israel Over Palestine*, London: Association of Arab-American University Graduates, 1984, 6.
3. Central Bureau of Statistics, General Census No. 1, *The West Bank of the Jordan, Gaza Strip and Northern Sinai, Golan Heights*, Jerusalem, 1968, 9 (in Hebrew). The number of Arabs in Jerusalem went up to 70,000 in late June 1967 following the Israeli incorporation of twenty-eight West Bank villages to Jerusalem.
4. *Memory of the Cactus: A Story of Three Palestinian Villages*, a documentary film by Al-Haq, Human Rights Defenders.
5. The following quotes are from Amos Kenan, *Israel: A Wasted Victory*, Tel Aviv: Devir, 1970, 18–21 (in Hebrew); also, Tom Segev, *1967: Israel, the War and the Year That Transformed the Middle East,* (henceforth: *1967*), London: Abacus, 2007, 490–91.
6. Naseer Aruri (ed.) *Occupation*, 128. In 1971, a Jewish settlement, Mevo Horon, was constructed on the ruins of Beit Nuba. The lands of Imwas and Yalu remained deserted until 1972, when, helped by donations from the Canadian Jewish community, the 'Canada Park' was constructed there. The rest of the lands were distributed among nearby Israeli settlements.
7. As cited in Shlomo Gazit, *Carrot and the Stick*, 41.
8. Uzi Narkiss, *Chayal she'l Yerushalaim (Soldier of Jerusalem)*, Tel Aviv, 1991, 333 (in Hebrew).
9. As cited in Tom Segev, *1967*, 482.
10. Interview with Major Eitan Ben-Moshe, *Yerushalaim*, 29 November 1999 (in Hebrew).
11. This testimony is in http://www.jpost.com/LandedPages/PrintArticle.aspx?id=64540.
12. Interview with Muhammed Abdel-Haq, 26 September 1999, in Tom Abowd, 'The Moroccan Quarter: A History of the Present', *Jerusalem Quarterly File*, no date, 9.
13. Moshe Dayan, *Story of My Life*, London: Sphere Books, 1976, 465.
14. Nadav Shragai, 'Scream Out in Tiny Letters', *Haaretz*, 3 November 2003 (in Hebrew).
15. In Shlomo Gazit, *Carrot and the Stick*, 198.
16. Nadav Shragai, 'Scream Out in Tiny Letters'.
17. Felner Eitan, *A Policy of Discrimination*, Jerusalem: B'Tselem, the web-

site of the Israeli Information Centre for Human Rights in the Occupied Territories (henceforth: B'Tselem), Report, May 1995, 10.

18. This and the following quotes are from Nadav Shragai, '26 June 1967: The Government Asks That the Press Refrain from Making a Fuss about the Annexation of East Jerusalem', *Haaretz*, 26 August 2005 (in Hebrew).

19. Anwar al-Khatib al-Tamimi (governor of Jerusalem District), 'Firsthand Account of the Fall of Arab Jerusalem', in http://www.palestine-studies. org/files/pdf/jps/9704.pdf.

20. Shlomo Gazit, *Carrot and the Stick*, 183.

21. Letter, 10 July 1967; see Palestinian Academic Society for the Study of International Affairs (PASSIA) Documents 100–101.

22. Memorandum concerning the measures taken by Israel with respect to the city of Jerusalem, submitted by Ruhi al-Khatib, 26 August 1967, in http://www.palestine studies.org/files/pdf/jps/9704.pdf.

23. Shlomo Gazit, *Carrot and the Stick*, 240.

24. Moshe Dayan, *Yoman Vietnam (Vietnam Diary)*, Tel Aviv: Dvir, 1977, 138 (in Hebrew).

25. Moshe Dayan's instructions to the military, 7 June 1967, in Martin Gilbert, *Israel: A History*, London: Black Swan, 2008, 396.

26. Moshe Dayan's instructions to military commanders, 17 June 1967, as quoted in Shabtai Teveth, *The Cursed Blessing: The Story of Israel's Occupation of the West Bank*, London: Weidenfeld & Nicolson, 1969, 110.

27. Shlomo Gazit, *Trapped Fools: Thirty Years of Israeli Policy in the Territories* (henceforth: *Trapped Fools*), London: Routledge, 2003, 163.

28. Summary of Moshe Dayan's meeting with Palestinian mayors, 24 October 1968, in the author's archive.

29. In a speech to the Arab Summit in Algiers, 7–9 June 1988, King Hussein reported that since Israel seized the West Bank and Gaza in 1967, Jordan had paid the salaries of 18,000 public servants on the West Bank, along with a further 6,000 in Gaza. During these years the Jordanian Treasury also paid the fees of West Bank students studying in Jordanian universities.

30. Moshe Dayan, *Story of My Life*, 399.

31. In Rosemary Sayigh, *Voices: Palestinian Women Narrate Displacement*, http://almashriq.hiof.no/palestine/300/301/voices/Westbank/hajji_fatima.html.

32. Ibid.

33. Interview published in the local Jerusalem newspaper *Kol Ha'ir*, November 1991 (in Hebrew).

34. Arie Barun, *Moshe Dayan ve'milchemet sheshet ha'yamim (Moshe Dayan and the Six Days War)*, Tel Aviv: Yediot Aharonot, 1997, 170 (in Hebrew).

35. Michael Shashar, *Milchemet ha'yom ha'shvi (The Seventh Day War)*, Tel Aviv: Sifriyat Ha'poalim, 1997, 240 (in Hebrew). He served as a staff officer and then as spokesman for the West Bank military government in 1967. This was said on 22 November 1967.

36. Shlomo Gazit, *Carrot and the Stick*, 282.

37. As cited in Tom Segev, *1967*, 553.

38. Shlomo Gazit, *Carrot and the Stick*, 284–5; also Michael Shashar, *Milchemet ha'yom ha'shvi*, 209.

39. Shabtai Teveth, *The Cursed Blessing*, 217.

40. 'Sumud' in David Grossman, *The Yellow Wind*, London: Jonathan Cape, 1988, 158–9.

41. Ibid., 159–60.

42. In Shlomo Gazit, *Carrot and the Stick*, 300–303.

43. As cited in Tom Segev, *1967*, 553.

44. Nadia Abu-Zahra and Adah Kay, *Unfree in Palestine: Registration, Documentation and Movement Restriction*, London: Pluto Press, 2012, 78.

45. Baruch Kimmerling, 'Jurisdiction in an Immigrant-Settler Society: The Jewish and Democratic State', *Comparative Political Studies*, 35, No. 10, December 2002, 1130–31.

46. David Kretzmer, *The Occupation of Justice: The Supreme Court of Israel and the Occupied Territories*, New York: State University of New York Press, 2002, 3.

47. Based on an interview with Ali Abu Shaeen in Ahron Bregman and Jihan el-Tahri, *Israel and the Arabs: An Eyewitness Account of War and Peace in the Middle East*, New York: TV Books, 2000, 173.

48. In B'Tselem, 21 August 1993, 17.

49. Testimony to B'Tselem, 11 August 1993, 61–2.

50. Source: Ronen Bergman, *Ve'Harashut Netunha (Authority Given)*, Tel Aviv: Yediot Aharonot, 2002 (in Hebrew), original document appears in the picture section. It seems that the Israelis got his age wrong.

51. 'A Doll at the Allenby Bridge' in David Grossman, *The Yellow Wind*, 161.

52. Yigal Allon, 'Israel: The Case for Defensible Borders', *Foreign Affairs*, October 1976, 55(1): 44, 41–2. In a later version of his plan, Allon would propose an even wider strip of some twenty kilometres, so as to include the eastern slopes of the West Bank mountain ridge.

53. Yigal Allon, 'Israel: The Case for Defensible Borders', 50.
54. Reuven Pedatzur, 'The Allon Plan is Unacceptable', *Haaretz*, 20 July 1990 (in Hebrew).
55. *The New York Times*, 16 August 1967.
56. Shlomo Gazit, *Carrot and the Stick*, 163.
57. Ibid., 152; Tuqan came from a prestigious Nablus family and was known for her strong opposition to the Israeli occupation.
58. Arie Brown, *Moshe Dayan ve'milchemet sheshet ha'yamim*, 11 (in Hebrew).
59. XX FRUS 1964–68, Doc. 320, *Telegram from the Department of State to the Embassy in Israel*, 13 November 1968, 633, 634 and 637.
60. According to legend it was given the name Machpelah ('double' in Hebrew) because it was a double cave, one level above the other, or perhaps because the forefathers and mothers were buried there in couples, Abraham and Sara, Isaac and Rebecca, Jacob and Leah; Rachel is buried near Bethlehem, where she died in childbirth, see Genesis 23; 49:29–32; 50:7–9, 12–14.
61. Dan Perry, 'Jewish Settlers, Crux of a Deepening Existential Quandary for Israel', *Associated Press*, 15 December 2003.
62. Yehiel Admoni, *Decade of Discretion: Settlement Policy in the Territories 1967–1977*, Tel Aviv: Devir, 1992, 58 (in Hebrew); also, Arie Dayan, 'Gazit: Kiryath Arba was Established Because Dayan was in Hospital', *Koteret Rashit*, 29 May 1985 (in Hebrew).
63. Rami Tal, 'Moshe Dayan: Soul Searching', *Yediot Aharonot*, 27 April 1997.
64. 'The Truth about Kiryath Arba Men', *Al Ha'mishmar*, 8 February 1980 (in Hebrew); also, Martin Gilbert, *Israel: A History*, 405.
65. Rami Tal, 'Moshe Dayan: Soul Searching'.
66. Ibid.
67. On this and other meetings between Israeli officials and King Hussein, see Avi Shlaim, *The Lion of Jordan: The Life of King Hussein in War and Peace*, London: Penguin Books, 2008, 280 and elsewhere. In this fascinating biography of King Hussein, Avi Shlaim very meticulously covers Israeli meetings with the king.
68. Reuven Pedatzur, 'The Allon Plan is Unacceptable'.
69. Gershom Gorenberg, *The Accidental Empire: Israel and the Birth of the Settlements 1967–1977*, New York: Henry Holt and Company, 2006, 164.
70. Reuven Pedatzur, 'The Allon Plan is Unacceptable'.
71. Reuven Pedatzur, 'The Secret Ritual of Hussein's Meetings', *Haaretz*, 6 July 1990.

72. Anwar al-Khatib al-Tamimi, 'Firsthand Account of the Fall of Arab Jerusalem', in http://www.palestine-studies.org/files/pdf/jps/9704.pdf.

73. Cited in Gordon Neve, *Israel's Occupation*, 63.

74. See paragraph 2 in www.monde-diplomatique.fr/cahier/procheorient/rabat74-en>.

75. James Lunt, *Hussein of Jordan*, London: Fontana/Collins, 1990, 253.

76. *The Washington Post*, 19 November 1974.

77. Ja'bari had been the undisputed mayor of Hebron since 1947 and he later had a few spells in ministerial roles in Amman. At King Hussein's request Ja'bari returned to Hebron as mayor and under the Israelis, in the years after the 1967 war, he was the perfect counter-balance to the growing influence of the nationalists – the PLO and the like – who wished to cut ties with Jordan.

78. Shlomo Gazit, *Trapped Fools*, 181.

79. *The New York Times*, 14 April 1976.

2 Gaza Strip

1. Yehiel Admoni, *Decade of Discretion*, 43.

2. Eshkol on 22 October 1967 in Yehiel Admoni, *Decade of Discretion*, 41.

3. Gershom Gorenberg, *The Accidental Empire*, 46; Yehiel Admoni, *Decade of Discretion*, 41.

4. Gidi Weitz, 'It's Our Defeat', *Yediot Aharonot*, 3 June 2005, 34; Tom Segev, *1967*, 643.

5. As cited in Gershom Gorenberg, *The Accidental Empire*, 142.

6. Ibid., 152.

7. Cited in Paul Cossali and Clive Robson, *Stateless in Gaza*, London: Zed Books, 1986, 84.

8. *Haaretz*, 25 August 1968 (in Hebrew).

9. Sara M. Roy, *The Gaza Strip: The Political Economy of De-Development*, Washington DC: Institute for Palestine Studies, 2001, 139.

10. Janet Abu Lughod, 'Demographic Consequences of the Occupation', in Naseer Aruri (ed.), *Occupation*, 404.

11. Ariel Sharon, *Warrior: The Autobiography of Ariel Sharon*, London: Macdonald, 1989, 250; see also Nathan Shachar, *The Gaza Strip: Its History and Politics from the Pharaohs to the Israeli Invasion of 2009*, Eastbourne: Sussex Academic Press, 2010, 80.

12. David Ben-Gurion's diary, 29 January 1960 (in Hebrew).

13. Interesting to note that, in his memoirs, Sharon seems to claim this tactic as his own whereas, in truth, others had used this technique in the past. The French General Marcel Bigeard, commander of the Colonial Parachute Regiment in Algiers in the 1950s, for instance, used this practice extensively to put down the FLN, adopting the culinary term 'quadrillage' to describe this system of sector-based surveillance, namely dividing a district up into manageable sectors or 'squares' to neutralize the enemy.

14. Ariel Sharon, *Warrior*, 251.

15. Phil Reeves, 'Sharon's Return Puts Wreckage Street in Fear', *Independent*, 21 January 2001.

16. Izzeldin Abuelaish, *I Shall Not Hate*, London: Bloomsbury, 2010, 61.

17. 7,217 from Jabalya, 4,836 from Shati and 3,802 from Rafah; see Sara M. Roy, *The Gaza Strip*, 105.

18. Uzi Benziman, *Sharon: An Israeli Caesar*, London: Robson Books, 1987, 116.

19. David Richardson, 'Last of the Aristocrats', *Jerusalem Post*, 17 May 1985.

20. Anan Safadi and Philip Gillon, 'Gaza after Shawa', *Jerusalem Post*, 27 October 1972.

21. Moshe Dayan, *Story of My Life*, 401–2.

22. *Jerusalem Post*, 24 April 1972.

23. 'Gaza Linked to Israel National Power Grid', *Jerusalem Post*, 27 November 1969.

3 Golan Heights

1. The animal wealth of the region included 37,000 cows, 1–2 million sheep and goats, 1,300 horses, 7,000 beasts of burden, 200,000 poultry and 7,000 beehives. At the end of 1966, orchards covered 40,000 dunams (a quarter of an acre, the standard measure of land in countries once under Ottoman rule), including 2,700,000 fruit trees with an annual production of 22,000 tons of various fruits; see Sakr Abu Fakhr, 'Voices from the Golan', *Journal of Palestine Studies*, Vol. 29, No. 4 (Autumn, 2000), 6.

2. Sakr Abu Fakhr, 'Voices from the Golan', 22.

3. Ibid., 14.

4. Ibid., 11, 15, 18.

5. Ibid., 17.

6. Ibid., 13.
7. According to Syrian sources the number of inhabitants on the Golan Heights on the eve of the 1967 war stood at 135,000. Another source puts the number at 130,000; see Muhammad Muslih, *The Golan: The Road to Occupation*, Washington DC: Institute for Palestine Studies, 1999.
8. Moshe Dayan, 'Hopeful Truth of the New Reality', *Life*, 29 September 1967.
9. As cited in Shay Fogelman, 'The Disinherited', *Haaretz*, 30 July 2010 (in Hebrew).
10. Sakr Abu Fakhr, 'Voices from the Golan', 12.
11. Ibid., 15.
12. Ibid., 12.
13. Report of the UN Secretary General, GA Resolution 2252 (ES-V); and Security Council Resolution 237-A/6797, and S/8158, 5.
14. As cited in Shay Fogelman, 'The Disinherited'.
15. Ray Murphy and Declan Gannon, 'Changing the Landscape: Israel's Gross Violations of International Law in the Occupied Syrian Golan', Washington DC: Al-Marsad: Arab Centre for Human Rights in the Occupied Golan, 2008, 27–30.
16. Ibid.
17. *Haaretz*, 12 September 1967 (in Hebrew); also 'The Disinherited: Syria's 130,000 Golan Heights refugees', in *Israel Occupation Archive*, 30 July 2010, http://www.israeli-occupation.org/2010-07-30/the-disinherited-syrias-130000-golan-height-refugees/.
18. Shay Fogelman, 'The Disinherited'.
19. Sakr Abu Fakhr, 'Voices from the Golan', 12.
20. Ibid., 23.
21. This and the following quotes are from Shay Fogelman, 'The Disinherited'.
22. Reuven Pedatzur, *Nitzachon ha'mevucha*, 110.
23. On the Druze, see Kais M. Firro, *A History of the Druzes*, Leiden: E. J. Brill, 1992.
24. Ray Murphy and Declan Gannon, 'Changing the Landscape', 34.
25. Sakr Abu Fakhr, 'Voices from the Golan', 14.
26. Ibid., 20.
27. Ibid., 30.
28. Memorandum of Conversation, 4 December 1968, XX FRUS, 1964–68, Doc. 339, 62 at 672–3.
29. Yehiel Admoni, *Decade of Discretion*, 25.
30. Michelle Stewart, Nancy Tuohy and Jonathan Molony, *From Settlement*

to the Shelf: The Economic Occupation of the Syrian Golan, Washington DC: Al-Marsad, 2009.

31. 'Golan's Capital Turns into Heap of Stones', *The Times*, 10 July 1974, 8.

32. Yehiel Admoni, *Decade of Discretion*, 125.

33. Sakr Abu Fakhr, 'Voices from the Golan', 20.

4 Sinai

1. On the removal of the Bedouin, see Nahum Barnea, *Davar*, 19 March 1972 (in Hebrew).

2. In 1974–5, the government would attempt to settle the evacuated Bedouins in permanent villages, giving them lands in the area of Dahniah and allocating them some water; 350 families accepted the offer.

3. See interview with Egypt's Chief of Staff, Saad el-Shazli, Cairo, 28 September 1996, for *The Fifty Years War*, in the author's archive.

4. Golda Meir, *My Life: The Autobiography of Golda Meir*, London: Futura, 1976, 377.

5. See text of the agreement in Henry A. Kissinger, *Years of Upheaval, 1973–1977*, Michael Joseph, 1982, 1250–51.

6. Matti Golan, *The Secret Conversations of Henry Kissinger: Step-by-Step Diplomacy in the Middle East*, New York: Bantam, 1976, 260.

7. 'Memorandum of Conversation' (Secret), 13 August 1974, The White House, Washington DC, 7, in the author's archive.

8. Ibid., 3, 7.

9. Ibid., 12.

10. Ibid., 13.

11. Letter from 71 Senators concerning reassessment to President Gerald Ford, 9 December 1974, in the author's archive.

12. Letter from US President Ford to Prime Minister Yitzhak Rabin, 1 September 1975, in the author's archive; also Donald Neff, 'It Happened in January', *Washington Report on Middle East Affairs*, January–February 1997.

13. David Hirst and Irene Beeson, *Sadat*, London: Faber & Faber, 1981, 193.

14. Letter from US President Ford to Prime Minister Yitzhak Rabin, 1 September 1975.

15. Donald Neff, 'It Happened in January'.

5 Likud Years

1. For the Likud party platform see Walter Laqueur and Barry Rubin (eds.), *The Israel–Arab Reader: A Documentary History of the Middle East Conflict*, 6th edn, London: Penguin Books, 2001, 206–7.

2. Arye Naor, *Begin ba'shilton: edut ishit* (*Begin in Power: Personal Testimony*), Tel Aviv: Yediot Aharonot, 1993, 47 (in Hebrew).

3. On this meeting see Eliahu Ben-Elissar, *Lo od milhama* (*No More War*), Jerusalem: Maariv, 1995, 33–6 (in Hebrew).

4. This was first published in Ahron Bregman, *A History of Israel*, London: Palgrave Macmillan, 2003, Appendix I ('The Dayan-el-Tohami Protocol, 1977'), 287–90. The following quotes are taken from this source.

5. Zbigniew Brzezinski, *Power and Principle: Memoirs of the National Security Advisor 1977–1981*, New York: Farrar, Straus and Giroux, 1983, 107; also, Uri Dan, *Mivtzha Gomeh* (*Operation Bulrush*), Tel Aviv: Maariv, 1981, 25 (in Hebrew).

6. Mohamed Heikal, *Secret Channels*, London: HarperCollins, 1996, 256.

7. This and the following quotes are from a letter from Jimmy Carter to Anwar Sadat, 21 October 1977, Declassified E.O.12958, Sec.3.6, Per 4/30/84, NLC-84-1, The Jimmy Carter Library.

8. Eric Silver, 'Begin's Secret Interviews', *The Jerusalem Report*, 21 May 1992. Nicolai Ceauşescu was held in high esteem in Israel. When the USSR cut off diplomatic relations with Israel in the wake of the 1967 war and forced other Eastern European nations to do the same, Romania continued to keep her links with Israel.

9. This and the following are from *Al-Ahram*, 10 November 1977.

10. Transcript of the Dayan–Tohami meeting, private source, note-taker the Mossad agent Yosef Ben-Porath, in the author's archive.

11. Ibid.

12. Anwar Sadat, *In Search of Identity*, New York: HarperCollins, 1978, 309; also, Ismail Fahmy, *Negotiating for Peace in the Middle East*, Baltimore, Md: Johns Hopkins University Press, 1983, 277; also, William B. Quandt, *Camp David: Peacemaking and Politics*, Berkeley, Calif.: California University Press, 2001, Appendix C.

13. Interview with Yitzhak Shamir, Tel Aviv, 21 January 1997, for *The Fifty Years War*, in the author's archive; also Uri Dan, *Mivtzha Gomeh*, 65.

14. As cited in Uri Dan, *Mivtzha Gomeh*, 54.

15. Kliot Nurit and Shemuel Albeck, *Sinai: anatomia shel prida* (*Sinai: Anatomy of a Settlement's Evacuation*), Tel Aviv: Defence Ministry Press, 1996, 44–5 (in Hebrew).

16. Zbigniew Brzezinski, *Power and Principle*, 116.

17. On the Begin plan, see *Jerusalem Post*, 29 December 1977; also Ilan Kfir, *Yediot Aharonot*, 20 January 1980 (in Hebrew); also 'Prime Minister Menachem Begin: Autonomy Plan for the Occupied Territories, 28 December 1977', in Walter Laqueur and Barry Rubin, *The Israel–Arab Reader*, 400–402.

18. David Hirst and Irene Beeson, *Sadat*, 299.

19. Ibid., 294.

20. Eliahu Ben-Elissar, *Lo od milhama*, 15.

21. Uri Dan, *Mivtzhah Gomeh*, 98.

22. William B. Quandt, *Camp David*, 161.

23. Israel Government Statement on Settlements, 12 February 1978, Israel Ministry of Foreign Affairs, Vols. 4–5, 1977–9.

24. Zbigniew Brezezinski, *Power and Principle*, 246.

25. Cheryl A. Rubenberg, *Israel and the American National Interest: A Critical Examination*, Chicago: University of Illinois Press, 1986, 231.

26. This and the following are from Jimmy Carter Library, Declassified E.O.12958, Sec.3.6.

27. Yoel Markus, *Camp David: ha'petach le'shalom* (*Camp David: The Road for Peace*), Tel Aviv: Schocken, 1979 (in Hebrew), 17; and Uri Dan, *Mivtzha Gomeh*, 202.

28. Yoel Markus, *Camp David*, 99; and Uri Dan, *Mivtzha Gomeh*, 212.

29. Uri Dan, *Mivtzha Gomeh*, 214.

30. Yoel Markus, *Camp David*, 101; and Uri Dan, *Mivtzha Gomeh*, 21.

31. Uri Dan, *Mivtzha Gomeh*, 219.

32. Ibid., 220.

33. Jimmy Carter, *Keeping Faith, Memoirs of a President*, London: Collins, 1982, 347, 351.

34. Ezer Weizman, *The Battle for Peace*, London: Bantam Books, 136–7.

35. Zbigniew Brzezinski, *Power and Principle*, 261.

36. Uri Dan, *Mivtzha Gomeh*, 246. Elyakim Rubinstein, 'Moshe Dayan and Sadat's Visit', lecture, 1 November 1987 (in Hebrew).

37. Zbigniew Brzezinski, *Power and Principle*, 270; Jimmy Carter, *Keeping Faith*, 396.

38. Letter from Begin to Carter, 17 September 1978, The Jimmy Carter Library.

39. Email communication with Prof. Yair Hirschfeld, 19 May 2010, in the author's archive.

40. As cited in Tom Segev, *1967*, 607.

41. Interview with Nasser Laham, http://www.justvision.org/portrait/76134/interview.

42. In *PLO Information Bulletin*, Vol. 4, No. 19, 1 November 1978.

43. 'Sadat Greeted Wildly on Arrival in Al Arish after Israelis Pull Out', *The New York Times*, 26 May 1979.

44. 'Nablus Mayor on Hunger Strike', *The New York Times*, 16 November 1979.

45. Martin Gilbert, *Israel: A History*, 501.

46. This and the following quotes are from the 'Druze National Document', March 1981, in the author's archive.

47. In the face of such strong opposition the Israelis eventually retreated and the Golanis were defined as 'residents' rather than 'citizens' of Israel.

48. Moshe Dayan in *Davar*, 17 April 1979 (in Hebrew).

49. Interview with Haila Hussein Abu Jabar in Brooke Kroeger, 'The Golan Heights: The Camp David Fear in the Occupied Golan Heights', 10 November 1980, http://brookekroeger.com/the-golan-heights-the-camp-david-fear-in-the-occupied-golan-heights/, accessed 11 August 2012.

50. Sakr Abu Fakhr, 'Voices from the Golan', 30–31.

51. Marvin Wingfield, *The Golan Heights: Occupation and Resistance*, Washington DC: ADC Research Institute, 2010, 18.

52. Michelle Stewart, Nancy Tuohy and Jonathan Molony, *From Settlement to the Shelf*, 30–31.

53. Sakr Abu Fakhr, 'Voices from the Golan', 31.

54. Ibid., 31.

55. *Jerusalem Post*, 2 September 1982.

6 Black December, 1987

1. 'Intifada: Recollections from the Past', *Palestine–Israel History*, 22 December 1997, in http://www.arabicnews.com/ansub/Daily/Day/971222/1997122234.html.

2. John Kifner, 'Kill Us or Get Out! Arabs Taunt as Rocks and Bullets Fly in Gaza', *The New York Times*, 16 December 1987.

3. Susan Warren, 'Palestinians Honour Dead on Martyr Street/Intifada Starts Its Fifth Year', *Houston Chronicle*, 12 September 1991.

4. Alan Sipress, 'Arafat Visits Cradle of Intifada', *Inquirer*, 3 July 1994.

5. As cited in Mark Tessler, *A History of the Israeli–Palestinian Conflict*, Bloomington, Ind.: Indiana University Press, 1994, 685.

6. 'Memories of the First Intifada', testimony of a woman from Khan Younis refugee camp in Gaza, 19 December 2011, http://lifeonbirzeitcampus.blogspot.be/2011/12/memories-of-first-intifada.html, accessed 10 August 2012.

7. John Kifner, 'Kill Us or Get Out'.
8. Izzeldin Abuelaish, *I Shall Not Hate*, 20-21.
9. Zeev Schiff and Ehud Yaari, *Intifada: The Palestinian Uprising, Israel's Third Front*, New York: Touchstone, 1990, 17, 83.
10. As quoted in Benny Morris, *Righteous Victims: A History of the Zionist–Arab Conflict, 1981–1989*, London: John Murray, 1999, 532.
11. 'The Other Barta'a', in David Grossman, *The Yellow Wind*, 119-20.
12. See First Communiqué of Hamas in Khaled Hroub, *Hamas: Political Thought and Practice*, Washington DC: Institute for Palestine Studies, 2000, Document No. 1, 265.
13. Charles Smith, *Palestine and the Arab–Israeli Conflict: A History with Documents*, New York: Bedford/St Martin's, 2000, 414.
14. Andoni Ghassan, 'A Comparative Study of *Intifada* 1987 and *Intifada* 2000', in Roane Carey et al., *The New Intifada: Resisting Israel's Apartheid*, London: Verso, 2001, 209.
15. In Arie Shalev, *The Intifada: Causes and Effects*, Boulder, Colo.: Westview Press, 1991, 13.
16. Yassir abd Rabbo, in Helena Cobban, 'The PLO and the Intifada', *Middle East Journal*. Vol. 44, No. 2 (Spring 1990), 229.
17. Melanie Kaye/Kantrowitz, 'Women and the Intifada', *Off Our Backs*, Vol. 19, No. 6 (June 1989), 1.
18. Ehud Barak to author, Tel Aviv, no date, in the author's archive.
19. Daoud Kuttab, 'A Portrait of the Stonethrowers', in Laleh Khalili, *Heroes and Martyrs of Palestine: The Politics of National Commemoration*, Cambridge: Cambridge University Press, 2007, 195.
20. In Thomas M. Ricks, 'In Their Own Voices: Palestinian High School Girls and Their Memories of the Intifadas and Non-Violent Resistance to Israeli Occupation, 1987–2004', *NWSA Journal*, Indiana University Press, 90, http://www.pwrdc.ps/Bibliography-%20New/6.pdf, accessed 12 August 2012.
21. 'Memories of the First Intifada', testimony of a woman from Khan Younis refugee camp in Gaza, 19 December 2001.

7 Intifada

1. Yehuda Litani, 'How the Protests are Organized', *Jerusalem Post International Edition*, 13 February 1988.
2. This and the following quotes are from Zachary Lockman (ed.) *Intifada*, Boston: South End Press, 1989, Communiqué No. 1, 328-9.

3. Mary Elizabeth King, *A Quiet Revolution: The First Palestinian Intifada and Nonviolent Resistance*, New York: Nation Books, 2007, 257.

4. Khalid Amayreh, in 'He Pointed the Finger and Pulled the Strings, But the Protection Ran Out', *Guardian*, 10 August 2002.

5. As quoted in Naria Abu-Zahra and Adah Kay, *Unfree in Palestine*, 89.

6. Hussein 'Awwad, a Testimony to B'Tselem, the Israeli Human Rights Centre, 11 August, 1993, 8.

7. Bernard E. Trainor, 'Israel vs. Palestinians: Tactics are Refined', *The New York Times*, 30 March 1989.

8. Daoud Kuttab, 'A Profile of the Stonethrowers', 198.

9. The testimony appears in Saree Makdisi, *Palestine Inside Out: An Everyday Occupation*, New York and London, W. W. Norton, 2008, 188.

10. 'Memories of the First Intifada', testimony of a woman from Khan Younis, Gaza, 19 December 2011, http://lifeonbirzeitcampus.blogspot. be/2011/12 memories-of-first-intifada.html, accessed 10 August 2011.

11. Thomas M. Ricks, 'In Their Own Voices', 91–2.

12. Don Peretz, *Intifada: The Palestinian Uprising*, Boulder, Colo.: Westview Press, 1990, 64.

13. Testimony in 'A Man is Like a Stalk of Wheat', in David Grossman, *The Yellow Wind*, 10.

14. UNLU Communiqué No. 24 in Daoud Kuttab, 'A Profile of the Stonethrowers', 200.

15. Torture is defined by the United Nations as 'any act by which severe pain or suffering . . . is intentionally inflicted on a person for such purposes as obtaining from him information or a confession, punishing him for an act he or a third person has committed or is suspected of having committed, or intimidating or coercing'. Article 5 of the Universal Declaration of Human Rights states: 'No one shall be subjected to torture or to cruel, inhuman or degrading treatment or punishment.'

16. B'Tselem, 'Violence against Minors in Police Detention', Jerusalem, 1990; the report focused on minors between the ages of twelve and eighteen. See also Norman G. Finkelstein, *The Rise and Fall of Palestine: A Personal Account of the Intifada Years*, Minneapolis, Min.: University of Minnesota Press, 1997, 48.

17. *Israel's Interrogation of Palestinians from the Occupied Territories: Human Rights Watch/Middle East*, New York, 1994, 21–2.

18. Aysha Odeh, in Buthina Canaan Khoury, *Women in Struggle*, H-Gender-MidEast, September 2005, http://www.h-net.org/reviews/showrev. php?id=15464, accessed 18 August 2012.

19. Joel Greenberg, 'Lynch Village Shows No Remorse', *Jerusalem Post International*, 4 September 1988.

20. See Amnon Straschnov, 'Don't Destroy Terrorists' Homes', *Haaretz*, 6 July 2008 (in Hebrew).

21. Testimony in Saree Makdisi, *Palestine Inside Out*, 108-9.

22. 'Sumud', in David Grossman, *The Yellow Wind*, 150-51.

23. 'The Terrorist's Father', in David Grossman, *The Yellow Wind*, 196.

24. Michal Shmulovich, '24 years later, Israel acknowledges top-secret operation that killed Fatah terror chief', *Times of Israel*, 4 November 2012.

25. In Ahron Bregman and Jihan el-Tahri, *The Fifty Years War: Israel and the Arabs*, London: Penguin Books/BBC Books, 1988, 193-5 (UK edn).

26. This and the following are quotes from the UNLU Communiqué No. 10, 11 March 1988, in the author's archive.

27. King Hussein, Address to the Nation, Amman, 31 July 1988, in Walter Laqueur and Barry Rubin (eds.) *The Israel-Arab Reader*, 338-41; see also James Lunt, *Hussein of Jordan*, 235.

28. King Hussein, Address to the Nation.

29. Youssef Ibrahim, 'PLO Proclaims Palestine to be an Independent State', *The New York Times*, 15 November 1988.

30. Palestinian Declaration of Independence in Walter Laqueur and Barry Rubin (eds.) *The Israel-Arab Reader*, 354-8.

31. Interview with George Shultz, Washington DC, 15 October 1997, for *The Fifty Years War*, in the author's archive.

32. Israel Ministry of Foreign Affairs, Statement by Yasser Arafat, 14 December 1988, Vols. 9-10, 1984-1988.

33. General Amram Mitzna to author, Haifa, 27 January 1997, in the author's archive; Ahron Bregman and Jihan el-Tahri, *The Fifty Years War*, 233 (US edn).

34. 'Israel Declines to Study Rabin Tie to Beatings', *The New York Times*, 12 July 1990.

35. Israeli Government Press Release, 14 May 1989, in the author's archive.

36. *Jerusalem Post International*, 27 May and 24 June 1989.

37. *Maariv*, 26 June 1992 (in Hebrew).

38. Joel Brinkley, 'Israel Says Army Will Get Tougher If Palestinians Reject Offer of Vote', *The New York Times*, 16 May 1989.

39. Sari Nusseibeh, *Once upon a Country: A Palestinian Life*, London: Picador, 2008, 315-16.

8 Gulf, Madrid, Oslo, 1991-1995

1. Lawrence Freedman and Efraim Karsh, *The Gulf Conflict*, Princeton, NJ: Princeton University Press, 1993, 101.

2. Gary Stein, 'Hussein a Hero to Palestinians on West Bank', SunSentinel. com, 15 August 1990.

3. Ahron Bregman and Jihan el-Tahri, *The Fifty Years War*, 202 (UK edn).

4. Lawrence Freedman and Efraim Karsh, *The Gulf Conflict*, 168.

5. Ahron Bregman and Jihan el-Tahri, *The Fifty Years War*, 217 (US edn).

6. A report in *Hadashot*, 24 February 1992 (in Hebrew), as appears in Norman G. Finkelstein, *The Rise and Fall of Palestine*, 49.

7. Walter Laqueur and Barry Rubin (eds.), *The Israeli–Arab Reader*, 577–82.

8. Ahron Bregman and Jihan el-Tahri, *The Fifty Years War*, 267 (US edn).

9. Ibid., 269.

10. Interview with Yair Hirschfeld, Ramat Yishai, 25 February 1997, for *The Fifty Years War*, in the author's archive.

11. Ahron Bregman, interview with Shimon Peres, Tel Aviv, 24 January 1997, for *The Fifty Years War*, in the author's archive.

12. 'The Closure of the West Bank and Gaza Strip: Human Rights Violations against Residents of the Occupied Territories', *B'Tselem, Information Sheet*, May 1993.

13. Ibid.

14. Testimony to B'Tselem. 11 August 1993, 61–2.

15. Ronen Bergman, 'Stories from the Couch', 7 Days, *Yediot Aharonot*, 15 March 2013 (in Hebrew).

16. The two letters appear in Shimon Peres, *Battling for Peace: Memoirs*, London: Weidenfeld & Nicolson, 1995, 377–8.

17. Ahron Bregman, interview with Warren Christopher, Los Angeles, 23 January 1998, for *The Fifty Years War*, in the author's archive.

18. Ahron Bregman, interview with Shimon Peres for *The Fifty Years War*.

19. Yoram Meital, *Peace in Tatters: Israel, Palestine and the Middle East*, Boulder, Colo.: Lynne Rienner Publishing, 2006, 34.

20. Rashid Khalidi, *The Iron Cage: The Story of the Palestinian Struggle for Statehood*, Boston: Beacon Press, 2006, 159.

21. Ahron Bregman, interview with Shimon Peres for *The Fifty Years War*.

9 Missed Opportunities, 1995–1999

1. Dan Naveh, *Sodot Memshalah* (*Executive Secrets*), Tel Aviv: Yediot Aharonot, 1999, 27 (in Hebrew).

2. Serge Schmemann, 'Ten More Die in Mideast Riots as Violence Enters 3rd Day; Mosque is Scene of a Clash', *The New York Times*, 28 September 1996.

3. Kotel Tunnel Incident, 1996, Palestine Facts, in http://www.palestine-facts.org/pf_1991to_now_kotel_tunnel_1996.php, accessed 20 August 2012.

4. Ahron Bregman, telephone interview with Benjamin Netanyahu [no date], in author's archive.

5. Dan Naveh, *Sodot Memshalah*, 40.

6. Testimonies of the survivors in the Ibrahimi mosque, see resistance. arabblogs.com/massacres/hebron/testimonies/index.htm, accessed 29 August 2012.

7. Ibid.

8. Danny Yatom, *Shutaf sod* (*The Confidant: From Sayeret Matkal to the Mossad*), Tel Aviv: Yediot Aharonot, 2009, 36 (in Hebrew).

9. Aaron David Miller, *The Much Too Promised Land: America's Elusive Search for Arab–Israeli Peace*, New York: Bantam Books, 2008, 271.

10. As cited in Akiva Eldar, 'The Har Homa Test', *Haaretz*, 10 December 2007 (in Hebrew).

11. Letter from King Hussein to Prime Minister Netanyahu, private source in the author's archive.

12. Dan Naveh, *Sodot Memshalah*, 71.

13. In his memoirs, the former director of Mossad, Yatom, refers to Haim Ha'Keini as 'H'; see Danny Yatom, *Shutaf Sod*, 13. The hit team that Ha'Keini assembled to carry out 'Operation Koresh' was headed by an agent nicknamed Tomy and some of its operatives had been involved in the 1995 assassination of the head of the Islamic Jihad, Fatchi Shkaki, in Malta; in the 1992 killing of Ataf Basiso in Paris; and in the March 1990 shooting in Brussels of Dr Gerald Vincent Bull, a Canadian engineer who had designed a supergun for the Iraqi government.

14. A later 'Top Secret' report on the failed operation, prepared by a three-man committee led by a Joseph Ciechanover, quotations from which are published here for the first time, concluded that 'Neither head of Mossad [Yatom] nor head of Caesarea [Ha'Keini] visited the theatre of operation before it took place and were not present there, or close to it, at the time the incident took place . . . it has been the practice of Mossad that, in such operations, the two top officials visit the place . . .' It also criticized Ha'Keini for ignoring 'a Shabak informer who . . . provided important information about Mashal's movements . . . we think that the head of Caesarea made a mistake in that he failed to give enough weight to the Shabak informer . . .' *Report on the Mashal Affair*, Chapter 13, 244. The committee's full report runs to 330 pages, only fifteen of which were made public.

15. The Ciechanover Commission commented in its report that 'the effects of [a failed] operation . . . on relationships with Jordan were hardly discussed

... neither within the intelligence community, nor in discussions with the prime minister. See ibid., 236, private source, in the author's archive.

16. The Ciechanover Commission would say in its secret report that 'the head of Mossad made a mistake by not giving the prime minister at once [namely *before* the operation] the king's message'. Ibid., 244.

17. Ronen Bergman, 'Ex-Mossad Officer Took Part in Failed 1996 Assassination Attempt on Hamas Leader, Gave Antidote That Saved His Life', *Yediot Aharonot*, 17 June 2005 (in Hebrew).

18. In Israel, the director of Mossad, Yatom, was forced to resign on 25 February 1998; the head of Caesarea, Haim Ha'Keini, also resigned, just before he was due to become deputy head of Mossad.

19. Ahron Bregman, interview with Yossi Beilin, Tel Aviv, 24 January 2005, for *Elusive Peace*, in author's archive.

20. Interview with Saeb Erekat, Jericho, 28 March 2004, for *Elusive Peace*, in author's archive.

21. Yossi Beilin, *Madrich le'yona petzuah*, (*Manual for a Wounded Dove*), Tel Aviv: Yediot Aharonot, 2001, 36 (in Hebrew); also Ahron Bregman, interview with Yossi Beilin.

22. For the text of the Wye River Memorandum, see Walter Laqueur and Barry Rubin (eds.), *The Israel–Arab Reader*, 529.

23. The relevant articles are: 6–10, 15, 19–23 and 30. There are also parts in articles 1–5, 11–14, 16–18, 25–7 and 29. See also letter from Yasser Arafat to President Clinton, 13 January 1998, www. Miftah.org.

24. This and the following quotes are based on Ahron Bregman, *Elusive Peace: How the Holy Land Defeated America*, London: Penguin Books, 205, xxvii.

10 Golan First, 1999–2000

1. The quotes are from a 'Brief to the President', 4 July 1999, private source, in the author's archive.

2. Letter from President Bill Clinton to Prime Minister Ehud Barak, 20 July 1999, private source, in the author's archive.

3. Private source, in the author's archive.

4. The following is based on a private source; see also *Tishreen* (Syria), 3 October 1999.

5. On these low-level talks, particularly between the Chief of Staff, Ehud Barak, and Syria's Chief of Staff, Shihabi; see Ahron Bregman and Jihan el-Tahri, *The Fifty Years War*, 264–66 (UK edn).

6. Transcript of a telephone conversation between Presidents Bill Clinton

and Hafez Assad, 24 August 1999 at 18.20, private source, in the author's archive.

7. A telephone conversation between Presidents Clinton and Assad, 2 September 1999.

8. The following is based on the transcript of a conversation between Prime Minister Ehud Barak and US envoy Dennis Ross, 5 September 1999, private source, in the author's archive; Ross's report on Assad's state of health also on 14 September 1999.

9. This and the following are based on the transcript of a conversation between Barak and Clinton, 15 December 1999, at 10.30.

10. Interview with Robert Malley for *Elusive Peace*.

11. This and the following are based on transcript of a conversation between Albright and Barak, 10 January 2000.

12. The following quotations are from the transcript of a telephone conversation between Clinton and Barak, 2 March 2000, 20.35 (Israeli time).

13. The quotations are from a telephone conversation between Clinton and Barak, 7 March 2000.

14. 'The Script', 10 March 2000, private source, in the author's archive.

15. Ibid.

16. Transcript of telephone conversation between Clinton and Barak, 26 March 2000, 13.30.

17. Interview with Sandy Berger, 18 April 2005, Washington DC, for *Elusive Peace*.

18. Indeed, in a meeting with Denis Ross on 13 September 1999, Barak said: 'I'm thinking about 200–300 metres east of the road which is running along the Kinneret.'

19. Interview with Bouthania Shaaban for *Elusive Peace*.

20. Ibid.

21. This and the following are based on the transcript of a telephone conversation between Clinton and Barak, 26 March 2000, 20.45.

11 Camp David II, 2000

1. Nimrod Novik to the prime minister based on Novik's meeting with Saeb Erekat, Washington DC, 23 July 1999, private source, in the author's archive. Erekat was the chief Palestinian negotiator, but also regarded as an obstacle. The UN representative, Terje Rød-Larsen, in a meeting with Barak's aide Dany Yatom, on 5 August 1999, said of Erekat: 'He can be counter-productive in the extreme. He has full control of the flow of information . . . You must be very careful with Saeb

Erekat . . . if you do the summits with Erekat it will not move . . .' And in another meeting with the Israelis Larsen and his wife, Muna, said: 'Saeb has many weaknesses . . . Saeb often lies even to Arafat . . . and this makes [Arafat] excited and say all sort of things . . .' Following these meetings the Israelis pressed the Americans to help replace Erekat, but to no avail.

2. This and following quotes are based on the transcript of a conversation between Barak and Arafat, Erez crossing, 27 July 1999, private source, in the author's archive.

3. This and the following quotes are from the transcript of a meeting chaired by Barak in Tel Aviv, 15 June 2000, 19.00, private source, in the author's archive.

4. Mohammed Bassiouni, report to Prime Minister Ehud Barak, 23 June 2000, private source, in the author's archive.

5. 'Arafat's Positions' (Secret), 27 June 2000, private source, in the author's archive.

6. Quoted from the transcript of a meeting between Albright and Barak, 27 June 2000, in the author's archive.

7. This and following quotes are based on a secret Shabak report, private source, in the author's archive.

8. Barak, in a meeting of the government, 9 July 2000; the following quotes are based on same source.

9. Quotes are from the transcript of a conversation between Malka and Barak, 9 July 2000, private source.

10. This and the following are based on the transcript of a meeting between Clinton and Barak, 11 July 2000.

11. The following is based on a Clinton–Barak meeting, 11 July 2000, at 17.35, private source, in the author's archive.

12. Transcript of Clinton–Barak conversation, 11 July 2000, 17.35, private source, in the author's archive.

13. Bill Clinton, *My Life*, London: Hutchinson, 2004, 912.

14. Secret letter from Secretary of State Madeleine K. Albright to Prime Minister Netanyahu, 24 November 1998, private source, in the author's archive.

15. Aaron David Miller, *The Much Too Promised Land*, 205.

16. Interview with Saeb Erekat for *Elusive Peace*.

17. This and the following are based on the transcript of a conversation between Clinton and Barak, 14 July 2000, private source, in the author's archive.

18. Bill Clinton, *My Life*, 855.

19. Meeting between Clinton, Barak and Arafat, 14 July 2000, at 23.35, private source, in the author's archive.

20. This and the following are based on the transcript of a conversation

between Barak and Dennis Ross, Dogwood, 15 July 2000, 10.25, private source, in author's archive.

21. Interview with Saeb Erekat for *Elusive Peace*.

22. Ibid.

23. Transcript of a conversation between Barak, Gilead Sher and Shlomo Ben-Ami, 16 July 2000, at 13.15, private source, in the author's archive.

24. Letter from Barak to Clinton, 16 July 2000, private source; the following quotations are all based on this document, which is in the author's archive.

25. Martin Indyk, *Innocent Abroad: An Intimate Account of American Peace Diplomacy in the Middle East*, New York: Simon and Schuster, 2009, 290.

26. Clinton, report to Barak, 16 July 2000, 21.00, private source; the following quotations are all based on this document, which is in the author's archive.

27. Clinton–Barak conversation, 16 July 2000, at 22.50, private source; the following quotations are all based on this report, which is in the author's archive.

28. Conversation between Clinton and Barak, 17 July 2000, private source, in the author's archive; the following quotations are all based on the transcript of their conversation.

29. A note for the record dictated by Barak to his aide, Yatom, and based on his conversation with Clinton, 18 July 2000, private source, in the author's archive.

30. Martin Indyk, *Innocent Abroad*, 322.

31. Interview with Sandy Berger for *Elusive Peace*.

32. This and the following are quotations from an interview with Sandy Berger.

33. Letter from Arafat to Clinton, 19 July 2000, private source, in the author's archive.

34. Letter from Barak to Clinton, 19 July 2000, private source, in the author's archive.

35. Transcript of a conversation between Clinton and Barak, 19 July 2000, at 19.18; private source, in the author's archive.

36. Clinton–Barak conversation, 19 July 2000, private source, in the author's archive.

37. As quoted in Clayton E. Swisher, *The Truth about Camp David*, New York: Nation Books, 2004, 307.

38. Clinton–Barak conversation, 19 July 2000, private source, in the author's archive.

39. Interview with Albright for *Elusive Peace*.

40. Transcript of a conversation between Clinton and Barak, 23 July 2000, private source, in the author's archive.

41. The papers of Akram Hanieh, editor-in-chief of the *Al Ayyam* news-

paper and adviser to Arafat, 'The Fifth Paper: The Summit According to Jerusalem Time', no date, no place, in the author's archive.

42. This and the following quotes are from the transcript of a conversation between Clinton and Arafat, 24 July 2000, at 19.00, private source, in the author's archive.

43. Interview with Mohammed Dahlan for *Elusive Peace*.

44. This and the following are from the transcript of a discussion among the Israeli team, 25 July 2000, at 08.10, private source, in the author's archive.

45. This and the following quotations are from the transcript of a conversation between Clinton and Barak, 25 July 2000, at 09.35, private source, in the author's archive.

46. Private source.

47. Henry Kissinger, *Years of Upheaval*, 201.

48. Transcript of a telephone conversation between Jacques Chirac and Barak, 28 July 2000, private source, in the author's archive.

49. This and following quotations are based on the transcript of a conversation between Barak, Ross and the US peace team, 30 August 2000, private source, in the author's archive.

50. This and following quotations are based on the transcript of a conversation between Clinton and Barak, 6 September 2000, private source.

51. This and following quotations are based on the transcript of a meeting between Barak and Arafat, Kochav Yair, 25 September 2000, private source, in the author's archive.

12 Al-Aqsa *Intifada*, 2000–2001

1. Interview with Haj Kamil for *Elusive Peace*, Jerusalem (no date, Roll 228).

2. Ted Gurr, 'A Casual Model of Civil Strife', *American Political Review*, Vol. 62, No. 4, 1968, 1104.

3. Jeremy Pressman, 'The Second Intifada: Background and Causes of the Israeli–Palestinian Conflict', *The Journal of Conflict Studies*, 2003, 136, 228.

4. Interview with Haj Kamil for *Elusive Peace*.

5. Akiva Eldar, 'Popular Misconceptions', *Haaretz*, 11 June 2004 (in Hebrew).

6. The following is based on the transcript of a conversation between Tarje Rød-Larsen and Barak, 30 September 2000, private source, in the author's archive.

7. This and following quotations are based on the transcript of a conversation between Albright and Barak, Paris, 4 October 2000, private source, in the author's archive.

8. Transcript of a conversation between Chirac and Barak, Elysée Palace, Paris, 4 October 2000, private source, in the author's archive.

9. This and the following are quoted in Raviv Drucker, *Harakiri. Ehud Barak: The Failure*, Tel Aviv: Yediot Aharonot, 2002, 313 (in Hebrew).

10. Saree Makdisi, *Palestine Inside Out*, 50, 53

11. Research interview with Mohaned Irbari, Umm el Fahm, 15 August 2004, for *Elusive Peace*, in the author's archive.

12. *Haaretz*, 12 March 2002 (in Hebrew).

13. Interview with Mohaned Irbari, no date, for *Elusive Peace*, in the author's archive.

14. Under mounting pressure, the government appointed a commission of inquiry – the Or Commission – to investigate the October 2000 events.

15. This is from the transcript of a conversation between Barak and Mubarak, 12 October 2000, at 15.05, private source, in the author's archive.

16. This and following quotations are based on the transcript of a telephone conversation between Clinton and Barak, 12 October 2000, private source, in the author's archive.

17. A letter from Barak to Clinton, 12 October 2000, private source, in the author's archive.

18. This is from the transcript of a telephone conversation between Barak and Mubarak, 12 October 2000, private source, in the author's archive.

19. Transcript of a telephone conversation between Clinton and Barak, 15 October 2000, at 21.05, private source, in the author's archive.

20. This and the following are based on the protocol of a meeting between Mubarak and Barak, Egypt, 16 October 2000, private source, in the author's archive.

21. Transcript of a meeting between Kofi Annan and Barak, Egypt, 16 October 2000, at 10.15, private source, in the author's archive.

22. Transcript of a conversation between Jordan's King Abdullah II and Barak, Egypt, 16 October 2000, at 11.05, private source, in the author's archive.

23. In the author's archive; also Annex B-1, Sharm el Sheikh Understanding, a letter dated 17 October 2000 from the Permanent Representative of the United States of America to the United Nations addressed to the Secretary General, *The Palestine Papers*, Al Jazeera, accessed 7 February 2011.

24. Transcript of a meeting between Barak and military commanders, 21 October 2000, private source, in the author's archive.

25. Transcript of a governmental meeting, 22 October 2000, private source, in the author's archive.

26. The following quotations are based on two transcripts of telephone con-

versations between Clinton and Barak, 22 October 2000, private source, in the author's archive.

27. Ehud Barak's instructions to army commanders, 24 October 2000, private source, in the author's archive.

28. Arafat in a meeting with Shimon Peres, Gaza, 1 November 2000, 22.00, private source, in the author's archive.

29. Haled Salam in a meeting with Peres, 1 November 2000, private source, in the author's archive.

30. Text of ceasefire, 2 November 2000, in the author's archive.

31. Transcript of a telephone conversation between Chirac and Barak, 2 November 2000, private source, in the author's archive.

32. 'Extra-Judicial Executions during the al-Aqsa Intifada', The Palestinian Society for the Protection of Human Rights and the Environment, 25 March 2001.

33. Ibid.

34. A report by Danny Abram, 25 November 2000, private source, in the author's archive.

35. This and following quotations are based on the transcript of a conversation between Clinton and Barak, 11 December 2000, private source, in the author's archive.

36. George W. Bush was elected US president on 7 November 2000. Clinton was to remain in office until the new president's inauguration on 20 January 2001.

37. This and following quotations are based on the Clinton Parameters as they appear in Walter Laqueur and Barry Rubin, *The Israel–Arab Reader*, 562–4; also in *Haaretz*, 31 December 2000 (in Hebrew).

38. This and following quotations are based on the transcript of a conversation between Barak and Egypt's President Mubarak, 26 December 2000, private source, in the author's archive.

39. Letter to the National Security Advisor, Samuel Berger, 28 December 2000, private source, in the author's archive.

40. This and following quotations are based on the transcript of a telephone conversation between Clinton and Barak, 1 January 2001, private source, in the author's archive.

41. Transcript of a telephone conversation between Clinton and Barak, 3 January 2001, at 17.00, private source, in the author's archive.

42. Ahmed Qurie, *From Oslo to Jerusalem: The Palestinian Story of the Secret Negotiations*, London: I. B. Tauris, 2006, 5–6.

43. As quoted in Raviv Drucker, *Harakiri*, 390.

44. Arieh O'Sullivan, 'IDF Kills Hizbullah Cell Leader in Gaza', *Jerusalem Post*, 14 February 2001.

45. Private source. On the legality of Israel's policy of assassination, see David Kretzmaer, 'Targeted Killing of Suspected Terrorists: Extra Judicial Executions or Legitimate Means of Defence?', *European Journal of International Law* 16, No. 2 (2005), 171–212.

13 Sharon and Arafat, 2001–2004

1. Cited in Charles Enderlin, *The Lost Years: Radical Islam, Intifada, and Wars in the Middle East 2001–2006*, New York: Other Press, 2007, 26.
2. Suzanne Goldenberg, 'War Jets Attack West Bank after Mall Bomb Carnage', *Guardian*, 19 May 2001.
3. Robert Pape, *Dying to Win: The Strategic Logic of Suicide Terrorism*, New York: Random House, 2005, 73–5, 32.
4. Baruch Kimerling, *Politicide: Ariel Sharon's War against the Palestinians*, London: Verso, 2003, 137.
5. Ahron Bregman, *Elusive Peace*, 156.
6. As cited in Amos Harel and Avi Isacharoff, *Hamilhama Ha'shvit* (*The Seventh War*), Tel Aviv: Yediot Aharonot, 2004, 115 (in Hebrew).
7. Interviews with Jibril Rajoub for *Elusive Peace*, 25 May 2004, 4 June 2004 and 13 October 2004, Jericho and Ramallah.
8. James Bennet and Joel Greenberg, 'Israel Breaks with Arafat after Palestinian Assault on Bus in West Bank Kills 10,' *The New York Times*, 13 December 2001.
9. Arafat's declaration in Gaza, Palestine Satellite Channel Television, 16 December 2001, at 16.00.
10. Ahron Bregman in an interview with Shaul Mofaz, Tel Aviv, 31 February 2005; and with Binyamin Ben Eliezer, Tel Aviv, 27 September 2004; both for *Elusive Peace*, in the author's archive.
11. Interview with Mohamad Abu Hamid, for *Elusive Peace*, no date (Roll 403–4); also http://www.guardian.co.uk/isreal/Story/o,2763,633643,oo.htm.
12. Ariel Sharon speaking to the press on 5 March 2002, as quoted in *Reporters Without Borders: Israel/Palestine. The Black Book*, London: Pluto Press, 1988, 58.
13. Interview with Muammar Shahrouri, 31 January 2005. The interview was conducted in an Israeli prison, where Shahrouri is imprisoned for his involvement in the Park Hotel bombing; for *Elusive Peace*, in the author's archive.
14. Interview with Fathi Khatib, 31 January 2005. The interview was con-

ducted in Beer Sheva prison, where Khatib is imprisoned for his involvement in the Park Hotel bombing; for *Elusive Peace*, in the author's archive.

15. Interview with General Giora Eiland, Ramat Ha'sharon, 28 September 2004, Ramat for *Elusive Peace*.

16. Interview with Mohammed Rashid, Paris, 3 November 2004, for *Elusive Peace*.

17. This testimony appears in Saree Makdisi, *Palestine Inside Out*, 183–4.

18. Ahron Bregman, *Elusive Peace*, 205.

19. Interview with Mohamad Abu Hamid, for *Elusive Peace*, no date, Jenin (Roll 403–4).

20. Interview with Hani al-Hassan, 9 June 2004, Ramallah, for *Elusive Peace*.

21. Tenth emergency special session, Agenda item 5, 'Illegal Israeli actions in Occupied East Jerusalem and the rest of the Occupied Palestinian Territory, Report of the Secretary General prepared pursuant to General Assembly resolution ES-10/10'.

22. Ahron Bregman, interview with Terje Rød-Larsen, Herzliya, 29 June 2004, for *Elusive Peace*.

23. Interview with Yasser Abed Rabbo, 26 June 2004, Ramallah, for *Elusive Peace*.

24. Interview with Anthony Zinni, 19 October 2004, Washington DC, for *Elusive Peace*.

25. Rita Giacaman, Anita Abdullah, Rula Abu Safieh and Luna Shamieh, 'Schooling at Gunpoint; Palestinian Children's Learning Environment in Warlike Conditions', 1 December 2002, as cited in Baruch Kimmerling, *Politicide*, 196.

26. Ahron Bregman, *Elusive Peace*, 229; Binyamin Ben Eliezer was not present in this meeting.

27. Danni Haloutz, *Begovah ha'einayim (Straightforward)*, Tel Aviv: Yediot Aharonot, 2010, 248 (in Hebrew).

28. Ahron Bregman, interview with Binyamin Ben Eliezer.

29. Interview with the Chief Commander of the Israeli Air Force, Dan Halutz, *Haaretz*, 23 August 2002 (in Hebrew).

30. George W. Bush, *Decision Points*, Washington DC: Broadway, 2011, 401.

31. As cited in Aaron David Miller, *The Much Too Promised Land*, 326.

32. Ten official Palestinian refugee camps are located in Jordan. They accommodate 307,785 registered refugees, or 17 per cent of the 1.7 million refugees registered with UNRWA in Jordan. Four of the camps were set up on the East Bank of the River Jordan just after the 1948

Arab–Israeli war, and six after the 1967 war. In addition, there are three neighbourhoods in Amman, Zarqa and Madaba which are considered refugee camps by the Jordanian government and 'unofficial' camps by UNRWA.

33. Interview with Marwan Muasher, 12 December 2004, Amman, for *Elusive Peace*.

34. The following is mainly based on interviews with Flynt Leverett, 15 October 2004, Washington DC, and with anonymous, for *Elusive Peace*.

35. Interview with Colin Powell, Washington DC, 22 February 2005, for *Elusive Peace*.

36. For the text of the roadmap see the US Department of State website, 30 April 2003.

37. Interview with John Wolf, 18 October 2004, Philadelphia, for *Elusive Peace*.

38. Interview with Nabil Shaath.

39. As quoted in Ahron Bregman, *Elusive Peace*, 269.

40. Guy Dunmore, 'Bush Attacks Israelis for Building of West Bank Wall,' *Financial Times*, 26 July 2003; also Brian Knowlton, 'Sharon Meets with Bush but Says Security Fence Will Still Go Up', *International Herald Tribune*, 30 July 2003.

41. Interview with Colin Powell for *Elusive Peace*.

42. George W. Bush, *Decision Points*, 400.

43. As cited in Saree Makdisi, *Palestine Inside Out*, 28.

44. Interviews with Mike Herzog, 11 October 2004, and Giora Eiland for *Elusive Peace*.

45. The following is based on an interview with Majd Zaatri, 1 February 2005, Beersheva prison, for *Elusive Peace*.

46. Shlomi Eldar, *Getting to Know Hamas*, Tel Aviv: Keter, 2012, 39 (in Hebrew).

47. As quoted in Ahron Bregman, *Elusive Peace*, 279.

14 Unilateralism and Its Rewards, 2004–2007

1. This and the following are based on the speech by Sharon at Herzliya, 18 December 2003, in the author's archive.

2. Ahron Bregman, interview with Shaul Mofaz for *Elusive Peace*.

3. This and the following are based on the testimony of Yassin's son, in Shlomi Eldar, *Getting to Know Hamas*, 53.

4. Ibid.

5. Interview with Marwan Muasher for *Elusive Peace*.

6. Interview with Colin Powell for *Elusive Peace*.

7. Source: Marwan Muasher.

8. See a letter from President George W. Bush to Sharon, 14 April 2004, in the author's archive.

9. White House transcript of the Bush–Sharon press conference regarding Sharon's Gaza Disengagement Plan, 14 April 2004, at http://electroncintifada.net/bytopic/historicalspeeches/262.shml.

10. As quoted in Ahron Bregman, *Elusive Peace*, 278–9.

11. Uri Dan, *Ariel Sharon: An Intimate Portrait*, New York: Palgrave, 2006, 246. Uri Dan was a close friend of Sharon.

12. Ariel Sharon in a TV interview, 24 April 2004, as quoted in Charles Enderlin, *The Lost Years*, 235.

13. Bassam Abu Sharif, *Arafat and the Dream of Palestine: An Insider's Account*, New York: Palgrave, 2009, 249.

14. Interview with Mohammed Rashid.

15. Telephone interview with Nabil Shaath, 15 April 2005, Tel Aviv, for *Elusive Peace*.

16. A 'Top Secret' Shabak document, 15 October 2000.

17. Aaron David Miller, *The Too Much Promised Land*, 355.

18. Dov Weisglass, interview, *Haaretz*, 8 October 2004 (in Hebrew).

19. Rocket threat from the Gaza Strip, 2000–2007, http://www.terrorism-info.org.il/malam_multimedia/English/eng_n/pdf/rocket_threat_e.pdf, accessed 29 August 2012.

Index